A Constitutional History of American Episcopal Methodism

John James Tigert

CONSTITUTIONAL HISTORY

OF

AMERICAN EPISCOPAL METHODISM.

(1)

A

CONSTITUTIONAL HISTORY

OF

AMERICAN EPISCOPAL METHODISM.

BY JNO. J. TIGERT, D.D.

———

Bassanio: . . . "I beseech you,
   Wrest once the law to your authority:
   To do a great right, do a little wrong."
Portia: "'Twill be recorded for a precedent,
   And many an error, by the same example,
   Will rush into the state.   It cannot be."
                    Shakespeare, Merchant of Venice.

———

NASHVILLE, TENN.:
PUBLISHING HOUSE OF THE M. E. CHURCH, SOUTH,
BARBEE & SMITH, AGENTS.
1894.

(4)

REVERENTLY INSCRIBED

TO THE MEMORY OF MY

Mother,

Mary Van Veghten Tigert,

A LIFE-LONG METHODIST OF THE OLDEN TYPE,

THE MELODY OF WHOSE VOICE

LIFTED IN

RAPTUROUS EXPERIENCE, SACRED SONG, OR PREVAILING PRAYER,

IN LOVE-FEAST, CLASS-MEETING, AND REVIVAL SERVICE,

YET LINGERS, A HALLOWING INFLUENCE,

IN THE HEART OF

HER FIRST-BORN SON.

PREFACE.

THIS history has been written from the sources, with due regard to recognized authorities. By sources are meant the journals and correspondence of the Wesleys, Coke, Asbury, Whatcoat, McKendree, and others; the memoirs of Ware, Watters, Gatch, and Garrettson; the official records of the Conferences in England and America; the literature of the governmental questions that have agitated the Church; and, in general, whatever contemporary data are now extant and accessible. By authorities are meant the histories of Smith, Bangs, Stevens, McTyeire, Atkinson, Neely, and some others; the biographies by Tyerman, Whitehead, Moore, Southey, Watson, Jackson, Drew, Bangs, Phoebus, Lee, Paine, Elliott, Clark, Emory, Hibbard, and others; and whatever later publications illustrate the inquiries here prosecuted. Jesse Lee's History of the Methodists is, for the most part, to be accepted as a source. It is not necessary, however, to attempt here a complete enumeration of the materials whence the narrative and its conclusions have been drawn: ample acknowledgment is made in the footnotes, and it is believed that no essential aid has been neglected.

Of a valuable collection of papers, of which considerable use has been made, some account should be given. Bishop Asbury's papers were left to Bishop McKendree; Bishop McKendree's to Bishop Soule, who, it was expected, would be his biographer. When Bishop Paine undertook this task, Bishop Soule placed both Mr. Asbury's (so far as not previously disposed of) and Mr. McKendree's papers in his hands. Later, Bishop Soule's own papers, and the collection in Bishop Paine's possession, of which he made large but by no means exhaustive use in his Life of McKendree, came into the hands of Bishop McTyeire. Since his death, they have been, by his direction, in my custody. Some of these papers ought not to be published, and will be submitted to judicious persons who have the best right to a judgment and voice in their final disposition; many are reserved for future uses; a considerable number—such as the notes of the first Bishops' meeting ever held in the Methodist Episcopal Church, at Philadelphia, in 1826, and the official correspondence of the Bishops at that time—are here published for the first time.

In this book, I do not pretend to have responded to a "long *felt* want." Nor has anybody urged me to write. The truth is that all of us, preachers as well as people, grow more or less indifferent to such inquiries, until some crisis in the affairs of the Church, perhaps unexpected and perilous, reveals to us our careless, if not sinful, neglect. But there is *real* need for a work like this. Hence, under a sense of duty, and in default of a more competent hand (or, indeed, of any hand turned to this task) I have undertaken to fill a hitherto unoccupied place in the literature of American Methodism, whose importance cannot be exaggerated. I wish I could have done the work better. I have not reached my ideal. The time for investigation and composition has been snatched from the many and exacting duties of a busy pastorate in a large city; but, though I have coveted abundant leisure, to perfect the literary form, and to make it more worthy of the theme, I think, after repeated review, that for "substance of doctrine," the book is about as good as I could make it. Otherwise, in this age of many books, I should have no right to publish it.

Whenever it was possible, my method of composition has been to combine the sources, especially on the many disputed points, into a consistent narrative, whose simplicity and directness should be the warrant of its truth. Sometimes I have been able to show, by brief extracts from many independent sources, that but one view could possibly represent the truth. For a time my mind inclined to the arrangement adopted by Gieseler, in his Church History, by which the evidence is thrown into footnotes; but this plan was

finally rejected as equally cumbersome and unnecessary. I have
not been satisfied to write a chapter or a paragraph, however, until
the results of a critical comparison of all the accessible sources and
authorities had crystallized in a clear conception, definite, concrete,
and satisfactory, at least to my own mind. Usually when in doubt,
I have said so. But I have written under the growing conviction
that in a work of this kind, the reader has a right to expect conclusions; and I have striven, without dogmatism or commentary unwarranted by the facts, to leave as few open questions behind me
as possible. This general method has been adopted, because (1)
it is the only conclusive one on points in dispute; (2) it is most
satisfactory on all points to the critical reader, who is generally put
in possession of sufficient evidence to test the validity of the conclusions arrived at; and (3) it is most entertaining to the general
reader, who is thus afforded a pleasing variety. Occasionally, short
excursions into the field of our general history have been indulged
in; for, as Hallam observes, at some periods constitutional and
general history nearly coincide. Presuming, however, upon the
reader's familiarity with this outlying territory, I have, in general,
confined the narrative to the strictly constitutional and governmental materials, which are rich and abundant.

Perhaps it ought to be added, that I have sought to pursue these
inquiries in a purely historical spirit. My aim has been first to get
at the truth—sometimes a task of considerable difficulty—and then
to tell it. No controversial aim or interest has consciously warped
a judgment or shaded a statement. I have no disposition to con-
ceal the fact that I am a member and minister of the Methodist
Episcopal Church, South; but, as the whole period covered by this
volume relates to the original, undivided household of our American Methodist faith, and is the common birthright of the two
Episcopal Methodisms, I trust that both the catholic spirit and the
truthful letter of this history will commend themselves to my
brethren of the Methodist Episcopal Church. It would be too
much to hope that all the conclusions herein expressed will be

universally accepted; but it is not too much to expect that all lovers and seekers of truth will find in this work little to hinder and something to aid them in their search.

Our constitutional epochs of 1773, when the first American Conference met; of 1784, when Mr. Wesley and the Christmas Conference organized the Methodist Episcopal Church; of 1787, when the American Church asserted its autonomy; of 1792, when the first Quadrennial General Conference assembled; of 1808, when the Delegated General Conference and its Constitution came into existence; and of 1820–1828, when the constitutional government of the Methodist Episcopal Church underwent its first severe strain, have, of course, been treated with special fullness. In this last-mentioned period, the evidence, not hitherto accessible in its entirety, has constrained the conclusion that the sectional severance of American Methodism, on constitutional issues which still divide it, was really effected. The fifth volume of Dr. Stevens' able history of the Methodist Episcopal Church, which will cover the period beginning with 1820, is announced as almost ready. I am sorry not to be able to consult it before going to press. Important later matters in 1844 and down to 1892—the centenary of the General Conference—have been treated, where chronological order has been sacrificed to topical completeness.

To Bishops Galloway and Hendrix, I must here express my appreciation of their kind encouragement.   J. J. T.

Kansas City, Mo., November 25, 1893.

CONTENTS.

BOOK I.

ENGLISH METHODISM TO 1784.

BOOK II.

AMERICAN METHODISM TO 1784.

BOOK III.

THE GRAND CLIMACTERIC YEAR: 1784.

BOOK IV.

FROM THE CHRISTMAS CONFERENCE TO THE IN-
STITUTION OF THE QUADRENNIAL
GENERAL CONFERENCE.

BOOK V.

THE QUADRENNIAL GENERAL CONFERENCES TO THE INSTITUTION OF THE DELEGATED GENERAL CONFERENCE.

BOOK VI.

THE DELEGATED GENERAL CONFERENCES OF THE UNDIVIDED METHODIST EPISCOPAL CHURCH.

BOOK I.

English Methodism to 1784.

(13)

CONSTITUTIONAL HISTORY

OF

AMERICAN EPISCOPAL METHODISM.

CHAPTER I.

ORIGIN OF THE CONFERENCE.

SINCE 1744 the two constant factors of Methodist polity, (1) a superintending and appointing power, and (2) a consulting body called the Conference, have been continuously operative.

These two factors are constitutional or elemental in the government of Methodism. The system itself changes as either of these elements changes or is variously combined with the other: the disappearance of either is the destruction of the system. Something better might take its place, but it would be also something different. The peculiar economy of Methodism would cease to exist.

The origin, development, history, and relations of these two factors, the former chiefly executive and the latter chiefly legislative, afford the principal, if not exclusive, materials for a constitutional history of Methodism, a task not hitherto accepted as the express province of any single work. It need hardly be added that our inquiry concerns itself altogether with polity and government and not at all with dogma and doctrine.

With the development and definition of the powers and prerogatives of the Conference, with its President, Secretary, other officers, and committees, in English Methodism,

(15)

after 1784, " the grand climacteric year of Methodism,'' *
which gave a determinate and permanent *status* to both its
English and American forms; or, at least, after 1791, the
year of the great Founder's death, we have nothing to do in
this volume.

From 1739, the year of the rise of the United Society, to
1791, it may be said in general, the supreme superintending
and appointing power, and the final legislative as well, in
both Methodisms, English and American, resided in Mr.
Wesley alone.   Even when he appointed Coke and Asbury
to their high office, Wesley had no thought of abandoning
his own jurisdiction over the American province of his pa-
triarchate.   He was not only a scriptural *episcopus* (as he
declared of himself),† for purposes of ordination, but in point
of power and its use a Bishop in fact,‡ freely exercising an
absolute authority such as has scarcely ever, before or since,
fallen to the lot of any one man.

Mr. Wesley's uniform defense and justification of his possession and exercise of these extraordinary powers was that
he was himself the creator, the sole author and finisher, of
the system which gave rise to them; and that all subordinate
agents had voluntarily entered into a compact with him on
stipulated and well-known conditions which they were free
at any time to dissolve and annul.   This absolutist, for such
he was in fact and principle, planted himself squarely on the
simple declaration that he was free to do what he would with
his own.   Whatever might be thought in our country and
time of the expediency of such a personal government, his-

---

* Dr. Whitehead, Life of Wesley, Amer. Ed., Boston, 1844, II. 248.

† Letter to Charles Wesley, Aug. 19, 1785: Tyerman, Life and Times,
III. 444.

‡ The first question in the American Minutes for 1789 is, " Who are the
persons that exercise the episcopal office in the Methodist Church in Europe
and America?"   The answer is, "John Wesley, Thomas Coke, and Francis
Asbury."   Tyerman adds (III. 437), " by regular order and succession," but
these words do not occur in the editions of 1813 and 1840 which lie before
me.   His authorities will appear later.   Thus John Wesley was virtually
dubbed " Bishop " two years before his death, despite his preference for
" knave, fool, rascal, or scoundrel," vigorously expressed in September, 1788.

tory has no other office than to record the fact. And wisdom is justified of her children. How these supreme powers of Mr. Wesley were modified in America after 1784 it will be a part of our task in the following pages to show.

From 1739, the true epoch of Methodism,* as we have assumed, to 1744, the year of the assembling of the first Conference, Mr. Wesley embodied in himself, without limitations of any kind or degree, springing either from a fundamental compact which bound or engaged him, or from the independent activities of personal agents, all controlling authority and power, of whatever nature, in Methodism. The calling of the Conference, though hardly a sharing of his powers, was his first movement toward a division of his burdens.

John Wesley arrived in England from America February 1, 1738, the day after George Whitefield had sailed for the continent Wesley had just left. His labors at Oxford and elsewhere before he went abroad as a missionary with General Oglethorpe, and his varied experiences as a parish priest in Georgia, while of intense personal interest and affording rich materials for a study of the man, have too remote a bearing upon his subsequent organization of Methodism in England and America to detain us here; his American adventures, however, may briefly engage our attention when we come to notice the beginnings of Methodism in America.

---

*In his Church History, Wesley assigns other dates, as the founding of the Holy Club at Oxford in 1729, ten years before, or the meeting begun at Fetter-lane, May 1, 1738, by the advice of Peter Böhler; but his well-known introduction to the General Rules begins, " In the latter end of the year 1739 eight or ten persons came to me in London, etc. . . . this was the rise of the United Society." The corner stone of the first Methodist chapel was laid in Bristol, May 12, 1739, and the Foundry was opened for public worship in London, Nov. 11, 1739. Wesley did not formally separate from the Moravians, however, until July 20, 1740, and Dr. Smith, in his History of Wesleyan Methodism, argues for this date. Tyerman seems to fix it three days later, at the first meeting of the seceders from the Moravians. Compare Stevens, History of Methodism, I. 124, 131, 132 and Tyerman, Life and Times of John Wesley, I. 282, 309, 310.

2

At a Moravian meeting in Aldersgate street, London, May 24, 1738, John Wesley experienced the grace of conversion. The servant became a son, and henceforth served in his Father's house with unremitting diligence.

His genius for organization and government finds early illustration in an agreement with Messrs. Gambold and Robson touching Moravian affairs. There is much truth in that view of history which, renouncing drum and trumpet, regards it as an accurate portrayal of the life of the people; but it verges on untruth when it disposes of epoch-makers and reformers as no more than the product of their times. History must indeed take account of the people, but its crises and changes, its free, fresh, full fountains are found in the biographies of its heroes. There can be no more interesting discovery than that of an influential system of thought or public policy as it lies in germ in the mind of a single person before it is put forth to mold the opinions or determine the actions of mankind. This little compact which Mr. Wesley drew up Nov. 12, 1739, embraces a sketch of what afterwards became (1) annual conferences, (2) quarterly meetings, (3) monthly advices of the progress of the work, and (4) systematic provision for its extension. Mr. Wesley says: "After much prayer and consultation we agreed: 1. To meet yearly in London, if God permit, on the eve of Ascension day. 2. To fix then the business to be done the ensuing year—where, when, and by whom. 3. To meet quarterly there, as many as can; namely, on the second Tuesday in July, October, and January. 4. To send a monthly account to one another of what God hath done in each of our stations. 5. To inquire whether Mr. Hall, Sympson, Rogers, Ingham, Hutchins, Kinchin, Stonehouse, Cennick, Oxlee, and Brown will join us herein. 6. To consider whether there be any others of our spiritual friends who are able and willing so to do." *

"But this plan," observes Dr. Whitehead, " was never

---

*Tyerman, Life and Times of John Wesley, I. 281; Whitehead's Life of Wesley, II. 79, Amer. Ed., Boston, 1844.

put into execution." * The evening before this arrangement at Wycombe with Gambold and Robson, Mr. Wesley had preached to seven or eight thousand people in the Foundry at London; and on July 20, 1740, occurred his formal separation from the Moravians.

Though the London Society, which has maintained an unbroken existence to this day, was organized in 1739, the first Yearly Conference did not convene until June 25, 1744. From that time until his death in 1791, Mr. Wesley held a Conference every year—forty-seven in all.

This annual English Conference Mr. Wesley called into existence. He made it. It exercised such powers as he accorded to it. It was his organ created to answer his ends. Methodist government from this beginning has continued to be the combination of the two factors, a personal executive and a Conference, first of the preachers, "in connection with Mr. John Wesley," and then, in recent times, of ministers and members. The system has found its mature expression and full embodiment in America—in the Episcopacy and the General Conference.

This first Conference, which met in the Foundry, London, consisted of six clergymen of the Church of England—the Revs. John Hodges, John Meriton, Henry Piers, and Samuel Taylor,† besides John and Charles Wesley—and four lay preachers, namely, Thomas Maxfield, Thomas Richards, John Bennet, and John Downes. Of these four, three afterwards abandoned Wesley: Downes only lived and died a Methodist.

June 24, the day before the opening of the Conference, a love-feast was held, at which the six English clergy were present, and the Lord's Supper was administered to the whole of the London Society, numbering more than two thousand members. The Conference was opened with prayer and a sermon by Charles Wesley, who baptized an adult, who there and then found peace with God.‡

---

* Life II. 79.   † For notices of these clergymen, see Tyerman, I. 442.
‡ Tyerman, Life and Times of John Wesley, I. 443.

The proceedings of the Conference were conducted in the form of question and answer, which is still the canonical Methodist usage, and Mr. Wesley opened the matters to come before the body as follows:

"It is desired that all things be considered as in the immediate presence of God; that we meet with a single eye, and as little children, who have everything to learn; that every point which is proposed may be examined to the foundation; that every person may speak freely whatever is in his heart; and that every question which may arise should be thoroughly debated and settled.

"*2.* Need we be fearful of doing this? What are we afraid of? Of overturning our first principles? *A.* If they are false, the sooner they are overturned the better. If they are true, they will bear the strictest examination. Let us all pray for a willingness to receive light, to know of every doctrine whether it be of God.

"*2.* How may the time of the Conference be made more eminently a time of watching unto prayer? *A.* 1. While we are conversing, let us have an especial care to set God always before us. 2. In the intermediate hours let us visit none but the sick, and spend all the time that remains in retirement. 3. Let us therein give ourselves to prayer for one another, and for a blessing upon our labor.

"*2.* How far does each of us agree to submit to the judgment of the majority? *A.* In speculative things, each can only submit so far as his judgment shall be convinced. In every practical point, each will submit so far as he can without wounding his conscience.

"*2.* Can a Christian submit any farther than this to any man, or number of men upon earth? *A.* It is undeniably certain he cannot; either to *Bishop, Convocation,* or *General Council.* And this is that grand principle of private judgment on which all the reformers proceeded, 'Every man must judge for himself; because every man must give an account of himself to God.' " *

*Myles, Chron. Hist. of Meth., pp. 23, 24.

The last two questions and answers assert the principles of Christian liberty which Methodism has always exemplified, but it might be inferred from the question about submitting to the majority that after debate decisions were made by vote of the Conference.* Such was not the case. The Conference debated, but the Chair decided. " Mr. Wesley was the government; and, though he invited the preachers to confer with him, he did not propose to abandon any of his original power. They had a voice by his permission, but he reserved the right to direct." †

That the Conference was thus constituted and continued with no more power than Mr. Wesley allowed it is abundantly evident from a defense of his course which Mr. Wesley issued at the Conference in Leeds in 1766, twenty-two years later, and from a letter which he wrote as late as January, 1780. In 1766 among other things he wrote:

" In 1744 I wrote to several clergymen, and to all who then served me as sons in the gospel, desiring them to meet me in London, to give me their advice concerning the best method of carrying on the work of God. *They* did not desire this meeting; but *I* did, knowing that ' in a multitude of counselors there is safety.' And when their number increased, so that it was neither needful nor convenient to invite them all, for several years I wrote to those with whom I desired to confer; and these only met at the place appointed, till at length I gave a general permission that all who desired it might come. Observe! I myself sent for these, of my own free choice; and I sent for them to *advise* not *govern* me. Neither did I at any of those times divest myself of any part of that *power* above described, which the providence of God had cast upon me without any design or choice of mine.

" What is that power? It is a power of admitting into and excluding from the societies under my care; of choosing

---

*Smith's "Disciplinary Minutes" of 1749, say, "How far does each of us agree to submit to the *unanimous* judgment of the rest?" (Hist. Wesleyan Meth., I., 227–229.)

†Neely, Governing Conference in Methodism, pp. 9, 10.

and removing stewards; of receiving or of not receiving helpers; of appointing them when, where, and how to help me; and of desiring any of them to meet me when I see good.   And as it was merely in obedience to the providence of God and for the good of the people that I at first accepted this power, which I never sought—nay, a hundred times labored to throw off—so it is on the same considerations, not for profit, honor, or pleasure, that I use it at this day.

"But several gentlemen are much offended at my having so much power.   My answer to them is this: 'I did not seek any part of this power; it came upon me unawares. But when it was come, not daring to bury that talent, I used it to the best of my judgment; yet I never was fond of it.   I always did, and do now, bear it as my burden—the burden which God lays upon me—and therefore I dare not yet lay it down.'   But if you can tell me any one or any five men to whom I may transfer this burden, who can and will do just what I do now, I will heartily thank both them and you.

"But some of our helpers say, ' This is *shackling free-born Englishmen,*' and demand a *free Conference;* that is, a meeting of all the preachers, wherein all things shall be determined by most votes.   I answer: ' It is possible, after my death, something of this kind may take place; but not while I live.   To *me* the preachers have engaged themselves to submit to serve me as sons in the gospel.   But they are not thus engaged to any man, or number of men, besides. To *me* the people in general will submit.   But they will not yet submit to any other.'   It is nonsense, then, to call my using *this power* 'shackling freeborn Englishmen.'   None needs to submit to it unless he will; so there is no shackling in the case.   Every preacher and every member may leave me when he pleases.   But while he chooses to stay, it is on the same terms that he joined me at first." *

In 1780, thirty-six years after the organization of the Conference, Wesley was not slow to defend the constitution he

---

*Tyerman, Life and Times, II. 578, 579; Wesley's Works, Amer. Ed., V. 220, 221.

had given it and under which it had continued to act. In a letter written in January of that year he says:

" You seem likewise to have quite a wrong idea of a Conference. For above six years after my return to England there was no such thing. I then desired some of our preachers to meet me, in order to advise, not control me. And, you may observe, they had no power at all but what I exercised through them. I chose to exercise the power which God had given me in this manner, both to avoid ostentation and gently to habituate the people to obey them when I should be taken from their head. But as long as I remain with them, the fundamental rule of Methodism remains inviolate. As long as any preacher joins with me, he is to be directed by me in his work. Do not you see, then, that Brother M., whatever his intentions might be, acted as wrong as wrong could be; and that the representing of this as the common cause of the preachers was the way to common destruction—the way to turn all their heads and to set them in arms? It was a blow at the very root of Methodism. I could not, therefore, do less than I did; it was the very least that could be done, for fear that evil should spread." *

In the Leeds deliverance of 1766, it is noteworthy (1) that Wesley expresses a willingness to share his powers and responsibilities, " if you can tell me any one or any five men to whom I may transfer this burden; " and (2) that he anticipates that a " free Conference," exercising his powers, may come into existence after his death. Already his mind was meditating provision for the perpetuity of Methodism after the personal bond which held it together should be dissolved. How this finally led to the enrollment of the Deed of Declaration in Chancery and the creation of the Legal Hundred we shall discover in following chapters.

Having seen how the English Conference was constituted, with limited, advisory powers, during Mr. Wesley's life, it may be of interest, in concluding this chapter, to note briefly

---

* Wesley's Works, Amer. Ed., VII. 228.

some of the doings, in matters governmental, of the first Conference in 1744. The three general heads of debate were, 1. What to teach; 2. How to teach; and 3. What to do, or how regulate discipline and practice. The doctrinal conclusions of the Conference do not here concern us.*

The Methodists were at this time divided into four sections: (1) the united societies, (2) the bands, (3) the select societies, and (4) the penitents. The united societies consisted of awakened persons, and it is worthy of note that from the beginning " seekers " have been eligible to membership; the bands, of those who professed conversion; the select societies, of those from the bands who seemed to walk in the light: the penitents were the backsliders. The lay assistants were to expound; to meet the united societies, bands, select societies, and penitents once a week; to visit the classes quarterly, and to decide differences; to receive on trial and to put the disorderly back on trial; to see that stewards, leaders, schoolmasters, and housekeepers faithfully discharged their duties, and to meet the stewards and leaders weekly to audit their accounts.

With reference to the Church of England, it was resolved to defend her doctrine, to obey the Bishops and canons as far as the Methodists conscientiously could; but to avoid to the utmost entailing a schism in the Church.†

Such were the more important decisions in matters of polity and administration reached in the first Methodist Conference of 1744.

---

* See, however, Tyerman, I. 443, 444, and Smith, Hist. of Wesleyan Meth., I. 229.

† Cf. Tyerman, I. 444–446.

CHAPTER II.

———

AT the twenty-sixth annual conference of English Methodism, which opened at Leeds, Aug. 1, 1769, two important measures were taken.

The first concerned America: "We have a pressing call from our brethren at New York, who have built a preaching house, to come over and help them. Who is willing to go?" Answer: "Richard Boardman and Joseph Pilmoor." Question: "What can we do further in token of our brotherly love?" Answer: "Let us now make a collection among ourselves. This was immediately done; and, out of it, £50 were allotted towards the payment of the debt, and about £20 given to our brethren for their passage."

It is, however, doubtful whether, as is commonly supposed, this was the first collection taken for the American Mission; for six months before this Wesley had permitted Robert Costerdine, in charge of the Sheffield circuit, to read publicly on any Sunday the letter which had been received from New York and "to receive what the hearers were willing to give." *

As the first important measure concerned the establishment of Methodism in America, so the second concerned its perpetuity in England. Friday, Aug. 4, Wesley read to the Conference the following paper:

"*My dear Brethren:* 1. It has long been my desire, that all those *ministers* of our Church, [*i. e.*, ordained clergy of the Church of England] who believe and preach salvation by faith, might cordially agree between themselves, and not hinder but help one another. After occasionally press-

---

* Tyerman, Life and Times, III. 48.

ing this, in private conversation, wherever I had opportunity, I wrote down my thoughts upon the head, and sent them to each in a letter. Out of fifty or sixty, to whom I wrote, only three vouchsafed me an answer. So I give this up. I can do no more. They are a rope of sand, and such they will continue.

"2. But it is otherwise with the *traveling preachers* in our connection. You are at present one body. You act in concert with each other, and by united counsels. And now is the time to consider what can be done, in order to continue this union. Indeed, as long as I live, there will be no great difficulty. I am, under God, a center of union to all our traveling, as well as local preachers. They all know me and my communication. They all love me for my works' sake; and, therefore, were it only out of regard to me, they will continue connected with each other. But by what means may this connection be preserved, when God removes me from you?

"3. I take it for granted, it cannot be preserved, by any means, between those who have not a single eye. Those who aim at anything but the glory of God, and the salvation of men; who desire or seek any earthly thing, whether honor, profit, or ease, will not, cannot continue in the connection; it will not answer their design. Some of them, perhaps a fourth of the whole number, will procure preferment in the Church. Others will turn Independents, and get separate congregations, like John Edwards and Charles Skelton. Lay your accounts with this, and be not surprised if some, you do not suspect, be of this number.

"4. But what method can be taken, to preserve a firm union between those who choose to remain together? Perhaps you might take some such steps as these. On notice of my death, let all the preachers, in England and Ireland, repair to London within six weeks. Let them seek God by solemn fasting and prayer. Let them draw up articles of agreement, to be signed by those who choose to act in concert. Let those be dismissed, who do not choose it, in the most friendly manner possible.   Let them choose by votes a *committee* of three, five, or seven, each of whom is to be *moderator* in his turn.   Let the committee do what I do now; propose preachers to be tried, admitted, or excluded; fix the place of each preacher for the ensuing year, and the time of next conference.

"5. Can anything be done now, in order to lay a foundation for this future union?   Would it not be well, for any that are willing, to sign some articles of agreement before God calls me hence?   Suppose something like these:

"'We, whose names are underwritten, being thoroughly convinced of the necessity of a close union between those whom God is pleased to use as instruments in this glorious work, in order to preserve this union between ourselves, are resolved, God being our helper: (1) *To devote ourselves entirely to God;* denying ourselves, taking up our cross daily, steadily aiming at one thing, to save our own souls, and them that hear us.   (2) To preach the *old Methodist doctrines*, and no other, contained in the minutes of the Conferences.   (3) To observe and enforce the whole *Methodist discipline*, laid down in the said minutes.'" *

In view of the obligation to preach the doctrines and to enforce the discipline contained in the Minutes, the preachers present wisely suggested to Mr. Wesley a publication embodying Methodist doctrine and discipline, as contained in the Minutes of the twenty-six yearly Conferences, to be sent to every "assistant," or preacher in charge of a circuit, to be by him communicated to all the "helpers," or junior preachers, in his work.   In 1753 Mr. Wesley had issued the first collection of this sort, made up of extracts from the Minutes to date.   This is known as the first edition of "The Large Minutes."   A second edition, containing the added legislation of the succeeding ten years, was issued in 1763.†   This request of the preachers at the Leeds Conference of

---

*Tyerman, Life and Times, III. 49, 50.

†Tyerman, II. 474–479, gives all the differences between the edition of 1753 and that of 1763 of "The Large Minutes."

1769 Mr. Wesley satisfied the following year when he issued the third edition of " The Large Minutes," an octavo pamphlet of sixty pages, entitled " Minutes of Several Conversations between the Rev. Messrs. John and Charles Wesley and Others," which included the minutes of Conferences down to 1770.[*]

This plan of Mr. Wesley's for the perpetuity of Methodism, embodying as it did a permanent doctrinal and disciplinary basis of union, as well as a central committee of control, was ordered inserted in the Minutes, after having received, as Dr. Whitehead thinks, the signatures of many of the preachers at the Conference of 1769. Mr. Wesley held the plan in suspense for some years, but brought it forward again at the Conferences of 1773, 1774, and 1775, when it received the signatures of all the preachers present at these sessions, more than one hundred in all.[†]

Thus for six years Mr. Wesley's deliberations led him to abide by this plan as the best he could devise. Dr. Whitehead more than hints that since the plan provided simply for the perpetual union of Methodism on the original basis, namely, not as a dissenting body, but as a society with unordained lay preachers, dependent upon the Church of England and her friendly clergy for the sacraments, the more ambitious Wesleyan leaders were not satisfied to be thus bound after Mr. Wesley's death. "Some years afterwards, [after 1769]" says the Doctor, " the mystery of innovations began to work secretly in the minds of several of the preachers who hoped to exalt themselves above all that had been known before among them. They knew Mr. Wesley did, and would let, or hinder, till he was taken out of the way: they had influence enough, however, to prevail upon him to relinquish the present plan, and leave the mode of union among the preachers after his death, to their own deliberations."[‡] The plan was relinquished; but

* Tyerman, III. 80.
† Stevens, Hist. of Meth., I. 442.
‡ Whitehead, Life of Wesley, II. 193. Compare the footnotes on p. 192.

Dr. Whitehead's testimony as to how, when, and why is doubtful.

Stevens is content to dismiss this proposal with the remark that it was superseded by the final plan of Wesley's Deed of Declaration recorded in Chancery.* So it was. But this Deed was not drawn until 1784, nine years after the original plan was last offered for signatures in the Conference. We are thus thrown back upon Whitehead's surmises and suspicious allegations, for a possible explanation. Dr. Neely imagines "that perhaps it had some application to Wesley's desire that the Rev. John Fletcher, vicar of Madeley, should be his active assistant during his old age, and his probable successor in the Methodist leadership after his decease," but finally concludes that "the points do not fit." †

But to the Rev. Jean Guillaume de la Flechiere—John William Fletcher—saint and scholar, pietist and polemic, (born 1729, died 1785, six years before Wesley) and Wesley's other scheme of a personal successor, we must now turn our attention. Whitehead, after mentioning in language none too friendly that Wesley by general suffrage had acted as "dictator," continues: "He had often found that all his authority was barely sufficient to preserve peace, and the mere external appearance of unanimity, and therefore concluded, that if his authority were to cease, or not to be transferred to another at his death, the preachers and people would fall into confusion."‡ Hence the letter following, which Wesley wrote to Fletcher in January, 1773, from Shoreham, whither he had doubtless gone to take counsel with the venerable Perronet:

"*Dear Sir:* What an amazing work has God wrought in these kingdoms in less than forty years! And it not only continues, but increases throughout England, Scotland, and Ireland; nay, it has lately spread into New York, Pennsylvania, Virginia, Maryland, and Carolina. But the wise

* Hist. of Meth., I. 442.   † Neely, Gov. Conf. in Meth., p. 26.
‡ Whitehead, Life, II. 217.

men of the world say: 'When Mr. Wesley drops, then all this is at an end.' And so it surely will, unless, before God . calls him hence, one is found to stand in his place. For

'Ονκ ἀγαθὸν πολυκοιρανίη· εἶς κοίρανός ἔστω.*

I see more and more, unless there be one προεσώτς, the work can never be carried on. The body of the preachers are not united, nor will any part of them submit to the rest; so that there must be one to preside over all, or the work will indeed come to an end.

"But who is sufficient for these things? Qualified to preside both over the preachers and people? He must be a man of faith and love, and one that has a single eye to the advancement of the kingdom of God. He must have a clear understanding; a knowledge of men and things, particularly of the Methodist doctrine and discipline; a ready utterance; diligence and activity; with a tolerable share of health. There must be added to these, favor with the people, with the Methodists in general. For unless God turn their eyes and their hearts toward him, he will be quite incapable of the work. He must likewise have some degree of learning; because there are many adversaries, learned as well as unlearned, whose mouths must be stopped. But this cannot be done unless he be able to meet them on their own ground.

"But has God provided one so qualified? Who is he? Thou art the man! God has given you a measure of loving faith, and a single eye to his glory. He has given you some knowledge of men and things, particularly of the whole plan of Methodism. You are blessed with some health, activity, and diligence, together with a degree of learning. And to all these he has lately added, by a way none could have foreseen, favor both with the preachers and the whole people. Come out, in the name of God! Come to the help of the Lord against the mighty! Come, while I am alive and capable of labor—

---

* "It is not good that supreme power should be lodged in many hands: let there be one governor."

"'Dum superest Lachesi quod torqueat, et pedibus me
Porto meis, nullo dextram subeunte bacillo.' *

"Come, while I am able, God assisting, to build you up in the faith, to ripen your gifts, and to introduce you to the people. *Nil tanti.* What possible employment can you have which is of so great importance?

"But you will naturally say: 'I am not equal to the task; I have neither grace nor gifts for such an employment.' You say true; it is certain you have not—and who has? But do you not know Him who is able to give them? Perhaps not at once; but rather day by day: as each is, so shall your strength be. 'But this implies,' you may say, 'a thousand crosses, such as I feel I am not able to bear.'

"You are not able to bear them *now*, and they are not *now* come. Whenever they do come, will He not send them in due number, weight, and measure? And will they not all be for your profit, that you may be a partaker of His holiness?

"Without conferring, therefore, with flesh and blood, come and strengthen the hands, comfort the heart, and share the labors of your affectionate friend and brother,

"JOHN WESLEY." †

"This was a momentous proposal," adds Tyerman, and asks, "Why was it not made to Wesley's brother?" This seems to have been Fletcher's thought, also, but such conundrums it is hardly the province of history to answer. Dr. Whitehead indulges in some uncharitable and unfounded surmises as to the grounds of Fletcher's refusal: he does not appear to have known that Fletcher ever sent the reply which is here appended:

"MADELEY, 6th February, 1773.

"*Reverend and Dear Sir:* I hope the Lord, who has so wonderfully stood by you hitherto, will preserve you to see

---

* While Lachesis has some thread of life to spin, and I walk on my own feet without the help of a staff. (Juvenal, Sat. iii.)

† Whitehead's Life of Wesley, II. 217-219; Tyerman, Life and Times, III. 147, 148; Smith, Hist. of Wesleyan Meth., I. 487-489.

many of your sheep, and *me* among the rest, enter into rest.
Should Providence call you *first*, I shall do my best, by the
Lord's assistance, to help *your brother* to gather the wreck
and keep together those who are not absolutely bent upon
throwing away the Methodist doctrine or discipline.   Every
little help will then be necessary, and I hope I shall not be
backward to throw in my mite.

"In the meantime, you stand sometimes in need of an
assistant to serve tables and occasionally to fill up a gap.
Providence visibly appointed me to that office many years
ago; and though it no less evidently called me hither, yet I
have not been without doubt, especially for some years past,
whether it would not be expedient that I should resume my
place as your deacon; not with any view of presiding over
the Methodists after you (God knows!), but to save you a
little in your old age, and be in the way of receiving, and
perhaps of doing, more good.   I have sometimes considered
how shameful it was that no clergyman should join you to
keep in the Church the work which the Lord had enabled
you to carry on therein; and, as the little estate I have in
my native country is sufficient for my maintenance, I have
thought I would one day or other offer you and the Methodists my *free* services.

" While my love of retirement, and my dread of appearing upon a higher stage than that I stand upon here, make
me linger, I was providentially called to do something in
Lady Huntingdon's plan; but being shut out there, it appears to me that I am again called to my first work.

"Nevertheless, I would not leave this place without a
fuller persuasion that the time is quite come.   Not that God
uses me much *now* among my parishioners, but because I
have not sufficiently cleared my conscience from the blood
of all men, especially with regard to ferreting out the poor,
and expostulating with the rich, who make it their business
to fly from me.   In the meantime, it shall be my employment to beg the Lord to give me light, and make me willing
to go anywhere or nowhere, to be anything or nothing.

"I have laid my pen aside for some time; nevertheless, I resumed it last week, at your brother's request, to go on with my treatise on Christian perfection. I have made some alterations in the sheets you have seen, and hope to have a few more ready for your correction, against the time you come this way. How deep is the subject! What need have I of the Spirit, to search the deep things of God! Help me by your prayers, till you can help me by word of mouth.

"I am, reverend and dear sir, your willing, though unprofitable, servant in the gospel,

"JOHN FLETCHER." *

In July following Wesley renewed his invitation in a personal interview with Fletcher and soon after wrote him as follows:

"LEWISHAM, July 21, 1773.

"*Dear Sir:* It was a great satisfaction to me that I had the opportunity, which I so long desired, of spending a little time with you; and I really think it would answer many gracious designs of Providence were we to spend a little more time together. It might be of great advantage, both to ourselves and the people, who may otherwise soon be as sheep without a shepherd. You say, indeed, 'whenever it pleases God to call me away, you will do all you can to help them.' But will it not then be too late? You may then expect grievous wolves to break in on every side, and many to arise from among themselves speaking perverse things. Both the one and the other stand in awe of me, and do not care to encounter me; so that I am able, whether they will or no, to deliver the flock into your hands. But no one else is; and it seems this is the very time when it may be done with the least difficulty. Just now the minds of the people in general are, on account of the Checks, greatly prejudiced in your favor. Should we not discern the providential time? Should we stay till the impression is worn away? Just now we have an opportunity of breaking the

---

* Tyerman, Life and Times, III. 149; quoted from Moore's Life, II. 259.

3

ice, of making a little trial. Mr. Richardson is desirous of making an exchange with you, and spending two or three weeks at Madeley. This might be done either now or in October, when I hope to return from Bristol; and until something of this kind is done you will not have that στοργή for the people which alone can make your labor light in spending and being spent for them. Methinks 'tis pity we should lose any time; for what a vapor is life!

"I am, dear sir, your affectionate friend and brother,

JOHN WESLEY." *

Wesley once more, in January, 1776, invited Fletcher to accompany him on his tours through England and Scotland, but, under date of January 9, Fletcher makes a decisive answer: "I received last night the favor of yours from Bristol. My grand desire is to be just what the Lord would have me be. I could, if you wanted a traveling assistant, accompany you, as my little strength would admit, in some of your excursions; but your recommending me to the societies, as one who might succeed you, (should the Lord call you hence before me,) is a step to which I could by no means consent. It would make me take my horse and gallop away. Besides, such a step would, at this juncture, be, I think, peculiarly improper, and would cast upon my vindication of your minutes such an odium as the Calvinists have endeavored to cast upon your 'Address.' It would make people suspect, that what I have done for truth and conscience sake, I have done with a view of being, what Mr. Toplady calls, 'the bishop of Moorfields.' We ought to give as little hold to the evil surmising and rash judgments of our opponents as may be. If, nevertheless, Providence throws in your way a clergyman willing to assist us, it would be well to fall in with that circumstance." †

Thus this project of designating a personal successor who should discharge, at least in some measure, Mr. Wesley's functions, came to naught. The plan of union on the basis of the " old Methodist doctrine " and the " whole Methodist

---

* Tyerman, III. 150.   † See the whole letter in Tyerman, III. 212, 213.

discipline '' was presented for signatures for the last time, as we have seen, at the Conference of 1775. For the reasons, possibly, assigned by Dr. Whitehead, or for others now unknown, it seems to have been abandoned. It was excellent as far as it went, and Mr. Wesley at this time probably regarded this conferential compact as binding until something better could be provided. In March, 1776, Mr. Wesley was seventy-three years old: it was high time that adequate provision for the perpetuity of Methodism were made. Both of his schemes, whether they were intended to be independent or in some way to be combined, as might have very well been done, had so far issued in no sufficient and final relief. An efficient personal superintendent, to whom preachers and people would yield a willing obedience, had not been secured; and the Conference had not been organized into a center of unity and government.

CHAPTER III.

THOMAS COKE AND THE DEED OF DECLARATION.

ABOUT the time that Fletcher's health, never robust, began to fail finally, Providence sent to Mr. Wesley, instead of his ardently desired and persistently designated successor, that remarkable young man whom he fondly regarded as his "right hand"—the Rev. Thomas Coke, LL.D. (born 1747, died 1814), the first Bishop of the Methodist Episcopal Church in America, and Mr. Wesley's chosen and accredited deputy in its organization. Forty-four years the junior of his chief, active, intelligent, devoted, vigilant, pious, he seemed at last the man for the hour.

Tuesday, Aug. 19, 1777, Mr. Wesley records in his Journal: "I went forward to Taunton with Dr. Coke who, being dismissed from his curacy, has bid adieu to his honorable name, and determined to cast in his lot with us." * The little Doctor—for he was small of stature, like Wesley himself—attended the Methodist Conference this year at Bristol, but, for unknown reasons (conjectured, however, by Samuel Drew, his biographer, to be connected with Mr. Wesley's supposed desire to retain him near his own person, lest the possible tender of preferment in the Establishment might entice him away from the Methodists before he was irrevocably committed to their cause)† his name does not appear in the Minutes until 1778, when he was appointed to labor in London, where he became superintendent of the circuit in 1780, about which time he also began to alternate with Mr. Wesley in annual visits to Ireland. In 1782 he was deputed to preside at the first Irish Conference, held in

---

* Wesley's Journal, Amer. Ed., II. 477.
† Drew, Life of Coke, Amer. Ed., p. 40.

the city of Dublin,* as subsequently, in 1784, he presided in the great American organizing Conference, commonly, but mistakenly, called the first General, at Baltimore.

At the English Conference of 1782, Coke took the most prominent part in steps toward the final and legal settlement of the title-deeds of the Methodist chapels, about which considerable difficulties, legal and other, to be more particularly described hereafter, had arisen.

At a very early period, Wesley published a model deed for the satisfactory settlement of chapels, the chief provisions of which were these two, namely: (1) The trustees were to permit Wesley himself and his appointees from the conference to have the free and undisturbed use of such chapels, for the purpose of preaching God's holy word therein—on Wesley's decease his rights were to descend to his brother Charles, and in case of the latter's death, to the Rev. William Grimshaw (a Yorkshire clergyman and graduate of Cambridge, who united with the Methodists in 1745, but died as early as 1763); (2) After the decease of these three clergymen— the Wesleys and Grimshaw—the chapels were to be held in trust for the sole use of the persons appointed at the Yearly Conference of the People called Methodists, *provided* that these appointees preached no other doctrines than those contained in Wesley's Notes on the New Testament and in his four volumes of Sermons.†

The origin and history of this deed is thus given by Mr. Wesley himself, under date of Jan. 3, 1783:

"4. I built the first Methodist preaching house, so called, at Bristol, in the year 1739. And knowing no better, I suffered the deed of trust to be drawn up in the Presbyterian form. But Mr. Whitefield hearing of it, wrote me a warm letter, asking, 'Do you consider what you do? If the trustees are to name the preachers, they may exclude even you from preaching in the house you have built! Pray let this deed be immediately canceled.' To this the trustees readily agreed. Afterward I built the preaching houses in

---

* Drew, Life of Coke, pp. 49, 50. † Tyerman, Life and Times, III. 417.

Kingswood, and at Newcastle-upon-Tyne. But none beside myself had any right to appoint the preachers in them.

"5. About this time a preaching house was built at Birstal, by contributions and collections. And John Nelson, knowing no better, suffered a deed to be drawn in the Presbyterian form, giving twelve or thirteen persons power not only of placing, but even of displacing, the preachers at their pleasure. Had Mr. Whitefield or I known this, we should have insisted on its either being canceled, like that at Bristol, or so altered as to insure the application of the house to the purpose for which it was built, without giving so dangerous a power to any trustees whatever.

" 6. But a considerable difficulty still remained. As the houses at Bristol, Kingswood, and Newcastle were my property, a friend reminded me, that they were all liable to descend to my heirs. (Pray let those consider this, who are so fond of having preaching houses vested in them and their heirs forever!) I was struck, and immediately procured a form to be drawn up by three of the most eminent counselors in London, whereby not only these houses, but all the Methodist houses hereafter to be built, might be settled on such a plan, as would secure them, so far as human prudence could, from the heirs of the proprietors, for the purpose originally intended." *

In 1784, the date of the Deed of Declaration, there were according to Myles (Chronological History) three hundred and fifty-nine Methodist chapels in the United Kingdom, most of which, it may be presumed, were settled according to the provisions of this " model deed."† Mr. Pawson declares,‡ that from the year 1750 all Methodist chapels were held according to the conditions of this deed; but there were certainly some exceptions, as Nelson's original Presbyterian deed to the Birstal chapel, to which Mr. Wesley refers above, and about which trouble arose, was drawn and

* Wesley's Works, Amer. ed., VII. 326, 327, " Case of Birstal House."
† Tyerman, III. 417, 418.
‡ MS. memoir of Dr. Whitehead; see Tyerman, III. 420.

dated in 1751. Still with the model deed itself there was dissatisfaction among the " wisest and best preachers," and at the Conference of 1767 the question was raised, "Are our preaching houses settled in our form safe? Should we not have the opinion of a counsel?" To these inquiries Mr. Wesley replied: "I think not. 1. Because the form was drawn up by three eminent counselors. But, 2. It is the way of every counsel to blame what another counsel has done; but you cannot at all infer that they think it wrong because they say so. 3. If they did in reality think it wrong, that would not prove that it was so. 4. If there was (which I do not believe) some defect therein, who would go to law with the body of Methodists? 5. And if they did, would any court in England put them out of possession, especially when the intent of the deed is plain and undeniable. *

But this reasoning, plausible as it was, did not long satisfy the preachers, especially Messrs. Hampson and Oddie, who, according to Pawson, "were men of remarkably deep understanding and sound judgment." Wesley began to yield, and various schemes were proposed. One was to consolidate all the chapels of Methodism into a general trust. Another was to have all the deeds brought to London and deposited in a strong box provided for the purpose: many were actually sent and, in consequence, some were lost.†

In 1782 the chapel at Birstal was rebuilt or enlarged and a new deed, for various reasons, detailed by Tyerman, was prepared, " which," says Wesley, " like the old [of 1751], gave a few persons the power of placing and displacing the preachers at their pleasure. This was brought and read to me at Daw Green. As soon as ever I heard it, I vehemently objected to it, and positively refused to sign it. . . . But in the evening several persons came again, and importunately urged me to sign it; averring that it was the same in effect with the old deed, and the old deed could not be altered. Not adverting that it was altered in the new

---

* Tyerman, III. 420; Neely, Governing Conference in Methodism, p. 49.
† Tyerman, III. 420, 421.

one, I, at length, unwillingly complied."* This new deed was dated May 14, 1782, and, says Tyerman, " was widely different from that of 1751, and, as the vice-chancellor ruled in 1854, so far as it purported to vary the trusts of the latter deed, it was void and of no effect, but it still contained the obnoxious clause, giving power to other parties than Wesley's Conference to appoint the preachers."†

Wesley, now an old man nearly eighty, had committed a blunder, shared in, however, by others. There was no predicting whereunto this thing might grow. The whole matter came up for review and settlement at the Conference of 1782, whose deliverance was explicit and decisive: "If the trustees still refuse to settle it on the Methodist plan; if they still insist that they will have the right of placing and displacing the preachers at their pleasure,—then, First, let a plain statement of the case be drawn up. Secondly, let a collection be made throughout all England in order to purchase ground, and build another preaching house as near the present as may be." ‡

The execution of this mandate of Conference was entrusted to Dr. Coke, who was at the same time directed to travel throughout England to see that all the chapels were settled according to the Conference plan. He promptly issued an "Address to the Inhabitants of Birstal," etc., in which, by way of a " plain statement " he narrates the history of their chapel deed and notifies them that he had been delegated to execute the Conference minute. It was a vital issue and a critical time. Methodism had reached the forks of the road; congregationalism or connexionalism, if not the perpetuity of Methodism itself, hung upon the issue. Wesley wrote to Bradford, " Birstal is a leading case, the first of an avowed violation of our plan; therefore the point must be carried for the Methodist preachers now or never, and I alone can carry it, which I will, God being my helper." In the paper on the Birstal House already cited,

---

* Wesley's Works, VII. 327. † Life and Times, III. 374, 375.
‡ Wesley's Works, VII. 327.

issued January 3, 1783, he lucidly discloses the evils which must arise from allowing such powers to trustees.

" Itinerant preaching is no more. When the trustees in any place have found and fixed a preacher they like, the rotation of preachers is at an end; at least, till they are tired of their favorite preacher, and so turned him out. While he stays, is not the bridle in his mouth? How dares he speak the full and the whole truth, since, whenever he displeases the trustees, he is liable to lose his bread? How much less will he dare to put a trustee, though ever so ungodly, out of the society! . . . I am not pleading my own cause. . . . I am pleading for Mr. Taylor, Mr. Bradburn, Mr. Benson, and for every other traveling preacher, that you may be as free, after I am gone hence, as you are now I am at your head; that you may never be liable to be turned out of any or all of our houses without any reason given, but that so is the pleasure of twenty or thirty men. . . . I insist upon that point, and let everything else go. No Methodist trustees, if I can help it, shall, after my death, any more than while I live, have the power of placing and displacing the preachers."*

The final result of this agitation was that a new deed was made, " giving the Conference power to appoint the preachers; and this serious hubbub, *pro tem.*, subsided."† Dr. Coke had actually purchased ground for the site of a new chapel, according to the direction of the Conference, and one reason why the trustees had claimed extraordinary powers was because of a debt of £350 on their new chapel, which they had advanced the money to pay. Wesley offered to relieve them of their debt and to present them with the ground Coke had bought, if they would make a satisfactory deed, which, according to the opinion of Mr. Maddocks, an eminent attorney, they were competent to do. Mr. Joseph Charlesworth, one of the trustees, in finally accepting Mr. Wesley's offer on behalf of his brethren, naïvely wrote:

---

* Wesley's Works, VII. 328.
† Tyerman, III. 382. See the whole account, III. 373-382.

" We cannot but acknowledge your goodness in promising the land, and the money towards paying our debt, which will be two very convenient articles at this place, as we are in great want of both."

But this Birstal trouble of 1782 led to a critical inquiry into the merits of the model deed itself, which had, hitherto, been adjudged sufficient. Was the " Yearly Conference of the People called Methodists " such a body as possessed a *legal* existence? Could it be legally described and legally identified? Of what followed Dr. Coke himself tells us in his "Address to the Methodist Society in Great Britain and Ireland on the settlement of the Preaching houses " :

" In the Conference held in the year 1782 several complaints were made in respect to the danger in which we were situated from the want of specifying, in distinct and legal terms, what was meant by the term, ' The Conference of the People called Methodists.' Indeed, the preachers seemed universally alarmed, and many expressed their fears that divisions would take place among us after the death of Mr. Wesley on this account; and the whole body of preachers present seemed to wish that some methods might be taken to remove this danger, which appeared to be pregnant with evils of the first magnitude.

"In consequence of this (the subject lying heavy on my heart), I desired Mr. Clulow, of Chancery Lane, London, to draw up such a case as I judged sufficient, and then to present it to that very eminent counselor, Mr. Maddocks, for his opinion. This was accordingly done, and Mr. Maddocks informed us, in his answer, that the deeds of our preaching houses were in the situation we dreaded; that the law would not recognize the Conference in the state in which it stood at that time, and, consequently, that there was no central point which might preserve the connection from splitting into a thousand pieces after the death of Mr. Wesley. To prevent this, he observed that Mr. Wesley should enroll a deed in chancery, which deed should specify the persons by name who composed the Conference, together with the mode of succession for its perpetuity; and at the same time such regulations be established by the deed as Mr. Wesley would wish the Conference should be governed by, after his death.

" This opinion of Mr. Maddocks I read in the Conference of 1783. The whole Conference seemed grateful to me for procuring the opinion, and expressed their wishes that such a deed might be drawn up and executed by Mr. Wesley as should agree with the advice of that great lawyer, as soon as possible.

" Soon after the Conference was ended, Mr. Wesley authorized me to draw up, with the assistance of Mr. Clulow, all the leading parts of a deed which should answer the above mentioned purposes. This we did with much care, and as to myself I can truly say with fear and trembling, receiving Mr. Maddocks' advice in respect to every step we took, and laying the whole ultimately at Mr. Wesley's feet for his approbation; there remained now nothing but to insert the names of those who were to constitute the Conference. Mr. Wesley then declared that he would limit the number to one hundred. This was indeed contrary to my very humble opinion, which was, that every preacher, in full connection, should be a member of the Conference; and that admission into full connection should be looked upon as admission into membership with the Conference; and I still believe it will be most for the glory of God, and the peace of our Zion, that the members of the Conference admit the other preachers who are in full connection, and are present at the Conference from time to time, to a full vote on all occasions. However, of course, I submitted to the superior judgment and authority of Mr. Wesley." *

This was the origin of, and this Dr. Coke's agency in procuring, the Magna Charta of English Methodism, the famous Deed of Declaration, dated Feb. 28, 1784: the further consideration of which, with the temporary troubles and lasting blessings which grew out of it, we defer to our account

* Drew, Life of Coke, pp. 47, 48.

of "the grand climacteric year." The Deed has stood the
test of litigation, and the strain and stress of changing times
and conditions: it remains to this day the sufficient instrument which has conserved and prospered the best interests
of English Methodism. For no act of his life, perhaps, was
Mr. Wesley more severely or more generally maligned: no
single deed of his has, perhaps, proved more signally bene-
ficial to his British followers. Time and experience have
brought a complete vindication of the wisdom of the independent course which he pursued.

BOOK II.

—

AMERICAN METHODISM TO 1784.

BEGINNINGS OF METHODISM IN AMERICA.

THE FIRST AMERICAN CONFERENCE.

THE ANNUAL CONFERENCES TO THE CLOSE OF RAN-
KIN'S ADMINISTRATION, 1777.

DISCORD AND DISUNION: 1778–1780.

PEACE AND PROSPERITY: 1781–1784.

(45)

CHAPTER IV.

BEGINNINGS OF METHODISM IN AMERICA.

THE Founder of Methodism resided in America as a clergyman of the Church of England, with Georgia for his parish, from Feb. 5, 1736, to Dec. 22, 1737. With his brother Charles, Benjamin Ingham, and Charles Delamotte, (who was his constant and intimate companion throughout the period of his American sojourn,) he landed at Savannah, Ga., on the former date, having set sail from England, Oct. 14, 1735. Charles Wesley, who was Oglethorpe's secretary, and Ingham, set out with the General to found Frederica; while John Wesley and Delamotte remained at Savannah, lodging for the time with Spangenberg, Nitschmann, and other Moravians. Wesley began his ministry at Savannah March 7, 1736, with a sermon on 1 Cor. xiii. 3.

Oxford Methodism, with its shining excellencies but serious defects, " misty, austere, gloomy, and forbidding," but " intensely sincere, earnest, and self-denying," * was now a thing of the past: its leaders had dispersed to both sides of the Atlantic, and apparently its work was done and its story told. The Methodism of the United Society was not yet born, and many sad American experiences must yet qualify its founder to return to England to begin that great work.

July 26, 1736, after spending little more than five months in Georgia, Charles Wesley embarked for England: in a little more than a year after his arrival Ingham also returned home.

In German, French, and Spanish, as well as in English, Wesley conducted his ministry in Georgia. German was his ordinary medium of intercourse with the Moravians;

---

* Tyerman, I. 107.

Spanish he learned that he might be able to instruct some Jews among his parishioners; and we learn of his giving French lessons to Miss Hopkey, afterwards Mrs. Williamson, association with whom was the source of many trials and tribulations to her parish priest, needless to be related here.

On a return trip from Frederica to Savannah in January, 1737, Wesley perused the works of Macchiavelli, and since his own genius for government and methods of administration have been rather freely likened to those of Richelieu and Loyola, it may be interesting to note the opinion which he formed and expressed, " that if all the other doctrines of devils, which have been committed to writing, were collected together in one volume, it would fall short of this; and that should a prince form himself by this book, so calmly recommending hypocrisy, treachery, lying, robbery, oppression, adultery, whoredom, and murder of all kinds, Domitian or Nero would be an angel of light compared to that man."

Wesley's ideas of religion at this period are freely expressed in a letter written in March, 1737: " I entirely agree with you, that religion is love, and peace, and joy in the Holy Ghost; that, as it is the happiest, so it is the cheerfulest thing in the world; that it is utterly inconsistent with moroseness, sourness, severity, and indeed with whatever is not according to the softness, sweetness, and gentleness of Christ Jesus. I believe it is equally contrary to all preciseness, stiffness, affectation, and unnecessary singularity. I allow, too, that prudence, as well as zeal, is of the utmost importance in the Christian life. But I do not yet see any possible case wherein trifling conversation can be an instance of it. In the following scriptures I take all such to be flatly forbidden: Matt. xii. 36; Eph. v. 4, and iv. 29; Col. iv. 6."

Other characteristics of the later Methodism, now latent in Wesley's mind and heart, also appear in the following: " When I first landed at Savannah, a gentlewoman said, ' I assure you, sir, you will see as *well dressed* a congregation on Sunday as most you have seen in London.' I did so;

and soon after I took occasion to expound those scriptures which relate to dress; and all the time that I afterward ministered at Savannah, I saw neither gold in the church, nor costly apparel, but the congregation in general was almost constantly clothed in plain clean linen or woolen."

In Savannah his manner of life, especially in the execution of his clerical duties, excited much comment. He was, in fact, regarded as a Romanist,—"(1) Because he rigidly excluded all Dissenters from the holy communion, until they first gave up their faith and principles and, like Richard Turner and his sons, submitted to be rebaptized by him; (2) because Roman Catholics were received by him as saints; (3) because he endeavored to establish and enforce confession, penance, and mortification; mixed wine with water at the sacrament; and appointed deaconesses in accordance with what he called the Apostolic Constitutions. He was, in point of fact," concludes Tyerman, " a Puseyite a hundred years before Dr. Pusey flourished." *

His conduct as a clergyman, while characterized by conscientiousness, studiousness, industrious application to incessant parish labors, self-denial, and diligent attention to public worship and the administration of the sacraments, was, indeed, " arrogant, foolish, offensive, intolerant; but the petty magisterial court at Savannah had no more right to try him for his high church practices than an Old Bailey judge and jury have to try the half-fledged papistical rectors, curates, and incumbents, who are playing such fantastic tricks in the Protestant churches of old England at the present day." † But the Williamson affair finally assumed such a shape that in disgust Wesley was driven from the colony, sailing Dec. 22, 1737, from Charleston, a town which he had twice before visited, once in July, 1736, when his brother Charles left for England, and again in April, 1737, when he preached on " Whatsoever is born of God overcometh the world." " He must have spoken as a Methodist preacher should, for after service a man of education and character

---

* Life and Times, I. 147, 148. † Tyerman, I. 159.

4

seriously objected to the sermon, saying, ' Why if this be Christianity, a Christian must have more courage than Alexander the Great.' " *

So ended Wesley's labors in Georgia, leaving no trace on the continental American Methodism that was yet to be. More humble men, under his inspiration and partly under his directions, were to lay its enduring foundations. Wesley was not yet ready for his task.

The Rev. Luke Tyerman, a laborious and exhaustive biographer, (to whom all after-comers must confess indebtedness,) but not always the most discreet, cannot forbear some wild speculations as to the possible consequences of Wesley's marriage with Miss Sophy Hopkey and his settlement in Savannah.   Only an Englishman, totally ignorant of the character, habits, and history of the American Indian could at this late date perpetrate the following: " Had John Wesley married Sophia Christiana Hopkey, the probability is that, instead of returning to England and beginning the greatest religious revival of modern times, he would have settled in Georgia, and, like another Xavier, have spent a most spiritual and devoted life in converting Indian and other kinds of heathen.   The results of such a life might have been glorious. Who can tell what might have been its influence upon the civilization and perpetuation of the nobly formed aboriginal inhabitants of the vast American continent?   Would America, in the decline of the nineteenth century, have been inhabited by European strangers or by educated, civilized, hard-working, prosperous descendants of the wild Indians of the woods? "

George Whitefield, as we have seen in a previous chapter, sailed for America the day before Wesley's arrival in England, Feb. 1, 1738.   Seven visits in all did this flaming evangelist make to America, at last laying down his body with his charge, ceasing at once to work and live, at New-

---

* McTyeire, Sermons, p. 52. Wesley also at this time issued what may be styled the first Methodist hymn book, whose title page bears date, Charleston, 1737.

buryport, Mass., Sept. 30, 1770, where his remains rest to
this day. His last sermon was preached at Exeter the day
before his death, when he held a vast multitude spell-bound
for two hours. The fruits of his evangelistic tours were
shared by all the Churches, Congregational, Presbyterian,
and Baptist, from Massachusetts to Georgia. In Philadelphia, New York, and Boston immense and delighted audiences waited on his ministry and great awakenings followed.
Jonathan Edwards was melted to tears under his preaching,
and Benjamin Franklin unconditionally surrendered to the
spell of his matchless oratory. He saw on one occasion
that Whitefield was going to lift a collection, but though he
had copper, gold, and silver in his pocket, he determined to
give nothing. But as the sermon progressed, " I began to
soften," he says, " and concluded to give the copper. Another stroke of his oratory determined me to give the silver;
and he finished so admirably that I emptied my pocket wholly into the collector's dish, gold and all."

In England eternity only will reveal the work accomplished
by Whitefield and his " female prelate, the grand, stately,
strong-minded, godly, and self-sacrificing Countess of Huntingdon ": in America, his labors were incomparably more
extensive and fruitful than those of Wesley. He was American Methodism's John the Baptist, bringing countless multi-
tudes to repentance, and, as a voice crying in the wilderness, preparing the way of the Lord.

Strawbridge, Embury, and Webb—local preachers all;
Boardman and Pilmoor—Wesley's first missionaries; Rankin and Asbury—the first general assistants for America,—
doubtless " gathered not a little of the fruit where Whitefield
had shaken the boughs." *

The labors of these heroes of the cross our prescribed
limits will not permit us to follow in detail: Strawbridge
planted Methodism in Maryland; Embury in New York;
and Webb in Pennsylvania. The two Irishmen, Strawbridge and Embury, came to America probably about the

---

* McTyeire, History of Methodism, p. 253.

same time—1760. Embury, inspired by Barbara Heck, began preaching in his own house in New York in the autumn
of 1766; in 1767 removed to the Rigging Lo ; and in 1768
built the John Street chapel, which he dedicated Oct. 30 of
that year. Strawbridge probably began preaching in his own
house on Sam's Creek as early as 1760, (as maintained by Dr.
Roberts,* a Baltimore local preacher of ability, who thoroughly investigated the case) and in 1762 had a second preaching place. The Rev. Wm. Hamilton states that by Strawbridge a "society consisting of twelve or fifteen persons
was formed as early as 1763 or 1764 and soon after a place
of worship was erected called the 'Log Meetinghouse.'"†
Without seeking to determine the question as to the relative priority of Strawbridge's or Embury's work, we may
content ourselves with recording Bishop Asbury's statement,
given in his Journal under date of April 30, 1801: "We arrived to dine at Alexander Warfield's, on Sam's Creek, and
pushed on to Henry Willis's, on Pipe Creek, where it had
been our intention to open Conference. We had about forty members present, and sat on Friday, Saturday, and Monday: on Tuesday morning we rose. . . . . There was
preaching every day and every night. Our own people and
our friends in the settlement were equally kind; and we had
rich entertainment. The settlement of Pipe Creek is the
richest in the state; here Mr. Strawbridge formed the first
society in Maryland—*and America.*" ‡

In 1769, Oct. 24, Boardman and Pilmoor were welcomed
at Philadelphia by Captain Webb, whom Dr. Stevens regards
as the chief founder of American Methodism. Richard
Boardman acted as Wesley's "assistant" or superintendent
for the work in America. In 1770, "America" appears for
the first time in the list of appointments from the English Conference. To this circuit, four preachers were assigned: Jo-

---

* Dr. Stevens, I. 54, calls him "one of our best authorities in Methodist
antiquarian researches."
† Meth. Quart. Rev. 1856, Art. "Early Meth. in Maryland."
‡ Asbury's Journal, ed. 1821, III. 27; the italics are in the original.

seph Pilmoor, Richard Boardman, Robert Williams, and
John King.   Williams, a volunteer, whom Wesley had endorsed, had reached America a few weeks before the regular itinerant missionaries, and enjoys the peculiar distinction
of being "the first Methodist minister in America that
published a book, the first that married, the first that located,
and the first that died."   His greater claim to grateful remembrance arises from the fact that he was the spiritual
father of Jesse Lee, the founder of New England Methodism.   King, who arrived in the country shortly after the
missionaries, was the first to preach the gospel according to
Methodism in the city of Baltimore, where it has ever since
maintained its primacy.

Francis Asbury, the apostle of American Methodism, and
Richard Wright, were Wesley's second brace of itinerant
appointees, and sailed from Bristol, Sept. 4, 1771.   They
reached Philadelphia, Oct. 27, 1771.   Thursday, Sept. 12,
Asbury indulged in self-examination: "Whither am I going?
To the new world.   What to do?   To gain honor?   No, if
I know my own heart.   To get money?   No, I am going to
live to God, and to bring others so to do. . . .   The
people God owns in England are the Methodists.   The doctrines they preach, and the discipline they enforce, are, I
believe, the purest of any people now in the world.   The
Lord has greatly blessed these doctrines and this discipline
in the three kingdoms: they must therefore be pleasing to
him.   If God does not acknowledge me in America, I will
soon return to England.   I know my views are upright now
—may they never be otherwise!" *

On their arrival in Philadelphia, the missionaries "were
directed to the house of one, Mr. Francis Harris, who,"
writes Asbury, "kindly entertained us in the evening, and
brought us to a large church, where we met with a considerable congregation.   Brother Pilmoor preached.   The
people looked on us with pleasure, hardly knowing how to
show their love sufficiently, bidding us welcome with fervent

* Asbury's Journal, I. 2.

affection, and receiving us as angels of God. . . . I felt my mind open to the people, and my tongue loosed to speak." *

This "large church," in which Pilmoor welcomed Asbury, as Asbury afterward welcomed Coke in Barratt's Chapel, was St. George's, revered as the "Old Cathedral" of Methodism in Philadelphia. For nearly fifty years it was the largest Methodist church in America. In it the first American Conference was held in 1773. It had been bought, in an unfinished state, from the German Reformed Church in 1770 by Miles Pennington, one of the first members of the first class, formed by Captain Webb in 1768.

In little more than two weeks, on Nov. 12, Asbury set out for New York, and at that place, Tuesday, Nov. 20, records in his Journal: "I remain in York though unsatisfied with our being both in town together. I have not yet the thing which I seek—a circulation of preachers to avoid partiality and popularity. However, I am fixed to the Methodist plan, and do what I do faithfully as to God. I expect trouble is at hand. This I expected when I left England, and I am willing to suffer—yea, to die—sooner than betray so good a cause by any means. It will be a hard matter to stand against all opposition as an iron pillar strong, and steadfast as a wall of brass; but, through Christ strengthening me, I can do all things." †

In New York he had found Boardman, "in peace, but weak in body." Two days later he adds: "At present I am dissatisfied. I judge we are to be shut up in the cities this winter. My brethren seem unwilling to leave the cities, but I think I shall show them the way. I am in trouble, and more trouble is at hand, for I am determined to make a stand against all partiality. I have nothing to seek but the glory of God, nothing to fear but his displeasure. I am come over with an upright intention, and through the grace of God I will make it appear: and I am determined that no man shall bias me with soft words and fair speeches;

* Journal, I. 4.   † *Ibid.*, I. 6

. . . but whomsoever I please or displease, I will be faithful to God, to the people, and to my own soul."

Boardman was the chief—Mr. Wesley's "Assistant" in charge of the American circuit; Asbury the subordinate— only a "helper." But perhaps there had been some talk with Wesley about evils he was to correct, with some special commission, before he left England, as Asbury declares he had expected trouble even before his departure. Moreover, Pilmoor had written to Wesley that Mr. Boardman and himself were "chiefly confined to the cities, and therefore cannot, at present, go much into the country:" both the policy and the reasons assigned for it, Wesley probably disliked; if so, Asbury had been told what he was to do. Of Boardman, Asbury writes, he "is a kind, loving, worthy man, truly amiable and entertaining, and of a childlike temper." His silence about his administrative gifts is noteworthy. It is not surprising, therefore, that under date of Oct. 10, 1772, we find Asbury making this record: "I received a letter from Mr. Wesley, in which he required a strict attention to discipline; *and appointed me to act as assistant.*"

Philadelphia and New York were good enough for Pilmoor (who subsequently became one of American Methodism's earliest contributions to the ministry of the Protestant Episcopal Church) and good Brother Boardman; Strawbridge was later settled over the Sam's Creek and Bush Forest congregations; and Asbury once had a "call" to an Episcopal Church in Maryland: "the Church and the nation owe the maintenance of the itinerancy," says Stevens, "with its incalculable blessings, chiefly to the invincible energy of Francis Asbury."

Asbury's promotion was effected apparently without friction, for on Oct. 19 he met Brother Boardman at Princeton and says, "We both agreed in judgment about the affairs of the society, and were comforted together," which seems to be a modest way of stating that the new "helper" accepted the views of the new "assistant" and easily adjusted himself to the changed situation, which relieved him of irksome responsibility.

The first Quarterly Conference in America of which we have any account was held at J. Presbury's on the western shore of Maryland, Dec. 23, 1772. Mr. Asbury says:

"We afterwards proceeded to our temporal business, and considered the following propositions:

" 1. What are our collections? We found them sufficient to defray our expenses.

" 2. How are the preachers stationed? Brother S. [Strawbridge] and Brother O. [Owen], in Frederick County; Brother K. [King], Brother W. [Webster], and I. R. [Isaac Rollins], on the other side of the bay; and myself in Baltimore.

" 3. Shall we be strict in our society meetings, and not admit strangers? Agreed.

" 4. Shall we drop preaching in the day time through the week? Not agreed to.

" 5. Will the people be contented without our administering the sacrament? J. K. was neuter; Brother S. pleaded much for the ordinances, and so did the people, who appeared to be much biased by him. I told them I would not agree to it at that time, and insisted on our abiding by our rules. But Mr. B. [Boardman] had given them their way at the quarterly meeting held here before, and I was obliged to connive at some things for the sake of peace.

" 6. Shall we make collections weekly, to pay the preachers' board and expenses? This was not agreed to: we then inquired into the moral character of the preachers and exhorters. Only one exhorter was found any way doubtful, and we have great hopes of him. Brother S. received £8 quarterage; Brother K. and myself, £6 each. Great love subsisted among us in this meeting, and we parted in peace." *

Here the great question of the ordinances, which subsequently came so near producing an early schism in American Methodism, meets us for the first time: Strawbridge appears

---

* Journal, I. 37, 38. Cf. Stevens, Hist. M. E. Ch., I. 133.

as the earnest advocate of the administration of the sacraments and Asbury falls heir to some difficulties arising from the lax administration of easy Brother Boardman.

At the British Conference of 1772, Captain Webb, recruiting for America, asked for two of the ablest men, Christopher Hopper and Joseph Benson, the commentator. Thomas Rankin and George Shadford were sent and were cordially received by Asbury at Philadelphia, June 3, 1773.[*]

"Thomas Rankin was one of the commanding men of the Wesleyan itinerancy. Wesley appointed him at once General Assistant or Superintendent of the American Societies, for he was not only Asbury's senior in the itinerancy, but was an experienced disciplinarian; and Wesley judged him competent to manage the difficulties which had arisen under the administration of Asbury, as represented in the correspondence of the latter. Asbury had probably asked to be relieved by such a successor, and welcomed him with sincere gratification."[†]

Mr. Asbury's plan of extending the work had carried him much into the country districts. To this policy, as we have seen, he steadfastly adhered. "But while he was thus engaged in visiting the plantations and villages, an undue eagerness to extend the work in the towns had unhappily led to a comparative neglect of discipline."[‡] Dr. Bangs declares that "notwithstanding the vigilance of Mr. Asbury . . . many disorders still existed for which an adequate remedy had not been provided. These things had been communicated to Mr. Wesley, and he therefore clothed Mr. Rankin with powers superior to any which had been vested in his predecessors in office."[§]

---

[*] Journal, I. 52.　　　　　　　　[†] Stevens, Hist. M. E. Church, I. 142.
[‡] Drew, Life of Coke, p. 61.　　[§] Bangs, Hist. M. E. Ch., I. 80.

CHAPTER V.

THE FIRST AMERICAN CONFERENCE: 1773.

THAT Thomas Rankin, the accomplished disciplinarian of eleven years' standing in the British Conference, and Mr. Wesley's General Assistant for America, specially appointed to rectify the American administration and to bring it into harmony with the English model, formed under Wesley's own eye and hand, should preside over the itinerants of the New World in their first Conference at Philadelphia in 1773, was a matter of course. He represented his chief. Mr. Wesley's right of appointment and control was undisputed, and, in the light of all the precedents in which these men had been trained, indisputable. The title of the Minutes of the first formal Conference ever held by Methodist preachers on the continent of America is "Minutes of Some Conversations between the Preachers in Connexion with the Reverend Mr. John Wesley." And this continued to be the official heading of the proceedings of the American Conference down to and including the Conference which sat in April and May of 1784. In 1785 begins the series of "Minutes Taken at the Several Annual Conferences of the Methodist Episcopal Church:" a series which in both branches of Episcopal Methodism has been perpetuated to this day.[*]

Thus from the beginning in both England and America, Methodism has been a "Connexion." The term is technical, and characteristic of the denomination. Connexionalism is of the essence of the system, equally opposed to congregationalism in the churches and to individualism in the preachers. Mr. Wesley, in America no less than in England, was, at the first, the center of union. Connexion with

---

[*] Minutes, ed. of 1813, pp. 2-49; ed. of 1840, pp. 5-21.

(58)

him was the living bond which held incipient American Methodism together. He was the fountain of authority, acknowledged by all as rightful, original, and supreme. Through him a closer organic union subsisted between the Methodism of America, recognized at home as scarcely more than a needy but promising and fruitful mission-field, and that of England, than between the colonies, now on the eve of revolt, and the mother country. Mr. Wesley was the patriarch and apostle, the founder and creator, of Ecumenical Methodism. Mr. Rankin was his American legate or viceroy. He took the President's chair in the first Conference without question and as of right. He directed the business and made the appointments of the preachers.

In St. George's Church, the "Methodist cathedral," in the city of Philadelphia, on the canonical day, Wednesday, July 14, 1773, the first American Methodist Conference assembled: it continued in session three days, adjourning Friday, July 16.* Asbury calls the Conference "*General,*"† but this was in contradistinction to the Quarterly Conferences hitherto held: the distinction between *Annual* and *General* Conferences did not yet exist. The Conference from this time became *annual*, as to its periodical meetings, and *general*, as to its representing and supervising and providing for the whole work. Its functions as we shall see were chiefly *executive*, though, also, under the necessities of the situation of the Americans and the watchful and sufficient authority of Mr. Rankin, partially *legislative*. Its legislation was of two general descriptions: (1) Declared agreement with, and subordination to, Mr. Wesley and the British Conference in the fundamentals of doctrine and polity; and (2) Special and local rules to guide the administration

---

*These dates are fixed with certainty by both Rankin's and Asbury's Journals. See A.'s Journal, I. 55. The printed minutes represent it as held in June—this is clearly a mistake, either clerical or typographical. Bangs' and Smith's Histories say July 4, but that day in 1773 was Sunday. Other dates are given by various authorities. Compare Stevens, Hist. M. E. Church, I. 160, footnote.

† Journal, I. 55.

of the American preachers, in the peculiar circumstances in which they found themselves.

The first American Conference, like the first English, of 1744, was composed of ten members, all Europeans, as follows: Thomas Rankin, Richard Boardman, Joseph Pilmoor, Francis Asbury, Richard Wright, George Shadford, Thomas Webb, John King, Abraham Whitworth, and Joseph Yearbry. To all of these we have previously been introduced in these pages save Whitworth and Yearbry: the latter came over with Rankin and Shadford,* and the former was an Englishman who had labored faithfully with Webb and Asbury in New Jersey in 1772,† and was received into full connection at the second Conference in 1774, when Yearbry was also admitted. Boardman and Pilmoor do not appear in the list of appointments, though they tarried in America for nearly six months after the Conference, embarking together for England, Jan. 2, 1774. Politically and ecclesiastically America was becoming somewhat unsuited to their tastes. They were loyal Englishmen and the clouds of the war of the Revolution were now lowering. Rankin, supported by Asbury, who makes some sharp and significant allusions in his Journal, was enforcing rigid discipline on preachers and people alike: and so the worthy pair, who had accomplished much good during their four years' sojourn in America, departed in peace. "Asbury labored hard to conform the American Societies to Wesley's model," remarks Stevens, " but had met with no little resistance from both the preachers and laymen; Rankin had been sent out for this purpose, and to these two thorough disciplinarians we owe the effective organization of the incipient Methodism of the new world. Without them it seems probable that it would have adopted a settled pastorate, and be-

---

* Asbury's Journal, I. 52.

† Stevens, Hist. M. E. Ch. I. 203: it is evidently an error, from which the most careful historian cannot altogether free his pages, by which Stevens represents Shadford as laboring in New Jersey in 1772. He did not come over till 1773.

come blended with the Anglican Church of the colonies, or like the fruits of Whitefield's labors, have been absorbed in the general Protestantism of the country." * Nor was our good friend Captain Webb in a position to take a regular appointment consistently with his other engagements. But these three vacancies in the ranks were filled by three noble men. Robert Strawbridge, Robert Williams, and William Watters—to whom is " now universally conceded the peculiar distinction of being the first native American itinerant of Methodism " †—received appointments, though they were not present.

The business of the Conference as recorded is digested into three distinct numerical series: (1) the first settles fundamental questions of doctrine and discipline in relation to Mr. Wesley and the English Conference, and might well be styled *constitutional;* (2) the second embraces "rules and regulations" for the government of the American preachers and people, and might fairly be designated *legislative* in the narrower sense; (3) the third includes what would now be called " minute business " in an Annual Conference.and is transacted under two *Questions:* " How are the preachers stationed?" and " What numbers are there in Society?" These questions fall within the limits of the ordinary *executive* functions of our present Annual Conferences. Under these heads we shall consider the various transactions of the First American Conference.

I. Constitutional: Doctrine and Discipline.

The first " query proposed to every preacher," doubtless from the Chair, as Rankin had seen Wesley do many times in England, was this: " Ought not the authority of Mr. Wesley and that Conference to extend to the preachers and people in America, as well as in Great Britain and Ireland?" The answer—by obvious implication the answer of " every preacher "—was, "*Yes.*"

The second was like unto the first, " Ought not the doc-

---

* Stevens, Hist. M. E. Church, I, 161. † Stevens, I. 175.   .

trine and discipline of the Methodists, as contained in the
[English] minutes to be the sole rule of our conduct, who
labor in the connexion with Mr, Wesley in America?"   A
similar answer was given, *"Yes."*

The words of the wise are as goads, and as nails fastened
by the masters of assemblies, which are given from one
shepherd; that this nail of union in one Methodist fold
under one Methodist shepherd might be driven through, until it should goad him who should kick against it, Rankin,
the "disciplinarian," propounded, and the preachers answered, a third question, "If so, does it not follow that if
any preachers deviate from the minutes we can have no fellowship with them till they change their conduct?" Again
a simple, and unanimous, *"Yes,"* settled the question.

Thus was the action of the Conference, in the preliminary
business of settling the foundations, concluded.   The proposal of the questions hardly involved the right of the body to
reach a contrary conclusion.   That contingency was not
contemplated.   To preacher or preachers who answered
these questions in the negative, it is obvious that Rankin and
the Conference would have straightway declared, "We can
have no fellowship with them till they change their conduct."
It was a sifting and settling time.   Rankin's business in
America was to consolidate a body of American Methodists
after the type of the primitive Wesleyan model.   The previous administration had not conformed entirely to these
principles.   Boardman was good, but easy; Asbury had
superseded him and encountered difficulties; Rankin had
come with an express commission from Wesley to set all
things in order.   Eleven hundred and sixty members were
reported in Society, but, writes Rankin, "Some of the
above number I found afterward were not closely united to
us.   Indeed our discipline was not properly attended to, except at Philadelphia and New York; and even in those
places it was upon the decline.   Nevertheless, from the accounts I heard, there was a real foundation laid of doing
much good, and we hoped to see greater things than these.

The preachers were stationed in the best manner we could, and *we parted in love, and also with a full resolution to spread genuine Methodism in public and private with all our might.*'' Of course it is conceivable that a majority or the whole of the Conference, under mistaken or mischievous influences, might have obstinately refused to answer affirmatively the preliminary questions which, according to primitive usage, Rankin doubtless felt it his duty to propound from the Chair. He desired a free and outspoken committal of the preachers on these vital points, and it was freely and manfully given. This course probably accorded strictly with his instructions from Wesley. Had a majority of the preachers refused compliance, the only result could have been a regular and an irregular, a primitive and a schismatic, Methodism in America. Both might have prospered, or one have come to naught: we cannot tell. If the whole Conference had set itself against union with, and subordination to, Wesley, Rankin would still have had the alternative of withdrawal to England, leaving the Americans in possession of the field to develop such a Methodism as their wisdom might frame or Providence shape. It might have succeeded; it probably would have failed: again we cannot tell. We cannot speculate sanely upon the results of a hypothetical statement of facts. These alternatives have been considered simply to show that Rankin sought and obtained a free and unanimous consent of the Americans to certain fundamental conditions of union with Mr. Wesley, without which the work could not have continued under Mr. Wesley's direction.

These and the other conclusions of the Conference were not reached without friction. The new administration was in some sense an impeachment of the old. Boardman and Pilmoor, as the first missionaries formally sent out by Wesley in 1769, had inaugurated that old administration and for four years had given it a complexion which even Asbury did not succeed in altering. Concerning the proceedings of the body, Asbury says: '' There were some debates amongst the preachers in this Conference relative to the conduct of some who had manifested a desire to abide in the cities and live like gentlemen. Three years out of four have been already spent in the cities. It was also feared that money had been wasted, improper leaders appointed, and many of our rules broken." * That these debates helped Messrs. Boardman and Pilmoor to reach conclusions and form decisions is highly probable. It is certain they received no appointments from General-Assistant Rankin and that, whether influenced by political or ecclesiastical considerations or a combination of both, they soon left the country. Asbury arrived at Philadelphia on Thursday, July 15, the second day of the Conference session, "but did not find such perfect harmony," he says, "as I could wish for." † There were, as we have seen, some grounds for such differences, though these were dissipated, and "We parted in love," as Rankin records. "First *pure*, then *peaceable*" is the divine order. But Asbury's attitude was evidently somewhat critical. It was a part of his temperament as a born leader. About true greatness a trace of human infirmity often lingers. It is not matter of record, though commonly conjectured, that Asbury had requested that Rankin, or some such superintendent, should be sent out. He had been the chief of administration. He was now superseded. He probably knew more about the work and the men than anybody else present— certainly more than the newly-arrived President of the Conference. The business may not have been transacted exactly as he would have brought it forward. Some things had gone wrong in America, as he had seen and had earnestly endeavored to correct. It is possible that the methods of reaching some of the conclusions, so briefly recorded in the minutes of the Conference, were not the best—rather English than American—and that the manner of General-Assistant Rankin, occupying the chair, toward Ex-Assistant Asbury, or possibly toward the Conference itself, was not always conciliatory. But whatever deductions are to be

---

* Journal, I. 56. † *Ibid.*, I. 55.

made for the personal equation, arising from human infirmities, the results reached were sound and enduring, and constitute no mean tribute to the ecclesiastical statesmanship of Rankin and the First American Conference.

The first edition of the "Large Minutes," as we have seen in a former chapter, had been issued in 1753; the second in 1763; and the third in 1770: this last publication it was, doubtless, which by the action of the Philadelphia Conference of 1773 became the original doctrinal and disciplinary basis of American Methodism.   It contained the record of the Leeds Conference of 1769 when the preachers, at Mr. Wesley's suggestion, bound themselves " to preach the *old Methodist doctrines*, and no other, contained in the Minutes of the Conferences," and " to observe and enforce the whole Methodist discipline, laid down in the said Minutes." *

This further commentary may conclude our notice of the first section of the action of the Conference: we find the *superintending* and *appointing* power present in the person of Mr. Rankin, and the Conference itself constituting the *consulting* element, with limited *legislative* privileges, exercised in the enactment of certain rules to be hereafter noticed.   The superintending power in the first American Conference derived its existence and authority directly and solely from Mr. Wesley; and the consulting element freely acknowledged the legitimacy and rightful authority of the superintendency.   Let it be borne in mind that we are not debating theories of government and weighing their comparative merits: we are studying history—constitutional history —and when we get back to the beginnings of American Methodist polity, this we find to be the shape which the government actually assumed; these the forms under which

. *Dr. Robert Emory, in his History of the Discipline, begins with a comparison between the original Discipline of the Methodist Episcopal Church, 1784, with the Large Minutes as found in Wesley's Works, V. 211–239, which were printed from a copy bearing date 1791—the year of Mr. Wesley's death—collated with the edition of 1789. This appears to have been the only copy accessible to Dr. Emory. See his Hist. of the Discipline of the M. E. Church, p. 26, footnote.

the elemental constitutional units first manifested themselves.

II. Legislative: Rules and Regulations.

Besides the three questions on doctrine and discipline, whose answers settled, in a manner not improperly described as constitutional, the fundamental relations of the Americans to Mr. Wesley and British Methodism, six rules "were agreed to by all the preachers present," of which the first two were as follows: " 1. Every preacher who acts in connection with Mr. Wesley and the brethren who labor in America, is strictly to avoid administering the ordinances of baptism and the Lord's supper. 2. All the people among whom we labor to be earnestly exhorted to attend the Church, and to receive the ordinances there; but in a particular manner, to press the people in Maryland and Virginia to the observance of this minute."*

The minutes at this point are not strictly correct; or, more probably, there was a private understanding as to a certain noteworthy exception to the operation of these rules. Asbury's Journal reveals the name of a preacher who was permitted to administer the sacraments: No preacher in our connection shall be permitted to administer the ordinances at this time; except Mr. S. [Strawbridge], and he under the particular direction of the assistant." †

Strawbridge's position was independent and influential. Though his name appears among the appointments, it was by no means certain that the Conference could exercise jurisdiction over, or execute discipline upon, the father of Methodism in Maryland, where there were five hundred members in Society. As early as 1762 or 1763 he baptized Henry Maynard, who died as late as 1837. There is reason to believe he had been ordained by a German minister, a certain Benedict Swoope, just as Otterbein afterwards assisted at the episcopal ordination of Asbury himself.‡ He had things in a mighty swing in Maryland. It is a tribute to his

---

* Minutes, ed. of 1813, p. 5. † Journal, I. 56.
‡ William Fort, in Christian Advocate and Journal, July 10, 1844.

unique relation to the work that, though not present at the Conference, he was excepted from the operation of the sacramental rule. Boardman, when he was Assistant, could not or did not stop him. Asbury "was obliged to connive at some things for the sake of peace" when he held the Quarterly Meeting, Dec. 23, 1772. General-Assistant Rankin concluded to follow in the footsteps of his illustrious predecessors, and the Conference dared not leave him off the plan of the work or abridge his privileges long recognized by the people, to whom he administered the sacraments before any English itinerants appeared in the country.

In the first Quarterly Conference of which any record exists; in the first Annual Conference that ever sat, Strawbridge won the day. "Being an Irishman, he shared not in the deferential sympathies of his English brethren for the Establishment; as for any other sentiments, the actual character of the representatives of the Establishment, clerical and lay, around him, could claim none from him but pity or contempt. Its clergy were known chiefly as the heartiest card-players, horse-racers, and drinkers of the middle colonies. Robert Strawbridge was doubtless imprudent in the Irish resolution with which he resisted the policy of the English itinerants; for the intuitive foresight, with which he anticipated the necessity of the independent administration of the sacraments, should have suggested to him the certainty of their concession in due time, and therefore the expediency of patient harmony in the infant Church till that time should come." * Whether Dr. Stevens' reasoning in the last sentence is conclusive or not, Strawbridge stood for the rights and liberties of American Methodists against the conservative English. It seemed as if he must win. The sacramental controversy came near disrupting American Methodism. Mr. Wesley conceded the point none too soon when in 1784 the Christmas Conference organized the "Methodist Episcopal Church in the United States of America."

But if the first three questions and answers settle the sub-

* Stevens, Hist. M. E. Ch., I. 164, 165.

ordination of the American Methodists to Mr. Wesley and
the British Conference, these first two rules, unanimously
adopted, equally settle the relation of the Societies in America to the Church of England, as it existed in the colonies
before the revolutionary war.   That relation, it was intended, should be identical with the relation of the United Society to the Church in England.   The sacraments were to
be sought at her altars from the hands of her clergy.   The
people were to be " exhorted " and " pressed " to attend
" the Church " and to receive the ordinances there.   These
American Methodists considered themselves Episcopalians,
with the peculiarities and improvements of Methodists su-
peradded.   In spirit and fact, they were submissive now
both to Mr. Wesley and to the Church of England: so the
Conference action indicates.   But by and by American
Methodism was confronted with the perplexities of a problem which involved the achievement of a twofold independence: (1) independence of Mr. Wesley and his British
Conference, and (2) independence of the Church of England.   Mr. Wesley in enabling them to achieve the latter
unwittingly afforded them the conditions for achieving also
the former.   Precisely how this double independence was
wrought out, it will be the province of the following pages
to delineate.

The third rule adopted by the Conference was designed
to enforce strictly in America a uniform observance of English Methodism: " No person or persons to be admitted into
our love-feasts oftener than twice or thrice, unless they become members; and none to be admitted to the society
meetings more than thrice." *

The fourth and fifth rules are intended to regulate the
book business, and thus in the very first Conference appear
the germs of the legislation which has established and fos-
tered the great publishing interests of American Methodism:

" 4. None of the preachers in America to reprint any of
Mr. Wesley's books without his authority (when it can be

---

*Minutes, ed. of 1813, p. 6.

gotten) and the consent of their brethren. 5. Robert Williams to sell the books he has already printed, but to print no more, unless under the above restrictions." *

Brother Williams' difficulty is hinted at by Mr. Asbury, " I was somewhat troubled to hear of Mr. W., who had printed some of Mr. Wesley's books for the sake of gain. This will not do. It does by no means look well." † This judgment is too severe. Probably Brother Williams' necessities—his distresses—were great. Jesse Lee, the first historian of Methodism, says: " Previous to the formation of this rule, Robert Williams, one of the preachers, had reprinted many of Mr. Wesley's books, and had spread them through the country, to the great advantage of religion. The sermons, which he printed in small pamphlets, had a very good effect, and gave the people great light and understanding in the nature of the new birth and in the plan of salvation; and withal, they opened the way in many places for our preachers to be invited to preach where they had never been before. But, notwithstanding the good that had been done by the circulation of the books, it now became necessary for all the preachers to be united in the same course of printing and selling our books, so that the profits arising therefrom might be divided among them or applied to some charitable purpose." ‡ Let us honor Williams then as the preacher who inaugurated the publishing business in American Methodism, and by his activity induced legislation to regulate it in the first Conference.

The sixth and last rule extends the supervision and authority of General-Assistant Rankin over the whole work and is in these words: " Every preacher who acts as an assistant [*i. e.,* has charge of a circuit] to send an account of the work once in six months to the General Assistant." §

III. *Minute or Executive Business.*

The administrative or executive business of the Confer-

* Minutes, ed. of 1813, p. 6. † Journal, I. 45.
‡ Lee, Hist. of Meth., p. 48. § Minutes, p. 6.

ence was formulated and transacted under two questions which have since grown very familiar, and which may be here reproduced in full:

"*Ques.* 1. How are the preachers stationed?

"*Ans.*

"New York, Thomas Rankin,   } to change in four
"Philadelphia, George Shadford, }   months.

"New Jersey, John King, William Watters.

"Baltimore,   { Francis Asbury, Robert Strawbridge,
              { Abraham Whitworth, Joseph Yearbry.

"Norfolk, Richard Wright.

"Petersburg, Robert Williams.

"*Ques.* 2. What members are there in the society?

"*Ans.*

New York.........	180	Maryland..........	500
Philadelphia.......	180	Virginia............	100
New Jersey........	200	(Preachers, 10.)———	
		Total ....1,160"*	

More than half the members—six hundred—it will be noticed were in Virginia and Maryland alone. These figures put beyond dispute that Strawbridge was the principal founder of American Methodism. Rankin had chosen the wrong end of the work for his labors, if he wished to establish a permanent and far-reaching influence. Asbury he sent to Baltimore, the pivotal city. In leadership and numbers, the Methodist center of gravity was now located in the South.

* Minutes, p. 6.

CHAPTER VI.

I. The Conference of 1774.

THE Second Annual Conference assembled as before in Philadelphia, Wednesday, May 25, 1774, and adjourned Friday, May 27. General-Assistant Rankin occupied the chair, managed the business, and made the appointments.

In this second session, it is easy to discern that the body is settling down to what subsequently became the routine minute business of Annual Conferences, the answers to six of the ordinary disciplinary questions being recorded. The first session was extraordinary. It had much to do in the way of general review and final settlement of what some of the irregulars might have been disposed to view as open questions. Enactments, such as we have ventured to style constitutional agreements, in view of their fundamental and permanent character, disappear from the record of business transacted at the Second Conference; confirming once more the view that such action by no means fell within the scope of the ordinary powers of the body, but was proposed by Mr. Rankin, as the newly-arrived plenipotentiary of Mr. Wesley, in the initial Conference, that there might be from the beginning a free, full, and frank understanding of the relations of the Americans to Mr. Wesley and the English, and that the preachers then in connection, or afterward to be received, might be informed of the conditions under which membership in the Conference could be held, the violation of which would issue in the withdrawal of fellowship from them, "till they change their conduct."

The six " Questions "propounded and answered were as follows:

"Ques. 1. Who are admitted [*i. e.,* into full connection] this year?

"Ques. 2. Who are admitted on trial?

"Ques. 3. Who are Assistants [*i. e.,* superintendents of circuits, or preachers in charge] this year?

"Ques. 4. Are there any objections to any of the Preachers?

"Ques. 5. How are the preachers stationed this year?

"Ques. 6. What numbers are there in Society?"

Five preachers are admitted into full connection, and seven on trial. Rankin's name appears first on the roll of Assistants and Asbury's immediately follows, Shadford's being third. The answer to Ques. 4 has since become stereotyped, "They were examined one by one." There were seventeen preachers, with a total of 2,073 members in Society, of whom 738 were reported from Baltimore, and 1,063 from Maryland—more than half of the denomination being in this state. Brunswick Circuit reported 218 members against 204 in Philadelphia and 222 in New York. The increase in the whole work had been nearly a thousand members, a result largely due to the efficiency of Rankin's administration. Asbury was appointed to New York (apparently, as we shall see, against his will, as he desired to labor in Baltimore) and Rankin to Philadelphia, these two to exchange at the end of the first quarter. Shadford was placed in charge of the Baltimore Circuit, with Dromgoole, (Drumgole is the spelling in the minutes) Webster, and Lindsay as "helpers." Strawbridge's name does not appear on the plan. Indeed none of Asbury's "helpers" of the preceding year are returned to Baltimore. Evidently Rankin was stirring things, and introducing a discipline under whose severity even Asbury, now in feeble health, smarted. To the list of appointments this note is appended, "All the preachers to change at the end of six months," of course as directed by the General-Assistant.

"The itinerancy was under a stern regimen at that day. Hitherto, as we have seen, it transferred the preachers from

New York to Philadelphia every four months; now it was more rigorous toward the laborers of the cities than before, for while the preachers on the country circuits exchanged semi-annually, those of Philadelphia and New York exchanged quarterly. The itinerancy was prized not only as affording variety of ministerial gifts to the Societies, but as a sort of military drill to the preachers. It kept them energetic by keeping them in motion. No great captain has approved of long encampments. The early Methodist itinerants were an evangelical cavalry; they were always in the saddle; if not in line of battle, yet skirmishing and pioneering; a mode of life which conduced not a little to that chivalric spirit and heroic character which distinguished them as a class. The system speedily killed off such as were weak in body, and drove off such as were feeble in character; the remnant were the 'giants of those days' morally, very often intellectually, and, to a notable extent, physically. Young men, prudently initiated into its hardships, acquired robust health, stentorian lungs, and buoyant spirits, 'a good humor,' a bon hommie which facilitated not a little their access to the common people; but many whose souls were equal to their work sunk under it physically. Its early records are full, as we shall hereafter see, of examples of martyrdom."[*]

The Conference "agreed to the following particulars" in the matter of rules and regulations touching the temporal economy of the Church: "1. Every preacher who is received into full connection is to have the use and property of his horse, which any of the circuits may furnish him with. 2. Every preacher to be allowed six pounds Pennsylvania currency per quarter and his traveling charges besides. 3. For every assistant to make a general collection at Easter in the circuits where they labor; to be applied to the sinking of debts on the houses and relieving the preachers in want. 4. Wherever Thomas Rankin spends his time he is to be assisted by those circuits."[†]

[*] Stevens, Hist. M. E. Ch., I. 230, 231.
[†] For all the preceding, see Minutes, 1813, pp. 7, 8.

At the Quarterly Conference which Asbury held on the
western shore of Maryland, Dec. 23, 1772, it will be remembered that Brother Strawbridge (a married man) was
allowed £8 quarterage, and Brother Asbury and Brother
King £6 each. The Annual Conference, it appears from
Regulation 2, now relieved the Quarterly Conferences of
this responsibility, and assumed jurisdiction of the matter of
fixing the compensation of the laborers in the vineyard, placing all the preachers on a uniform basis of support. So this
financial arrangement continued for many years afterward.
Not until quite late in the history of the Church was this
primitive jurisdiction of the Quarterly Conference restored,
and the principle established that those who pay shall determine what is necessary for the support of the ministry, and
what they are able to contribute. In this rule, also, appears
the distinction between "quarterage" and "traveling expenses" which has hardly yet become extinct, the writer of
these pages having had his traveling expenses to his last appointment allowed by the stewards.

The Quarterly Conference is the body of supreme authority and jurisdiction in the local Church: the Annual Conference originally exercised general supervision until the General Conference was developed from it by processes which
will be fully noticed in the progress of our history. In England there is still but a single Conference supervising the
whole work. It meets annually.

In the third rule, we see the germs (1) of the Church-
extension fund and (2) of the Conference collection. Build-
ing church-houses soon came to be looked upon as the
business of the local society, and the general collection for
paying debts on chapels and meeting-houses disappeared.
But the organization of Church-extension Boards is only a
reversion to the primitive type. The principle of community
of interest and obligation, even in the erection of local
houses of worship, was recognized in the beginning and re-
appears at last in more formal appliances and organizations.

In the fourth regulation we discover the beginnings of the

Bishops' Fund. It makes little difference whether the person exercising a general superintendency is known as General-Assistant, Superintendent, Presiding-elder, or Bishop; his relation to the work is practically the same. Mr. Rankin sustained by Mr. Wesley's appointment such a general relation to the whole work. His claim for support was accordingly placed on a general basis.

General-Assistant Rankin gives the following account of the Conference session: " Everything considered, we had reason to bless God for what he had done in about ten months. Above a thousand members are added to the Societies, and most of these have found peace with God. We now labor in the provinces of New York, the Jerseys, Pennsylvania, Maryland, and Virginia. We spoke our minds freely, one to another in love; and whatever we thought would further the work we most cheerfully embraced. We had now more than seventeen preachers to be employed the ensuing year, and upward of two thousand members, with calls and openings into many fresh places. We stationed the preachers as well as we could, and all seemed to be satisfied."

Ex-Assistant Asbury says: " Wednesday 25. Our Conference began. The overbearing spirit of a certain person had excited my fears. My judgment was stubbornly opposed for a while, and at last submitted to. But it is my duty to bear all things with a meek and patient spirit. Our Conference was attended with great power; and, all things considered, with great harmony. We agreed to send Mr. W. [Wright] to England; and all acquiesced in the future stations of the preachers. My lot was to go to New York. My body and mind have been much fatigued during the time of this Conference. And if I were not deeply conscious of the truth and goodness of the cause in which I am engaged, I should by no means stay here. Lord! what a world is this! yea, what a religious world! O keep my heart pure, and my garments unspotted from the world! Our Conference ended on Friday with a comfortable intercession." *

* Journal, 1. 81.

Dr. Bangs' comment is that Rankin, in the faithful exercise of his superintendency, " set himself to purifying the societies from corrupt members and restoring things to order," and " it was soon found that the discharge of this duty, however painful, instead of abridging the influence of ministerial labor, greatly extended it, and exerted a most salutary effect upon the societies." *

Dr. Stevens also records some judicious observations on the methods and results of Rankin's administration at this juncture: " The disciplinary views of Rankin, enforced during the preceding year, upon the preachers and Societies, with a rigor which seemed to some of them hardly tolerable, had produced salutary effects generally, as evinced by the growing efficiency of the denomination and an unexpected increase of its members. It had been regulated and consolidated and now presented generally an attitude of strength which gave assurance of a prosperous future. Rankin insisted with English firmness, if not obstinacy, that the method of procedure established in the British Conference should be rigorously followed by the present session. The principles of his administration were good, and necessary for the infant Church; but he seems to have been unhappy in his official manners. He had not the tact of Asbury to adapt himself to the free and easy spirit of the Americans, whose democratic colonial training had thrown off punctiliousness without impairing their energy and devotion to general order. Even Asbury hesitated at his rigor, but was conciliated by seeing his own judgment followed in detail, though ' stubbornly opposed ' at first." †

The " certain person " referred to in the extract from Asbury's Journal is undoubtedly Rankin. We cannot now determine what were the precise differences between them. So far as these differences concerned the business of the Conference, Asbury prevailed; so far as they related to Asbury's appointment, Rankin moved him from Baltimore to New York, to exchange in three months with him-

<hr/>

* Hist. M. E. Church, I. 80, 81.   † *Ibid.*, I. 227, 228.

self at Philadelphia. Asbury on the floor was more than a match for Rankin in the chair, since "his judgment was at last submitted to." He could afford to be "meek and patient" as regards his appointment, since his official superior was guided by his better knowledge of the work and its needs. Let us judge Rankin, however, by results, and accord him his due meed of praise. His own Journal as well as Asbury's reveals that he was often discouraged and despondent. In '73, '74, and '75, he speaks in his Journal of the assembling of the "little conference:" it was in great contrast with what he had been accustomed to in England, and this day of small things in America was a disappointment to him. But he clung to his mission and, if not always with the best grace, yet with persistence and success, he carried forward the administration on Wesleyan lines.

The alienation between him and Asbury, however, continued. The following extracts from Asbury's Journal in the autumn of 1794 reveal its existence, and something of its nature:

"Friday, Nov. 2. Mr. R. came to Burlington to-day, and desired me to go to Philadelphia. So, after preaching in the evening from Prov. xxviii. 13, I set off the next morning for the city; and found the Society in the spirit of love.

"Lord's-day 4. I preached twice with some freedom. The next day my mind was in a sweet, calm frame, and I felt a strong determination to devote myself wholly to God and his service. I spoke my mind to Mr. R., but we did not agree in judgment. And it appeared to me, that to make any attempt to go to Baltimore would be all in vain [*i. e.*, against the will of the General-Assistant, as the next entry shows].

"Tuesday 6. Visited some of my friends in the city [of Philadelphia]; and wrote a letter to Mr. Wesley, which I read to Mr. R. that he might see I intended no guile or secret dealings. It is somewhat grievous that he should prevent my going to Baltimore, after being acquainted with my engagements and the importunities of my friends there. . . .

The next day Mr. R. appeared to be very kind; so I hope all things will give place to love.

"Lord's-day 11. Mr. R. preached a close sermon on the neglect of public worship

"Wednesday 14. Mr. R. was sick, and Captain W. was busy, so I spent my time in study and devotion. . . . But what need can there be for two preachers here to preach three times a week to about sixty people? This is indeed a very gloomy prospect.

"Lord's-day 18. My soul was happy while preaching in the morning. Mr. S. gave us an old piece at Church; and Mr. R. was very furious in the evening [presumably violent in preaching].

"Friday 23. In the evening I preached from these words, ' Neither give place to the devil:' and believe it was good for some that they were present."

"Monday, Jan. 2, [1775]. At Mr. B.'s, where we dined to-day, I was much grieved at the manner of Mr. R.'s conversation: but let it be a caution to me to be prudent and watchful.

"Lord's-day 8. A letter from my friend W. L. informed me that three of my friends were coming to conduct me, if possible, to Baltimore. But it is a doubt with me if I shall, with consent, be permitted to go.

"On Monday the 30th some letters came from Baltimore earnestly pressing me to go. And Mr. R. was so kind as to visit me [Asbury was sick]; when all was sweetness and love.

"Thursday 16 [Feb.]. R. S. [Robert Strawbridge] wrote me a letter with his usual kindness; and informed me that Mr. D. concurred in sentiment relative to my going to Baltimore. And it is thought by many, that there will be an alteration in the affairs of our Church government.

"Saturday 26. I packed up my clothes in order to depart on Monday morning for Baltimore.

"Thursday, March 2. We then pursued our journey to Baltimore. The next day I had the pleasure of seeing our new house. Here are all my own with increase.

" Lord's-day 12. I saw Brother S. and entered into a free
conversation with him. His sentiments relative to Mr. R.
corresponded with mine. But all these matters I can silently
commit to God, who overrules both in earth and heaven." *

These extracts abundantly indicate that Asbury was deeply dissatisfied that Mr. Rankin would not permit him to return to labor in Baltimore. Both were good men. We
have now no means of judging of the merits of Mr. Rankin's
appointments. Rankin was firm. Asbury was not inclined
to yield. He submitted the case to Mr. Wesley; but frankly showed his letter to Rankin before sending it. Asbury
took the matter so seriously that he began to anticipate, with
others, " an alteration in the affairs of our Church government." It will be remembered that under the Boardman
administration he had declared, " I have not yet the thing I
seek—a circulation of preachers to avoid partiality and popularity. I am fixed to the Methodist plan. I am determined to make a stand against all partiality." But it looks
a little as if it was difficult for him, under Rankin, to take
his own medicine. His friends were continually beseeching
him by letter and embassy to come to Baltimore. At last,
before the meeting of the next Conference, he " packed
up" and went; whether with or without the " consent" of
the General-Assistant we are not told.

Rankin also wrote to Wesley. " It was Asbury's misfortune as long as Wesley lived," says Bishop McTyeire, " to
be misrepresented to him by weak but well-meaning men
whom he overshadowed, or by designing men whom he
overruled."† As a general proposition this is perhaps true.
It is also true that by every token and standard Asbury was
a greater man than Rankin, better adapted to, and better
acquainted with, the American work. But in this affair of
his Baltimore appointment, Asbury himself made the appeal
to Wesley against the legitimate authority, whether wisely
or unwisely exercised, of his American representative. In
his reply to Rankin under date of March 1, 1775, Mr. Wes-

---

* Asbury's Journal, I. 101–109 (extracts).   † McTyeire, Hist. of Meth., p. 285.

ley says: "As soon as possible, you must come to a full and clear explanation, both with brother Asbury (if he is recovered) and with Jemmy Dempster. But I advise brother Asbury to return to England the first opportunity." *

The Revolution was coming on; the preachers were in danger of political entanglements; Mr. Wesley inclosed in his communication to the General-Assistant a letter to all the preachers, whose pertinency and wisdom in those troublous times warrants its reproduction here:

"LONDON, March 1, 1775.

"*My dear Brethren:* You were never in your lives in so critical a situation as you are at this time. It is your part to be peace makers; to be loving and tender to all; but to addict yourselves to no party. In spite of all solicitations, of rough or smooth words, say not one word against one or the other side. Keep yourselves pure; do all you can to help and soften all; but beware how you adopt another's jar.

" See that you act in full union with each other: this is of the utmost consequence. Not only let there be no bitterness or anger, but no shyness or coldness, between you. Mark all those that would set one of you against the other. Some such will never be wanting. But give them no countenance; rather ferret them out, and drag them into open day.

" The conduct of T. Rankin has been suitable to the Methodist plan: I hope all of you tread in his steps. Let your eye be single. Be in peace with each other, and the God of peace will be with you.

"I am, my dear brethren,

" Your affectionate brother,

"JOHN WESLEY." †

April 21, 1775, Wesley writes Rankin again, " Brother Asbury has sent me a few lines, and I thank him for them. But I do not advise him to go to Antigua. Let him come home without delay. If one or two stout, healthy young men would willingly offer themselves to that service, I should have no objection." ‡ Again, May 19, 1775, he

---

Wesley's Works, Amer. ed., VII. 7, 8.   † *Ibid.*   ‡ *Ibid.*, p. 9.

writes, "I doubt not but Asbury and you will part friends: I shall hope to see him at the [English] Conference. He is quite an upright man. I apprehend he will go through his work more cheerfully when he is within a little distance from me."* July 28, Mr. Wesley says, "I rejoice, too, over honest Francis Asbury, and hope he will no more enter into temptation." Finally, Aug. 13, when he had learned of Asbury's appointment for another year's labor, Wesley writes, "I am not sorry that Brother Asbury stays with you another year. In that time it will be seen what God will do with North America, and you will easily judge whether our preachers are called to remain any longer therein. If they are, God will make their way plain, and give them favor even with the men that delight in war." †

And so the matter ended. It will be noticed that in his letter of April 21, Wesley advises against Asbury's going to Antigua—partly, no doubt, on account of his feeble health. It appears that previously he had favored the project. So this extract from Asbury's Journal implies: "Wednesday 23 [Feb. 1775]. I received a letter from Miss G. [Gilbert], at Antigua, in which she informed me that Mr. G. [Francis Gilbert] was going away; and as there are about three hundred members in society, she entreats me to go and labor amongst them. And as Mr. Wesley has given his consent, I feel inclined to go, and take one of the young men with me. But there is one obstacle in my way—the administration of the ordinances. It is possible to get the ordination of a presbytery; but this would be incompatible with Methodism; which would be an effectual bar in my way." ‡

Upon the possible consequences of this early removal of the Apostle of American Methodism it is useless to speculate: more important is it to note, in view of his subsequent ordination as Deacon, Elder, and Bishop, that this Episcopalian, whatever may have been the force of Strawbridge's example, did not regard the "ordination of a presbytery" as compatible with Methodism.

---

* Wesley's Works, Amer. ed., VII. 9. † Page 11. ‡ Journal, I. 107.

II. The Conference of 1775.

The Third Annual Conference assembled as before under the presidency of Mr. Rankin in the city of Philadelphia, Wednesday, May 17, 1775, and adjourned Friday the 19th. It followed by a few months the session of the Colonial Congress in the same city. The same questions are asked in the same order as at the preceding Conference, with the omission of Question 4; though the preachers, of course, passed an examination of character. "Question 5. What numbers are there in Society?" was answered as follows: "New York, 200; Philadelphia, 190; New Jersey, 300; Chester, 74; Kent, 253; Baltimore, 840; Frederick, 336; Fairfax, 30; Norfolk, 125; Brunswick, 800:" the total was 3,148, with nineteen preachers.

In the list of appointments, James Dempster appears as the Assistant at New York; Martin Rodda, at Baltimore; George Shadford, on the Brunswick work, with William Glendenning among his "helpers;" Asbury is sent alone to Norfolk, and Strawbridge's name again appears as a "helper" on the Frederick work, of which William Watters is preacher in charge.

At the close of the list of appointments are the following directions and agreements:

"Thomas Rankin is to travel till the month of December, and then take a quarter in New York.

"The preachers in New Jersey to change in one quarter.

"Webster and Cooper to change with Gatch and Watters at the end of six months.

"The preachers in Brunswick and Hanover, to change as the Assistant thinks proper.

"Thomas Rankin's deficiencies to be paid out of the yearly collection.

"The preachers' expenses from Conference to their circuit to be paid out of the yearly collection.

"A general fast for the prosperity of the work, and for the peace of America, on Tuesday, the 18th of July." *

---

* Minutes, ed. of 1813, pp. 9, 10.

The Conference collection, it will be noticed, was now burdened with the deficiencies in the General-Assistant's support, and with the expenses of the preachers from the seat of the Conference to their circuits.

The names of three new English preachers appear on the Conference roll: Rodda and Dempster were new missionaries who had arrived at New York in the autumn of 1774, and had relieved Asbury at John Street, when he joined Rankin at Philadelphia and was anxious to proceed still further south. Glendenning appears to have accompanied them as a volunteer, as Yearbry did Rankin and Shadford. Dempster and Glendenning finally abandoned Methodism; and Rodda left the country on account of political imprudences.

Of the Conference, Rankin says, " We conversed together and concluded our business in love. We wanted all the advice and light we could obtain respecting our conduct in the present critical situation of affairs. We came unanimously to this conclusion, to follow the advice that Mr. Wesley and his brother had given us,* and leave the event to God."

Brother Asbury was gratified with a " circulation of preachers," for he was sent, not to Baltimore but to Norfolk, a feeble and undisciplined Society. " From Wednesday till Friday we spent in Conference," he says, " with great harmony and sweetness of temper." He departed for his new work uncomplainingly and with the hopefulness of a true Methodist preacher: " I am now bending my course towards Norfolk to preach the glad tidings of salvation to perishing sinners there. . . . With a thankful heart I landed at Norfolk." † And at Norfolk and Portsmouth he did a good work. He reports finding only " 30 persons in society after their manner; but they had no regular class-meetings." One hundred and twenty-five members had been reported at the Conference: so even in those days there was some looseness all around. However, he men-

* See Wesley's Works, Amer. ed., vii. 8, with footnote. † Journal, I. 114.

tions preaching to 150 souls immediately on his arrival and having an audience of 50 at 5 o'clock in the morning.*

III. The Conference of 1776.

For the first time the Conference met in the city of Baltimore, Tuesday, May 21, 1776, Rankin presiding as usual. It was held in Lovely Lane Chapel, the second Methodist house of worship built in the city.

Five preachers were admitted into full connection, and nine on trial, among whom were Freeborn Garrettson and Francis Poythress. "I attended," says Garrettson, "passed through an examination, was admitted on trial, and my name was, for the first time, classed among the Methodists; I received of Mr. Rankin a written license." Poythress, Asbury, in 1797, nominated for the episcopate. Nine preachers are named as Assistants, the first four being Thomas Rankin, Francis Asbury, Martin Rodda, and George Shadford; Rankin, however, left his own name off the list of regular appointments, partly, perhaps, because his general duties no longer admitted of his giving a definite period of service to any circuit, and partly because the war of the Revolution was making his stay in America uncertain. Asbury is again appointed superintendent of the Baltimore circuit. 4,921 members are reported in Society, of whom 1,611 are from Brunswick, 900 from Baltimore, and 683 from North Carolina. In the north there is a falling off, New York reporting but 132, Philadelphia but 137, and New Jersey 150: this is largely due to the war, military operations pressing heavily upon those regions. Twenty-four preachers receive appointments: with the General-Assistant, there were twenty-five itinerants. July 26th is appointed a day of general fasting.†

Of the Conference, Watters says, "We were of one heart and mind, and took sweet counsel together, not how we should get riches or honors, or anything that this poor world

---

*Journal, I. 114. †Minutes, ed. of 1813, pp. 11, 12.

could afford us; but how we should make the surest work for heaven, and be the instruments of saving others."

Asbury did not attend the Conference. Sunday, May 5, he is at Philadelphia, but in a dejected frame of mind: "Lord's-day 12. Divine grace assisted and comforted me in all the exercises of the day. But the next day I was seized with a severe chill, and was carried to my lodging very sick; nevertheless set out the next day, if possible, to reach the Conference: and came to Chester that night. Wednesday 15. Attempted to reach a quarterly meeting, but when I got to the place was obliged to go to bed. Though the next day, weak as I was, I went.and held a love-feast, and afterward preached. . . . . Was very unwell all the Lord's-day, [Sunday, May 19] but my great desire to be at Conference induced me to make an attempt, on Monday, to travel. But by the time I had rode three miles, I found if I traveled, it would be at the hazard of my life: and was therefore obliged to decline it, though the disappointment was very great." The next day the Conference sat. On the following Monday the sick itinerant says, " Expecting the preachers were on their return from the Conference, I appointed preaching at my lodgings, but had to preach myself, to a small, attentive, tender company, and felt much quickened in my soul. At night brother R. arrived and informed me that I was appointed for Baltimore: to which I cheerfully submit, though it seems to be against my bodily health."*

IV. The Conference of 1777.

The Fifth Annual Conference convened "At a Preaching-House, near Deer Creek, in Harford County, Maryland," Tuesday, "May 20, 1777."† Over this Conference Rankin presided, as he had over all preceding ones.

The Minutes record eight questions, asked and answered. The first six are the same in matter and order as those asked

---

* Asbury's Journal, I. 137, 138.

† Minutes, ed. of 1813, p. 13: the day of the week is fixed by Asbury's Journal.

at the Conference of 1774. " Question 4. Are there any
objections to any of the Preachers?" having been omitted
during two sessions, so far as the Minutes show, is now restored. "They were examined one by one " is the answer
as before.   Eight preachers are admitted into full connection, and fourteen on trial, among whom are Caleb B. Pedicord, John Tunnell, John Littlejohn, Lee Roy Cole, John
Dickins, and Reuben Ellis.   Fourteen Assistants, or Superintendents of circuits, are named, of whom the first seven
are, "Thomas Rankin, Francis Asbury, Martin Rodda,
George Shadford, Edward Drumgole, William Watters,
Philip Gatch;" but the names of Rankin and Asbury do
not appear in the list of appointments: neither was definitely assigned to work.   Before the next Conference Rankin
returned to England.   Asbury was seriously debating the
question.   But the same is true of Rodda and Shadford,
both of whom, like Rankin, returned to England before the
next Conference; yet they were placed in charge of important circuits, Kent and Baltimore.   Asbury's failure to take
an appointment, therefore, is not fully explained; though
Rankin's general duties excuse him, as at the preceding Conference.   There were fifteen circuits in all; but New York
is left without a preacher, doubtless on account of the war,
the city being then occupied by the British.   There are 6,-
968 members in Society, of whom 1,360 are reported from
Brunswick; 900 from Baltimore; 930 from North Carolina;
726 from Kent; 160 from New Jersey; and 96 each from
New York and Philadelphia.   Friday, July 25, was appointed as a fast-day.   Two questions are appended, one touching the consecration and steadfastness of the preachers in
those times that tried men's souls, and the other concerning
the abuse of funeral sermons: "*Ques.* 7. As the present
distress is such, are the preachers resolved to take no step to
detach themselves from the work of God for the ensuing
year? *Ans.* We purpose, by the grace of God, not to take
any step that may separate us from the brethren, or from
the blessed work in which we are engaged.   *Ques.* 8. Has

not the preaching of funeral sermons been carried so far as
to prostitute that venerable custom, and in some sort to render it contemptible? *Ans.* Yes: therefore let all the preachers inform every society, that we will not preach any but
for those who we have reason to think died in the fear and
favor of God." *

From the Minutes, it would appear that this was all the
business transacted. But there are other contemporaneous
and reliable sources of information. At this very Conference, as we have seen, Philip Gatch was named an Assistant. To Gatch's MS. journal, Dr. Leroy M. Lee had access and makes this extract of questions asked at the Conference of 1777: "*Ques.* What shall be done with respect
to the ordinances? *Ans.* Let the preachers and people
pursue the old plan as from the beginning. *Ques.* What
alteration may we make in our original plan? *Ans.* Our
next Conference will, if God permit, show us more clearly." †

There is other evidence that the question of the sacraments was still a burning one. Asbury, whether designedly
or by seizing an unexpected and most favorable opportunity,
held a "caucus" before the meeting of Conference, and
outlined its business, as well as made a "slate" of appointments. A long note in his Journal gives an account of this
preliminary meeting, and also most affecting details of
scenes at the Conference itself:

"Monday 12. Set out for our yearly conference, and
having preached at Mr. P.'s by the way, came safe to Mr.
G.'s, and was glad to see the preachers who were there.
We had some weighty conversation on different points: and
among other things, it was asked whether we could give our
consent that Mr. R. [Rankin] should baptize, as there appeared to be a present necessity. But it was objected that
this would be a breach of our discipline; and it was not
probable that things would continue long in such a disor-
dered state. The next day, with great harmony and joint

* Minutes, ed. of 1813, pp. 14, 15. † Life and Times of Jesse Lee, p. 78.

consent, we drew a rough draught for stationing the preachers the ensuing year.   And on Friday we conversed on the
propriety of signing certificates avouching good conduct for
such of the preachers as chose to go to Europe.   But I
could not see the propriety of it at this time.   We also conversed on such rules as might be proper for the regulation
of the preachers who abide on the continent.   And it was
judged necessary that a committee should be appointed to
superintend the whole.   And on Monday we rode together
to attend the Conference at Deer-Creek.

" So greatly has the Lord increased the number of traveling preachers within these few years, that we have now
twenty-seven who attend the circuits, and twenty of them
were present at this conference.   Both our public and private business was conducted with great harmony, peace,
and love.   Our brethren who intend to return to Europe,
have agreed to stay till the way is quite open.   Our Conference ended with a love-feast and watch-night.   But when
the time of parting came, many wept as if they had lost
their first-born sons.   They appeared to be in the deepest
distress, thinking, as I suppose, they should not see the
faces of the English preachers any more.   This was such a
parting as I never saw before. . . .   A certificate, as
mentioned above, had been acceded to, and signed in the
Conference." *

Part of the prearranged programme, it is seen, miscar-
ried: the departing English preachers were granted certificates, which were signed in open Conference.   In view of
Rankin's approaching departure, which would leave the
American work without an official head, government by a
committee, as suggested in Asbury's preliminary meeting,
was adopted.   The Minutes say nothing of it; but this is
not strange: there is satisfactory evidence, as we have
seen, of their incompleteness on other heads.   " There appearing no probability of the contest between Great Britain
and this country ending shortly," says Watters, " several

* Asbury's Journal, I. 186.

of our European preachers thought that, if an opportunity should offer, they would return to their home in the course of the year. To provide against such an event five of us, Gatch, Dromgoole, Ruff, Glendenning, and myself, were appointed a committee to act in the place of the general assistant in case they should all go before the next Conference. It was also submitted to the consideration of this Conference whether in our present situation, of having but few ministers left in many of our parishes to administer the ordinances of baptism and the Lord's supper, we should not administer them ourselves. . . . In fact, we considered ourselves, at this time, as belonging to the Church of England. After much conversation on the subject, it was unanimously agreed to lay it over for the determination of the next Conference, to be held in Leesburg, the 19th of May."

The Rev. John Lednum, in his History of the Rise of Methodism in America, also names the Committee of Control: William Watters, Philip Gatch, Daniel Ruff, Edward Dromgoole, and William Glendenning.* Watters as the oldest native itinerant presided in the succeeding Conference of 1778, and was clearly the head of the committee and of the provisional government.

This government by committee, until the distress of the times should be overpast, was doubtless suggested by Asbury: he carefully records it as part of the proceedings of the meeting held a week before Conference, in which he was the master spirit. Why he was not placed at the head of the committee is unaccountable, unless American antagonism to the English made it expedient, if not necessary, that an American should be at this time the official head of American Methodism. McKendree became later the first American Bishop: to Watters must be given the honor of being the first American chief of administration, exercising, with his colleagues, a superintendency for a time during the troublous period of the Revolution. If the unacceptability

---

* Page 190.

of an English preacher was Asbury's reason for not taking an appointment at this Conference, all the more was it inexpedient that he should be appointed head of the Committee of Control.

This completes, we believe, the sum total of what is known of this important Conference, the last of General-Assistant Rankin's administration. The view that Asbury's disabilities arose from the political complications of the times, is rendered highly probable, if not certain, by his Journal: if the prudent Asbury was thus handicapped and finally forced into retirement, it cannot be a matter of surprise that the other English preachers felt compelled to leave the country. Thursday, June 20, 1776, Asbury "went to Nathan Perrig's, and was fined five pounds for preaching the gospel." * Tuesday, Jan. 21, 1777, he records: "A messenger from Mr. G.'s met me at the Widow B.'s, informing me that Mr. R—a [Rodda] and Mr. G. S. [George Shadford] were there waiting to see me. After preaching I set out, and met my brethren the same night, and found them inclined to leave America and embark for England. But I had before resolved not to depart from the work on any consideration. After some consultation it was thought best that Mr. R—a should go to Mr. R—n [Rankin] and request his attendance here." † March 26, he received a letter from Shadford "intimating that according to rule, the time was drawing near for us to return." Asbury makes significant comment, " But St. Paul's rule is, that our spiritual children should be in our hearts to live and die with them." ‡ His resolution " not to depart from the work " began, however, to be shaken. Monday, March 30, he " was under some exercise of mind in respect to the times: my brethren are inclined to leave the continent, and I do not know but something may be propounded to me which would touch my conscience," but April 2, " Having received information that some of my brethren had determined on their departure, I wrote to Brother S. [Shadford]

---

* Journal, I. 141. † *Ibid.*, I. 176. ‡ *Ibid.*, I. 182.

that as long as I could stay and preach without injuring my conscience, it appeared as my duty to abide with the flock. But I must confess that Satan has harassed me with violent and various temptations." * This is his last entry bearing on the subject before the Conference of 1777. It leaves the question of remaining or departing unsettled, but with the scale very decidedly inclined toward "abiding with the flock." Either (1) the probability of departure, or (2) the unacceptability of a non-juring English preacher, to the civil authorities and partly to his congregations, constituted a sufficient reason for Asbury's not taking an appointment, and still more for his not being placed on the Committee of Control. Yet, as we have seen, both Rodda, the most injudicious and offensive of the English preachers, and Shadford, took appointments; and Glendenning was on the Committee of Control. There is an irreducible remainder of mystery in every explanation of Asbury's failure to take work at this Conference, or to be assigned to a share in the provisional government. That he was not in close sympathy with the departing Englishmen (except Shadford, who lingered to the last) is evident. He was personally opposed to granting them certificates of character to be presented in England on their return. His language implies that he hardly shared in the general grief at parting with them at Conference. "*They* [the other preachers] appeared to be in the deepest distress, thinking, as I *suppose*, they should not see the faces of the English preachers any more." Some lingering root of bitterness may have caused Rankin to refuse him, or Asbury to decline, work. If Rankin appointed or nominated the Committee of Control, he may have designedly left off Asbury's name.

About two months after Conference, July 21, 1777, Asbury makes a sad entry in his Journal: "Heard Mr. Rankin preach his last sermon. My mind was a little dejected; and I now felt some desire to return to England, but was willing to commit the matter to the Lord." † Mr. Rankin

---

*Journal, I. 182, 183. †*Ibid.*, I. 190.

spent the winter in Philadelphia, left the capes of Delaware, March 17, 1778, and arrived at Cork, April 15.

After a careful and candid survey of all the material facts, I am inclined to a more favorable judgment of General-Assistant Rankin and his administration than our historians generally have embodied in their pages. His great services in the founding of American Methodism have scarcely been appreciated to the full. He remained in America more than four years, faithfully administering his high trust in the midst of ecclesiastical difficulties and political convulsions which would have speedily sent a weak man flying from his post. He convened the first Annual Conference, and presided with dignity, firmness, and much wisdom in five of these general assemblies. He purified and consolidated the American societies, conforming them more closely to the English disciplinary model. When he came there were 1,160 members, with ten preachers; when he departed, 6,968 members, with 36 preachers. To be sure, these results were not all due to his personal labors; but some men in his position could have cast ruin and blight all about them: he conserved the fruits and extended the work. He retained the confidence and affection of Wesley, who habitually addresses him as "Dear Tommy." He made mistakes; but possibly no more and no other than were inseparable from his limitations as an Englishman, newly arrived in America. "Peculiarities he certainly had," says a contemporary, "which sometimes prevented his being as useful as otherwise he would have been." Asbury was in every respect an abler man and, as a natural leader, saw these mistakes clearly. Even in a subordinate position he chafed under them; sometimes he succeeded in overruling them. Human nature being constituted as it is, this chafing was in part unavoidable; but in the matter of his own appointment to Baltimore, he seems, with unnecessary if not ill-judged persistence, to have embarrassed the administration of his ecclesiastical superior, even though that administration was confessedly not faultless. So Mr. Wesley judged, after hearing both parties to the issue, and that without impeaching the integrity of either. Rankin departed. Asbury remained; and, as the Apostle of American Methodism, made a sublime and splendid record of suffering and achievement, hardly paralleled since the days of St. Paul, which has totally eclipsed the humbler and briefer labors of his faithful predecessor in the general superintendency. But the American Church would dishonor herself, should she withhold his meed of praise from Thomas Rankin, first President of an American Methodist Conference, and first General-Assistant,* superintending the interests and molding the destinies of our Methodism. Appropriately does Stevens grace the first volume of his great History of the Methodist Episcopal Church with a frontispiece which reproduces the lineaments of his noble countenance. We may rejoice for the sake of the departing Superintendent, that his last Conference was "a season of uncommon affection," and that "when the time of parting came, many wept as if they had lost their firstborn sons."

Thus closed the first period in the history of the American Conferences: the period of close communication with England and of the occupancy of the Conference Chair by Mr. Wesley's appointed delegate and representative. But the war effectually cut off communication with the home office; and with the Conference of 1778, William Watters, the American, in the Chair, begins a new era, which continues till 1784, when Mr. Wesley's hand again appears and his control again asserts itself.

This era, however, naturally divides itself into two periods: the first of discord and disunion, 1778–1780; the second of peace and prosperity, 1781–1784. With these two periods the two chapters following will be occupied.

---

* Boardman and Asbury had borne only the title "Assistant," the work in its infancy being regarded as a single circuit.

CHAPTER VII.

DISCORD AND DISUNION: 1778–1780.

I. The Conference of 1778.

THE Sixth Annual Conference convened at Leesburg, Va., May 19, 1778. The office of General-Assistant had been, to use the English phrase, " put in commission;" and William Watters, the senior native itinerant, and the chief of this commission, presided in the Conference. He was but twenty-seven years of age and modestly says:

> Having no old preachers with us, we were as orphans bereft of our spiritual parents; but though young and inexperienced in business, the Lord looked graciously upon us, and had the uppermost seat in all our hearts, and of course in our meeting. As the consideration of the administration of the ordinances was laid over, at the last Conference, till this, it of course came up and found many advocates. It was with considerable difficulty that a large majority was prevailed on to lay it over again till the next Conference, hoping that we should, by that time, be able to see our way more clear in so important a change.

Watters' name is placed first in the list of Assistants on account of his seniority and presidency: it thus stands in the place Rankin's had filled in the Minutes of every Conference since 1774, when the Assistants were first enumerated under a separate question.

This was the first session held in Virginia, " the chief field of Methodism, comprising nearly two thirds of its members." [*] The returns from the circuits are not given in detail. The total number of members is 6,095. Only twenty-nine itinerants receive appointments. It is the first time in the history of American Methodism that the Minutes show a decrease of ministers and members.

The following new questions appear:

> Ques. 6. Who shall act as general stewards? Ans. William Moore, Henry Fry.

> Ques. 7. What was done with the balance of the collection? Ans. Lodged with Henry Fry.

---

[*] Stevens, Hist. M. E. Ch., II. 43.

Ques. 8. What shall the preachers be allowed for quarterage? Ans. Eight pounds Virginia currency.*

The depreciation of the currency, Jesse Lee explains, brought about the increased allowance—£32 *per annum*— to the preachers. The last Friday in August was appointed for a fast day.

Stevens says there were thirty preachers;† the Minutes say twenty-nine: Stevens includes, the Minutes exclude, Asbury. He was not present; he did not receive an appointment; his name does not appear in the list of Assistants. Strictly speaking he was a local preacher. Of course nobody supposed his retirement to be permanent; his connection with the Conference was easily resumed; "supplies," as we should call them now, were so frequently called in from the local ranks that scarcely any distinction existed between local and traveling preachers; moreover, the question, "Who are located this year?" or "Who desist from traveling?" was not yet asked at the Conference sessions, so that no record of location occurs in Asbury's case, any more than in scores of others. Asbury's position and influence were undiminished; but at this juncture the name of the great Bishop disappears completely from the records of the Annual Conference. Officially speaking, it was now but a slender thread that bound him to American Methodism.

Ezekiel Cooper says, in his Funeral Discourse at the death of Bishop Asbury, that in March, 1778, George Shadford and Mr. Asbury observed a season of fasting and prayer, to know the will of God concerning their withdrawal from America, and that "Shadford concluded, and observed that he had an answer to leave the country and return to England; but Asbury, who received an answer to stay, replied: 'If you are called to go, I am called to stay; so we must part.'" Thus, then, and at this comparatively late date, did Asbury reach his all-important decision, so fraught with unnumbered blessings to Methodism and America.

---

*Minutes, ed. 1813, pp. 16, 17. † Hist. M. E. Ch., II. 44.

According to Jesse Lee, "Mr. Asbury began to lie by at Thomas White's in Delaware, March 5, 1778." Asbury himself dated his "confinement" from March 10, as the following entry under Saturday, April 11, will show:

And I know not what to determine, whether to deliver myself into the hands of men, to embrace the first opportunity to depart, or to wait till Providence shall farther direct. The reason of this retirement was as follows: From March 10, 1778, on conscientious principles I was a non-juror, and could not preach in the State of Maryland, and therefore withdrew to the Delaware State, where the clergy were not required to take the State oath, though with a clear conscience I could have taken the oath of the Delaware State had it been required.*

Asbury's headquarters, during his retirement, were at Judge White's, in Kent County, Delaware. It afforded opportunity for close study and protracted devotions, which he faithfully improved. He was "confined" only about five weeks; with the exception of eleven he traveled more or less. His improved treatment is supposed to have been due to the fact that about 1779 "a letter which he wrote to Rankin in 1777, in which he gave it as his opinion that the Americans would become a free and independent nation, that he was too much knit in affection to many of them to leave them, and that Methodist preachers had a great work to do under God, in this country, had fallen into the hands of the American officers, and had produced a great change in their opinions and feelings toward him." †

Gatch and Garrettson confirm the testimony of Watters that the sacramental question was unanimously deferred to the Conference of 1779. "I was present," says Mr. Garrettson, "and the answer was, 'Lay it over until the next Conference,' which was appointed to be held in Fluvanna County, Virginia, May 18, 1779, at what was called the Brokenback Church." Thus the Conference stood adjourned to meet the following year at a designated time and place. But before that time and at another place, a Conference assembled whose proceedings our narrative will have to take into account.

---

*Journal, I. 208.   †Lednum, p. 226.

*II. The Two Conferences of 1779—A Threatened Schism:
A Conservative North* versus *A Progressive South.*

The first Conference of the year was held at the home of
Judge White, in Kent County, Del., beginning Wednesday,
April 28. This was done chiefly for the convenience of
Asbury, who, as we have seen, had been there confined, and
could not yet safely venture into Maryland and Virginia.
He, doubtless, presided and brought forward the business.
Of the meeting he says:

> Our Conference for the Northern stations began at Thomas White's.
> All our preachers on these stations were present, and united. We had
> much prayer, love, and harmony; and we all agreed to walk by the same
> rule and to mind the same thing. As we had great reason to fear that our
> brethren to the southward were in danger of separating from us, we wrote
> them a soft, healing epistle. On these Northern stations we have now about
> seventeen traveling preachers. We appointed our next Conference to be
> held in Baltimore town, the last Tuesday in April next.*

Postponing the questions of the authority by which this
Conference was called and of the strict legality of its transactions, we first consider what was done. "Ques. 3. Who
desist from traveling?" appears for the first time in the
Minutes of this session. Trouble with the preachers of the
Southern and regular Conference is further indicated by the
following pledge which the preachers present made, "Ques.
6. Who of the preachers are willing to take the station this
Conference shall place them in, and continue till next Con-
ference?" Sixteen preachers sign this agreement, with
Francis Asbury at their head, and including such men as
William Watters, Freeborn and Richard Garrettson, Caleb
B. Pedicord, William Gill, and Daniel Ruff.

The authority of an Assistant, or preacher in charge, is
defined and formally increased, though these powers he had
doubtless long exercised by custom and common consent.
"No helper," say the Minutes, "is to make any alteration
in the circuit, or appoint preaching in any new place, without consulting the Assistant: every exhorter and local
preacher to go by the directions of the assistants where,

---

* Journal, I. 237, 238.

and only where they shall appoint." Exhorters, local preachers, and junior preachers, or "helpers," continue thus under the direction of the preacher in charge, or "assistant," to this day.

"Ques. 8. Why was the Delaware Conference held?" is intended to justify the somewhat extraordinary proceedings of the Conference. The answer is, "For the convenience of the preachers in the Northern stations, that we all might have an opportunity of meeting in Conference; it being unadvisable for brother Asbury and brother Ruff, with some others, to attend in Virginia; it is considered also as preparatory to the Conference in Virginia. Our sentiments to be given in by brother Watters."

On these points more remains to be said. "Ques. 10. Shall we guard against a separation from the Church, directly or indirectly?" is answered "By all means." The final questions, which complete the business of the Conference, are quite remarkable in their character; especially if these sixteen preachers regarded themselves merely as a preparatory Conference.

Ques. 12. Ought not brother Asbury to act as General Assistant in America? He ought: 1st, on account of his age; 2d, because originally appointed by Mr. Wesley; 3d, being joined with Messrs. Rankin and Shadford, by express order from Mr. Wesley. Ques. 13. How far shall his power extend? On hearing every preacher for and against what is in debate, the right of determination shall rest with him, according to the Minutes.*

When the Delaware Conference adjourned the legal or governmental situation is perhaps not inaccurately described as follows:

(1) An irregular Conference composed of a small minority of preachers had been unexpectedly, if not illegally, convened, in advance of the regular and unquestionably legal session. Watters, the only preacher who attended both the "preparatory" and "regular" sessions, received "no notice" of the irregular meeting, but, hearing of it, "determined, if possible" to get there, that he might persuade

---

* For all the preceding, see Minutes, ed. of 1813, pp. 18-20.

"Asbury to attend the regularly appointed Conference, to be held on the 18th of May, 1779, in Fluvanna County." * Garrettson calls it "a little Conference," "called by the Northern brethren," for their "convenience," and adds, " In May, 1779, the regular Conference was held, according to appointment," etc.† If Watters was not notified, it is not likely that others in the South were: only those were invited, it would seem, who were known to agree on the main sacramental point at issue. Asbury describes it as " a Conference for the Northern stations."

(2) Sixteen preachers, including Watters, agree to receive their appointments at the "preparatory" Conference (no doubt from Asbury himself, in view of the answers to Questions 12 and 13) and to remain in their stations until the next session of the irregular body, no matter what might be the action and appointments at the regular Conference. As a matter of fact no one of the sixteen, except Watters, even gave his presence at the regular session.

(3) Though styling themselves a " preparatory " Conference, these sixteen, by their answer to Question 10, concerning separation from the Church of England, decided the sacramental controversy, absolutely and finally, against the administration of the sacraments by Methodist preachers, without waiting to consult the sentiments, or attempting to change the convictions, of the majority of the preachers, who were about to assemble in regular session the next month at Fluvanna.

(4) This minority designated "Brother Asbury" General-Assistant for America, and insured his supremacy by enacting that " On hearing every preacher for and against what is in debate, the right of determination shall rest with him according to the Minutes "—" that is," adds Stevens, according to the usage of Wesley, as seen in the British Minutes, these being the only Minutes yet extant. The Ameri-

---

* Watters' Life, p. 72; Stevens, Hist. M. E. Ch., II. 60, 61.

† Semi-centennial Sermon; Stevens, II. 60, 61; L. M. Lee's Life of Jesse Lee, p. 81.

can Minutes were not published till 1795." *   These powers,
however, did not seem so unusual to the preachers who submitted to them, as to us, since General-Assistant Rankin,
as well as Wesley, had exercised them.   " The determination of questions in the early Conferences was a prerogative
of the General-Assistant, qualified, however, by the opinion
of the majority when this was obvious." †   " In imitation of
the practice of Mr. Wesley, after hearing all that could be
said *pro* and *con*, the presiding officer decided the point." ‡

On the other hand, some considerations may be urged in
extenuation of what appears to be the hasty action of the
Delaware Conference.

(1) The evident drift of opinion among preachers and
people may have been, and probably was, such as to render
it certain that the decision of the sacramental controversy at
the regular session would be in favor of the administration
of the ordinances.   It must not be forgotten, however, that
this Southern majority afterwards proved singularly tractable
and self-sacrificing.

(2) Asbury, though not the General-Assistant, was now
the only preacher in America who had been sent out under
a commission from Mr. Wesley: this, added to his commanding personal influence, based on his character, abilities,
and services, rendered him in some sort the real head of
American Methodism.

(3) Wesley's position on the sacramental question was
well known.   The practice of English Methodism had been
uniform.   The " United Societies " had no sacraments; to
administer them was " to separate from the Church."
Methodists, in Europe and America, were Episcopalians,
looking to "the Church" for sacramental provisions.   In
addition to all this, the Americans in their first Annual Conference, held under the presidency of the now departed
Rankin, in 1773, had bound themselves by a solemn compact, which we have elsewhere § ventured to describe as

* Hist. M. E. Ch., II. 58.   † *Ibid.*, II. 13, footnote.
‡ Bangs, Hist. M. E. Ch., I. 132.   § See the present work, pp. 61–66.

constitutional, that "the authority of Mr. Wesley and that Conference" should "extend to the preachers and people in America;" that "the doctrine and discipline of the Methodists, as contained in the Minutes," should "be the sole rule of our conduct;" and "that if any preachers deviate from the Minutes, we can have no fellowship with them till they change their conduct." Thus the sacramental question was the fundamental test in both England and America: while the Methodists declined to administer, they were "societies;" when they decided to empower their own preachers to dispense the sacraments, they became a Church. Asbury doubtless believed that he, more than any other man, would be held responsible by Mr. Wesley for such a radical revolution in American Methodism: therefore to meet an extraordinary emergency he assumed and exercised extraordinary powers. His "preparatory" Conference he esteemed "regular" because its action was in harmony with what had hitherto been uniformly recognized as essentially Methodistic: his principles among Methodists had been accepted, "*ab omnibus, semper, et ubique.*" The "regular" Conference he had determined in advance to regard as schismatic, because, in his view, it was not constitutionally capable of deciding the sacramental question: Mr. Wesley must be heard from. Yet, it must be allowed, by the impartial historian, that both before and after this time, Asbury was not passively submissive to the authority of Wesley on other points; Rankin, Wesley's deputy, had found him persistent if not stubborn; and in 1784, only five years later, Asbury determined to protect himself against the supremacy of Wesley, by demanding election to the Episcopal office by the Conference, after he had received appointment from Wesley. After all it is probable that had Asbury agreed with the Southern majority in their conviction that the administration of the sacraments was now a necessity, or in the expediency and legitimacy of presbyterial ordinations, he would have found a way to get rid of all constitutional and Wesleyan difficulties.

Having thus endeavored to set clearly before the reader, impartially and thoroughly, the merits of this controversy which threatened what might have proved a fatal schism in the infant Methodism of America, we shall be permitted, (since in a Constitutional History much space must be assigned to such a question,) to exhibit briefly the opinions of others.

Dr. Neely, after citing from Asbury's Journal an account of his endeavors " to prevent a separation among the preachers in the South," says:

> He fears the brethren from the South are in danger of separating, and he writes certain parties to endeavor to prevent a separation; and yet these Northern preachers, who rally around Mr. Asbury, have practically withdrawn from the Southern preachers, and stand in the attitude of separatists. If they had all met together, and the Southerners had seceded, then the case would have been different; or even if all had met at the place legally designated, and the Southerners, having a majority, had carried measures to which the Northern preachers were conscientiously opposed, and then the Northern minority had withdrawn on principle, the case would have been different.*

Bishop McTyeire denominates this Delaware assembly a "*quasi* Conference" and says: " The opening breach was, at last, closed by the moderation of the sacramental party, who compromised on a reference of the whole subject [to Mr. Wesley] backed by such official statements of the case as had never before been made." †   The tone of his judicial narrative carries with it sympathy with, and admiration for, the independent and yet moderate course of the sacramental party; coupled with a qualified recognition of the wisdom and conservatism of Asbury's action, which, however, he does not fail to see was irregular.   Of the sacramentarians (if we may so employ the word) he says: " The ground was not yielded without a struggle—not of arguments, for the brethren administering the ordinances were satisfied with their position—but it was a struggle of entreaties and tears, of love and pleas for continued union."   Of Asbury's party and its victory he writes: " The trained conservatism of

---

* Neely, Gov. Conf. in Meth., pp. 133, 134.   † Hist. of Meth., pp. 316, 318.

Wesleyan Methodists triumphed, though it bore hard upon them [the American Methodists]. They waited till all could be united in measures of relief, and until relief could come in regular order." *   Five years later, at the Christmas Conference of 1784, the relief came " in regular order."

Dr. Leroy M. Lee expresses a very decided judgment of the irregularity of the Delaware proceedings:

The meeting held in Kent county, Delaware, April 28th, 1779, preceding the one whose acts we are now reviewing, was not a regular session of the Conference of "Preachers in connexion with the Rev. John Wesley," although it is so styled in the "Printed Minutes." It is true, the circumstances that kept Mr. Asbury from his usual labors in the Church, prevented his attendance at *the* Conference. But this fact neither lessened the authority of the Virginia Conference, on the one hand, nor augmented the power of the meeting at which he was present, in Delaware, on the other. And it is due to historical accuracy to state that the Northern meeting was convened, in part, for the purpose of preventing the adoption of any measures with regard to the Ordinances. . . . And both Messrs. Watters and Garrettson, in their journals, refer to the "little Conference," called for the " convenience" of the Northern Preachers; all of whom knew the question of Ordinances would receive the final decision of the regular Conference, then near at hand; and Mr. Watters, who was present at both, was specially commissioned to communicate to the Virginia Conference the "sentiments" of this meeting, as a kind of protest against the adoption of any measures upon the subject. Under these circumstances, the Virginia Conference complained that an illegal Conference had been held, to keep as many of the Northern Preachers from the session as possible, lest they should join with them in adopting the Ordinances.†

Dr. Abel Stevens declares, " The Kent session was not only an informal one, called after the ' regular Conference ' had been appointed, but was probably unknown to the Southern preachers till after its adjournment," and continues at length in the same vein:

Any student of Methodist history must dissent with diffidence from the judgment of so high an authority as Dr. Nathan Bangs. That historian says that, "Although the Kent Conference was considered as 'a preparatory Conference,' yet, if we take into consideration that the one, afterward held in Virginia, was held in the absence of the General Assistant, we shall see good reason for allowing that this, which was held under the presidency of Mr. Asbury, was the *regular* Conference, and hence their acts and doings are to be considered valid." The historical evidence is, however, decisively

* Hist. of Meth., p. 315.   † Life and Times of Rev. Jesse Lee, pp. 81, 82.

to the contrary. Wesley had superseded Asbury, in the office of "General Assistant," by the appointment of Rankin. Rankin had held that office and presided in every Annual Conference down to the preceding session. At the latter Asbury was not present; he was in retirement at Judge White's house; and as he received no appointment, his name is not even mentioned, in any way whatever, in the Minutes for the year; Watters presided, and the Conference appointed its next session to be held at Fluvanna. The session at Fluvanna was, therefore, as Watters calls it, the "regularly appointed Conference." Instead of Asbury being the General Assistant at this time, that office had been, as we have noticed, put in commission at the Conference of 1777, being vested in a committee of five, Gatch, Dromgoole, Glendenning, Ruff, and Watters, in view of the probable return of Rankin to England. All these commissioners, except Ruff, were within the territory of the Fluvanna Conference; one of them, Gatch, presided at its session, and was the champion of its proposed reforms. Asbury was designated to the office of General Assistant by the informal Conference in Kent; he had, therefore, no previous official authority to call that Conference, nor could his new appointment be considered legal till the majority of his brethren, who were within the Fluvanna Conference, should confirm it.*

The reader has now before him about all that has been relevantly said—perhaps all that can be judiciously said—about this " irregular " session. Irregular it certainly was, and it was probably Asbury's influence which brought about the insertion of its proceedings in the Minutes, when these were first collected and printed in 1795. Of the three reasons assigned in the answer to Question 12 for electing Asbury General-Assistant, the third about his " being joined with Messrs. Rankin and Shadford, by express order from Mr. Wesley," is historically inaccurate. Shadford was not appointed co-General-Assistant; but Rankin was appointed to supersede Asbury in the office, and the latter was actually ordered to England. During the administration of Rankin, Asbury was subordinate to his authority. As President of the Conference, he made the appointments, sometimes sadly disappointing Asbury. Asbury had never before presided in any body that aspired to be recognized as an Annual Conference.

The Seventh regular Conference assembled, according to adjournment, at Brokenback Church, Fluvanna Co., Va., May 18, 1779. William Watters, the president of the pre-

* Stevens, Hist. M. E. Church, II. 62, 63.

ceding year, was in attendance: his name, however, is significantly dropped to the bottom of the list of Assistants, and it is not probable that he presided. He had attended the irregular session in Kent, and at the following meeting of the Northern body, his name is placed next to Asbury's in the list of Assistants. Philip Gatch was the leading spirit of the Conference, and, as he was also a member of the Committee of Control, appointed two years before, it is probable that he presided. Dr. Stevens says he presided, but gives no authority for the statement. The Church owes to him a most important rule of administration: the trial of accused members by committee, instead of the previous clerical right of excommunication.

The name of Asbury is nowhere mentioned in the Minutes of this " regular " session. There is no name common to the two lists of Assistants, six of whom were appointed at the Northern Conference, and eleven at the Southern. The Baltimore and Frederick Circuits appear in both lists of appointments, the same preachers being sent to them by each Conference, except that at the regular session Freeborn Garrettson is substituted for his brother Richard on the Frederick work.

The statistics of *all* the circuits are given in the regular Minutes: with the exception of the name of Watters, this is almost the only indication of union between the two Conferences. There are 8,577 members in society, of whom all but 2,987, even when Baltimore and Frederick are counted as belonging to the Northern Conference, hold their membership in the circuits constituting the Virginia Conference. The Minutes give the number of traveling preachers as 49; but this result is obviously obtained by adding the number of names on the roll of the irregular Conference (17) to the number on the roll of the regular body (32): there were but 44, since five names are common to the two rolls. Allowing Baltimore and Frederick to the Asbury Conference, it contained seven circuits, while the regular body had fourteen. The proceedings of that session not only represented a majority of the circuits, preachers, and people, but were enacted in the legal assembly of the Church, and by a legal majority of its recognized legislators.

The answer to Ques. 6 marks the change from one year of probation for a traveling preacher to two years, before he is eligible to admission into full connection: a rule which has continued in force to this day. The next answer excludes effective men who do not travel from the benefits of quarterage in the circuits where they live and probably, also, from any claim on the Conference collection. The final answer regards the preacher who receives a subscription which is not reported as quarterage as unfaithful to the brotherhood and excluded from the connection.

Strangely enough, the printed minutes contain no reference to the most momentous transaction of the Conference. The sacramental controversy received a positive solution which no anticipatory action of the irregular Conference could prevent. "The Fluvanna Conference," says Stevens, "being the ' regularly appointed ' session of this year, had the question therefore legitimately before it—referred directly to it by the preceding session." From Philip Gatch's manuscript journal we extract the following series of questions and answers:

Ques. 14. What are our reasons for taking up the administration of the ordinances among us? *Ans.* Because the Episcopal establishment is now dissolved, and, therefore, in almost all our circuits the members are without the ordinances—we believe it to be our duty.

Ques. 15. What preachers do approve of this step? *Ans.* Isham Tatum, Charles Hopkins, Nelson Reed, Reuben Ellis, P. Gatch, Thomas Morris, James Morris, James Foster, John Major, Andrew Yeargan, Henry Willis, Francis Poythress, John Sigman, Leroy Cole, Carter Cole, James O'Kelly, William Moore, Samuel Roe.

Ques. 16. Is it proper to have a committee? *Ans.* Yes, and by the vote of the preachers.

Ques. 17. Who are the committee? *Ans.* P. Gatch, James Foster, L. Cole, and R. Ellis.

Ques. 18. What powers do the preachers vest in the committee? *Ans.* They do agree to observe all the resolutions of the said committee, so far as the said committee shall adhere to the Scriptures.

Ques. 19. What form of ordination shall be observed, to authorize any Preacher to administer? *Ans.* By that of a Presbytery.

Ques. 20. How shall the Presbytery be appointed? *Ans.* By a majority of the Preachers.

Ques. 21. Who are the Presbytery? *Ans.* P. Gatch, R. Ellis, James Foster, and, in case of necessity, Leroy Cole.

Ques. 22. What power is vested in the Presbytery by this choice? *Ans.* 1. To administer the ordinances themselves. 2. To authorize any other Preacher or Preachers, approved of by them, by the form of laying on of hands.

Ques. 23. What is to be observed as touching the administration of the ordinances, and to whom shall they be administered? *Ans.* To those who are under our care and discipline.

Ques. 24. Shall we rebaptize any under our care? *Ans.* No.

Ques. 25. What mode shall be adopted for the administration of baptism? *Ans.* Either sprinkling or plunging, as the parent or adult shall choose.

Ques. 26. What ceremony shall be used in the administration? *Ans.* Let it be according to our Lord's command, Matt. xxviii. 19: short and extempore.

Ques. 27. Shall the sign of the cross be used? *Ans.* No.

Ques. 28. Who shall receive the charge of the child, after baptism, for its future instruction? *Ans.* The parent or persons who have the care of the child, with advice from the Preacher.

Ques. 29. What mode shall be adopted for the administration of the Lord's Supper? *Ans.* Kneeling is thought the most proper; but, in cases of conscience, may be left to the choice of the communicant.

Ques. 30. What ceremony shall be observed in this ordinance? *Ans.* After singing, praying, and exhortation, the Preacher delivers the bread, saying, 'The body of our Lord Jesus Christ,' etc., after the Church order." *

The governmental situation in American Methodism on the adjournment of the Fluvanna Conference may be represented in detail as follows:

(1) The Fluvanna action carefully distinguishes between the new Committee of Control and the formally constituted Presbytery. To be sure both bodies are composed of the same men: the men fit for the one position are naturally also those best qualified for the discharge of the duties of the other. The Committee business is determined in Questions 16, 17, 18; and Gatch's selection at the head of the new organ of government lends additional probability to his

* Dr. L. M. Lee, Life and Times of Jesse Lee, pp. 79-81.

presidency of this Conference. The Presbytery matter is decided in Questions 19, 20, 21, 22.

(2) The appointment of a new Committee of Control deliberately ignores the recognition by the Kent Conference of Asbury's powers as General-Assistant. Watters doubtless communicated to the regular body what had been done, if the "healing epistle" did not also contain the news. But they took no notice of the election of Asbury. Moreover, it is to be remarked that the Kent Conference permitted itself no appeal from the decisions of the General-Assistant, whereas the Fluvanna brethren expressly reserved to themselves the privilege of passing upon the scriptural character of the acts of their Committee.

(3) Jesse Lee records that "the committee [presbytery] thus chosen first ordained themselves, and then proceeded to ordain and set apart other preachers for the same purpose, that they might administer the holy ordinances to the Church of Christ. The preachers thus ordained went forth preaching the gospel in their circuits as formerly, and administered the sacraments wherever they went, provided the people were willing to partake with them."[*] That this action was decent, rational, and scriptural, Methodists of our day would have little disposition to deny. The regular and legal character of the body that reached this decision has already been sufficiently vindicated. There are no reasons why "Philip Gatch, John Dickins, Nelson Reed, Reuben Ellis, John Major, Henry Willis, Francis Poythress, and others as eminent, should be represented, however indirectly, as they have hitherto been by some of our authorities, as, practically, revolters from and disturbers of the Church. They were in every legal sense the Church itself."[†]

Yet this action completed, apparently irreparably, the breach which the Northern Conference had opened. Not only was a different form of government adopted in each body, one essentially episcopal and the other as evidently

---

[*] Hist. of Meth., p. 69. [†] Stevens, Hist. M. E. Ch., II. 66.

presbyterial, but by ordinations and sacraments the Southern Methodists had deliberately erected themselves into a Presbyterian Church. From this step it seemed impossible to recede. The two Conferences had drifted widely apart; and at this stage of the proceeding, it was difficult to see how they could come together again.

(4) The regular Conference had departed from the recognized principles of old Methodism. But if they thus ceased to be Methodists, in a little more than five years afterward John Wesley, also, ceased to be one. How much this action of theirs determined and hastened the measures of Wesley for the organization of the Methodist Episcopal Church cannot be estimated; but no doubt it contributed no little to this auspicious result.

The Fluvanna Conference adjourned to hold its next session at Manikintown, Va., May 8, 1780.

III. The Two Conferences of 1780.

Asbury's Conference of conservatives assembled at Baltimore, in the new Lovely Lane Chapel, Monday, April 24, 1780. This is the date given in the printed minutes. But the preceding Conference had adjourned to "the last Tuesday in April," and Asbury says under date of Tuesday, April 25, "Our Conference met in peace and love." Probably the preachers began arriving on Monday; some informal conversations were held that day; and on Tuesday the Conference began its session, with Asbury in the Chair. On the 24th Asbury prepared his list of appointments.*

Since the last session Asbury's Conference of conservative or constitutional irregulars had been gaining some ground. The action taken at the regular Conference in Virginia had been supported by a large majority, but was not unanimous. Some of the older lay members, perhaps a considerable number, trained in the traditions of Methodism, were doubtful about receiving the ordinances from other than episcopally-ordained men, especially without Mr. Wes-

---

*Journal, I. 280, 281.

ley's consent. The few preachers who could not approve the action of the Virginia Conference transferred their membership and labors to the Northern body.

The first question propounded is this, "What preachers do now agree to sit in Conference on the original plan as Methodists?" The names of twenty-four preachers are appended. This is an increase of eight over the number that had signed Question 6 in the last Conference; but several of these were now admitted on trial and none of the eighteen progressives who approved the administration of the sacraments—like Tatum, Reed, Ellis, Gatch, Willis, Poythress, Cole, and O'Kelly—are included. John Tunnell is perhaps the most influential man that had come over. The Southern Conference is still strong in leaders and numbers; but the Northerners have gained a signal advantage in the phraseology of this first question, which plants them squarely on the "original plan"—the constitutional enactments of 1773. Here was Asbury's strength, and he knew it. He alone of all the preachers now itinerating in America had been sent out by Wesley; he alone had been commissioned as Assistant for America: his Conference now stood on the Wesleyan platform. Irregular he was, but in defense of Wesleyanism and the fundamental compact of the Americans adopted at Rankin's first Annual Conference.

The list of appointments shows ten circuits, including Baltimore and Frederick, and twenty two preachers assigned to work. Asbury, as recognized General-Assistant, did not take an appointment. Of the twenty two appointees several were young men, however, just admitted on trial, so that as regards the older and more influential men the relative strength of the parties to the controversy is but little changed.

Asbury speaks in his Journal more than once, during the period just preceding the assembling of this Conference, of "preparing papers" for the body. The statesmanship of the natural leader is asserting itself in deliberate mastery of the emergencies of the times and the peculiarities of his situation. He is consolidating his preachers and people by the imposition of new and timely rules and regulations. No one could foresee how long the struggle with the Southern Conference might be protracted: like a wise general Asbury prepared for the shock and strain of sharp and continuous conflict by unifying and strengthening his own forces and binding them more closely to their commander. This policy is outlined in a series of twenty questions and answers, almost all of which bear visibly the marks of having been proposed from the Chair, with whom " the right of determination " rested. More legislation is now enacted than had heretofore, so far as the Minutes show, been considered in any annual assembly: even if the recalcitrant Virginians should return, it was desirable that they should find the government solid, and shaped to the General-Assistant's hand. While Asbury was a local preacher, they had strayed from the old paths of Methodism. But even in that lowly capacity he had proved himself too much for them. If, on returning to the constitutional fold, they find him securely seated in the General-Assistant's Chair, their commission of superintendency as well as their presbytery, will dissolve into thin air, and the man who is authorized to exercise all the powers that ever belonged to Thomas Rankin, or to Wesley himself in the British Conference, will see that the progressive Southerners do not again slip their halters.

The most of these twenty questions and answers, as incorporating several principles and measures which have remained permanently operative in American Methodism, as well as the Asburyan *ultimatum* to the regular Conference, are here cited:

Ques. 7. Ought not all the Assistants to see to the settling of all the preaching houses by trustees, and order the said trustees to meet once in half a year, and keep a register of their proceedings; if there are any vacancies choose new trustees for the better security of the houses, and let all the deeds be drawn in substance after that in the printed Minutes? *Ans.* Yes.

Ques. 8. Shall all the traveling preachers take a license from every Conference, importing that they are Assistants or helpers in connection with us? *Ans.* Yes.

Ques. 9. Shall Brother Asbury sign them in behalf of the Conference? *Ans.* Yes.

Ques. 10. Ought it to be strictly enjoined on all our local preachers and exhorters, that no one presume to speak in public without taking a vote every quarter (if required) and be examined by the Assistant with respect to his life, his qualification, and reception? *Ans.* Yes.

Ques. 12. Shall we continue in close connection with the Church, and press our people to a closer communion with her? *Ans.* Yes.

Ques. 13. Will this Conference grant the privilege to all the friendly clergy of the Church of England, at the request or desire of the people, to preach or administer the ordinances in our preaching houses or chapels? *Ans.* Yes.

Ques. 16. Ought not this Conference to require those traveling preachers who hold slaves to give promises to set them free? *Ans.* Yes.

Ques. 17. Does this Conference acknowledge that slavery is contrary to the laws of God, man, and nature, and hurtful to society; contrary to the dictates of conscience and pure religion, and doing that which we would not others should do to us and ours? Do we pass our disapprobation on all our friends who keep slaves, and advise their freedom? *Ans.* Yes.

Ques. 20. Does this whole Conference disapprove the step our brethren have taken in Virginia? *Ans.* Yes.

Ques. 21. Do we look upon them no longer as Methodists in connection with Mr. Wesley and us till they come back? *Ans.* Agreed.

Ques. 22. Shall brother Asbury, Garrettson, and Watters attend the Virginia Conference, and inform them of our proceedings in tl is, and receive their answer? *Ans.* Yes.

Ques. 23. Do we disapprove of the practice of distilling grain into liquor? Shall we disown our friends who will not renounce the practice? *Ans.* Yes.

Ques. 24. What shall the Conference do in case of brother Asbury's death or absence? *Ans.* Meet once a year, and act according to the Minutes.

Ques. 25. Ought not the Assistant to meet the colored people himself, and appoint as helpers in his absence proper white persons, and not suffer them to stay late, and meet by themselves? *Ans.* Yes.

Ques. 26. What must be the conditions of our union with our Virginia brethren? *Ans.* To suspend all their administrations for one year, and all meet together in Baltimore.

Questions 12, 13, 20, 21, 22, and 26 constitute the *ultimatum* to the Virginians. Reserving these for more minute consideration, let us first notice the purport and bearing of some of the remaining enactments.

(1) "Minutes" are mentioned in two answers—those to Questions 7 and 24. The American as well as the English Minutes are doubtless included in the latter case. But in the former, "*printed* Minutes" are exclusively referred to.

These could only be the English Minutes, since all authorities from Jesse Lee, the original, contemporary historian, down, agree that the American Minutes were never printed before 1795. This answer is important as being the *earliest* recognition, in the official transactions of the American Conferences, of the doctrinal standards of Methodism. The American chapels and meeting-houses had been generally settled according to the form of the deed used in England since 1750: but now the Conference specially enjoins on all the Assistants that (1) trustees shall everywhere be appointed; that (2) they shall meet semi-annually, and (3) keep a record of their proceedings; that (4) all vacancies on these boards shall be promptly filled; and that (5) "all the deeds shall be drawn in substance after that in the *printed* [*i. e.* English] Minutes." But that deed provided that the trustees should hold the property for the sole use of such persons as might be appointed at the yearly Conference of the people called Methodists, provided the said persons preached no other doctrines than those contained in Wesley's Notes on the New Testament and in his four volumes of sermons.* This question is of far-reaching importance, and will come up again. Only in recent times by those who have permitted the history to drop out of their memories, has the question been raised as to the scope and intention of that part of the first Restrictive Rule which forbids the General Conference to "establish any new standards or rule of doctrine contrary to our present existing and established standards of doctrine." For American Methodism the progress of our history will clearly establish that these standards of doctrine are (1) the Twenty-five Articles, (2) Wesley's Notes on the New Testament, and (3) his four volumes of Sermons, the limits of which will be more particularly fixed hereafter. From this Conference of 1780 to the General Conference of 1808, which adopted the Restrictive Rule, the testimony is uniform and convincing.

Nor is this question purely theoretical and doctrinal in its

---

*Tyerman, II. 478 and III. 417.

8

bearing. As long as two Conferences existed in America, each claiming '' connexion with Mr. Wesley,'' and each exercising an independent and supreme jurisdiction, it is evident that questions of titles to Church property were more than likely to arise. Asbury, a prudent man, foresaw the evil and hid himself. This minute direction concerning trustees and the form of deeds would secure to the Northern Conference all the property they were then holding and using: if the Southerners persisted in their independent course, and an issue were raised for settlement in the courts, it might be in evidence that they had so far departed from the '' original plan'' of Wesleyan Methodism as to forfeit their title to the property they were holding. All this Asbury had carefully thought out, and he had this minute ready for adoption by the Conference. In his subsequent administration, he, no doubt, carefully looked to its enforcement.

(2) Questions 9 and 10 were further designed, it is evident, to furnish an easy touchstone by which the Asburyan preachers might be instantly identified and distinguished from the traveling preachers of the Southern Conference. Moreover, since this license under Asbury's hand was subject to annual renewal by the Conference, it enabled the General-Assistant to keep all his forces well in hand: when a brother became weak on the sacramental question, or took work under the other Conference, his license could be suffered to lapse, and that would be the end of the matter. After the schism was healed, this continued a most wholesome and useful provision. Question 10 was also intended to put the local preachers and exhorters into more closely fitting harness, with the reins in a traveling preacher's hand.

(3) Questions 16 and 17 mark the introduction of antislavery legislation into American Methodism. ''Methodism thus early recorded its protest against negro slavery, anticipating its abolition in Massachusetts by three years, in Rhode Island and Connecticut by four years, the thesis of Clarkson, before the University of Cambridge, by five years;

and the ordinance of Congress against it, in the Northwestern Territory, by seven years." *

(4) Question 23 is sufficient evidence that Methodism was not only an anti-slavery, but also a temperance society, from the beginning.

(5) Question 24 is conclusive proof that Asbury was not actuated by personal motives or ambitions in forming and continuing the Northern Conference. He did not intend that its existence should hinge on the accident of his presence or absence, his life or death. He regarded it as the bulwark of Wesleyanism in America and the exponent of original Methodism. Therefore he provided that, in the event of his absence or death, the body should not be absorbed in the Virginia Conference, which, from his standpoint, was made up of separatists, "no longer to be looked upon as Methodists in connection with Mr. Wesley and us." Therefore, if brother Asbury should die, the Northern Conference must "meet once a year and act according to the Minutes"—doubtless both English and American, including the Minutes of this present momentous session.

(6) Question 25 amply attests that from the beginning to, spread the gospel among the slaves was accepted as part of the Heaven-appointed mission of Methodism. The Assistant was to meet the people of color himself, and in no case to leave them under improper or incapable "helpers" of their own race. "This probably gave the preachers an opportunity," remarks Neely, "to preach to the slaves without exciting the suspicion of their owners, who even at that day did not know what schemes might be resorted to by the slaves for the purpose of gaining their freedom." †

Asbury's Journal reveals the fact that the *ultimatum*, which in effect excommunicated the Southern Conference "till they come back," was not reached until after a protracted debate on a plan, or conditions, of union proposed by himself. Tuesday, April 25, he says:

We settled all our Northern stations; then we began in much debate

---

*Stevens, Hist. M. E. Ch., II. 78.   † Gov. Conf. in Meth., pp. 158, 159.

about the letter sent from Virginia. We first concluded to renounce them. Then I offered conditions of union:

I. That they should ordain no more.

II. That they should come no further than Hanover Circuit.

III. That we would have our delegates in their Conference.

IV. That they should not presume to administer the ordinances where there is a decent Episcopal minister.

V. To have a Union Conference.

These would not do, as we found upon long debate, and we came back to our determinations; although it was like death to think of parting. At last a thought struck my mind, to propose a suspension of the ordinances for one year, and so cancel all our grievances and be one. It was agreed on both sides; and Philip Gatch and Reuben Ellis, that had been very stiff, came into it, and thought it would do.*

As we have already gathered from the Minutes (Ques. 22) Asbury, Garrettson, and Watters were the Committee appointed to attend the Virginia Conference. Asbury's plan of union, it is seen, was a little awkward and complex, as he doubtless saw after the sifting of Conference debate. It involved (1) the recognition of existing ordinations, but the cessation of the practice for the future; (2) a boundary line between the Northern and Southern jurisdictions; (3) Asburyan delegates in the Virginia Conference; (4) the ordained Methodists to refrain from administering the sacraments, where there was a "decent Episcopal minister;" and (5) a Union Conference, in which it was intended, no doubt, that a final and faithful effort should be made to adjust all differences. This plan was abandoned, however, and that embodied in the Minutes substituted.

The regular Conference at Fluvanna had adjourned to meet at Manakintown, Powhattan County, Va., May 8, 1780.† No separate Minutes of this session are known to exist: the official printed Minutes of the denomination simply incorporate the returns of numbers in society with the similar statistics in the Baltimore Conference, and by inserting, "Question 27. How are the preachers stationed in Virginia?" in the proceedings of the Asburyan body, in-

---

* Journal, I. 281.

† Mr. Justice McLean's Life of Gatch, p. 75; Garrettson's Semi-centennial Sermon.

clude the Southern appointments in the Northern minutes. The Southerners have ten circuits, and to them twenty preachers are appointed, mostly men of experience and weight, like Dickins, Poythress, O'Kelly, Reed, Willis, Cole, and others. Stevens regards the omission or suppression of the Manakintown Minutes as "a grave defect in the official records of the denomination." * He continues:

> The Fluvanna session being, as has been shown, the "regularly appointed" Conference, legitimately adjourned from the preceding year, under the authoritatively appointed commissioners of superintendency, presided over by one of those commissioners, and comprising a majority of the circuits, preachers, and people, was unquestionably the legal or rightful session of the body. The legitimate session for the next year must therefore be that to which the Fluvanna session adjourned. . . . This statement of the facts of the case is, I repeat, due to the integrity of history and to the memory of the Fluvanna brethren, who, as has been seen, were no schism or faction, but really, at the time of their session, the Church, represented in its legitimate Conference. Their measures were equally legitimate; they were conducted with dignity and solemnity; and they were at last effectuated, to the signal advantage of American Methodism.†

Though the essential injustice, involved in the omission or suppression of the Minutes of the regular session of 1780 (the *eighth* regular session of the American Conference) must be allowed, it can be satisfactorily shown from other sources, that nothing material has been lost. Asbury was present at the beginning of the Conference, and almost certainly to its close. The sacramental controversy, and union with the Northern Conference, were the topics immediately introduced, and it is certain that we have the substance of the conclusions reached. Moreover, it can be shown that it is not at all improbable that, after conditions of union were agreed upon, Asbury himself made the Southern appointments; and, as this was the only other important business transacted, he probably at the time inserted these appointments in the Northern Minutes, or, at least, did so when the Minutes were first printed in 1795. He may have thought it wise to suppress the evidences of disunion, and, however we may regret his action from the

---

* Hist. M. E. Ch., II. 66, 73.   † *Ibid.*, II. 73–76.

standpoint of official punctilio, we may not impeach his motives.   Asbury, Watters, and Garrettson, the three commissioners, have all left full and interesting accounts of their embassy.   Let us attentively consider then the extant, contemporary sources of information, and the foregoing conclusions will be forced upon us.   And first Asbury's Journal:

Monday, May 1, 1780. I am going to Virginia.

Thursday 4. Prepared some papers for Virginia Conference.—I go with a heavy heart; and fear the violence of a party of positive men!

Friday 5. Set out in company with brother Garrettson. . . . We found that the plague was begun; the good man Arnold was warm for the ordinances.

Sunday 7. On entering into Virginia, I have prepared some papers for the Conference, and expect trouble, but grace is almighty.

Monday 8. These people are full of the ordinances. We talked and prayed with them, then rode on to the Manakintown ferry, much fatigued with the ride; went to friend Smith's, where all the preachers were met. I conducted myself with cheerful freedom, but found there was a separation in heart and practice. I spoke with my countryman, John Dickins, and found him opposed to our continuance in union with the Episcopal Church. Brothers Watters and Garrettson tried their men, and found them inflexible.

Tuesday 9. The Conference was called: Brother Watters, Garrettson, and myself stood back; and being afterward joined by Brother Dromgoole, we were desired to come in, and I was permitted to speak.—I read Wesley's thoughts against a separation; showed my private letters of instruction from Mr. Wesley; set before them the sentiments of the Delaware and Baltimore Conferences; read our epistles, and read my letter to Brother Gatch, and Dickins's letter in answer. After some time spent in this way, it was proposed to me, if I would get the circuits supplied, they would desist; but that I could not do. We went to preaching; I spoke on Ruth ii. 4, and spoke as though nothing had been the matter among the preachers or people; and we were greatly pleased and comforted; there was some moving among the people. In the afternoon we met. The preachers appeared to me to be farther off; there had been, I thought, some talking out of doors. When we—Asbury, Garrettson, Watters, and Dromgoole—could not come to a conclusion with them, we withdrew, and left them to deliberate on the conditions I offered, which was to suspend the measures they had taken for one year. After an hour's conference, we were called to receive their answer, which was that they could not submit to the terms of union. I then prepared to leave the house to go to a near neighbor's to lodge, under the heaviest cloud I ever felt in America. O what I felt! Nor I alone, but the agents on both sides! They wept like children, but kept their opinions.

Wednesday 10. I returned to take leave of the Conference, and to go off immediately to the North; but found they had been brought to an agreement while I was praying, as with a broken heart, in the house we went to lodge at; and Brothers Watters and Garrettson had been praying upstairs, where the Conference sat. We heard what they had to say—surely the hand of God has been greatly seen in all this. There might have been twenty promising preachers and three thousand people seriously affected by this separation, but the Lord would not suffer this. We then had preaching by Brother Watters on " Come thou with us, and we will do thee good " —afterward we had a love-feast; preachers and people wept, prayed, and talked, so that the spirit of dissension was powerfully weakened, and I hoped it would never take place again. *

Thus we see that Asbury was present three days—the usual term of a Conference session at that time—and that almost the whole time was taken up with interviews with him and his colleagues, and the exciting discussions that resulted therefrom. It was proposed to desist from the administration of the ordinances, if Asbury could get Episcopal ministers to supply the circuits with sacraments, but this he could not do.

William Watters, who was also one of the commissioners of union, and was, therefore, a participator in, and eye and ear witness of, these proceedings, has left us a detailed account of his mission, its progress and results. He says:

We found our brethren as loving and as full of zeal as ever, and as determined on persevering in their newly adopted mode; for to all their former arguments they now added (what with many was infinitely stronger than all other arguments in the world) that the Lord approbated and greatly blessed his own ordinances, by them administered the past year. We had a great deal of loving conversation, with many tears; but I saw no bitterness, no shyness, no judging each other. We wept and prayed and sobbed, but neither would agree to the other's terms. In the meantime, I was requested to preach at twelve o'clock. As I had many preachers and professors to hear me, I spoke from the words of Moses to his father-in-law: " We are journeying unto the place of which the Lord said, I will give it to you; come thou with us, and we will do thee good; for the Lord hath spoken good concerning Israel." After waiting two days, and all hopes of an accommodation failing, we had fixed on starting back early in the morning; but *late in the evening it was proposed by one of their own party in Conference (none of the others being present) that there should be a suspension of the ordinances for the present year, and that our circumstances should be laid before Mr. Wesley, and his advice solicited; also that Mr. Asbury should be requested to ride through the different circuits, and superintend the work at large. The proposal, in*

---

* Asbury's Journal, I. 282, 283.

*a few minutes, took with all but a few. In the morning, instead of coming off in despair, we were invited to take our seats again in the Conference, where, with great rejoicings and praises to God, we, on both sides, heartily agreed to the accommodation.**

The Baltimore terms were accepted and, most wonderful of all, forcing us to recognize the overwhelming personal influence of the man, Mr. Asbury was "*requested to ride through the different circuits, and* SUPERINTEND THE WORK AT LARGE." This proposal instantly took with nearly the entire Conference, and, in the morning, the Northern commissioners took their seats in the Conference, and both sides "heartily agreed to the accommodation." Since Mr. Asbury's powers as General-Assistant were thus cordially and generally recognized before the adjournment of the session, we repeat that, as the Committee of Control in the South was practically abolished by this arrangement, it is by no means improbable that Asbury himself arranged the appointments and afterwards inserted them in the minutes of the Baltimore Conference.

Garrettson's accounts, both in his Autobiography and in his Semi-centennial Sermon, add nothing to the particulars already before us except that " a letter, containing a circumstantial account of the case, written by John Dickins, was signed and sent to Mr. Wesley." As Dickins corresponded with Wesley on behalf of the Conference, so Asbury rested Friday, May 12, " to write to Mr. Wesley," and on Saturday, Sept. 16, he says he " wrote to Mr. Wesley, at the desire of the Virginia Conference, who had consented to suspend the administration of the ordinances for one year." †
Thus the case was appealed by consent of both parties to the Methodist patriarch in England, while the General-Assistant in America is again exercising undisputed superintendence over the whole work.

---

* Life of Watters, p. 79.   † Asbury's Journal, I. 284, 309.

CHAPTER VIII.

PEACE AND PROSPERITY: 1781–1784.

I. The Conference of 1781.

THIS Conference, at which were finally consummated the proposals and measures for reunion so auspiciously begun in 1780, marks the beginning of a new era of peace and prosperity. United American Methodism, under the single leadership of Asbury, presents an unbroken front, and, as the revolutionary war draws to a close, enters, under favorable conditions of civil and religious peace, upon an aggressive career of almost uninterrupted prosperity and conquest.

A "preparatory" and a "regular" session was held, of which more will be said: of the regular session Asbury wrote: "Tuesday [April] 24. Our Conference began in Baltimore, where several of the preachers attended from Virginia and North Carolina.—All but one agreed to return to the old plan, and give up the administration of the ordinances: our troubles now seem over from that quarter; and there seems to be a considerable change in the preachers from North to South: all was conducted in peace and love."* Watters, the peacemaker, gratefully records that he "was not a little comforted in finding all so united in the bonds of the peaceable gospel of Jesus Christ. We rejoiced together," he adds, "that the Lord had broken the snare of the devil, and our disputes were all at an end." The Minutes show an increase of more than two thousand members as the result of the peaceful and harmonious labors of the year, reporting as they do, 10,539 in Society, distributed in twenty-five circuits, and served by fifty-five preachers,

* Asbury's Journal, I. 328.

including General-Assistant Asbury, whose labors and travels are now so extensive that, according to established custom, he takes no appointment. Well might Jesse Lee declare, "the Lord had wonderfully favored the traveling preachers, so that we spread our borders, and our numbers increased abundantly." "Of the more than 10,500 Methodists now reported in the country, there were but 873 north of the southern boundary of Pennsylvania; 9,666 were below it." *

This year there appears for the first time a unique heading of the official minutes which continues in the same form until it is succeeded by the announcement of minutes taken at "the several Annual Conferences of the Methodist Episcopal Church." This heading speaks of the Conference as "held at Choptank, State of Delaware, April 16, 1781, and adjourned to Baltimore the 24th of said month." Here we discover the germ of the modern American Annual Conference. In England, with compact territory and dense population, it has never been found necessary to divide the work by the organization of these subordinate bodies; the Irish Conference, in its relation to the British, as the Americans cited in justification of their action, is found to be the best precedent and analogy for the American plan, now begun on a small scale, but afterwards to become the only adequate solution of ecclesiastical government for the millions of members and for the immense territorial expansion, of the Methodist Episcopal Churches, hitherto unparalleled among Protestant communions. To be sure two Conferences had been held in each of the preceding years. But only one of the bodies meeting in 1779 and 1780 was "regular": the other must be set down as extraordinary in its call and session. Nevertheless, experience had shown the plan to be possessed of obvious advantages, especially for the convenient attendance of preachers, who were now widely scattered upon circuits, some of which were very remote from any single center at which the Conference could convene.

---

* Stevens, Hist. M. E. Ch., II. 92.

The statement in the minutes of 1779 that the Delaware Conference was held "for the convenience of the preachers in the Northern stations" and "as preparatory to the Conference in Virginia," while it did not assign all the reasons which brought about that gathering, was by no means devoid of foundation in fact.   Consequently, after the reunion of 1780 had rendered unnecessary the existence of two Conferences on the basis of doctrinal or governmental differences, the conveniences arising from this arrangement during the two years of estrangement, had so commended themselves to Asbury's judgment, and doubtless also to that of the body of preachers, that in 1781, when harmony and unity were restored, the General-Assistant thought it expedient to appoint two Conferences.   Such were the small beginnings from which have sprung the one hundred and seventy-five Annual Conferences of the Methodist Episcopal Church and the Methodist Episcopal Church, South.   The minutes contain a formal statement and justification of this new departure.

"On the twenty-fourth day of April," says Jesse Lee in his History, "the Ninth Conference met in Baltimore.   But previous to this a few preachers on the Eastern Shore held a little Conference in Delaware State, near Choptank, to make some arrangements for those preachers who could not go with them, and then adjourned (as they called it) to Baltimore; so, upon the whole, it was considered but one Conference."   Thus these "preparatory" Conferences, owing to their irregular origin in 1779 and 1780, were still, in some quarters, regarded with suspicion; but "upon the whole" everybody soon fell in with the new plan.

To this day, according to the language of the Discipline, a preacher is "admitted on trial," not into a particular Annual Conference, but "into the traveling connection."   The Annual Conferences arose and continue to arise from subdivisions of the Church, its territory, and its one body of ministers, who form what is technically called the "traveling connexion."   The Church did not arise from the amalgamation of Annual Conferences. The Annual Conference is thus a unit of administration, created first by the Superintendents for their convenience and that of the preachers, and later by the authority of the General Conference. This unit of administration is territorial, for, within its prescribed boundaries, every Annual Conference, great or small, exercises precisely the same powers, under the same rules and regulations. In the beginning, however, before the organization of the Quadrennial General Conference in 1792, since legislative powers were exercised by the whole body of the ministry, with the approval of the General-Assistant or Superintendent, these local Conferences were considered simply as adjourned meetings of the undivided ministry. Such is the plain implication of the heading of the Minutes, which continued till the organization of the Methodist Episcopal Church.

At this Ninth Annual Conference of 1781, the first question was intended to cement indissolubly the union of 1780:

What preachers are now determined, after mature consideration, close observation, and earnest prayer, to preach the old Methodist doctrine, and strictly enforce the discipline as contained in the Notes, Sermons, and Minutes published by Mr. Wesley so far as they respect both preachers and people, according to the knowledge we have of them, and the ability God shall give, and are firmly resolved to discountenance a separation among either preachers or people?

The answer embraces the names of thirty-nine preachers, beginning with Francis Asbury, and including Lee Roy Cole, Reuben Ellis, Francis Poythress, Nelson Reed, Richard Ivy, and Henry Willis, who had been leaders of the Southern sacramental party. Gatch had previously ceased to travel, and the last question asked at this Conference of 1781, "Who desist from traveling this year?" includes in its answer the names of John Dickins and Isham Tatum, who had likewise been conspicuous and able leaders of the sacramentarians, and of William Moore and Greenberry Green, who had been identified with the Southern Conference. Cole, Willis, Ivy, Ellis, Reed, and Poythress are all appointed Assistants. Asbury thus wisely recognized the gifts of the Southern leaders and accorded them this expression of his esteem and confidence. O'Kelly was not present at the Conference: his name does not appear among those appended to Question 1, nor does he receive an appointment. Is he the preacher intended by Asbury, when he declares, as already noticed, that "All *but one* agreed to return to the old plan?"

Freeborn Garrettson is our sole and yet sufficient authority for the statement that at or before this Conference, a reply had been received from Mr. Wesley in answer to the letters written by Dickins and Asbury. "We met," he says, "and received Mr. Wesley's answer, which was that we should continue on the old plan until further direction. We unanimously agreed to follow his counsel and went on harmoniously."*

At the Conference of 1780 we have seen the order given to the Assistants, "let all the deeds be drawn in substance after that in the printed minutes." We know that the deed contained in these English or printed minutes named Wesley's four volumes of Sermons and his Notes on the New Testament as doctrinal standards of Methodism. At the Conference of 1781, in this answer to the first question, which was designed to heal existing dissensions and become once more an enduring bond of union, these doctrinal standards are explicitly mentioned. The "old" plan, the "old" Methodist doctrine, the "old" Methodist discipline—on these original foundations alone would Asbury and his Conference consent to build the temple of American Methodism, one and undivided. Of the fact, the historian cannot fail to take notice: our discussion of what it involved is once more postponed to a later date.

It is not necessary that we should take further notice of what have since become the ordinary disciplinary or minute questions under which the regular business of Annual Conferences is transacted. The questions and answers which embrace the legislation of this Conference, the rules and

---

*Semi-centennial Sermon.

regulations imposed on preachers and people, need not detain us, except the explicit recognition of two years as the legal period of ministerial probation.

Ques. 4. Should we take the preachers into full connection after one year's trial? Or, would it not be better, after considering how young they are in age, grace, and gifts, to try them two years; unless it be one of double testimony, of whom there is general approbation? *Ans.* Yes.*

At the Fluvanna, or regular, Conference of 1779, the period of probation for admission into full connection had been extended to two years; but as Asbury and the northern brethren were not present, the Conference of 1781 formally enacted the two years' term, which has continued to this day. A necessity also arose for directing preachers in charge not to undo the action of their predecessors with regard to preaching places, without inquiring as to its grounds. Very wholesome legislation against the readmission of expelled members without evidence of repentance may be profitably considered in our own day. Courses of study had not yet been appointed for traveling preachers, but their germ may be discovered in the answer to Question 8, which directed the preachers to read the "Rules," the "Character of a Methodist," and the "Plain Account of Christian Perfection." The practical and experimental character of this reading recommended by the Conference is significant. Commenting upon a correspondence which Wesley had in 1746 with Dr. Philip Doddridge, who was then at the head of a Dissenting Seminary, asking for suggestions of books to be studied by his preachers, Mr. Tyerman observes:

Of necessity, then, preaching was solely on the fundamental points of experimental and practical religion; and hence, their unequaled success in awakening and converting sinners. . . . The effect of this unadorned preaching of the greatest of all virtues was surprising. Under these untutored discourses, people found themselves emerging out of thick darkness into light, which St. Peter aptly describes as '*marvelous.*' These were glorious results, and almost make one wish, that among the cultivated and captivating preachers of the present day, who can discourse most eloquently

*Minutes, ed. of 1813, p. 28.

upon any subject, from Eve's fig leaves up to Aaron's wardrobe, or from the architecture of Noah's ark down to the whale that swallowed Jonah, there were a sprinkling of men whose preaching powers, like those of Wesley's first helpers, were confined to an incessant utterance, in burning if somewhat boorish words, of the glorious old truths now-a-days too much neglected." *

II. The Conference of 1782.

The Tenth Annual Conference was "held at Ellis's Preaching-house in Sussex county, Virginia, [Wednesday] April 17, 1782, and adjourned to Baltimore, [Monday] May 21." † Of the legislative relations of the two sessions Jesse Lee remarks:

As the Conference in the North was of the longest standing, and withal composed of the oldest preachers, it was allowed greater privileges than that in the South, especially in making rules and forming regulations for the societies. Accordingly, when anything was agreed to in the Virginia Conference, and afterwards disapproved of in the Baltimore Conference, it was dropped. But if any rule was fixed and determined on at the Baltimore Conference, the preachers in the South were under the necessity of abiding by it. ‡

After the Conferences became more numerous, however, the legislative power was recognized as common to them all, and general approval in all the sessions of a year was necessary for the passage of a given measure.

Asbury's Journal contains the following interesting notices of the session of the Virginia Conference at Ellis's:

Tuesday [April] 16. We set out; and on the next day, (17th) reached Ellis's, at whose house we held the conference. The people flocked together for preaching: Mr. Jarratt gave us a profitable discourse on the 14th chapter of Hosea. In the evening the preachers met in conference: as there had been much distress felt by those of them of Virginia, relative to the administration of the ordinances, I proposed to such as were so disposed, to enter into a written agreement to cleave to the old plan in which we had been so greatly blessed, that we might have the greater confidence in each other, and know on whom to depend: this instrument was signed by the greater part of the preachers without hesitation. . . . With the exception of one, all the signatures of the preachers present were obtained. §

---

* Life and Times, I. 516, 517.
† Minutes, ed. 1813, p. 33. The days of the week are fixed by Asbury's Journal.
‡ Hist. of the Methodists, pp. 78, 79. Cf. Dr. L. M. Lee, Life of Jesse Lee, pp. 100, 101. Dr. Lee adds, "A preacher in one division possessed the right to sit and vote in the other.
§ Journal, I. 344, 345.

In Asbury's Journal we have a most instructive picture of the ecclesiastical relations which Methodism gladly sustained in those days to the Episcopal Church in America, as well as in England, whenever a friendly rector permitted and encouraged it. The General-Assistant preaches at the humble "chapel" of the Methodist society, and then attends "Church" to receive the sacrament, and, by invitation, to read the lessons of the day before the loving sermon of the pious rector. The Methodist preacher becomes the guest of his clerical friend, and the two set out together for the Conference, where the rector preaches the opening sermon. The same preacher delivers the closing discourse and we do not wonder that the Conference adopted a minute acknowledging their obligations to the Rev. Mr. Jarratt, for his kind and friendly services to the preachers and people, and advising the preachers in the South to consult him in the absence of Mr. Asbury.*

It will be noticed that, according to Asbury's memorandum, "with the exception of one, all the signatures of the preachers present were obtained" to the agreement concerning the ordinances. Though he may have been the single exception of the preceding year, James O'Kelly is not intended by Asbury's present entry; for he not only received an appointment, but on March 28, preceding the Conference, had promised Asbury "to join heartily in our connection." † In truth the last stand for the sacraments was made by the local preachers, who, disaffected toward their traveling brethren, sought to influence the people against them also. Thursday, Dec. 6, 1781, Asbury writes:

Came to Baltimore. Here I received letters from Virginia, by which I learn that affairs are not so bad in Virginia as I feared: a few of the local preachers have made some stir, and the traveling preachers have withdrawn from them and their adherents. . . . Virginia, Wednesday 19. . . . I find the spirit of party among some of the people: the local preachers tell them of the ordinances, and they catch at them like fish at a bait; but when they are informed that they will have to give up the traveling preachers, I apprehend they will not be so fond of their new plan; and

*Minutes, ed. of 1813, p. 37. †Journal, I. 343.

if I judge right, the last struggle of a yielding party will be made at the approaching [Quarterly] Conference to be held at Manakintown. . . . Tuesday, January 1, 1782. . . . There is considerable distress amongst our societies, caused by some of the local preachers, who are not satisfied unless they administer the ordinances without order or ordination.*

Thus the traveling preachers had all at last been brought into line: that the battle went quickly and decisively against the local brethren, there is little room to doubt.

Of the Baltimore session, Asbury gives but a short notice:

Monday, 21st. A few of us began Conference in Baltimore. Next day we had a full meeting. The preachers all signed the agreement proposed at the Virginia Conference, and there was a unanimous resolve to adhere to the old Methodist plan. We spent most of the day in examining the preachers.

Wednesday, 23d. We had many things before us. Our printing plan was suspended for the present for want of funds.

Friday 25th. Was set apart for fasting and prayer. We had a love-feast. The Lord was present and all was well. The preachers, in general, were satisfied. I found myself burthened with labors and cares. We now have fifty-nine traveling preachers, and eleven thousand and seven hundred and eighty-five in society.†

His statistics are identical with those given in the Minutes: ‡ including himself, there were now sixty American itinerants, who were appointed to the charge of twenty-six circuits.

In addition to the usual disciplinary or minute questions, the following concerning rules and regulations were asked:

Ques. 13. How shall we more effectually guard against disorderly traveling preachers? Write at the bottom of every certificate: The authority this conveys is limited to next Conference.

Ques. 14. How must we do if a preacher will not desist after being found guilty? Let the nearest assistant stop him immediately. In brother Asbury's absence let the preachers inform the people of these rules.

Ques. 15. How shall we more effectually guard against disorderly local preachers? Write at the bottom of the certificate: This conveys authority no longer than you walk uprightly, and submit to the direction of the assistant preacher.

Ques. 16. By what rule shall we conduct ourselves toward the preachers and people that separate from us? Disown them. §

Dr. L. M. Lee had in his possession a manuscript copy of

---

*Journal, I. 337, 338. ‡ Ed. of 1813, p. 36.
†Journal, I. 346. § Minutes, p. 36.

9

the minutes of the Conferences held at Ellis's Meeting-house for the years 1782, 1783, and 1784: the questions and answers, according to this manuscript, correspond with those of the printed minutes, with the exception of the answer to Question 16, which reads: "Put the people out of Society when they receive, and the preachers when they administer, the ordinances, if they have been previous-ly warned." * It is not improbable that this fuller answer, given at the session at Ellis's, was altered at Baltimore to the shorter, as being sufficiently obvious.

For the first time a certificate of membership is ordered for the laity when removing, (Ques. 17) and the next question affords an explanation of how it comes to pass that both Gatch and Garrettson depose, as we have seen, to the consideration of the sacramental question at the Conference of 1777, the last in which Mr. Rankin presided, while the printed minutes contain no reference to the matter: "Ques. 18. Shall we erase that question proposed in Deer Creek Conference respecting the ordinances? Undoubtedly we must. It can have no place in our Minutes while we stand to our agreement signed in Conference: it is, therefore, disannulled."

Doubtless the same principles were applied to the expur-gation of the Fluvanna minutes; and so the printed minutes, first collected in 1795, contain no reference to the ordina-tions of Methodist preachers and their administration of the sacraments before 1784.

The next question is important: "Ques. 19. Do the brethren in Conference unanimously choose brother As-bury to act according to Mr. Wesley's original appoint-ment, and preside over the American Conferences and the whole work? Yes."

We have seen how this action had been previously taken at the irregular Delaware Conference of 1779 and how in 1780, at the time of reconciliation in the Virginia Confer-ence, Mr. Asbury's superintendency had apparently been

* Life of Jesse Lee, pp. 100–102.

quietly acquiesced in; no formal action had been deemed necessary in 1781; but in 1782 Mr. Asbury was unanimously chosen to "preside over the American Conferences and the whole work." "Mr. Wesley's original appointment" was also mentioned, however, and thus Mr. Asbury's authority rested upon the double foundation of original appointment by Wesley and election by the preachers. He was growing familiar with election by the Conference, and these precedents doubtless suggested to his mind the alternative of election to the Episcopal office in 1784, by which he sought and secured independence of Mr. Wesley's hitherto unquestioned supremacy.

For the first time the following question was asked in Conference: "Where and when shall our next Conferences be held?" and the answer was given "For Virginia the first Tuesday, and in Baltimore the last Wednesday, in May." And thus, as Jesse Lee remarks, "it was now settled and fixed to have two Conferences in each year."

III. *The Conference of 1783.*

The Eleventh Annual Conference, according to adjournment of the preceding year, began its session at Ellis's Preaching-house, Sussex County, Va., Tuesday, May 6, 1783, whence it adjourned to assemble again at Baltimore, Wednesday, May 27. General-Assistant Asbury was present and presided in both sessions. "After long rides through Fluvanna and Orange circuits," he writes, "I came to Petersburg on Monday the fifth of May; and the next day to Ellis's chapel." Thus the faithful itinerant superintendent was promptly on hand, on the day appointed a year before, to meet his Virginia Conference, though it is probable the Conference did not formally assemble until Wednesday morning. Asbury says, "Wednesday 7. Our Conference began at this place. Some young laborers were taken in to assist in spreading the gospel, which greatly prospers in the North. We all agree in the spirit of African liberty, and strong testimonies were borne in its favor in our love-feast: our affairs were conducted in love.'' His notice of the Baltimore session is very brief: " Tuesday, 26. We began our Conference with what preachers were present. On Wednesday we had a full assembly, which lasted until Friday.'' *

The statistics show thirty-nine circuits, (New York and Norfolk reappearing on the list,) with 13,740 members, an increase of 1,955, served by eighty-two itinerants, excluding the General-Assistant   " There were now but 1,623 Methodists north of Mason and Dixon's line; 12,117 south of it.'' †

The Conference maintained its advanced ground on slavery and temperance:

Ques. 10. What shall be done with our local preachers who hold slaves, contrary to the laws which authorize their freedom, in any of the United States? *Ans.* We will try them another year. In the meantime let every Assistant deal faithfully and plainly with every one, and report to the next Conference. It may then be necessary to suspend them.

Ques. 11. Should our friends be permitted to make spirituous liquors, sell, and drink them in drams? *Ans.* By no means; we think it wrong in nature and consequences, and desire all our preachers to teach the people by precept and example to put away this evil.

At the preceding Conference it had been enacted that members removing to different parts of the Connexion should take a certificate of membership in the Society. The revolutionary war being now over and intercourse opened between England and America, it was natural to expect an influx of European Methodists, both preachers and people. Accordingly, in answer to the next question, the Conference determined, "We will not receive them without a letter of recommendation, which we have no reason to doubt the truth of.'' At the Conference of 1778 general stewards for the Conference had been appointed; in 1782 the amount of the Conference collection is stated in the minutes, and specific directions are given for the supply of the " deficiencies " of the preachers; accordingly the final question of this session is, " Who are appointed as General Stewards? *Ans.* Samuel Owings, John Orick.''

---

* For all these extracts, see Journal I. 356.

† Stevens, Hist. M. E. Ch., II. 112.

The Conference adjourns to meet in "Baltimore, the fourth Tuesday in May." So fully and generally are the Virginia and Baltimore sessions now recognized as the separate meetings of a single Conference, that though no mention of a preliminary session is made in the adjournment of 1783, such an assembly gathers as usual at Ellis's in 1784. It was found necessary, also, to limit the attendance at the Conference sessions to " the Assistants, and those who are to be received into connexion." The supply of the circuits during the time of Conference, and not the entertainment of the body, was the difficulty. Hence at this Conference, the Assistants are directed, in time of Conference, to " engage as many local preachers as can be depended upon, and such among them as are needy to be allowed for their labor in proportion with the traveling preachers." *

About three months after Conference, Asbury wrote to Shadford concerning the American work. After giving the statistics, he mentions four clergymen who have " behaved themselves friendly in attending Quarterly Meetings." They were Mr. Jarratt, in Virginia; Mr. Pettigrew, in North Carolina; Dr. McGaw, of Philadelphia; and Dr. Mogden, in East Jersey. He briefly rehearses the sacramental difficulties, and concludes:

I travel 4,000 miles in a year, all weathers, among rich and poor, Dutch and English. O my dear Shadford, it would take a month to write out and speak what I want you to know. The most momentous is my constant communion with God as *my* God; my glorious victory over the world and the devil. I am continually with God. I preach frequently, and with more enlargement of heart than ever. ˙ O America! America! it certainly will be the glory of the world for religion! I have loved, and do love America. I think it became necessary after the fall that Government should lose it. Your old national pride, as a people, has got a blow. You must abate a little.†

IV. The Conference of 1784.

The Twelfth and last Annual Conference before the Episcopal organization of American Methodism was " be-

---

* For all the preceding, see Minutes, ed. 1813. pp. 41, 42.
† Quoted from a forgotten periodical, by Stevens, II. 127, 128.

gun at Ellis's Preaching-house, Virginia, April 30, 1784, and ended at Baltimore, May 28th, following.'' * Asbury presided in both sessions. Of the meeting at Ellis's he says, '' Our business was conducted with uncommon love and unity.'' Of the Baltimore session he writes, '' Our Conference began, all in peace. William Glendenning had been devising a plan to lay me aside, or at least to abridge my powers: Mr. Wesley's letter settled the point, and all was happy. The Conference rose on Friday morning.'' †

This entry introduces an important topic which cannot be passed over. On Christmas eve, 1783, Asbury reached the home of Mr. Pettigrew, the friendly Episcopal clergyman before mentioned, in North Carolina, and makes this important minute:

Here I received a letter from Mr. Wesley, in which he directs me to act as general assistant, and to receive no preachers from Europe that are not recommended by him; nor any in America who will not submit to me and to the Minutes of the Conference. ‡

Stevens says the letter was addressed to the Conference, and Jesse Lee gives ''an extract:''

BRISTOL, October 3, 1783.

1. Let all of you be determined to abide by the Methodist doctrine and discipline, published in the four volumes of Sermons, and the Notes upon the New Testament, together with the Large Minutes of the Conference.

2. Beware of preachers coming from Great Britain or Ireland without a full recommendation from me. Three of our traveling preachers here eagerly desired to go to America, but I could not approve of it by any means, because I am not satisfied that they thoroughly like either our discipline or doctrine. I think they differ from our judgment in one or both. Therefore, if these or any others come without my recommendation, take care how you receive them.

3. Neither should you receive any preachers, however recommended, who will not be subject to the American Conference, and cheerfully conform to the Minutes both of the English and American Conferences.

4. I do not wish our American brethren to receive any who make any difficulty of receiving Francis Asbury as the General Assistant.

Undoubtedly the greatest danger to the work of God in America is likely to arise either from preachers coming from Europe, or from such as will arise from among yourselves speaking perverse things, or bringing in among you new doctrines, particularly Calvinian. You should guard

*Minutes, ed. 1813, p. 43. †Asbury's Journal, ed. 1821, I. 367. ‡Journal, I. 363.

against this with all possible care, for it is far easier to keep them out than to thrust them out.

I commend you all to the grace of God, and am your affectionate friend and brother,   JOHN WESLEY.*

It is not improbable that this letter was suggested by an epistle of Edward Dromgoole's to Wesley, under date of May 24, 1783, in which he said:

> The preachers at present are united to Mr. Asbury, and esteem him very highly in love for his work's sake, and earnestly desire his continuance on the continent during his natural life; and to act as he does at present, to wit, to superintend the whole work and go through all the circuits once a year. He is now well acquainted with the country, with the preachers and people, and has a large share in the affections of both; therefore they would not willingly part with him.

Asbury received the letter from Mr. Wesley exactly one year before the assembling of the Christmas Conference. Mr. Wesley had appointed no General-Assistant for America since Mr. Rankin's return in 1777. Asbury had been unanimously chosen to the office by the Conference of 1782. Mr. Wesley now formally confirms this election, of which he had doubtless been informed, wishing no preachers to be received into the American Conference who made " any difficulty of receiving Francis Asbury as the General-Assistant." On the eve of the Episcopal organization of our Methodism, Asbury holds alone the general superintendency by a double tenure: Wesley's appointment protects him against a rebellious Glendenning at home; the Conference election leaves him not absolutely in the hands of the Methodist patriarch abroad. We can clearly see why he clung to the privilege and support of Conference election, when, in this very year, Wesley promoted him to the office of General Superintendent or " Bishop." Yet by this letter Wesley asserts his continued authority over American Methodism, and that authority is not disputed either by Asbury or the Conference. Mr. Wesley's first direction defines clearly, once more, the single doctrinal and disciplinary basis of Methodism. European preachers holding other views are to be excluded from

---

* Hist. of Methodists, pp. 85, 86.

the American Connexion. The American minutes are to have equal authority with the English; and Asbury is to continue, by his authority, as General-Assistant. The effects of this letter are clearly discernible in the legislation of the Annual Conference held in the spring of 1784, most of its suggestions being summed up in the answer to a single question:

Ques. 21. How shall we conduct ourselves toward European preachers? *Ans.* If they are recommended by Mr. Wesley, will be subject to the American Conference, preach the doctrine taught in the four volumes of Sermons and Notes on the New Testament, keep the circuits they are appointed to, follow the directions of the London and American Minutes, and be subject to Francis Asbury as General Assistant, whilst he stands approved by Mr. Wesley and the Conference, we shall receive them; but if they walk contrary to the above directions, no ancient rite or appointment shall prevent their being excluded from our connection.

Asbury's double tenure, it will be observed, is carefully guarded by the language, "whilst he stands approved by Mr. Wesley and the Conference." The doctrinal standards, here once more formally adopted by Conference action, it seems most appropriate should be reserved for presentation in the separate chapter following. We are now on the eve of the transformation of the Societies into a Church: a new nation has been born, and the Protestant ecclesiasticism which has largely supplied its religious needs is about to be formed. At this juncture it seems fitting that we should take a formal survey of its standards of doctrinal belief and public religious teaching.

Anti-slavery legislation, concerning members, local preachers, and itinerants, was passed in these terms:

Ques. 12. What shall we do with our friends that will buy and sell slaves? *Ans.* If they buy with no other design than to hold them as slaves, and have been previously warned, they shall be expelled, and permitted to sell on no consideration.

Ques. 13. What shall we do with our local preachers who will not emancipate their slaves in the States where the laws admit it? *Ans.* Try those in Virginia another year, and suspend the preachers in Maryland, Delaware, Pennsylvania, and New Jersey.

Ques. 22. What shall be done with our traveling preachers that now are, or hereafter shall be, possessed of slaves, and refuse to manumit them where the law permits? *Ans* Employ them no more.

Jesse Lee, who was present when these regulations were placed on the statute book, and witnessed their operation among preachers and people, observes: " However good the intention of the preachers might be in framing these rules, we are well assured that they never were of any particular service to our societies. Some of the slaves, however, obtained their freedom in consequence of these rules."

For the first time the question is asked in the Minutes, " What preachers have died this year?" The General-Assistant is allowed "twenty-four pounds, with his expenses for horses and traveling, brought to, and paid at Conference." Thirteen wives of preachers are allowed £302, against £206 for eleven the year before. The preachers are directed carefully to avoid superfluity in dress and to speak frequently and faithfully against it in all the societies.

Question 8 enacts a very important measure: " How · shall we keep good order among the preachers and provide for contingencies in the vacancy of Conference and absence of the General-Assistant? *Ans.* Let any three Assistants. do what may be thought most eligible, call to an account, change, suspend, or receive a preacher till Conference." Thus the provisions for arrest and trial were increasing and the itinerants were being held to a more rigid supervision and account. The office of presiding elder did not yet exist. The Assistants had charge of the " Helpers " in their circuits, but there was no officer intermediate between them and the General-Assistant, who must travel throughout all the circuits from North Carolina to New York and by personal knowledge of the men and the work, form his judgment for making the appointments and directing affairs at Conference.

As far back as 1774, as we have seen, it was ordered that every Assistant should take a general collection, " to be applied to the sinking of the debts on the houses and relieving the preachers in want." This primitive Church extension movement is now a little further developed:

Ques. 10. What can be done towards erecting new chapels, and discharging the debts on those already built? *Ans.* Let the assistant preacher put a yearly subscription through the circuits, and insist upon every member that is not supported by charity to give something; let them subscribe the first quarter and pay the second; and the money to be applied by two General Stewards."

For the first time, *three* Conference sessions are appointed for the following year, " The first at Green Hill's (North Carolina), Friday 29th and Saturday 30th of April; the second in Virginia, at Conference Chapel, May 8th; the third in Maryland, Baltimore, the 15th day of June." * So is the work expanding: before these three Annual Conferences, as we may venture to call them, shall assemble, the Methodist Episcopal Church will have been organized, and General Superintendents Coke and Asbury, with their associated Elders and Deacons, will be the leaders of the American itinerancy. All three of these Conferences were in the South. The last statistics reported before the organization of the Church give " but 1,607 Methodists north of Mason and Dixon's line, and 13,381 south of it." †

Of the last Conference of the colonial period of American Methodism, and of Asbury its chief, Thomas Ware, who was present, shall sketch the picture:

I doubt whether there ever has been a Conference among us in which an equal number could be found in proportion to the whole so dead to the world and so gifted and enterprising as were present at the Conference of 1784. Among these pioneers, Asbury, by common consent, stood first and chief. There was something in his person, his eye, his mien, and in the music of his voice which interested all who saw and heard him. He possessed much natural wit, and was capable of the severest satire; but grace and good sense so far predominated, that he never descended to anything beneath the dignity of a man and a Christian minister. In prayer he excelled. Had he been equally eloquent in preaching, he would have excited universal admiration as a pulpit orator. But when he was heard for the first time, the power and unction with which he prayed would naturally so raise the expectation of his auditors that they were liable to be disappointed with his preaching; for, although he always preached well, in his sermons he seldom, if ever, reached that high and comprehensive flow of thought and expression—that expansive and appropriate diction—which always characterized his prayers. This may be accounted for, in part at least, from the fact stated by the late Rev. Freeborn Garrettson in preaching his funeral sermon. "He prayed," said the venerable Garrettson, " the best, and he prayed the most of any man I ever knew." ‡

---

* For all the preceding, see Minutes, ed. of 1813, pp. 46–48. † Stevens, Hist. M. E. Ch., II. 132.
‡ Autobiography, p. 83.

CHAPTER IX.

THE DOCTRINAL STANDARDS OF ECUMENICAL METHODISM.

THE first restrictive rule limiting the powers of the General Conference distinguishes between "Articles of Religion" and "our present existing and established standards of doctrine." The Articles, twenty-five in number, are set forth at length in the first section of the first chapter of the Discipline. Unfortunately we cannot gather from this volume itself any information concerning the "established standards of doctrine," existing when this rule was framed in 1808. History, therefore, must be our recourse for supplying this defect and giving a correct interpretation of the language. We may congratulate ourselves that on so vital a head the materials are adequate and afford conclusive results.

The first section of the first chapter of the first part of the Discipline of "The Methodist Church of Canada" reads as follows:

STANDARDS OF DOCTRINE.

The doctrines of the Methodist Church of Canada are declared to be those contained in the Twenty-five Articles of Religion, and those taught by the Rev. John Wesley, M.A., in his Notes on the New Testament, and in the first fifty-two Sermons of the first series of his discourses, published during his life-time.*

It were well if this declaration formed the first section of the first chapter of the first part of the Discipline of every Methodist Church in the world. The declaration is true of every Methodist Church throughout the world, but our Canadian brethren enjoy the distinction and advantage of prefacing their Articles of Religion with this explicit and perspicuous statement. This declaration enumerates the three elements of the *Ecumenical Creed* of Methodism. From

---

* Doctrines and Discipline of the Methodist Church of Canada, 1882, p. 9.

(139)

the beginning to this date, there has been no doctrinal division in Methodism. World-wide Methodism receives these standards. As Professor Burwash has well pointed out, the first fifty-two Sermons constitute the *standard of preaching;* the Notes on the New Testament, the *standard of interpretation;* and the Twenty-five Articles, the *standard of unity* with the Churches of the Reformation.[*]

The first restrictive rule, limiting the powers of the General Conference, reads: "The General Conference shall not revoke, alter, or change our Articles of Religion, or establish any new standards or rule of doctrine contrary to *our present existing and established standards of doctrine.*" What are the "present existing and established standards of doctrine" here referred to? The rule was adopted by the General Conference of 1808, and consequently nothing of later date can be placed among the "existing standards." Unquestionably the standards "existing and established" in 1808 were, besides the Articles, Mr. Wesley's first fifty-two Sermons and his Notes on the New Testament, as will be shown at length in the sequel. It was unfortunate, however, that those who framed and passed the restrictive rules in 1808 took for granted that posterity would possess that familiar knowledge of the standards which belonged to themselves. As a consequence they did not formally enumerate the standards either in the restrictive rules or elsewhere in the Discipline. As the fathers passed away, the Church gradually lost sight of the exact works which constituted the standards mentioned in the restrictive rule. The doctrinal uniformity of American Methodism, and its freedom from controversy and heresy, could receive no more striking illustration than in this fact that the Church suffered to drop out of notice the standards to which there never arose occasion for serious appeal. Even a man so cautious and correct as Bishop McTyeire was at a loss. In the earlier editions of his "Manual of the Discipline," after quoting the first restrictive rule, he says:

---

[*] Wesley's Sermons, edited by Rev. N. Burwash, S.T.D., Professor of Theology in the University of Victoria College. Introduction, p. xi.

Some of the leading and characteristic doctrines of Methodism are not mentioned in the twenty-five technically called "Articles of Religion;" and these "established standards of doctrine" the Church is as fully pledged to and as much obliged to maintain as the Articles. Usage and general consent indicate these standard expositions of the Bible to be Wesley's Sermons and his Notes on the New Testament, Watson's Theological Institutes and the Wesleyan Methodist Catechisms, and the Hymn-book.*

But Watson's "Theological Institutes" cannot be referred to in the restrictive rule, for that masterly body of divinity was not then published or even written. The preface bears date, "London, March 26, 1823," but this is really the date of the issue of Part I., embracing only the Evidences of Christianity.† The preparation and publication of the entire work covered a period of about seven years, from 1822 to 1829. It was issued in six parts, Part II. appearing early in 1824, Part III. in the autumn of 1825, Part IV. in the autumn of 1826, Part V. in May, 1828, and Part VI. as late as July 1, 1829.‡ Accordingly, in the later editions of his "Manual," we find Bishop McTyeire making some corrections:

American Methodists (1781) vowed to "preach the old Methodist doctrine" of Wesley's "Notes and Sermons." May, 1784, "the doctrine taught in the four voiumes of Sermons [the first fifty-two of our edition] and Notes on the New Testament" was reaffirmed. The Deed of Declaration (February, 1784) legally established these standards in the parent body. The Rule (1808) guards them equally with the Articles. Usage allows Watson's Theological Institutes and the authorized Catechisms and Hymn-book to be high expository authority.§

Note a difference: Institutes, Catechisms, and Hymn-book are "high expository authority," but the restrictive rule does not guard them; the first fifty-two Sermons of Mr. Wesley and his Notes on the New Testament " the Rule guards *equally with the Articles*," and Sermons, Notes, and Articles are by a common boundary fenced within the same enclosure.

Recurring now to the Minutes of the Conference of 1781,

---

* Manual of the Discipline, Ed. of 1876, p. 131.
† Jackson's Life of Watson, p. 265.
‡ Jackson's Life of Watson, pp. 278, 304, 322, 340, and 353.
§ Manual of the Discipline, Ed. of 1883, and all later editions, p. 131.

we find the first question to be this: "What preachers are now determined, after mature consideration, close observation, and earnest prayer, to preach the old Methodist doctrine, and strictly enforce the discipline, as contained in the Notes, Sermons, and Minutes published by Mr. Wesley, so far as they respect both preachers and people, according to the knowledge we have of them, and the ability God shall give?" The same standards, we have seen, are nominated in the chapel deeds which were directed to be drawn by the action of the American Conference in 1780.

In the Minutes of 1784 occurs the following with regard to European preachers:

> If they are recommended by Mr. Wesley, will be subject to the American Conference, *preach the doctrine taught in the four volumes of Sermons, and Notes on the New Testament*, keep the circuits they are appointed to, follow the direction of the London and American Minutes, and be subject to Francis Asbury as general assistant, while he stands approved by Mr. Wesley and the Conference, we will receive them, etc.

This question we know embodies precisely the points indicated by Mr. Wesley's letter to the Conference, received by Asbury Christmas Eve, 1783, and quoted by Jesse Lee.

When the chapel deeds were reduced to permanent form, the Doctrinal Standards were nominated in the "Deed of Settlement." In the "Deed of Settlement" of each chapel it was placed in the hands of local trustees, who, after the decease of Mr. Wesley, should "permit such persons as shall be appointed at the yearly conferences of the people called Methodists, in London, Bristol, Leeds, Manchester, or elsewhere, specified by name in a deed enrolled in chancery, under the hand and seal of the said John Wesley, and bearing date the 28th of February, 1784, and no others, to have and enjoy the said premises for the purposes aforesaid; provided, always, that the persons preach no other doctrine than is contained in Mr. Wesley's Notes upon the New Testament and four volumes of Sermons." *

---

* See in full the "Model Deed for the Settlement of Chapels" in Smith's Hist. of Wesleyan Meth., I. 736. It is the ordinary legal trust deed and must be distinguished from the "Deed of Declaration" enrolled in chancery in 1784 and designed to define and protect the Deeds of Settlement under

Referring to the Course of Study as contained in the current edition of the Discipline (1890), we find that the bishops have made some significant changes. The present generation of preachers may have forgotten the works which constitute the standards: the bishops have so adjusted the Course of Study that in a few years hence every deacon in the Connection will be as familiar with all the standards as each itinerant now is with the Articles of Religion. Instead of assigning one volume of Wesley's Sermons to each year in the four years' course, as heretofore, the bishops have omitted the third and fourth volumes. The first fifty-two sermons of the edition issued by our Publishing House include all the sermons embraced in the original four-volume edition; and these fifty-two sermons are the ones nominated as standards of doctrine in Mr. Wesley's original "Deeds of Settlement" for his chapels and referred to by the American Methodists in their Conference resolutions of 1780, 1781, and 1784. Accordingly, the Book Editor of the Methodist Episcopal Church, South, has edited the fifty-two sermons, with introductions, analyses, and questions, and they have been published in two volumes with the distinctive title of "*Wesleyan Standards.*" In the Course of Study for the first and second years, as it appears in the Discipline, these two volumes are denominated "Wesley's Doctrinal Standards." The general introduction to Vol. II. concludes with this language: "In accordance with this construction of the Constitution of the Church [the obvious import of the first restrictive rule, as recited above] the bishops of the Methodist Episcopal Church, South, have placed these Wesleyan Standards in the Course of Study for young ministers." * The Notes on the New Testament are also included in the Course of Study for the first two years.

---

it. This "Model Deed" was first published in the English Minutes of 1788, (Smith, I. 586) but a deed, precisely the same so far as the nomination of doctrinal standards is concerned, had been in use from a very early date, according to John Pawson, since 1750.

* The Wesleyan Standards, Introduction to Vol. II., p. 6.

Students and examining committees have been laid under great obligations by the work which Dr. Harrison has so skillfully done for them. In his Introduction to Volume I. he lucidly sets forth the advantages of standards in this full sermonic form:

There is, however, a marked difference between the doctrinal standards of Methodism and those of other Churches. Protestant Churches have adopted, almost without exception, confessions of faith or articles of religion as the sole standard of doctrinal teaching. These they regard as brief summaries of the gospel contained in the New Testament. Mr. Wesley departed from the custom of ages by giving to his followers not merely the outlines of a system of truth to be subscribed and believed, but the method and substance of doctrine in the form of sermons delivered from the pulpit. The wisdom of this method the experience of more than a century has demonstrated. The brief, and often ambiguous, forms of a creed may sometimes promote, instead of preventing, dissension and controversy. In such a concise statement the mere *letter* of the truth can be recorded. In the Wesleyan Standards we have the *spirit* of the truth also. The manner of presenting the great doctrines of the gospel, the arguments by which the truth of God may be most successfully defended, and the objections which the sinful nature of man presents in the form of excuse or extenuation for neglect or abuse of the divine mercy, are all set forth with felicity of diction and comprehensiveness of knowledge. The forms of error which Mr. Wesley attacks are not those which are peculiar to a country or an age. However they may change the distinctive expressions which apply to them in the eighteenth century, these errors are still in existence, and must be overthrown if the gospel is to meet the wants of the world and destroy the kingdom of Satan.

In a similar vein writes Professor Burwash:

The precise form which the standards of any Church will take will thus naturally depend on the circumstances of its origin. A Church arising out of a great *intellectual* movement, like the Churches of the Reformation, will naturally fortify itself with creeds, confessions, and catechisms; inasmuch as its existence and success depend so largely upon the logical validity of its teachings. A Church arising out of a great *evangelistic* movement quite as naturally finds its standard in a *grand, distinctive norm or type of preaching*. . . . The Church of the Apostles was an evangelistic Church. Its standard of doctrine was first of all a *type of preaching*, of which we doubtless have a compressed yet faithful exhibit in the synoptic Gospels. The Pauline and the Petrine, Luke and Mark, set forth one Christ, in essentially one gospel, of which John, a little further on, sets forth the more perfect unification and expansion—just as Matthew had given the foundation. To this consensus of preaching, this normal or standard gospel, Paul makes constant reference in his Epistles, although it had not been reduced to written form. . . . We, therefore, claim for the "Sermons" and "Notes" a foremost place among the Christian symbols. The sermons set before us *that great, distinc-*

tive type and standard of gospel preaching by which Methodism is what she is as a great living Church. When she ceases to preach according to this type and standard she will no longer be Wesleyan Methodism. No other Church of modern times can boast of such *a standard of preaching, so mighty and pervasive* in its power to preserve the perfect doctrinal as well as spiritual *unity* of the entire body. God save us from the day when the Methodist ministry shall cease to study this standard, and to preach according thereto!*

Moreover, it is a great mistake to suppose that these sermons are put together without a doctrinal method and intent. Dr. Burwash gives us the following clear analysis of the doctrines taught in them:

1. The universality and impartiality of God's grace to man as manifested in the provisions of the atonement.

2. The freedom of the human will, and man's individual probational responsibility to God.

3. The absolute necessity, in religion, of holiness in heart and life.

4. The natural impossibility of this to fallen human nature.

5. The perfect provision for this necessity and impossibility, as well as for the pardon of past sins, in the salvation offered by Christ.

6. The sole condition of this salvation—faith.

7. The conscious witness of the Spirit to this salvation.

This full-orbed conception of spiritual religion embraced the great scriptural verities of all ages and schools of Christian thought. It grasped the wideness of God's love with the old Greek Christian and the modern Arminian, and it sounded the depths of the human heart with Augustine. It maintained the necessity of good works with the Roman Church, and it recognized the peculiar import of faith with Protestantism. With the Churchman it held the importance of means, and with the evangelical mystic it recognized the peculiar office of inward grace; and it built the doctrines of inward holiness and Christian perfection of the English mystics upon their true foundation by uniting them to the evangelical principle of saving faith.†

A final quotation from Dr. Burwash will suffice to place the remaining standards—namely, the Notes and the Articles —in their proper light before the reader:

The Notes have also their peculiar and unique value. They open up to us the mode of interpretation by which the grand type of preaching contained in the Sermons was derived from its fountain-head—the New Testament of our Lord and Saviour Jesus Christ. They are thus the link which binds our subordinate standards with the original apostolic standard. Without that link our form of preaching would be deprived of its divine authorization.

But the Articles of Religion have their own appropriate place in our doc-

---

* Dr. Burwash, Wesley's Doctrinal Standards: The Sermons. Introduction, pp. viii.-x.
† Dr. Burwash's Introduction, pp. xii., xiii.

trinal foundations. They indicate that which we have received as our common heritage from the great principles of the Protestant Reformation, and from the still more ancient conflicts with error in the days of Augustine and Athanasius. They represent the Methodist Church in its unity with Christendom and Protestantism; but the " Sermons and Notes " represent it in its one completeness as a living form of religion, called into being by the Spirit and Providence of God.*

Until 1882 the parent body of Methodism, the English Wesleyan Methodists, received the entire Thirty-nine Articles of the Church of England as a standard of doctrine—a fact which will explain some statements in Pope's Compendium of Christian Theology. But in that year the Conference adopted the Twenty-five Articles instead, of course properly altering the XXIII. on civil government. Thus in 1882 was the doctrinal unity of Ecumenical Methodism rendered complete, by the final acceptance in England of the Articles which Mr. Wesley prepared for the Methodist Episcopal Church in America. If the English Wesleyans, and all other bodies of Methodists throughout the world, could be brought to adopt the Episcopal form of Church government, we should have universal Methodism conforming to Mr. Wesley's ideal and plan, in respect of both doctrine and polity. It is not likely to be misunderstood if we venture to add that there can be little doubt that the Methodist Episcopal Churches are truer exponents and examples of Mr. Wesley's views and intentions respecting the constitution of the Church and the government of his followers than the non-episcopal bodies. But this question will come up again. How those views and intentions were carried into execution in the organization of the Methodist Episcopal Church in the United States of America will be narrated in our next Book.

It is scarcely necessary to add that the doctrinal standards which we have been considering are conditions of admission to, and continuance in, the ministry, but have no bearing on private membership in the Church. The " General Rules " are the recognized terms of communion throughout Methodism. They are free from dogmatic definitions or re-

---

* Burwash, Introduction to The Sermons, p. x.

quirements. "There is *only one condition* previously required of those who desire admission into these societies—a 'desire to flee from the wrath to come, and to be saved from their sins,'" which, however, must continue to be evidenced by the fruits described at length under the three divisions of the General Rules. The General Conference has no power either to abrogate this one term of communion or to add another to it.* When Wesley gave the Articles of Religion to the American Church he did not make them a condition of membership. "The 'Articles of Religion' and the 'General Rules' are both parts of the constitutional law of American Methodism; but the General Rules still prescribe the 'only condition' of membership, and mention not the Articles or any other dogmatic symbols." † Private members may be tried and expelled for sowing dissensions in the Societies and inveighing against Methodist doctrine and discipline, but not for opinions or beliefs they may hold. "While Wesley thus sacredly maintained the catholicity of Church communion, he nevertheless guarded with care the theology of Methodism. His Notes and some of his Sermons were made standards in this respect. This was in fact

---

* Of a provision in the Discipline of the M. E. Church, similar to one in our own, Dr. Abel Stevens says: "It has sometimes been a question whether doctrinal opinions are not required for *admission* by the administrative prescription adopted since Wesley's day: ' Let none be received until they shall, on examination by the minister in charge before the Church, give satisfactory assurances both of the correctness of their faith and their willingness to keep the rules.' It may be replied, 1. That, according to Wesley's definition, of the faith essential to a true Church, there could be no difficulty here. 2. That, as the requisition is merely an administrative one for the preachers, and prescribes not what are to be " satisfactory assurances," etc., the latter are evidently left to the discretion of the pastor, and the requirement is designed to afford him the opportunity of further instructing the candidate, or of receiving from him pledges that his opinions shall not become a practical abuse in the society. 3. If the rule amounts to more than this, it would probably be pronounced, by good judges of Methodist law, incompatible with the usages and general system of Methodism, an oversight of the General Conference which enacted it, and contrary to the General Rules, as guarded by the Restrictive Rules." (Hist. of Meth., II. 449, footnote.)

† *Ibid.*, p. 448.

necessary for his catholic purpose; for what could more ef-
fectively promote theological variations or dissensions among
his people, than continual variations or contradictions in their
public instruction?'' * Wesley declared to his preachers,
'' I have no more right to object to a man for holding a different opinion from my own, than I have to differ with a
man because he wears a wig and I wear my own hair, though
I have a right to object if he shakes the powder about my
eyes,'' and hence he prescribed a character and life, rather
than subscription to doctrines, as essential to membership
in the United Societies.

---

* Hist. of Meth., II. 447.

BOOK III.

THE GRAND CLIMACTERIC YEAR: 1784.

(149)

CHAPTER X.

———

" THE year 1784," says Dr. Whitehead, " brings us to
the grand climacterical year of Methodism. Not, indeed, if we number the years of its existence [the 63d year
is esteemed the grand climacteric of human life] but if we
regard the changes which now took place in the form of its
original Constitution. Not that these changes destroyed
at once the original Constitution of Methodism: this would
have been too great a shock; but the seeds of its corruption and final dissolution were this year solemnly planted,
and have since been carefully watered and nursed by a powerful party among the preachers. The changes to which I
allude were 1, The Deed of Declaration; and 2, Ordination." * The medical practitioner's knowledge enabled the
doctor to borrow an apposite term, descriptive of supposed
changes in the human constitution, and apply it to the critical transition period in the development of Methodism, both
at home and across the seas; but subsequent events, compared with this record, have totally eclipsed his fame as a
prophet, just as the fidelity of other chroniclers has robbed
him of repute as the biographer of Wesley and the would-be
historian of Methodism.† Robert Southey, however, un-

---

* Life of Wesley, II. 248.

† My copy of Whitehead's Wesley was once the property of an eminent
Methodist preacher, now deceased, who, after reading it in two weeks, while
yet a young man, says on the fly-leaf: " I wonder not that the Methodists
were at loggerheads with Dr. W. They had a right to oppose *him*, in setting himself up as John Wesley's biographer and the historian of Methodism, *because*, (1) He was a bungler as a writer; with a wealth of fresh material at command he has made a poor book. His selections from MSS. are
not always good. His comments are flat and impertinent. (2) He was a
bull-headed, self-conceited, prejudiced creature—saw not John Wesley's

fortunately treated him as an authority, and echoes his sentiment, minus his dismal prophecies, about the " grand climacterical year," so called, " because Wesley then first arrogated to himself an episcopal power; and because in that year the legal settlement of the Conference was effected, whereby provision was made for the government of the Society after his death." *

Undoubtedly it was the " grand climacteric " year. Wesley was eightyone years old. But seven years of life, as the event proved, remained to him. Many among preachers and members—some of them plotters and schemers—were awaiting his end with pious resignation. His dissolution, it was confidently expected, would prove also the dissolution of the Methodist Connexion, united by a personal bond, which death should loose. Methodism, spread defenseless throughout the British Isles, was a rich prey. Hovering over it were eagles—and other birds hardly worthy the aquiline name or company—with sharpened beak and claw, ready for the feast. Chapels and congregations were ready to the hand of popular favorites who would soon settle with all the freedom of Independents, rid at last of the ceaseless martial music to which Wesley had kept the itinerant ranks of Methodism moving. 'Twas a pleasing prospect. To be

strong points—took Charles for the greater man of the two—objects to the great and leading acts of his hero's life, and that he may back up his objections, he begins early and loses no opportunity to discredit Wesley's judgment—his knowledge of men—his firmness in adhering to his well-advised purposes, etc. If Dr. Whitehead really was selected by John Wesley as a biographer or literary executor, it is the most conclusive evidence of the book against his judgment and penetration.—Much damage has been done Methodism by this spiteful, anti-Methodistic book.—It is full of the author's own grudges, and personal and party dislikes—a cheat—an imposition." In another place the same writer says: " Dr. John Whitehead, the *author* of this Life of Wesley, which is rejected by all Wesleyans, and of this history of Methodism, which none but its enemies receive, was one of those *spoonies* that never tire of extolling the Establishment and would have had English Methodism play second fiddle to it until it 'played out '—which it would soon have done. Imagine a Life of George Washington written by a tory! Such is this ' Life.' "

* Southey's Life of Wesley, Amer. ed. 1858, II. 284.

sure for more than thirty years the title-deeds of the chapels had bound trustees, preachers, and people to Wesley's doctrinal standards. But then the preachers were to be appointed by the "Yearly Conference of the People called Methodists." And such a body had no legal existence. Scarcely should Wesley be laid in his grave, before the lawyers would help the trustees into permanent possession and control of the chapels, and the preachers into pulpits, over which neither a Methodist Conference nor an English Bishop could exercise supervision. In America, Asbury had suppressed the sacramentarians, and the presbyterian organization of Methodism, only after protracted and strenuous effort; and then had succeeded by joining the recalcitrants, in a common appeal to Wesley, and thus holding out the hope of speedy and effectual relief from that source. Had Wesley died without episcopally organizing American Methodism, it is difficult to see how these trans-Atlantic Societies could have had a future. If Asbury's consecrated will and tact could have held the Americans together until his death, the English dissolution, on Wesley's death, must then have repeated itself in America. Methodism's contributions to the ministry and membership of Episcopal and Independent bodies, in England and America, from the beginning to this good day, have been innumerable. But for Wesley's foresight and firmness, Methodism would long ago have been swallowed up. It is not too much to say that, notwithstanding its glorious successes won under the personal leadership and control of Wesley, Methodism, but for the measures adopted in 1784, "the grand climacteric year," when the seeds of its perpetual union and, we trust, immortal usefulness, were planted, to be carefully watered and nursed by powerful confederacies of itinerant preachers, would have long since disappeared from the face of the earth. To-day, Methodist Churches and Methodist Societies, out of which the Churches were formed, would have been alike unknown to the world.

The evil showed itself in prominent overt acts, previous to this period.

Mr. Wesley, having striven to prevail on some trustees, in Yorkshire,* to settle their chapels, so that the people might continue to hear the same truths and be under the same discipline as heretofore, was assailed with calumny, and with the most determined opposition, as though he intended to make the chapels his own! Another set of trustees, in the same county, absolutely refused to settle a lately erected chapel; and, in the issue, engaged Mr. Wesley's book-steward in London,† who had been an itinerant preacher, to come to them as their minister. This man, however, was "*wise in his generation;*" and insisted upon having an income of sixty pounds *per annum,* with the chapel-house to live in, settled upon him during his life, before he would relinquish his place under Mr. Wesley. What will not party spirit do! I was a witness, when, after Mr. Wesley's death, it was found, that the preachers continued united and faithful in their calling, how deeply those men repented of their conduct in this instance. In vain they represented to the man of their unhappy choice, how lamentably their congregations had declined, and how hardly they could sustain the expenses they had incurred. The answer was short: they might employ other preachers, if they should think it proper; but the dwelling-house and the stated income belonged to him! . . . In that day of uncertainty and surmise, there were not wanting some, even among the itinerant preachers, who entertained fears respecting a settlement of this kind. They had but little hope that the work would continue, after Mr. Wesley's death, as it had during his life; and they thought it probable, that the largest Societies and, of course, the principal chapels would become independent. . . . Some of the itinerant preachers brought the charge, at the first Conference after the Deed was enrolled, that it was the work of Dr. Coke, who had joined Mr. Wesley a few years before. Mr. Wesley only replied to this in the words of Virgil, *Non vult, non potuit!* "He had neither the will nor the power."

The truth is: the Conference had requested Mr. Wesley to get such an instrument drawn up, as would define or explain what was meant by that expression, used in the various deeds of the chapels so settled; viz., "THE CONFERENCE OF THE PEOPLE CALLED METHODISTS;" upon the meaning of which terms the authority so appointing must rest, so long as there should be an itinerant ministry. The elder Mr. Hampson was particularly earnest with Mr. Wesley, to have such an instrument executed without delay. He immediately set about it; and having given directions to his solicitor, who took the opinion of counsel upon the most proper and effectual way of doing it, he committed it chiefly to the care of Dr. Coke, as his own avocations would not admit of a constant personal attendance. He, however, wrote, with his own hand, a list of a hundred names, which he ordered to be inserted, declaring his full determination that no more should be appointed; and as there never had been so great a number at any Conference, and generally from twenty to thirty less, the number so fixed would not, it was

* See the case of Birstal House, pp. 38–42, of this work.

† Mr. John Atlay, nine years an itinerant preacher, and fifteen years book-steward in London: see four letters to him from Mr. Wesley, Works, VII. 331, and the "Case of Dewsbury House," which is the chapel referred to in the text, VII. 329, 330. Cf. "A Word to Whom it May Concern," VII. 332.

thought, have excited either surprise or displeasure. I can state with the fullest certainty, that what Dr. Whitehead has asserted, respecting Mr. Wesley having repented of this transaction, is totally unfounded. On the contrary, he reviewed it always with high satisfaction; and praised God, who had brought him through a business which he had long contemplated with earnest desire, and yet with many fears.*

The full title of that famous and important document, the " Deed of Declaration," the Magna Charta of British Methodism, is " The Rev. John Wesley's Declaration and Establishment of the Conference of the People called Methodists." † According to the Deed itself its object was " to explain the words ' Yearly Conference of the People called Methodists,' contained in all the said trust deeds, and to declare what persons are members of the said Conference, and how the succession and identity thereof is to be continued." The preamble recites the origin, composition, and functions of Wesley's Conference, and the nature, object, and conditions of the trust deeds by which the chapels and other property were held for the use of the Methodist preachers, with all of which we have previously become familiar. The Deed then enumerates the names of one hundred preachers, with their addresses, and declares that they " being preachers and expounders of God's Holy Word, under the care and in connection with the said John Wesley, have been, now are, and do, on the day of the date thereof [Feb. 28, 1784] constitute the members of the said Conference, according to the true intent and meaning of the said several gifts and conveyances wherein the words, ' Conference of the people called Methodists,' are mentioned and contained; and that the said several persons before named, and their successors forever, to be chosen as hereafter mentioned, are and shall forever be construed, taken, and be the Conference of the people called Methodists." All this hinged upon prescribed conditions and regulations which may be briefly summarized as follows: (1) That they and their successors, for the time being forever, shall assemble once a year; (2) That the act of the majority

---

* Moore's Life of Wesley, II. 295-300. † Whitehead, Life, II. 248

shall be the act of the whole; (3) That their first business, when they assemble, shall be to fill up vacancies; (4) That no act of the Conference shall be valid unless forty of its members are present; (5) That the duration of the yearly Conference shall not be less than five days, nor more than three weeks; (6) That, immediately after filling up vacancies, they shall choose a President and Secretary from themselves; (7) That any member of the Conference, absenting himself from the yearly assembly for two years successively, without the consent of the Conference, and who is not present on the first day of the third yearly assembly, shall forthwith cease to be a member, as though he were dead; (8) That the Conference may expel any member, or any person admitted into connection, for any cause which to the Conference may seem fit or necessary; (9) That they may admit into connection any person, of whom they approve, to be a preacher of God's holy word, under direction of the Conference; (10) That no person shall be elected a member of the Conference, who has not been admitted into the connection, as a preacher, for twelve months; (11) That the Conference shall not appoint any person to the use of chapels, who is not either a member of the Conference, or admitted into connection with the same, or upon trial; and that no person shall be appointed for more than three years successively, except ordained ministers of the Church of England; (12) That the Conference may appoint the place of holding the yearly assembly at any other town than London, Bristol, or Leeds; (13) That the Conference may, when it shall seem expedient, send any of its members as delegates to Ireland, or other parts out of the kingdom of Great Britain, to act on its behalf, and with all the powers of the Conference itself; (14) That all resolutions and acts of the Conference shall be written in the journals and be signed by the President and Secretary for the time being; (15) That whenever the Conference shall be reduced under the number of forty members, and continue so reduced for three years successively; or whenever the members shall decline or neglect to meet together annually during the space of three years, the Conference of the people called Methodists shall be extinguished, and all its powers, privileges, and advantages shall cease; (16) That nothing in this deed shall extinguish or lessen the life estate of John and Charles Wesley in any of the chapels in which they now have, or may have, any estate or interest, power or authority.*

At the Conference of 1783, the year before the enrollment of the Deed, one hundred and ninety-two preachers had been given appointments. Twenty-two of these had not yet been admitted into full connection. Tyerman thinks it would have been prudent to have named the whole of the remaining one hundred and seventy in the Deed. Wesley's reasons seem to have been conclusive against this. Sixteen, however, were selected who had traveled less than four years, whereas the following were among the rejected: Thomas Lee, who had traveled 36 years; John Atlay, 21; James Thompson, 25; John Poole, 25; William Ashman, 19; J. Hern, 15; William Eels, 12; Thomas Mitchell, 36; and Joseph Pilmoor, 19.

Why a man who afterward developed such traits as Atlay, the renegade book-steward, and one like our old friend, Brother Pilmoor, formerly of the American circuit—afterwards the Rev. Dr. Pilmoor, an estimable Protestant Episcopal clergyman of the city of Philadelphia—should have been omitted, we can readily understand. Perhaps if we were intimately acquainted with the characters and careers of the remainder of this corps of ancient worthies we could better appreciate the sweet reasonableness of the course which Wesley, who knew them well, pursued toward them.

When the delegated General Conference was determined

---

* This summary substantially reproduces Tyerman's, Life and Times of Wesley, III. 418, 419. Other summaries may be found in Whitehead's Life, II. 248–253; Southey's Life, II. 284–286. The Deed is printed in full in Wesley's Works, Amer. ed., IV. 753–759; in Smith's Hist. of Wesleyan Meth., Appen. E., I. 731–735; and in Neely's Governing Conference in Methodism, pp. 60–69.

on in America a keen and protracted debate turned on whether the delegates should be appointed by election or by seniority and, at last, the dispute was settled by leaving that alternative with the Annual Conferences: as a matter of fact no Conference ever appointed its representatives by seniority.

Immediately, John Hampson, Sr., sent forth a printed circular, entitled, "An Appeal to the Reverend John and Charles Wesley; to all the preachers who act in connection with them, and to every member of their respective societies in England, Scotland, Ireland, and America." "In this document," says George Smith, "the curious may find all the allegations put forth in every agitation of Methodism from that time to the present. Here is an alleged great breach of faith, an asserted act of injustice and tyranny, which is said to have been committed under the influence of a favored few; and the complainants are represented as persecuted and injured." *

The Deed of Declaration [continues Dr. Smith] was violently opposed in Wesley's time by those preachers who regarded themselves as equal, in repect of standing and ability, to any of their brethren; but whose names were not inserted by Wesley in the Deed. The mention of this class is a sufficient explanation of their objection.

Besides these, there were others, itinerant and local preachers, who had become united to Methodist Societies, but who never calculated on the permanence of the body, or its continued and energetic action as a whole, after the death of Wesley. Some of these, it is believed, unfaithful to their principles and calling, looked forward to the death of their founder as a time when, by the favor of friendly trustees, they might secure the pulpits of respectable chapels, and escape from the toil, privations, and dangers of itinerancy.

There were, also, men who believed that Methodism was, in its origin, a very good and useful means of rousing a slumbering Church and nation to a sense of God and religion; but that, having brought out the sterling doctrines of the Reformation from neglect and obscurity, and imbued the clergy and the people to some extent with a conviction of their spiritual vitality and practical importance, as well as having afforded, in thousands of instances, proofs of the experimental and practical godliness which they could impart in life and in death, it ought to have retired from the scene, and never to have formed a permanent body, but to have left these lessons of holy faith and practice for the edification of the Church whence

---

* Hist. of Wesleyan Meth., London ed., I. 523, 524.

the founder of Methodism had been raised. Had this been done, Wesley would have been lauded as an apostle by Dr. Southey and many others, who have spoken of him in a very different tone. The Deed of Declaration alone prevented such a dislocation of the Societies on the death of Wesley.

For this reason, those persons who deplore the continued existence of Methodism as a great and lamentable ecclesiastical irregularity; who believe, that on the demise of Wesley, if not before, the Societies which he had gathered should have fallen back into the bosom of the National Church; naturally look on the Deed of Declaration as the master evil of the whole system.*

As early as April, 1785, Mr. Wesley placed in the hands of Joseph Bradford a letter to be delivered to the Conference at the first session after his death:

CHESTER, April 7, 1785.

My Dear Brethren: Some of our traveling preachers have expressed a fear, that, after my decease, you would exclude them either from preaching in connection with you, or from some other privileges which they now enjoy. I know no other way to prevent such inconvenience, than to leave these my last words with you.

I beseech you, by the mercies of God, that you never avail yourselves of the deed of declaration to assume any superiority over your brethren; but let all things go on, among those itinerants who choose to remain together, exactly in the same manner as when I was with you, so far as circumstances will permit.

In particular, I beseech you, if you ever loved me, and if you now love God and your brethren, to have no respect of persons in stationing the preachers, in choosing children for Kingswood school, in disposing of the yearly contribution, and the preachers' fund, or any other public money: but do all things with a single eye, as I have done from the beginning. Go on thus, doing all things without prejudice or partiality, and God will be with you even to the end.   JOHN WESLEY.†

At the Conference of 1791, the first after Mr. Wesley's death, this letter was read, when it was unanimously resolved:

That all the preachers who are in full connection with them shall enjoy every privilege that the members of the Conference enjoy, agreeably to the above written letter of our venerable deceased father in the gospel. ‡

We conclude our account of the Deed of Declaration and take our leave, in this history, of English Methodism, established to this day upon the legal rock which Mr. Wesley, as-

---

* Hist. of Wesleyan Meth., London ed., I. 526, 527.
† Wesley's Works, Amer. ed., VII. 310, 311.
‡ *Ibid.*, VII. 311, footnote.

sisted by Dr. Coke, quarried for its sufficient foundation, with the great Founder's own final defense of his action, under date of March 3, 1785:

In naming these preachers, as I had no adviser, so I had no respect of persons; but I simply set down those that, according to the best of my judgment, were most proper. But I am not infallible. I might mistake, and think better of some of them than they deserved. However, I did my best; and if I did wrong it was not the error of my will, but of my judg-ment.

This was the rise and this is the nature of that famous "Deed of Decla-ration"—that vile, wicked deed!—concerning which you have heard such an outcry. And now, can any one tell me how to mend it, or how it could have been made better? "O yes, you might have inserted two hundred, as well as one hundred preachers." No, for then the expense of meeting would have been double, and all the circuits would have been without preachers. "But you might have named other preachers instead of these." True, if I had thought as well of them as they did of themselves. But I did not; therefore I could do no otherwise than I did, without sinning against God and my own conscience.

"But what need was there for any deed at all?" There was the utmost need of it. Without some authentic deed fixing the meaning of the term, the moment I died the Conference had been nothing. Therefore any of the proprietors of the land on which our preaching-houses were built might have seized them for their own use, and there would have been none to hin-der them; for the Conference would have been nobody—a mere empty name.

You see, then, in all the pains I have taken about this absolutely neces-sary deed I have been laboring, not for myself (I have no interest therein), but for the whole body of Methodists, in order to fix them upon such a foundation as is likely to stand as long as the sun and moon endure. That is, if they continue to walk by faith, and to show forth their faith by their works; otherwise I pray God to root out the memorial of them from the earth.*

---

*"Thoughts upon Some Late Occurrences," Wesley's Works, VII. 309, 310.

CHAPTER XI.

THE CHRISTMAS CONFERENCE AND WESLEY'S FINAL SET-TLEMENT OF EPISCOPAL METHODISM.

AS late as 1805, Asbury, the Apostle of America, soberly summing up the elements of his Churchly status, and evincing a decent respect for the opinions of the thoughtful and virtuous portion of mankind, said: "I will tell the world what I rest my authority upon. 1. Divine authority. 2. Seniority in America. 3. The election of the General Conference. 4. My ordination by Thomas Coke, William Philip Otterbein, German Presbyterian minister, Richard Whatcoat, and Thomas Vasey. 5. Because the signs of an apostle have been seen in me." *

This is a sensible and solid statement by which the staunch old Bishop sought to satisfy himself no less than the world. In an eminent sense he was the first Bishop of American Methodism, though ordained a Superintendent by Coke, the "Foreign Minister of Methodism," who had been himself solemnly set apart to the same office by the imposition of the hands of Wesley himself. This is the staple, then, whence the chain of Methodist Episcopacy is pendent. Is it sufficient to bear the weight?

We are now introduced to the transaction, which, estimated according to any standard, must be pronounced the weightiest in Wesley's long and eventful career. He deliberately assumed and exercised the power of ordination, contrary to the canons of the Church of England, of which he was a member and a minister. More: he bestowed a third ordination upon a co-equal presbyter of the English Church, provided him with proper credentials, and sent him to America empowered and directed to ordain others. As in the

---

* Journal, III. 168, May 22, 1805.

sixteenth century Luther created a new Church for regenerated Germany, so, in a scarcely subordinate sense, Wesley, in the closing years of the eighteenth, constituted a Church providentially adapted to the conditions and needs of newly-liberated and sparsely-settled America.

From the beginning to this good hour, Wesley's conduct at this juncture has been fiercely assailed and bitterly misrepresented—sometimes ignorantly, sometimes designedly. He lost many old friends and made many new enemies, when the time was short for appeasing the latter or regaining the former. "I can scarcely yet believe it," wrote Charles, " that, in his eighty-second year, my brother, my old, intimate friend and companion, should have assumed the episcopal character, ordained elders, consecrated a bishop, and sent him to ordain our lay preachers in America!" * In doggerel and ditty from the pen of his good brother † and from that of meaner poets, the venerable Founder of the people called Methodists was mercilessly lampooned. It was a somewhat more refined, but scarcely less cruel, weapon than those employed by the mobs of earlier days. Pitifully but firmly the old man pleads with his brother, " I walk still by the same rule I have done for between forty and fifty years. I do nothing rashly. It is not likely I should. The high day of my blood is over. If you will go on hand in hand with me, do. But do not hinder me, if you will not help. Perhaps if you had kept close to me, I might have done better. However, with or without help, I creep on." ‡ Churchmen have endeavored to overlay the simple dignity and apostolic grandeur of Wesley's act with forced interpretations of its significance, far-fetched

---

* Letter to Dr. Chandler, April 28, 1785.

† Since bishops are so easy made

By man or woman's whim

Wesley his hands on Coke has laid

But who laid hands on him? —an epigram which

enlivens the pages of many Churchmen's tracts, otherwise a little prosy, and occasionally strays into ponderous tomes.

‡ Letter to Charles, Aug. 19, 1785.

and grotesquely inadequate, impertinently assuming to declare for Wesley " that he did not design to confer upon Coke the character of a Bishop; that Coke's new office was designed to be a species of supervisory appointment, vague and contingent—something widely different from episcopacy, however difficult to define; and that, therefore, the distinct existence of American Methodism, as an Episcopal Church, is a fact contrary to the intentions of Wesley." Nor have satire and invective been left to the use of external foes alone. By those who in England claimed the Wesleyan name and in America that of Methodist, in earlier and later narratives, which aspire to the character of sober history or truthful biography, the grand old man of Methodism has been stigmatized as inconsistently surrendering lifelong principles in a moment of sentimental enthusiasm. Or, if his consistency and character are saved, it is at the expense of his discretion and sense, since, in the house of his friends, are to be found those who play into the hands of the prelatists and deliberately declare that his solemn ordination of Coke meant little or nothing, and that he never anticipated any important consequences in the organization of the American Methodists. But, fortunately, the ancient performances of this general type sufficiently reveal their origin in pique and disappointment, and the modern imitations usually betray their design to establish or to defend some newly-devised theory of Methodism and its government, which would fain root itself in the past, even if false to the fathers and the facts.* Poor old Dr. Whitehead, buried though he is in the selfsame grave with Wesley, must be allowed his fling. " Thus we see," he declares in regard to Coke's ordination, " that Mr. Wesley's principle and practice in this affair directly oppose each other," etc., etc.†

---

* " Some read in all this only the pride and ambition of Coke and Asbury. The reading is false to the writing of the fathers. For myself, I shall never assail the Methodist Episcopacy through such an impeachment of these faithful servants of God and Methodism."—Dr. John Miley, Proceedings of Centennial Conference, 1884, p. 116.

† Life of Wesley, II. 260.

Even Tyerman blots his fair pages by transferring to them an anonymous screed which this venomous physician safely attributes to " one of the preachers."   " Who is the father of this *monster* [ordination!]," asks this unknown itinerant, " so long dreaded by the father of his people, and by most of his sons?   Whoever he be, time will prove him to be a felon to Methodism, and discover his assassinating knife sticking fast in the vitals of its body.   Years to come will speak in groans the opprobrious anniversary of our religious madness for gowns and bands." *   The one hundredth " opprobrious anniversary " of this monstrous ordination, was fittingly celebrated in the city of Baltimore by the Bishops and representatives of about four millions of American Episcopal Methodists!   So does history revenge itself upon those who venture too boldly upon the rôle of prophecy.

According to the critics who occupy such standpoints as we have been cursorily reviewing, before entering upon a detailed examination of the events involved, the driveling weakness of a semi-imbecile octogenarian gave unpremeditated and instantaneous birth to a scheme of ecclesiastical government, so solid, so symmetrical—in a word, so sufficient—that, after the lapse of more than a century, when the Churches, whose polity is essentially but a continuation or reproduction of this model, number their communicants by the millions, this form of Church government shows no sign of fracture or strain but, on the contrary, evinces an expansive adaptability to indefinitely increasing demands, inferior to no similar solution of the confessedly complex problem of civil or ecclesiastical government wrought out by the genius of men.   The younger Pitt, chancellor of the exchequer before he had completed his twenty-third year, need not, in his palmiest days, have been ashamed of the paternity of a plan of administration so simple, original, comprehensive, and, as the event proved, signally and permanently adequate and successful.   It is not claimed, according to the example of others, that the pattern was shown to

* Tyerman, III. 439; Whitehead, II. 257.

Wesley in the mount; but if wisdom has ever been unmistakably justified of her children, the deeds of this marvelous octogenarian may lay claim to that high providential distinction.

If criticism fails to establish the doting idiocy and irresponsible second childhood of the man who abridged the Articles and Liturgy of the English Church for the use of his American children, and penned Coke's letters of episcopal orders and the address to "Dr. Coke, Mr. Asbury, and our brethren in North America," it may at least essay the easier task of aspersing the characters and motives of the advisers by whom he was surrounded. A man who for fifty years had proved singularly firm and immovable in his convictions and decisions might, in age and feebleness extreme, become a tool in the hands of ambitious and designing men, who should at once thwart his judgment and betray his confidence. That Coke, whom Asbury, who knew him well, pronounced "the greatest man of the last century," and whose shining track of world-wide evangelism is like the flight of the apocalyptic angel, had characteristic weaknesses and was guilty of many indiscretions, we have no interest in denying. His peculiarities of character laid him open to many insinuations and imputations, but his vindication in this crisis is complete and convincing, as we shall see, in some detail, hereafter. "But do you not allow," writes Charles to his brother, "that the Doctor has separated? Do you not know and approve of his avowed design and resolution to get all the Methodists of the three kingdoms into a distinct, compact body? Have you seen his ordination sermon? Is the high day of his blood over? Does he do nothing rashly? Have you not made yourself the author of all his actions? I need not remind you, *qui facit per alium facit per se.* I must not leave unanswered your surprising question, 'What then are you frighted at?' At the Doctor's rashness, and your supporting him in his ambitious pursuits," etc.* To which John calmly replied, after the official record of the Doctor's acts in America had

---

* Letter, Sept. 8, 1785.

been laid before him, " I believe Dr. Coke is as free from ambition as from covetousness. [He gave more money to religion than any other Methodist, if not any other Protestant, of his day.] He has done nothing rashly that I know." * Fletcher was present at the Leeds Conference of 1784, and with his sagacious counsels the American policy was determined upon. Coke's reluctance when Wesley's plan was first broached to him will become evident in the sequel.

If all other sources of impeachment fail, it still remains possible, as we have noticed, to deny that Mr. Wesley's acts at this crisis possessed any special significance or were intended by him to produce the results which have actually proceeded from them.† The venerable man was partly a dupe and partly the hero of a chapter of accidents. The imagination of posterity, or the vanity of Methodists, has done the rest—has endowed him with statesmanlike prescience and has attributed to wise design what was the unforeseen but happy result of blind chance.

It lies beyond the scope of our history to enter into any formal refutation of these several theories of how Mr. Wesley came to ordain a presbyter of the Church of England to the office of a Methodist Superintendent and to provide for the organization of the Methodist Episcopal Church in the United States. The literature is voluminous and as curious as voluminous. Its production has not yet ceased. Happily a plain narrative which shall embody all the material facts in their proper sequence and relations is likely to lead to but one conclusion in candid minds, thus leaving to the office of historical construction and interpretation the simple task of bringing the multitudinous rays which flash from many and unexpected quarters to a final focus. To this narrative, from which the reader has perhaps been too long detained, we now proceed.

* Letter, Sept. 13.

† "Wesley meant the ceremony to be a mere formality likely to recommend his delegate to the favor of the Methodists in America." Tyerman, III. 434.

I. Wesley's Ordination of Thomas Coke.

In February, 1784, the month in which the Deed of Declaration was enrolled in Chancery, Mr. Wesley called Dr. Coke into his private chamber in London and introduced the subject of providing for the American Methodists in nearly the following manner:

That, as the revolution in America had separated the United States from the mother country for ever, and the Episcopal Establishment was utterly abolished, the societies had been represented to him in a most deplorable condition. That an appeal had also been made to him through Mr. Asbury, in which he was requested to provide for them some mode of church government, suited to their exigencies; and that having long and seriously revolved the subject in his thoughts, he intended to adopt the plan which he was now about to unfold. That as he had invariably endeavored, in every step he had taken, to keep as closely to the Bible as possible, so, on the present occasion, he hoped he was not about to deviate from it. That, keeping his eye upon the conduct of the primitive churches in the ages of unadulterated Christianity, he had much admired the mode of ordaining bishops which the church of Alexandria had practiced. That, to preserve its purity, that church would never suffer the interference of a foreign bishop in any of their ordinations; but that the presbyters of that venerable apostolic church, on the death of a bishop, exercised the right of ordaining another from their own body, by the laying on of their own hands; and that this practice continued among them for two hundred years, till the days of Dionysius. And finally, that, being himself a presbyter, he wished Dr. Coke to accept ordination from his hands, and to proceed in that character to the continent of America, to superintend the societies in the United States.*

Dr. Coke was startled and expressed his doubts. Mr. Wesley recommended to his attention the arguments of Lord King, which had satisfied his own mind; but still nearly two months elapsed before Coke gave a qualified assent to Wesley's proposal. And here we may briefly review the process by which Mr. Wesley had reached the conclusions which he privately urged upon the notice of Dr. Coke. January 20, 1746, nearly forty years before the period at which we are now arrived, Wesley set out on a journey to Bristol, and read Lord King's " Inquiry into the Constitution, Discipline, Unity, and Worship of the Primi-

---

* Drew, Life of Coke, pp. 71, 72. Mr. Drew incloses this narrative in quotation marks, to intimate, I suppose, that it represents a memorandum or dictation of Dr. Coke's, from whom alone it could have originated.

tive Church."* The Dissenting Lord High Chancellor's
argument convinced the High-church clergyman, and, after
the perusal, he wrote, " In spite of the vehement prejudice
of my education, I was ready to believe that this was a fair
and impartial draught; but, if so, it would follow that bishops and presbyters are essentially of one order," etc. Accordingly in the Minutes of the Conference of 1747 we find
the following questions and answers on the subject of Church
government:

Q. What instance or ground is there, then, in the New Testament for a
national Church? *A.* We know none at all. We apprehend it to be a merely political institution. *Q.* Are the three orders of bishops, priests, and deacons plainly described in the New Testament? *A.* We think they are; and
believe they generally obtained in the Churches of the apostolic age. *Q.*
But are you assured, that God designed the same plan should obtain in all
Churches, throughout all ages? *A.* We are not assured of this; because we
do not know that it is asserted in Holy Writ. *Q.* If this plan were essential
to a Christian Church, what must become of all the foreign reformed
Churches? *A.* It would follow, that they are no parts of the Church of
Christ! A consequence full of shocking absurdity. *Q.* In what age was
the Divine right of episcopacy first asserted in England? *A.* About the
middle of Queen Elizabeth's reign. Till then all the bishops and clergy in
England continually allowed, and joined in, the ministrations of those who
were not episcopally ordained.

In 1756, Wesley wrote, " I still believe ' the espiscopal
form of church government to be scriptural and apostolical.' I mean well agreeing with the practice and writings
of the apostles; but that it is prescribed in Scripture, I do not
believe. This opinion, which I once zealously espoused, I
have been heartily ashamed of, ever since I read Bishop
Stillingfleet's ' Irenicon.' I think he has unanswerably
proved that neither Christ nor his apostles prescribe any
particular form of Church government; and that the plea of
Divine right for diocesan episcopacy was never heard of in
the primitive Church."† In 1761, he declared that Stillingfleet had convinced him that it " was an entire mistake that
none but episcopal ordination is valid." In 1780, he
shocked Charles with the claim, " I verily believe I have as

---

*Amer. Ed., New York, Lane & Scott, 1851.   †Works, Amer. ed., VII. 284.

good a right to ordain as to administer the Lord's Supper."
And finally, in August, 1785, defending his course in a letter
to his brother, he writes, "I firmly believe I am a scriptural
ἐπίσκοπος, as much as any man in England, or in Europe;
for the uninterrupted succession I know to be a fable, which
no man ever did or can prove." Here is provided a catena
of deliverances extending over a period of forty years from
1746 to 1785 which must forever set at rest the hasty charge
that under the impulse of excitement or the demands of an
unexpected emergency the octogenarian Wesley canceled
his lifelong convictions.

But the ambitious Coke has not yet consented to the ordination. In about two months, as intimated above, he wrote
acceding to it, though still suggesting delay, or, if possible,
some modification of the plan. Here is his letter:

NEAR DUBLIN, *April* 17, 1784.

Honored and very dear Sir: I intended to trouble you no more about my
going to America; but your observations incline me to address you again
on the subject.

If some one, in whom you could place the fullest confidence, and whom
you think likely to have sufficient influence and prudence and delicacy of
conduct for the purpose, were to go over and return, you would then have
a source of sufficient information to determine on any points or propositions. I may be destitute of the last mentioned essential qualification (to
the former I lay claim without reserve); otherwise my taking such a voyage
might be expedient.

By this means you might have fuller information concerning the state of
the country and the societies than epistolary correspondence can give you;
and there might be a cement of union, remaining after your death, between
the societies and preachers of the two countries. If the awful event of your
decease should happen before my removal to the world of spirits, it is almost certain, that I should have business enough, of indispensable importance, on my hands in these kingdoms.

I am, dear sir, your most dutiful and most affectionate son,

THOMAS COKE.

Here the matter rested until the Leeds Conference of
1784. Pawson relates that ordination was first proposed by
Wesley himself in his select committee of consultation.
Says he: "The preachers were astonished when this was
mentioned, and, to a man, opposed it. But I plainly saw
that it would be done, as Mr. Wesley's mind appeared to

be quite made up." * And he proved a match for all of them.

Coke, Whatcoat, and Vasey were selected for the American work. Shortly after the close of the Conference, Dr. Coke addressed Mr. Wesley the following epistle:

August 9, 1784.

Honored and dear Sir: The more maturely I consider the subject, the more expedient it appears to me, that the power of ordaining others should be received by me from you, by the imposition of your hands; and that you should lay your hands on brother Whatcoat and brother Vasey, for the following reasons: (1) It seems to me the most scriptural way, and most agreeable to the practice of the primitive churches. (2) I may want all the influence, in America, which you can throw into my scale. Mr. Brackenbury informed me at Leeds, that he saw a letter from Mr. Asbury, in which he said that he would not receive any person, deputed by you, with any part of the superintendency of the work invested in him; or words which evidently implied so much. I do not find the least degree of prejudice in my mind against Mr. Asbury; on the contrary, I find a very great love and esteem; and am determined not to stir a finger without his consent, unless necessity obliges me; but rather to be at his feet in all things. But, as the journey is long, and you cannot spare me often, it is well to provide against all events; and I am satisfied that an authority, formally received from you will be fully admitted; and that my exercising the office of ordination, without that formal authority, may be disputed, and perhaps, on other accounts, opposed. I think you have tried me too often to doubt, whether I will, in any degree, use the power you are pleased to invest me with, further than I believe absolutely necessary for the prosperity of the work.

In respect of my brethren Whatcoat and Vasey, it is very uncertain whether any of the clergy, mentioned by brother Rankin, except Mr. Jarratt, will stir a step with me in the work; and it is by no means certain, that even he will choose to join me in ordaining; and propriety and universal practice make it expedient, that I should have two presbyters with me in this work. In short, it appears to me, that everything should be prepared, and everything proper be done, that can possibly be done, on this side the water. You can do all this in Mr. C——n's house, in your chamber; and afterwards, (according to Mr. Fletcher's advice,) give us letters testimonial of the different offices with which you have been pleased to invest us. For the purpose of laying hands on brothers Whatcoat and Vasey, I can bring Mr. Creighton down with me, by which you will have two presbyters with you.

In respect to brother Rankin's argument, that you will escape a great deal of odium by omitting this, it is nothing. Either it will be known, or not known. If not known, then no odium will arise; but if known, you will be obliged to acknowledge, that I acted under your direction, or suffer me to sink under the weight of my enemies, with perhaps your brother at the head of them. I shall entreat you to ponder these things.

Your most dutiful,   THOMAS COKE.

_____
* MS. memoir of Whitehead.

Whitehead thinks this letter affords materials for observations both " serious and comic." Tyerman concludes from it that Wesley had never intended ordaining Coke, but, at his request, acquiesced. This conclusion, in view of the attendant facts, is, as we shall see, unwarranted. But, if it were, it is difficult to see how it affects either Coke's character or the foundations of Methodist Episcopacy. Wesley, whether by persuasion or of his own motion, did ordain Coke with the convictions and purposes which have been considered at length. But the letter is susceptible of a natural and, it might be added, necessary interpretation. Pawson, whose testimony at a later date when he was President of the Conference is decisive of what Wesley intended by Coke's and later episcopal ordinations, declared positively, as Mr. Tyerman cites, that, at Conference, Mr. Wesley's select committee of consultation were " to a man" opposed to the ordination project. Yet Mr. Wesley's mind was " quite made up" and Mr. Pawson " plainly saw it would be done." It was determined in Conference that Coke, Whatcoat, and Vasey should go to America. That point being fixed beyond recall, it was of the first importance to Coke in what character and with what powers he should go. The opposition to the ordinations could not be unknown to him. He knew what influences were now at work about his chief. While the saintly Fletcher indorsed the step, the returned Rankin counseled against it. Where Charles Wesley stood everybody knew. Any prudent man could foresee the delicate position in which the new envoy and joint superintendent would be placed in relation to Mr. Asbury. He came to share his powers and in some respects to assume a superior position, as Mr. Wesley's delegate, a clergyman of the Church of England, and the organizing officer of the new Church. Coke's conduct at this juncture and after his arrival in America, when Mr. Dickins advised him to carry out his mission on Mr. Wesley's authority without consulting Mr. Asbury, must win our admiration for its obvious delicacy and nice sense of propriety. In these transactions, the foreign minister of Methodism showed himself a diplomat as well as a gentleman and a Christian.

Dr. Coke's reference to his having seen "a letter from Mr. Asbury, in which he observed that he would not receive any person, deputed by you, with any part of the superintendency," is perhaps best understood in the light of a letter of Asbury's addressed to Wesley under date of September 20, 1783:

> No person can manage the lay preachers here so well, it is thought, as one that has been at the raising of most of them. No man can make a proper change upon paper to send one here and another [there] without knowing the circuits and the gifts of all the preachers, unless he is always out among them. My dear sir, a matter of the greatest consequence now lies before you. If you send preachers to America, let them be proper persons. We are now united; all things go on well considering the storms and difficulties we have had to ride through. I wish men of the greatest understanding would write impartial accounts, for it would be better for us not to have preachers than to be divided. This I know, great men that can do good, may do hurt if they should take the wrong road. I have labored and suffered much to keep the people and preachers together, and if I am thought worthy to keep my place I should be willing to labor and suffer till death for peace and union.

At the close of the Leeds Conference of 1784 Mr. Wesley went to Bristol and Dr. Coke to London, to prepare for his voyage to America. While in London he received a letter from Wesley asking his immediate presence in Bristol and directing him to bring with him the Rev. Mr. Creighton, a regularly ordained presbyter of the Church of England, who had long officiated in Wesley's London chapels. "The Doctor and Mr. Creighton accordingly met him in Bristol, when, with their assistance, he ordained Mr. Richard Whatcoat and Mr. Thomas Vasey presbyters for America; and being peculiarly attached to every rite of the Church of England, did afterward ordain Dr. Coke a superintendent, giving him letters of ordination under his hand and seal." * Whatcoat, one of the most exact and reliable of our primitive sources, in his Journal says:

September 1, 1784, Rev. John Wesley, Thomas Coke, and James Creigh-

---

* Coke and Moore's Life of Wesley, Eng. ed., p. 459.

ton, presbyters of the Church of England, formed a presbytery and ordained Richard Whatcoat and Thomas Vasey deacons. And on September
2d, by the same hands, etc., Richard Whatcoat and Thomas Vasey were ordained elders, and Thomas Coke, LL.D., was ordained superintendent for
the Church of God under our care in North America.

"On Wednesday, September 1st," says Wesley in his
Journal, "being now clear in my own mind, I took a step
which I *had long weighed*, and appointed three of our brethren to go and serve the desolate sheep in America, which I
verily believe will be much to the glory of God." Charles
Wesley was present at the time in Bristol, but he was not invited to assist in the ordinations. His help was not needed,
neither was he left in ignorance for the sake of concealment.
It was well known that he would not coöperate: his brother,
having decided, resolved to give him no opportunity to oppose and hinder. It proves the clearness and strength of
Wesley's resolution, rather than hesitancy or doubt. That
he did not regret the step is evident from the language inserted in the Conference Minutes of 1786:

> Judging this to be a case of necessity, I took a step which, for peace and
> quietness I had refrained from taking many years; I exercised that power
> which I am fully persuaded the great Shepherd and Bishop of the Church
> has given me. I appointed three of our laborers to go and help them, by
> not only preaching the word of God, but likewise administering the Lord's
> supper, and baptizing their children throughout that vast tract of land.

Thus on the second of September, 1784, in the city of
Bristol, England, the Rev. Thomas Coke, LL.D., presbyter of the Church of England, was by John Wesley, Founder of the people called Methodists, assisted by the Revs.
James Creighton, Richard Whatcoat, and Thomas Vasey,
ordained by the imposition of his hands the first "superintendent or bishop of the Methodist societies in America; an
act of as high propriety and dignity as it was of urgent necessity." * The "letters of episcopal orders," as they were
soon after described to be in the discipline of the Methodist
Episcopal Church, delivered by Wesley into the hands of

---

* Stevens, Hist. of Meth., II. 215.

Coke were couched in these clear, direct, and comprehensive terms:

> To all to whom these presents shall come, John Wesley, late Fellow of Lincoln College in Oxford, Presbyter of the Church of England, sendeth greeting.
>
> Whereas many of the people in the southern provinces of North America, who desire to continue under my care, and still adhere to the doctrines and discipline of the Church of England, are greatly distressed for want of ministers to administer the sacraments of baptism and the Lord's supper, according to the usage of the said Church; and whereas there does not appear to be any other way of supplying them with ministers:
>
> Know all men, that I, John Wesley, think myself to be providentially called, at this time, to set apart some persons for the work of the ministry in America. And, therefore, under the protection of Almighty God, and with a single eye to His glory, I have this day set apart as a superintendent, by the imposition of my hands, and prayer, (being assisted by other ordained ministers,) Thomas Coke, doctor of civil law, a presbyter of the Church of England, and a man whom I judge to be well qualified for that great work. And I do hereby recommend him to all whom it may concern, as a fit person to preside over the flock of Christ. In testimony whereof, I have hereunto set my hand and seal, this second day of September, in the year of our Lord one thousand seven hundred and eighty-four. JOHN WESLEY.*

How greater formality and decency could have characterized the proceeding it is difficult to conceive. But that the new American Superintendent might be fully equipped for his weighty mission, Wesley placed in his hands the well-known circular letter, a solid and stately document of transparent simplicity, which might well lie at the base of sacred franchises, civil or ecclesiastical:

> BRISTOL, *September* 10, 1784.
>
> *To Dr. Coke, Mr. Asbury, and our Brethren in North America.*
>
> BY a very uncommon train of providences, many of the provinces of North America are totally disjoined from the mother country, and erected into independent states. The English government has no authority over them, either civil or ecclesiastical, any more than over the states of Holland. A civil authority is exercised over them, partly by the congress, partly by the provincial assemblies. But no one either exercises or claims any ecclesiastical authority at all. In this peculiar situation, some thousands of the inhabitants of these states desire my advice, and, in compliance with their desire, I have drawn up a little sketch.

---

*A facsimile of this ordination parchment of the first Methodist bishop, reproduced for presentation at the London Ecumenical of 1881, lies before the writer. The above is a verbatim copy.

Lord King's account of the primitive church convinced me, many years ago, that bishops and presbyters are the same order, and consequently have the same right to ordain. For many years, I have been importuned, from time to time, to exercise this right, by ordaining part of our traveling preachers. But I have still refused; not only for peace sake, but because I was determined, as little as possible, to violate the established order of the national church to which I belonged.

But the case is widely different between England and North America. Here there are bishops, who have a legal jurisdiction; in America there are none, neither any parish minister; so that, for some hundreds of miles together, there is none either to baptize, or to administer the Lord's supper. Here, therefore, my scruples are at an end; and I conceive myself at full liberty, as I violate no order, and invade no man's rights, by appointing and sending laborers into the harvest.

I have accordingly appointed Dr. Coke and Mr. Francis Asbury to be joint superintendents over our brethren in North America; as also Richard Whatcoat and Thomas Vasey, to act as elders among them, by baptizing and administering the Lord's supper. And I have prepared a liturgy, little differing from that of the Church of England, (I think the best constituted national church in the world,) which I advise all the traveling preachers to use on the Lord's day, in all the congregations, reading the litany only on Wednesdays and Fridays, and praying extempore on all other days. I also advise the elders to administer the supper of the Lord, on every Lord's day.

If any one will point out a more rational and scriptural way of feeding and guiding these poor sheep in the wilderness, I will gladly embrace it. At present, I cannot see any better method than that I have taken.

It has indeed been proposed to desire the English bishops to ordain part of our preachers for America. But to this I object, 1. I desired the bishop of London to ordain one, but could not prevail. 2. If they consented, we know the slowness of their proceedings; but the matter admits of no delay. 3. If they would ordain them now, they would expect to govern them. And how grievously would this entangle us! 4. As our American brethren are now totally disentangled, both from the state and the English hierarchy, we dare not entangle them again, either with the one or the other. They are now at full liberty, simply to follow the Scriptures and the primitive church. And we judge it best that they should stand fast in that liberty wherewith God has so strangely made them free.   JOHN WESLEY.

Thus empowered, Superintendent Coke and his attendant presbyters set sail for America, September 18. All things were now ready. Soon we shall join them with Asbury and the American itinerants at Baltimore in the Christmas Conference. But first let us briefly consider Mr. Wesley's other ordinations.

II. Mr. Wesley's Ordinations for Scotland and England.

These Scotch and English ordinations do not directly concern our theme, except as they conclusively establish, all contemporary rumors and gossip to the contrary notwithstanding, that Wesley had now deliberately entered upon a course of conduct which he unregretfully and undeviatingly pursued to the end of his life. A little less than a year after Coke's ordination, Wesley ordained three ministers for Scotland. He gives us this account in his Journal: "1785: August 1.—Having, with a few select friends, weighed the matter thoroughly, I yielded to their judgment, and set apart three of our well-tried preachers, John Pawson, Thomas Hanby, and Joseph Taylor, to minister in Scotland." These ordinations occurred during the session of the Conference, which adjourned August 3. "Our peaceful Conference ended," says Wesley, "the God of power having presided over all our consultations." * At the Conference of 1786 Wesley ordained Joshua Keighley and Charles Atmore for Scotland; William Warrener for Antigua; and William Hammett for Newfoundland. In 1787, Tyerman states, five others were ordained, whose names he does not mention. In 1788, while Wesley was traveling in Scotland, he ordained John Barber and Joseph Cownley, and "at the ensuing Conference, seven others, including Alexander Mather, who was ordained to the office, not only of deacon and elder, but of *superintendent*." † If Wesley hesitatingly bestowed on Coke at his earnest solicitation a nondescript third ordination which meant little more than a paternal blessing; and if he regarded himself as really incapable of bestowing anything more than presbyterial orders, as some maintain, it is quite impossible to understand what the good man meant by bestowing the orders of deacon, elder, and superintendent upon Mather by three successive impositions of hands. But such conduct agrees exactly with his directing Coke to bestow three ordinations upon Asbury, and his inserting the three ordination forms of the English Church

---

* Journal, Amer. ed., II. 622.   † III. 441.

in the first prayer-book of American Methodism. Was not the man who did these things still an Episcopalian?* Does not such an act as the threefold ordination of Mather when Wesley was eighty-five years old, just three years before his death, look as if he meant to organize and perpetuate an Episcopal Church in England as well as in America? Or, at least, to give his followers the means of readily so doing after his death? In 1789 Wesley ordained Henry Moore and Thomas Rankin, they with Mather being designed for service in England. Thus, when Wesley departed this life, he left in England a Superintendent and at least two presbyters of the most eminent station and character—Mather was elected President of the second Conference after Wesley's death (1792) and Moore served twice in that capacity (in 1804 and 1823)—from whom the ultra-conservative and divided English, if they would, might have originated a British Church fashioned after Wesley's American model. We begin to see light, now, on some of Charles Wesley's fears and accusations. "When once you began ordaining in America," he writes, "I knew and you knew that your preachers here would never rest till you ordained them. You told me they would separate by and by. The Doctor tells us the same. *His Methodist Episcopal Church in Baltimore was intended to beget a Methodist Episcopal Church here.* You know he comes, armed with your authority, to make us all Dissenters. One of your sons assured me that not a preacher in London would refuse orders from the Doctor."† In his reply of five days later John entered no denial or demurrer to any of these radical accusations. Tyerman quotes a brief passage from a letter of John Pawson's, written in 1793 while he was President of

---

*Certain objectors seem never to tire of the argument that since Wesley held that bishops and presbyters are of the same order, he therefore believed that a presbyter is a bishop, and a bishop is a presbyter, despite his bestowing a third ordination on presbyters. Such reasoning has the same logical value as concluding that because a *tiger* and a *cat* are of the same order, therefore a tiger is a cat and a cat is a tiger.

† Letter of Aug. 14, 1785.

12

the Conference, but places it in connections which tend to break the force of the small section he cites.* It will be well to consider the whole:

> It will by no means answer our ends to dispute one with another as to which is the most scriptural form of Church government. We should consider our present circumstances, and endeavor to agree upon some method by which our people may have the ordinances of God, and, at the same time, be preserved from division. I care not a rush whether it be Episcopal or Presbyterian; I believe neither of them to be purely scriptural. But our preachers and people in general are prejudiced against the latter; consequently, if the former will answer our end, we ought to embrace it. Indeed, I believe it will suit our present plan far better than the other. The design of Mr. Wesley will weigh much with many, which now evidently appears to have been this: He foresaw that the Methodists would, after his death, soon become a distinct people; he was deeply prejudiced against a Presbyterian, and was as much in favor of an Episcopal form of government. In order, therefore, to preserve all that was valuable in the Church of England among the Methodists, he ordained Mr. Mather and Dr. Coke bishops. These he undoubtedly designed should ordain others. Mr. Mather told us so at the Manchester Conference, but we did not then understand him. I see no way of coming to any good settlement but on the plan I mentioned before. I sincerely wish that Dr. Coke and Mr. Mather may be allowed to be what they are, bishops. We must have ordination among us at any rate.†

Rev. Dr. James Dixon, President of the Wesleyan Conference in 1841, did not hesitate to declare in a sermon preached before the Conference that "the constitution of the American Methodist Episcopal Church is only a legitimate development of the principle [of Wesley's ordinations]; and, it may be added, that an imitation of that great transaction in this country would be perfectly justifiable on the ground assumed by Mr. Wesley himself, and held sacred by his followers." ‡ In another connection, the same authority says, "If we mistake not, it is to the American Methodist Episcopal Church that we are to look for the real mind and sentiments of this great man." § So President Pawson

---

* Life, III. 443.

† Smith, Hist. of Wesleyan Meth., II. 3, 4.

‡ Methodism in its Origin, Economy, and Present Position, N. Y., Lane and Scott, 1848, pp. 221, 222.

§ *Ibid.*, p. 248.

thought in 1791 and, says Stevens, "some of the most commanding members of the Conference concurred with him, and received his suggestion as the most likely solution of their formidable difficulties."

This leads to an easy and natural explanation of one of the most serious charges of "ambition," against Bishop Coke, with which this section of our narrative may fitly close. "In 1784, he secretly summoned a meeting at Litchfield of the most influential of the English preachers and passed a resolution that the Conference should appoint an order of bishops, to ordain deacons and elders, he himself, of course, expecting to be a member of the prelatical brotherhood." * It was the year of Pawson's proposal of Episcopacy and of the widespread agitations of Alexander Kilham, who stigmatized the Litchfield meeting as "a conspiracy to place pretentious prelates over the people." President Pawson, Superintendents Coke and Mather, Dr. Adam Clarke, Henry Moore, Bradburn, Taylor, and Rogers were present at the meeting—an eminently weighty and respectable company, entitled by every token to take measures for the relief of the distractions of Zion. Coke addressed the assembly and enlarged upon the prosperity of Episcopal Methodism in America, and the relief which Wesley's plan had given in a similar sacramental controversy there. All present had been ordained by Wesley, save Dr. Clarke, Bradburn, and Rogers. Coke suggested the rational and scriptural plan of originating from among themselves a Wesleyan ministry in three orders—as, no doubt, Mr. Wesley, as Pawson had suggested, had intended they should do.

Most of the meeting approved his proposition; but Moore very wisely suggested that they should confine their proceedings to the discussion of its practicability, and defer its decision to the next Conference. He, however, pronounced the measure a scriptural and suitable expedient for the government of any Christian Church. Mather concurred with Moore. They adjourned after adopting a series of resolutions which were to be submitted with all their signatures to the Annual Conference. They proposed "an

*Tyerman, III. 434.

order of superintendents," to be annually chosen "if necessary;" the ordination of the preachers as deacons and elders; the division of the Connection into seven or eight districts, each to be under the care of one of the superintendents who should have power to call in the assistance of the President in any exigency. They all agreed to "recommend and support" this scheme in the Conference as "a thing greatly wanted, and likely to be of much advantage to the work of God." *

The excitement of the times, the negotiations pending between the Conference and the body of delegated trustees, etc., were unfavorable to calm consideration and the wisest action; consequently the Litchfield resolutions were voted down. Otherwise such a body of united, weighty, and determined men ought to have carried their plan through. So nearly did English Methodism come to the adoption of the Episcopal form of Church government.

III. Mr. Asbury and the Calling of the Christmas Conference.

Superintendent Coke and Presbyters Whatcoat and Vasey landed at New York, November 3, 1784. Dr. Coke immediately revealed his character and mission to John Dickins, the preacher stationed in that city. In his Journal, under the date of his landing, he says:

I have opened Mr. Wesley's plan to Brother Dickins, the traveling preacher stationed at this place, and he highly approves of it; says that all the preachers most earnestly long for such a regulation, and that Mr. Asbury he is sure will agree to it. He presses me most earnestly to make it public, because, as he most justly argues, Mr. Wesley has determined the point, and therefore *it is not to be investigated, but complied with.*

So the entry reads in the London edition of "extracts" from Coke's Journals (1793); in the original Journal printed in the Philadelphia *Arminian Magazine* (1789), the italicized words quoted above are replaced by these: "*though Mr. Asbury is most respectfully to be consulted in respect to every part of the execution of it.*" This accurately represents what Coke actually did, and doubtless insisted on in his first interview with Dickins, whose advice, it will be

---

* Stevens, Hist. of Meth., III. 52, 53. The resolutions, bearing the signature of Adam Clarke, are printed in Smith's Hist. of Wesleyan Meth., II. Appendix 9.

seen, was not followed. On the night of his arrival, Coke preached his first sermon in America in John Street chapel. The third day he set out for Philadelphia, arriving on Saturday evening. Sunday morning the Methodist Superintendent filled the pulpit of Dr. McGaw, (a clergyman mentioned by Asbury as friendly to the Methodists) at St. Paul's Protestant Episcopal Church—or, rather, what soon afterwards became such, as that eminently respectable denomination of Christians had not yet been organized in America. In the evening he preached at St. George's, the Methodist cathedral, where Rankin had held the first Conference more than eleven years before. Drs. McGaw and White—the latter afterward the first Bishop of the Protestant Episcopal Church in Pennsylvania—called to see him Monday, and Dr. White tendered him the use of his church for the following Sunday, which, however, he was obliged to decline. On Friday, November 12, Coke preached at the "Cross Roads" in Delaware, and the next day was received by Mr. Richard Bassett, a member of the executive council of the state, and afterward of the convention which framed the constitution of the United States, and governor of Delaware, who, though not a member of the Methodist Society, was, like the Capernaum centurion, erecting a large chapel at his own expense. Here he met Freeborn Garrettson whom he describes as "all meekness, love, and activity." "On Sunday, the fourteenth of November, the day on which a bishop for Connecticut [Samuel Seabury] was consecrated at Aberdeen, [by Scotch non-juring prelates] he preached in a chapel in the midst of a forest to a noble congregation." * Of this meeting Dr. Coke writes:

After the sermon a plain, robust man came up to me in the pulpit and kissed me. I thought it could be no other than Mr. Asbury, and I was not deceived. I administered the sacrament, after preaching, to five or six hundred communicants, and held a love-feast. It was the best season I

* George Bancroft, Hist. of United States, Author's Last Revision, 1886, VI. 162. On pages 160-164, Mr. Bancroft gives a vivid and, as to facts, entirely accurate account of the origin of the "new Episcopal Church." He misconstrues Wesley's motives, however, when he says he "resolved to get the start of the English hierarchy." How long he had waited, we have seen.

ever knew, except one at Charlemont in Ireland. After dinner Mr. Asbury and I had a private conversation on the future management of our affairs in America. He informed me that he had received some intimations of my arrival on the continent, and had collected a considerable number of the preachers to form a council, and if they were of opinion that it would be expedient immediately to call a Conference, it should be done. They were accordingly sent for, and, after debate, were unanimously of that opinion. We therefore sent off Freeborn Garrettson, like an arrow, from north to south, directing him to send messengers to the right and left, and to gather all the preachers together at Baltimore on Christmas eve. Mr. Asbury has also drawn up for me a route of about a thousand miles in the meantime. He has given me his black, (Harry by name,) and borrowed an excellent horse for me. I exceedingly reverence Mr. Asbury; he has so much wisdom and consideration, so much meekness and love; and under all this, though hardly to be perceived, so much command and authority. He and I have agreed to use our joint endeavors to establish a school or college. I baptized here thirty or forty infants, and seven adults.

An eye-witness gives a most affecting account of this first meeting of American Methodism's first Bishops:

It was in full view of a large concourse of people—a crowded congregation, assembled for public worship. While Dr. Coke was preaching, Mr. Asbury came into the congregation. A solemn pause and deep silence took place at the close of the sermon, as an interval for introduction and salutation. Asbury and Coke, with great solemnity and much dignified sensibility, and with full hearts of brotherly love, approached, embraced, and saluted each other. The other preachers, at the same time participating in the tender sensibilities of the affectionate salutations, were melted into sweet sympathy and tears. The congregation also caught the glowing emotion, and the whole assembly, as if divinely struck with a shock of heavenly electricity, burst into a flood of tears.[*]

Asbury says in his Journal:

Sunday 15. [14] I came to Barratt's chapel; here, to my great joy, I met those dear men of God, Dr. Coke, and Richard Whatcoat; we were greatly comforted together. The Doctor preached on "Christ our wisdom, righteousness, sanctification, and redemption." Having had no opportunity of conversing with them before public worship, I was greatly surprised to see brother Whatcoat assist by taking the cup in the administration of the sacrament. I was shocked when first informed of the intention of these my brethren in coming to this country: it may be of God. My answer then was, if the preachers unanimously choose me, I shall not act in the capacity I have hitherto done by Mr. Wesley's appointment. The design of organizing the Methodists into an Independent Episcopal Church was opened to the preachers present, and it was agreed to call a general conference, to meet at Baltimore the ensuing Christmas; as also that brother Garrettson go off to Virginia to give notice thereof to our brethren in the South.[†]

---

[*] Ezekiel Cooper in his Funeral Discourse for Asbury.   [†] I. 376.

Coke's account closely agrees with Asbury's and similarly indicates some doubt and hesitation on Asbury's part. He says: "After dining, in company with eleven of the preachers, at our sister Barratt's, about a mile from the chapel, I privately opened our plan to Mr. Asbury. *He expressed considerable doubts concerning it, which I rather applaud than otherwise.*" *

When we correlate the antecedent history in both England and America with the circumstances in which Asbury and the American Methodists were now placed, and duly ponder the character in which Mr. Wesley had sent Dr. Coke and the declared aims of his mission, it is not surprising that the American General Assistant was "shocked" when he learned the ministerial standing of Coke, Whatcoat, and Vasey, and declared "if the preachers unanimously choose me, I shall not act in the capacity I have hitherto done, by Mr. Wesley's appointment." He had hitherto acted in the capacity of sole Captain-general of the American itinerants and Societies. He did not propose the instant surrender of this position to a stranger. For years he had exercised the functions of a General Superintendent, save those of ordination and the administration of the sacraments. If these additional powers were now to be conferred upon him, he intended that his new position should be based upon the consent of the preachers and not alone upon the jurisdiction of Mr. Wesley, extended to America in the person of his envoy. We have seen how Mr. Asbury was first recognized as General Assistant by the irregular Delaware Conference of 1779, after the retirement of Mr. Rankin and the other English preachers, and after William Watters had presided at the Conference of 1778. After the reunion of the Northern and Southern Conferences, he was again unanimously chosen in 1782 to "preside over the American Conferences and the whole work," it being added, however, that this was "according to Mr. Wesley's original appointment." During Rankin's administration, it will be remembered, the differences be-

* Philadelphia Arminian Magazine, 1789, pp. 243, 244.

tween him and Asbury had become so serious, that Mr. Wesley ordered the latter's return to England. But during the revolutionary war Mr. Wesley's control of the Americans had been cut off, and thus Asbury's leadership had become thoroughly established on the basis of the unanimous consent of the preachers. Wesley's letter which Asbury received on Chrismas eve, 1783, exactly one year before the Christmas Conference, was not so much an appointment to the office of General Assistant as it was an authoritative recognition of Asbury's rightful occupancy of that position. He could not easily surrender the advantages of this unique relation which he sustained to the preachers and the work. Hence his proposal to call a Conference, which was neither suggested by Coke nor contemplated by Wesley.

Of course, Wesley was aware that the Americans had been holding an Annual Conference since 1773. Rankin (1773–1777), Waters (1778), Asbury (1779–1784) had been the presidents. Rankin had used the same presidential powers which Wesley did in England. When Asbury was recognized in 1779, it had been expressly provided that " on hearing every preacher for and against what is in debate, the right of determination shall rest with him according to the minutes.'' That a Conference of these limited powers might be assembled, if convenient, to which certain privileges might be accorded by Coke and Asbury, as Wesley increasingly did in England,* Wesley doubtless supposed was not improbable. But Asbury's aim, in deciding on a Conference of all the preachers, in that initial interview at Barratt's chapel, was something quite different. Of course he did not propose, as an ordained Superintendent, to hand over to the Conference all those powers which he had freely exercised in the presidential chair and elsewhere

* " From the beginning he was the center and seat of all power and authority; and although, as time advanced, he gradually, and almost imperceptibly, devolved nearly the whole administrative government of the Societies on the Conference and the Assistants, still all matters of peculiar difficulty were carried to him, and from his judgment there was no appeal." (Smith's Hist. of Wesleyan Meth., I. 513.)

when he was simply an elected General Assistant. Down to 1792, he did many things, as his revision and rearrangement of the Discipline in 1787 and his developing and enlarging the office of presiding elder, which had not been authorized by Conference action. But he did mean by placing the election of the Conference behind his new position to interpose a sufficient authority between himself and Mr. Wesley. The Christmas Conference of 1784 is not properly the beginning of the government of the Church by the General Conference, though it exercised larger powers than had ever before been accorded an American Conference. It conveys an erroneous impression to call it a General Conference, if the associations of later years are allowed to cluster around the name. It was general only in the sense that it was intended to be an assembly of all the American itinerants, and that it did determine by majority vote the fate of the measures submitted to it. But in it there was not a single deacon or elder. Ministerial orders came to it from Mr. Wesley through Dr. Coke. It was a mass convention of young itinerants called to assist in organizing a Church. The body did not provide for any successor or any future session. When it adjourned it dissolved. It no longer possessed either actual or potential existence, except as the several Annual Conferences increasingly, but still not universally, exercised legislative powers. Nobody could tell when, if at all, another such general body would be convened. Not until eight years later, in 1792, did another general assembly meet. In the meantime, just because of the felt want, of which the General Conference proper was the final solution, was the disastrous experiment of the Council attempted. Nevertheless Mr. Asbury's proposal was the *germ* of General Conference government. The situation of the Americans during the war had brought about his own designation to office by election of the preachers. He now followed up that precedent, and interposed the Conference as an effectual barrier against the supremacy of Mr. Wesley.

It must be held in mind that this year 1784 is the date of

the full empowering of the English Conference by the Deed
of Declaration.   As English Methodism was given a definite,
legal status by a clear and rigid constitution framed for the
Conference, it seems to some writers all the more incompre-
hensible that a Conference should not have been the chief
feature in Wesley's organization of Episcopal Methodism on
this side the water.   The absence of provision for a Conference has created so urgent a doubt in the minds of a few
chroniclers that they have ventured in late years to maintain
that Mr. Wesley did not intend the organization of what
Asbury, in his account of his first interview with Coke,
styles an " Independent Episcopal Church," independent,
that is, of the Church of England, or its languishing remains
in the States.   That Coke, Asbury, and the Christmas Conference so understood, and accordingly executed, the designs of the Founder is not disputed, or, indeed, disputable.
But this proceeding is attributed to excess of zeal and the
overweening ambition of Coke, who transcended his powers
and overleaped the modest designs of Wesley.   It cannot be
denied that Wesley constituted a ministry in three grades or
orders; that he abridged the thirty-nine articles to constitute
a doctrinal basis for the new organization; that from the
English Book of Common Prayer he framed a liturgy for
public worship; and that he embodied these provisions in a
work entrusted to Coke's custody entitled, " The Sunday
Service of the Methodists in North America, with other
Occasional Services; London: Printed in the year 1784,"
which contained a form of public prayer, " The Form and
Manner of Making and Ordaining of Superintendents, Elders, and Deacons," and " The Articles of Religion.''
Thus the three-fold ministry and the organization itself
were evidently intended to be permanent.   Else these provisions for their perpetuity had been irrelevant and unnecessary.   This Episcopal regimen was expressly justified on the
ground that in America there were now neither bishops nor
parish ministers; that if the English bishops could at last be
induced to ordain for the Methodists of America, " they

would likewise expect to govern them, and how grievously
would this entangle us;" and that, since "our American
brethren are now totally disentangled both from the State and
from the English hierarchy, we dare not entangle them again
either with the one or the other." * "No extant forensic argument" says Stevens, "founded upon documentary evidence, is stronger than would be a right collocation of the
evidence which sustains the claim of American Methodists
respecting this question. . . . Presented in their right
series they become absolutely decisive, and must conclude
the controversy with all candid minds."†

A comprehensive survey will sufficiently explain Wesley's
failure to provide, in this Independent Episcopal Church,
for a governing body such as some years afterward the
General Conference became. Unfortunately the survey has
hitherto been made, either by English writers who encountered on one side of the Atlantic the anomaly of a Conference, or supreme ecclesiastical synod, without an ordained
ministry, or by American writers who, on this side the
Atlantic, encountered the difficulties of the contrary anomaly of a Church with an ordained ministry in three orders,
for which no controlling Conference was provided. The
writer of these lines trusts he may be pardoned for suggesting that after a familiar and extensive acquaintance with the
literature of the question in both England and America, he
has perused no author who has generalized his solution of
the manifest difficulties involved, from the combined elements afforded equally by the English and the American
constitutions. Was Wesley responsible for this fractional
or truncated organization in either case? Let us see.

The evidence is conclusive that nothing lay nearer Wesley's heart than the continued union of Methodists throughout the world after his decease. He did not intend the separation of the American and English Methodists into two

---

*Wesley's Circular Letter, presented by Dr. Coke to the Christmas Con-
ference as the basis of its action.

† Hist. of Meth., II. 217.

communions, one under the government of Bishops and the other under that of the Conference. Among the first regulations adopted by the Christmas Conference was this:

During the life of the Rev. Mr. Wesley, we acknowledge ourselves his sons in the gospel, ready in matters belonging to Church government to obey his commands. And we do engage, after his death, to do everything that we judge consistent with the cause of religion in America and the political interests of these States, to preserve and promote our union with the Methodists in Europe.*

This stood until 1787. Mr. Wesley regarded this as no empty compliment. September 6, 1786, he wrote to Dr. Coke, "I desire that you would appoint a General Conference of our preachers in the United States to meet at Baltimore on May 1, 1787, and that Mr. Whatcoat may be appointed Superintendent with Mr. Asbury." Such a General Conference did not assemble, and Mr. Whatcoat did not become a Superintendent until thirteen years later (1800) when he was chosen by the free suffrages of the American itinerants. On the contrary, the resolution of submission to Mr. Wesley was expunged, much to his grief. It is enough here to cite from Mr. Wesley's letter to Whatcoat sufficient proof of his desire for continued union between the American and English Methodists.

It was not well judged of Brother Asbury [said he] to suffer, much less indirectly encourage, the foolish step in the last Conference. Every preacher present ought, both in duty and in prudence, to have said, "Brother Asbury, Mr. Wesley is your father, consequently ours." Candor will affirm this in the face of the world. It is highly probable that disallowing *me* will, as soon as my head is laid, occasion a total breach between the English and American Methodists. They will naturally say, "If they can do without us, we can do without them."

Thus, it is seen, the Conference, under Asbury's sufferance, exercised powers which Wesley had never intended should fall within its province. The beginning of this was in his own election to the Superintendency; its continuation in the rejection of Whatcoat, as Wesley's nominee, for the same office.

Reverting to the Deed of Declaration, we find the follow-

---

* Dr. Emory's Hist. of the Discipline, pp. 26, 27.

ing provision for the extension of the supervision and powers of the Conference beyond the limits of Great Britain:

Thirteenth. And for the convenience of the chapels and premises already, or which may hereafter be given or conveyed upon the trusts aforesaid, *situate in Ireland or other parts out of the Kingdom of Great Britain*, the Conference shall and may, when and as often as it shall seem expedient, but not otherwise, appoint and delegate any member or members of the Conference with all or any of the powers, privileges, and advantages, herein before contained or vested in the Conference; and all and every the acts, admissions, expulsions, and appointments whatsoever of such member or members of the Conference, so appointed and delegated as aforesaid, the same being put into writing and signed by such delegate or delegates, and entered into the Journals or Minutes of the Conference, and subscribed as after mentioned, shall be deemed, taken, and be the acts, admissions, expulsions, and appointments of the Conference to all intents, constructions, and purposes whatsoever, from the respective times when the same shall be done by such delegate or delegates, notwithstanding anything herein contained to the contrary.

It will be remembered that Dr. Coke presided in the first Irish Conference of 1782, and, until he prepared to visit India, on the voyage to which he died, he almost invariably presided in Ireland, " thus filling the presidential chair with honor, approbation, and great utility for nearly thirty years." * After Mr. Wesley's death this appointment was made by virtue of the above-cited regulation incorporated in the Deed of Declaration. In 1805 the Irish Conference, for example, took this action: " Your readiness of mind to comply with our request, so often made, for our greatly respected friend and brother, Dr. Coke, convinces us still more and more of your affection toward us. We do, therefore, with confidence, unanimously request that he may be appointed our president the ensuing year." To which the English Conference responded: "In compliance with your request, we appoint the Rev. Dr. Coke to be the president of the next Irish Conference, to be held in Dublin on the first Friday in July, 1806."

We now begin to see how Wesley expected to maintain a bond of union among the Methodists throughout the world after his decease. It is intelligible why, in organizing Amer-

---

* Drew, Life of Coke, p. 51.

ican Methodism into an Episcopal Church, he did not provide for a supreme General Conference, since he had deliberately adopted measures by which the authority of the British Conference might be extended to any part of the world.   If the central Conference extended in its oversight and government to America, so that the Americans were not really without Conference government, it is just as true that the English Methodists were not left without an ordained ministry, and that in three orders.   If any question be raised about Coke's being a Bishop among the Wesleyans— though President Pawson, as we have seen, did not doubt it in 1793—there can be none about Alexander Mather's position, thrice ordained by Wesley, and himself the second President of the Conference, in 1792.   The reader will now perceive why large space in this history has been devoted to Wesley's ordinations for England and Scotland, subsequent to his ordination of Coke, Whatcoat, and Vasey.   We see why Charles Wesley charged, and John Wesley did not deny, that Dr. Coke's Methodist Episcopal Church in America was designed to beget a like Methodist Episcopal Church in England.   Biographer after biographer and historian after historian have treated this language as the vain ravings of an outraged opponent.   When light is thrown into it from all directions—from the transactions in England and from the events in America—it is seen to be a sober representation of John Wesley's intentions, or, at least, of the results, which he believed would naturally, if not necessarily, flow from his actions after his decease: hence Pawson's letter; hence the Litchfield meeting, and the deliberate proposals of Coke, Mather, Pawson, Adam Clarke, Henry Moore, Samuel Radburn, Rogers and Taylor.   Until we bring together the American and English elements of the situation, it seems inexplicable that the Methodist Episcopal Church in America entered on its great career with an ordained ministry but without a General Conference, and that English Methodism, on the death of Wesley, began with fully organized Conference government, but without an ordained ministry, the imposition of hands by the President, Ex-president, and Secretary beginning as late as 1834. American Methodism, in the year after Wesley's death (1792) secured to itself the first General Conference properly so called. Such full and final assertion of independence was hardly possible at any earlier date. As long as Mr. Wesley lived the forms of union between the American and British Methodists must be kept up. He died in 1791. In 1792 the first Quadrennial General Conference assembled, and the organization of this supreme legislative tribunal is the final announcement by the Americans of their irrevocable independence. The government of American Episcopal Methodism was thus completed; but English Methodism has continued to this day, in the eyes of some of its most cultured ministers and members, a hybrid somewhat, a cross between a Church and a Society.

At that memorable first interview between Coke and Asbury at Barratt's Chapel, in Delaware, November 14, 1784, Asbury by his proposal to call a Conference, cordially seconded by the American preachers present, ultimately secured independence of Mr. Wesley and English Methodism, and self-government to American Methodism. Mr. Wesley did not include in his scheme the assembling of the American itinerants to pass judgment upon his proposals and plans, and to accept the one and elect the other of his appointees to the general superintendency. Wesley never intended to originate an American General Conference. Upon this fact proper historical emphasis has not, as yet, been placed. It was the germ of Conference authority, manifesting itself in the Annual Conferences in America, that gradually separated the American from the English Methodists; that subsequently declined to elect Whatcoat and Garrettson, upon Mr. Wesley's nomination, to the episcopate; and that omitted Mr. Wesley's name from the Minutes. It was not the Christmas Conference, however, by its unforeseen organization, or by any subsequent action, that separated these Methodists of North America from any shadow of churchly authority which the Church of England may have possessed in the United States after the revolutionary war: this fragile bond, if it did not fall away of itself, Mr. Wesley himself unhesitatingly severed. In a word, it was the unexpected organization of the Christmas Conference—which grew out of the stand which Mr. Asbury took in the interview at Barratt's Chapel, and whose powers and authority he recognized as capable of being set over against those of Mr. Wesley alone—that gave the American Church autonomy; *i. e.*, independence of Mr. Wesley and the English Conference. Dr. Coke was always uneasy at this point; not about the ordination—he came to make a man already superintendent a bishop, in fact if not in name; not about the organization of an Episcopal Church independent of, and indeed a successor to, the Church of England, then practically defunct in the States; but about the autonomy, the independence of Mr. Wesley and the home Conference. This Conference had not entered into Wesley's platform or Coke's. In Asbury's platform, however, it was the chief plank. This sufficiently explains Coke's language in his letter to Bishop White, in 1791, that he probably went further in the organization of the American Church than Mr. Wesley intended.

All the indications are that Mr. Wesley meant his superintendents to ordain whom they chose, and to be the sole ecclesiastical rulers, under himself, of both preachers and people in America. They were not to wait on the election of a Conference before they conferred deacon's or elder's orders, for no executive or legislative assembly of preachers had been provided for by Mr. Wesley; and such was not the habit of the English Bishops or the law of the English Church. He, in turn, expected to name the superintendents with as much freedom as an English premier issues his *congé d'élire* to fill the vacancies in the sees of the Church of England. As the originator of the United Societies, he had been the fountain of authority, both legislative and executive, in England and, up to this time, in America. He therefore intended that Coke and Asbury should be the general superintendents of the American work as himself was of the English, making regulations and enforcing them, distributing the preachers according to their own judgment, and having entire and unquestioned oversight, *with this exception:* Coke and Asbury were to continue subject to Mr. Wesley's authority, he not unnaturally considering himself as the proper head of the whole Methodist Connection in Europe and America. Mr. Wesley took it upon himself, assisted by other presbyters, solemnly to ordain, and to accredit with the authority to ordain others, a man who was already a presbyter of the Church of England. He did not call this man a bishop, but by the equivalent title of Superintendent; neither did he call himself the senior bishop, or the archbishop, of Methodism; yet that he esteemed himself a scriptural bishop and by appointment of Divine Providence the patriarch and apostle of Methodism throughout the world is not open to question. In this conjoint episcopal and patriarchal capacity he regarded himself as competent to the government, even of the two men whom he constituted General Superintendents of American Methodism. If Asbury had accepted on these conditions, there would have been no independent American Conference, but certainly a Church, for Mr. Wesley intended complete independency of any jurisdiction which the Church of England may have been supposed still to exercise in America. It would have been an Episcopal Church of the most ultra type, governed wholly by bishops, and destitute of a General Conference or legislature of any sort, except as the British Conference stood in this relation to the American work. The bishops would have been subject to Mr. Wesley during his life, but in America would have governed as he did in England. They would have called the preachers together at sundry times and in divers convenient places, in an Annual Conference capacity—the capacity in which the British Conference really met during Mr. Wesley's life—to discuss local matters, and to receive their appointments: but

13

all legislative and executive powers would have been resident in the bishops themselves, subject to Mr. Wesley during his life, and to the British Conference after his decease. This was Mr. Wesley's plan; and it is due to the sagacity and far-sighted statesmanship of Asbury, in declining to accept office on such terms, that a General Conference—first general in fact, and afterward delegated and limited—was subsequently incorporated in the fundamental organization of American Episcopal Methodism. Had the British Conference, after Mr. Wesley's death, assumed the same attitude toward the episcopacy of Coke and Asbury in America that it did toward that of Coke and Mather in England, and had the American Methodists submitted to the authority of the home Conference, Episcopal Methodism, answering to Wesley's own design, would have become extinct in the world. The Episcopacy would have been decapitated or ignored, and the American General Conference would not have come into existence. Thus Asbury opposed and overruled Wesley in America, but it proved the condition of carrying the Founder's own plan into successful operation in the United States at least, despite the comparative failure in England, and that on a scale so magnificent that Wesley in his most optimistic mood never dreamed of such Episcopal Churches as now exist among the Methodists of America.

IV. *The Christmas Conference and Its Work.*

On the 17th of December, Coke and Asbury, having completed their evangelistic itineraries, arrived under the roof of Mr. Gough, at Perry Hall, about fifteen miles from Baltimore. William Black, a preacher from Nova Scotia, and Vasey were also of the company. "Here," writes Coke, "I have a noble room to myself, where Mr. Asbury and I may, in the course of a week, mature everything for the Conference." Whatcoat joined them on the 19th, and the next day they began the revision of "the Rules and Minutes." Asbury observed Friday, November 26, as a day of fasting and prayer, to know "the will of God in the matter that is shortly to come before our Conference. The preachers and people," he adds, "seem to be much pleased with the projected plan; I myself am led to think it is of the Lord. I am not tickled with the honor to be gained—I see danger in the way. My soul waits upon God. O that he may lead us in the way we should go! Part of my time is, and must necessarily be, taken up with preparing for the Conference." *

The Christmas Conference began its session on Friday, December 24, at 10 A.M. in Lovely Lane chapel, Baltimore. Whatcoat says, "On the 24th we rode to Baltimore; at 10 o'clock we began our Conference." Coke's entry is "On Christmas eve we opened our Conference." Asbury writes that they "continued at Perry Hall until Friday the twenty-fourth. We then rode to Baltimore, where we met a few preachers." Coke's certificate of Asbury's ordination also shows that he was ordained deacon Saturday, December 25. The joint testimony of Coke, Asbury, and Whatcoat is thus decisive of the date. The first Discipline of the Methodist Episcopal Church, framed at this Conference, bears, however, this title: "Minutes of several Conversations between the Rev. Thomas Coke, LL.D., the Rev. Francis Asbury, and others, at a Conference, begun in Baltimore in the State of Maryland, on Monday the 27th of December, in the year 1784. Composing a Form of Discipline for the Ministers, Preachers, and other Members of the Methodist Episcopal Church in America."† The harmony of the two dates is probably found in the order of proceedings. It is likely that the consideration of Mr. Wesley's circular letter, the settlement of the organization and title of the new Church, and the determination with regard to Mr. Asbury's ordination, at least, occupied the time on Friday and Saturday. On Monday morning, possibly with a fuller Conference, the coversations began touching the revision of discipline, which continued throughout the week. No official records of the Christmas Conference are extant, save the preliminary reference in the Minutes of 1785 and the Discipline framed by this Conference and afterwards published, which Dr. Robert Emory gives entire in his History of the Discipline. Asbury's notice of the Conference is as follows:

It was agreed to form ourselves into an Episcopal Church, and to have superintendents, elders, and deacons. When the Conference was seated, Dr. Coke and myself were unanimously elected to the superintendency of the Church, and my ordination followed, after being previously ordained deacon and elder, as by the following certificate may be seen:

Know all men by these presents, That I, Thomas Coke, Doctor of Civil Law; late of Jesus College, in the university of Oxford, Presbyter of the Church of England, and Superintendent of the Methodist Episcopal Church in America; under the protection of Almighty God, and with a single eye to his glory; by the imposition of my hands, and prayer, (being assisted by two ordained elders,) did on the twenty-fifth day of this month, December, set apart Francis Asbury for the office of a deacon in the aforesaid Methodist Episcopal Church. And also the twenty-sixth day of the said month, did by the imposition of my hands, and prayer, (being assisted by the said elders,) set apart the said Francis Asbury for the office of elder in the said Methodist Episcopal Church. And on this twenty-seventh day of the said month, being the day of the date hereof, have, by the imposition of my hands, and prayer, (being assisted by the said elders,) set apart the said Francis Asbury for the office of a superintendent in the said Methodist Episcopal Church, a man whom I judge to be well qualified for that great work. And I do hereby recommend him to all whom it may concern, as a fit person to preside over the flock of Christ. In testimony whereof I have hereunto set my hand and seal this twenty-seventh day of December, in the year of our Lord 1784.   THOMAS COKE.

Twelve elders were elected, and solemnly set apart to serve our societies in the United States, one for Antigua, and two for Nova Scotia. We spent the whole week in Conference, debating freely, and determining all things by a majority of votes. The Doctor preached every day at noon, and some one of the other preachers morning and evening. We were in great haste, and did much business in a little time.

Monday, January 3, 1785. The Conference is risen, and I have now a little time for rest.*

The "Minutes taken at the several Annual Conferences of the Methodist Episcopal Church for the year 1785" contain this preliminary notice: "As it was unanimously agreed at this Conference that circumstances made it expedient for us to become a separate body, under the denomination of

---

* Journal, I. 377, 378.

the *Methodist Episcopal* Church, it is necessary that we should here assign some reasons for so doing." The circular letter of Mr. Wesley, dated Bristol, September 10, 1784, and directed " to Dr. Coke, Mr. Asbury, and our Brethren in North America" is then cited as the Magna Charta of American Episcopal Methodism.* After the letter, this conclusion is stated, " Therefore, at this Conference we formed ourselves into an Independent Church: and following the counsel of Mr. John Wesley, who recommended the Episcopal mode of Church government, we thought it best to become an Episcopal Church, making the Episcopal office elective, and the elected superintendent or bishop † amenable to the body of ministers and preachers."

In the first Discipline, framed by the Christmas Conference, the question following the resolution of submission to Mr. Wesley, previously quoted in another connection, is this:

Ques. 3. As the ecclesiastical as well as civil affairs of these United States have passed through a very considerable change by the revolution, what plan of Church government shall we hereafter pursue? *Ans.* We will form ourselves into an Episcopal Church, under the direction of superintendents, elders, deacons, and helpers, according to the forms of ordination annexed to our Liturgy, and the Form of Discipline set forth in these Minutes.‡

Whatcoat says in his Memoirs, already cited, " We agreed to form a Methodist Episcopal Church, *in which the Liturgy* (as presented by the Rev. John Wesley) *should be read*, and the sacraments be administered by a superintendent, elders,

---

*To the sentence " I have accordingly appointed Dr. Coke and Mr. Francis Asbury to be joint *Superintendents* " this footnote is attached, "As the translators of our version of the Bible have used the English word *Bishop* instead of *Superintendent*, it has been thought by us, that it would appear more scriptural to adopt their term Bishop." This was probably added by Mr. Asbury in 1787, when the title *Superintendent* was changed to *Bishop* in the Discipline.

† I know of no reason for supposing that the alternative word "bishop" was not in the original Minutes of 1785. The adjective Episcopal was incorporated in the official title of the Church and occurs no less than three times in this sentence. Jesse Lee gives us a sufficient account of its first introduction into the Discipline in 1787; but it seems to be a piece of conjectural and hypercritical emendation which would exclude it from the Minutes of 1785. Abel Stevens accepts it without question.

‡ Robert Emory's Hist. of Discipline, p. 27.

and deacons, who shall be ordained by a presbytery, using the Episcopal form, as prescribed in the Rev. Mr. Wesley's prayer book. Persons to be ordained are to be nominated by the superintendent, elected by the Conference, and ordained by imposition of the hands of the superintendent and elders; *the superintendent has a negative voice.*" * He further gives us the most minute and accurate chronology of the session, stating that Coke and his presbyters ordained Asbury deacon on the second day, and elder on Sunday, the third day; on Monday Otterbein joined Coke, Whatcoat, and Vasey in his third ordination, to the Superintendency. This agrees with Coke's ordination parchment, cited above from Asbury's Journal: the settlement of Asbury's position was thus regarded of such importance that all three orders were bestowed upon him before the other preachers were elected and ordained. Tuesday, Wednesday, and Thursday were occupied with the revision and framing of the Discipline and the election of preachers to orders. Friday several deacons were ordained; Saturday, January 1, 1785, the college matter was under consideration; Sunday, twelve elders, previously ordained deacons, and one deacon were ordained; "and we ended our Conference" says Whatcoat, "in great peace and unanimity."

The elders chosen were Freeborn Garrettson and James O. Cromwell, for Nova Scotia, Jeremiah Lambert for Antigua, and for the United States, John Tunnell, William Gill, LeRoy Cole, Nelson Reed, John Haggerty, Reuben Ellis, Richard· Ivey, Henry Willis, James O'Kelly, and Beverly Allen. Of the ten original elders, first constituted in the Methodist Episcopal Church, it is remarkable that no less than six—Cole, Reed, Ellis, Ivey, Willis, and O'Kelly —had been master spirits in the old Southern "regular" Conference, which had contended so stoutly for the sacraments among Methodists. Cole and Ellis had been members of the presbytery appointed at Fluvanna in 1779, and all of these six had previously received ordination from that

---

* Page 21. The italics are his own.

presbytery. For renouncing their rights and patiently waiting, they had now their reward in being numbered among
the elders first ordained by Superintendents Coke and Asbury. John Dickins—another able Fluvanna leader—Ig-
natius Pigman, and Caleb Boyer were elected deacons.
Coke says:

> They [the Conference] are indeed a body of devoted, disinterested men,
> but most of them young. The spirit in which they conducted themselves,
> in choosing the elders, was most pleasing. I believe they acted without be-
> ing at all influenced by friendship, resentment, or prejudice, both in choos-
> ing and rejecting. The Lord was peculiarly present while I was preaching
> my two pastoral sermons.

In the sermon at the episcopal ordination of Asbury, he
delivered himself with all the weight of a prophet's fire, both
in denouncing existing evils in the English Church and in
anticipating the unequaled success of Asbury's continental
episcopate:

> You may now perceive [said he] the dreadful effects of raising immoral
> or unconverted men to the government of the Church. The baneful influ-
> ence of their example is so extensive that the skill and cruelty of devils can
> hardly fabricate a greater curse than an irreligious bishop. But thou, O
> man of God, follow after righteousness, godliness, patience, and meekness.
> Do the work of an evangelist, and make full proof of thy ministry, and thy
> God will open to thee a wide door, which all thy enemies shall not be able to
> shut. *He will carry his Gospel by thee from sea to sea, and from one end of the*
> *continent to another.*

The Rev. Thomas Ware, who was present, bears explicit
testimony to important points, particularly the choosing of a
name for the new Church:

> The order of things devised by him [Wesley] for our organization as a
> Chuch, filled us with solemn delight. . . . We did, therefore, according
> to the best of our knowledge, receive and follow the advice of Mr. Wesley,
> as stated in our form of Discipline. After Mr. Wesley's letter, appointing
> Dr. Coke and Mr. Asbury joint superintendents over the Methodists in
> America, had been read, analyzed, and cordially approved by the confer-
> ence, a question arose what name we should take. I thought to myself, I
> was content that we should call ourselves the Methodist Church, and so
> whispered to a brother that sat near me. But one proposed, I think it was
> John Dickins, that we should call ourselves the Methodist Episcopal
> Church. Mr. Dickins was, in the estimation of his brethren, a man of ster-
> ling sense and sterling piety; and there were few men on the conference
> floor heard with greater deference than he. The most of the preachers had

been brought up in what was called the Church of England; and all being agreed that the plan of general superintendency was a species of Episcopacy, the motion was carried, without, I think, a dissenting voice. There was not, to the best of my recollection, the least agitation on this question. Had the conference indulged the least suspicion that the name they were about to take, would in the least degree cross the views or feelings of Mr. Wesley, it would have been abandoned; for the name of Wesley was inexpressibly dear to the Christmas Conference, and to none more so than to Asbury and Coke. After our organization, we proceeded to elect a sufficient number of elders to visit the quarterly meetings, and administer the ordinances; and this it was that gave rise to the office of presiding elders among us.*

In his letter of December 1, 1828, Ware declares that " Dr. Coke was in favor of taking the name Methodist Episcopal Church." It is not improbable that Dickins proposed this title on the floor of the Conference at the suggestion of Coke and Asbury, and, as there is evidence that the Doctor " argued " the point before the Conference, it is not surprising that the name was adopted without dissent or debate, for, says Ware, in the article on " The Christmas Conference " just cited, Dr. Coke " was the best speaker in a small circle, or on a Conference floor, I ever heard." †

Ware vindicates the fair names of Coke and Asbury against the aspersions of schismatic agitators of the times in which he wrote, little dreaming that there would arise men who, a century after the Christmas Conference, would labor to prepare an historical basis for the same allegations, deliberately reiterated:

Had I, at the close of the Christmas Conference, been told that, in some future time, even before I should go the way of all flesh, men would arise calling themselves Methodists, who would report, and even put forth their most skillful exertions to make the world believe that Asbury and Coke did, from sheer ambition, conspire against Mr. Wesley, whom they professed so much to love and honor, and on him surreptitiously father a spurious Episcopacy, and thereby with falsehood stain, not only the fame of the man Wesley, but the first page of their Discipline, to be perpetuated throughout all future generations, I should have said, No, surely, that can never be, that from ourselves men should arise who could excogitate, or even retail, so foul a slander:—that be far from them. ‡

---

* Methodist Magazine and Quarterly Review; Art. "Christmas Conference," by Thomas Ware, January number, 1832, p. 98.

† p. 104.

‡ Ware's Art., " The Christmas Conference," in Meth. Mag. and Quart. Rev., p. 100.

In pursuance of our plan to gather the testimony of the participants in the Christmas Conference as to what the Conference itself understood Mr. Wesley to intend, and as to what the body actually did, and thus, as far as possible, to remedy the defect arising from the lack of an official journal of the proceedings, we may now introduce the Rev. Freeborn Garrettson. In a letter to Rev. A. M'Caine, dated September 29, 1826, in answer to inquiries which were intended to elicit information discreditable to Methodist Episcopacy and to the origin of the Methodist Episcopal Church, he says:

With respect to your first query, I am fully of opinion the Christmas conference was authorized by Mr. Wesley, to organize themselves under an episcopal form of church government. Dr. Coke did receive ordination to the superintendency by the laying on of the hands of Mr. Wesley and the presbyters present, and had directions to consecrate Mr. Asbury. Mr. Wesley's letter in the discipline satisfies me, and I have seen from his pen where he asserts his opinion in favor of episcopacy as the best form of church government. . . . Remember Mr. Wesley speaks of a moderate episcopacy, in which I do most cordially agree.

With regard to your second query, nearly forty years have passed away, and I cannot charge my memory with every minutia; however, instructions were communicated from Mr. Wesley, and as we were all young, humble, happy, and sincere, and well pleased with what he offered, (would to God we were all so now,) I doubt not but that we followed his wishes to a punctilio.

With regard to your third query, actions speak louder than words. Dr. Coke was ordained deacon and presbyter, and Mr. Wesley laid hands on him a third time for the general superintendency in our church, and directed the setting apart Asbury for the same office; and in the year 1787, he appointed two others [Garrettson himself and Whatcoat] to be set apart for the same office. The word bishop in the primitive church was as simple as that of elder or presbyter, and perhaps more so; but it rose by slow degrees, till there was arch over arch, till an infallible monster was brought forth. Mr. Wesley designed we should have a moderate episcopacy, and therefore he gave us the word superintendent instead of bishop; and the change of the word was cause of grief to that dear old saint, and so it was to me.*

Our old friend, William Watters, first native American itinerant, and President of the Conference of 1778 when Rankin had returned to England and Asbury was a local preacher in retirement, says:

---

* Meth. Mag. and Quart. Rev., July, 1830, pp. 340, 341.

We formed ourselves into a separate Church. This change was proposed to us by Mr. Wesley after we had craved his advice on the subject, but could not take effect until adopted by us; which was done in a deliberate, formal manner, at a Conference called for that purpose, in which there was not one dissenting voice. Every one, of any discernment, must see from Mr. Wesley's Circular Letter on this occasion, as well as from every part of our mode of Church government, that we openly and avowedly declared ourselves Episcopalians, though the doctor and Mr. Asbury were called Superintendents.*

William Phoebus, another member of the Conference, deposes as follows:

We assembled at the city of Baltimore, in the State of Maryland, and received Thomas Coke, LL.D., with his testimonials from the greatest man to *us* in the world. He proceeded to form the first Church that ever was organized under a pure republican government, and the first that was ever formed in this happy part of the world. In the year of our Lord 1785, and in the ninth year of the independence of the United States, on the first day of January, we thought it not robbery to call our society a Church, having in it, and of it, several presbyters and a President.†

Dr. Coke, in his sermon at the third ordination of Mr. Asbury, already quoted, says that Mr. Wesley, " after long deliberation saw it his duty to form his Society in America into an independent Church; but he loved the most excellent liturgy of the Church of England, he loved its rites and ceremonies, and therefore adopted them in most instances for the present case." From the beginning, as we have seen, " bishop " was used in the Minutes of 1785, as an explanatory synonym for " superintendent." By July, 1785, Coke was with Wesley at the British Conference.

Coke also took to England the American Minutes, and they were printed on a press which Wesley used, and under his own eye. The Baltimore proceedings were therefore known to Wesley, but we hear of no remonstrance from him. They soon became known, by the Minutes, to the public; and when Coke was attacked publicly for what he had done, he replied, as we have seen, through the press, that " he had done nothing but under the direction of Mr. Wesley." Wesley never denied it. ‡

Nearly four years elapsed after the organization of the Church with the adjective " Episcopal " in its title, and after the publication on Wesley's press of the Minutes of

---

* Autobiography, p. 104.   † See Myles, Chron. Hist. of Methodists, p. 165.
‡ Stevens, Hist. Meth. II. 227; cf. Hist. M. E. Ch., II. 191.

1785 containing the word "bishop" as a synonym for "superintendent" before Wesley rebuked Asbury (September 20, 1788 is the date of Wesley's famous and oft-quoted letter) for permitting himself to be personally described and addressed as "bishop."

Finally in 1789, there was inserted in the Discipline for the first time, "Sec. 3. On the Nature and Constitution of our Church," of which the concluding paragraph reads as follows:

> For these reasons we have thought it our duty to form ourselves into an independent church. And as the most excellent mode of church government, according to our maturest judgment, is that of a moderate episcopacy, and as we are persuaded that the uninterrupted succession of bishops from the apostles can be proved neither from Scripture nor antiquity, we therefore have constituted ourselves into an Episcopal Church, under the direction of bishops, elders, deacons, and preachers, according to the forms of ordination annexed to our Prayer-book, and the regulations laid down in this Form of Discipline.

Under the following section, the first question is "What is the proper origin of the Episcopal authority in our Church?" and the answer is:

> In the year 1784 the Rev. John Wesley, who, under God, has been the father of the great revival of religion now extending over the earth by the means of the Methodists, determined, at the intercession of multitudes of his spiritual children on this continent, to ordain ministers for America, and for this purpose sent over three regularly-ordained clergy; but preferring the Episcopal mode of church government to any other, he solemnly set apart, by the imposition of his hands and prayer, one of them, namely, Thomas Coke, doctor of civil law, late of Jesus College, in the University of Oxford, for the episcopal office; and having delivered to him letters of episcopal orders, commissioned and directed him to set apart Francis Asbury, then general assistant of the Methodist Society in America, for the same Episcopal office, he, the said Francis Asbury, being first ordained deacon and elder. In consequence of which, the said Francis Asbury was solemnly set apart for the said Episcopal office by prayer and the imposition of the hands of the said Thomas Coke, other regularly-ordained ministers assisting in the sacred ceremony. At which time the General Conference held at Baltimore did unanimously receive the said Thomas Coke and Francis Asbury as their bishops, being fully satisfied of the validity of their Episcopal ordination.*

---

*Robert Emory's Hist. of Discipline, ed. 1844, pp. 93, 94. The writer of these lines has in his possession a copy of the Discipline of 1790 which contains the same language unaltered. Bishop Hendrix has a copy of 1791: no change in the form of statement was made until 1792.

This corresponds with the sentiments of Bishops Coke and Asbury expressed in their Notes on the Discipline, prepared by request of the General Conference of 1796, and impliedly sanctioned by the General Conference of 1800, which directed them to be bound up with the Form of Discipline. In Section I. "Of the Origin of the Methodist Episcopal Church" these first Bishops say:

The late Rev. John Wesley recommended the episcopal form to his societies in America; and the General Conference, which is the chief synod of our church, unanimously accepted of it. Mr. Wesley did more. He first consecrated one for the office of a bishop, that our episcopacy might descend from himself. The General Conference unanimously accepted of the person so consecrated, as well as of Francis Asbury, who had for many years exercised every branch of the episcopal office, excepting that of ordination. Now, the idea of an apostolic succession being exploded, it follows, that the Methodist Church has everything which is Scriptural and essential to justify its episcopacy. Is the unanimous approbation of the chief synod of a church necessary? This it has had. Is the ready compliance of the members of the church with its decision, in this respect, necessary? This it has had, and continues to have. Is it highly expedient, that the fountain of the episcopacy should be respectable? This has been the case. The most respectable divine since the primitive ages, if not since the time of the apostles, was Mr. Wesley.

Under Section IV. "Of the Election and Consecration of Bishops and of their duty," Coke and Asbury declare:

In considering the present subject, we must observe, that nothing has been introduced into Methodism by the present episcopal form of government, which was not before fully exercised by Mr. Wesley. He presided in the conferences; fixed the appointments of the preachers for their several circuits; changed, received, or suspended preachers wherever he judged that necessity required it; traveled through the European connection at large; superintended the spiritual and temporal business; and consecrated two bishops, Thomas Coke and Alexander Mather, one before the present episcopal plan took place in America, and the other afterward, besides ordaining elders and deacons.*

The preceding is a complete *résumé* of the evidence, derivable from contemporary sources, of Mr. Wesley's intentions, of the understanding of Superintendents Coke and Asbury, of Presbyter Whatcoat, and of participants in the Christmas Conference, as to what that body did when it organized the Methodist Episcopal Church. Almost every

* Emory's Hist. of the Discipline, ed. 1844, pp. 282, 287.

step, from Wesley's ordination of Coke to the adjournment of the Conference, has been stubbornly disputed, and the evidence critically sifted by objectors, within and without the limits of Methodism, who have sought in one interest or another, to minify or discredit the results reached and permanently embodied in the constitution of the Methodist Episcopal Church. That a "moderate episcopacy" was constituted; that an Episcopal Church was organized; that a ministry in three grades or orders was permanently provided for; that the Christmas Conference understood itself and Mr. Wesley; that the "ambition" of Coke and Asbury did not lead them to impose upon Wesley, on the one hand, and on the American Methodists on the other, a "spurious episcopacy," never designed by the Founder or intelligently accepted by the Church; that Wesley himself fully approved, against his brother Charles and other malcontents in England, what Dr. Coke had done as his envoy and representative: all this has been made indubitable by a patient and candid survey of the extant contemporary records. The ten days' work of this historic organizing convention has been before the world for more than a century and, for the ends aimed at by its authors, may challenge comparison with the imperishable results achieved by those unselfish patriots, who assembled less than three years later, and, under the presidency of the Father of his country, wrought out the Constitution of the United States. When it became evident that the eleven states represented in the Convention at Philadelphia, in 1787, had unanimously endorsed the Constitution, Benjamin Franklin, surveying an image of the sun, emblazoned on the back of the president's chair, said to those about him, "I was not able to tell whether it was rising or setting; now I know that it is the rising sun." *
Over America's plains and rivers, mountains and valleys, when the Christmas Conference adjourned, the Sun of righteousness was rising with healing in his wings. "Proclaim liberty throughout all the land unto all the inhabitants

---

* Bancroft, Hist. U. S., Author's Last Revision, VI. 367.

thereof:" Church and Nation were now ready to run the race of the mighty Nineteenth century that lay all unknown before them. The Lord reigneth: let the earth rejoice!

We may be permitted to remind the reader, in concluding this section of our studies, that the preceding inquiry is purely historical. The writer has no aspiration in these pages to win the honors of the controversialist or polemic. He has not sought to compose an essay on the principles of Church government. He has not even raised the question as to what Methodist Episcopacy ought to be, or whether the Church is now competent to improve it. His investigation has been confined to the single point of determining what Methodist Episcopacy and the Methodist Episcopal Church were in their origin: what Mr. Wesley designed them to be and what the Christmas Conference actually constituted them. "Whatever view we take of the subject," concludes Abel Stevens, "we are compelled to one conclusion: that Wesley did create and establish the American Methodist episcopacy. The man who gainsays such evidence must be given up as incorrigible. There can be no reasoning with him." * "Episcopal" is the chief word in the title of the two Methodist Episcopal Churches, and "Methodist" is a qualifying term to point out the kind of Episcopalians we are. The grammar and the logic, as well as the history of our name, make *Episcopal* the *genus* and *Methodist* the *species*. As Dr. Whedon forcefully said in the old *Quarterly*, we are neither Methodist Congregational nor Methodist Presbyterian, but Methodist Episcopal Churches. The one ground of the use of the term "Episcopal" in the name of our Churches is generally overlooked. The word does not imply simply that the government is episcopal, as distinguished from presbyterial or congregational. Asbury and his coadjutors, and our early English membership, were Episcopalians; and history will sustain the point that our name was meant to indicate the organization on scriptural principles of the first, (and there-

---

* Hist. of Meth., II. 229.

fore at that time the one,) Episcopal Church on the American continent. Hitherto the American Methodists had received the sacraments from the English clergy resident in the colonies, and regarded themselves as members of that Church. In 1784, when the Methodist Episcopal Church in America was organized, neither the English nor the Protestant Episcopal Church existed here in legal or complete organic form. The American Methodists, by the help of Mr. Wesley, therofore organized themselves into an American Episcopal Church, taking the name and style already indicated. They regarded themselves as the successors of the old Church, then defunct, and entered upon their work accordingly. The Methodist Episcopalians still adhered " to the doctrines and discipline of the Church of England," and this historical truth is fittingly embalmed in the parchment of their first bishop. American Methodism, according to the design of its founders, has for more than a century approved itself as the great popular Episcopal Church of America. "The Methodist bishops were the first Protestant bishops, and Methodism was the first Protestant Episcopal Church of the New World; and as Mr. Wesley had given it the Anglican articles of religion (omitting the seventeenth, on predestination), and the liturgy, wisely abridged, it became, both by its precedent organization and its subsequent numerical importance, the real successor to the Anglican Church in America." *

---

* Stevens, Hist. of Meth., II. 215.

CHAPTER XII.

FIRST DISCIPLINE OF THE METHODIST EPISCOPAL CHURCH.

THE " Form of Discipline for the Ministers, Preachers, and other Members of the Methodist Episcopal Church in America " adopted by the Christmas Conference, was formulated in one continuous series of questions and answers, eighty-one in number. It was printed in Philadelphia in 1785, and may be indifferently referred to as the Discipline of 1784, in the last week of which year it was established, or of 1785, the date of its publication. It was based on the " Large Minutes " of the British Conference, though matter from the American Minutes and much new legislation, suited to the changed conditions of the new Church, were incorporated. In Dr. Robert Emory's History of the Discipline* may be found an exact record of the differences between this first American Methodist Discipline and the edition of the Large Minutes for 1789, the last revision made before Mr. Wesley's death. Any reader who may have been led to suppose that American Methodism was, in its rules and regulations, a comparatively independent development, or that the year 1784 marks a total breach between the Disciplines of the two Connexions, or what afterwards became two distinct ecclesiastical bodies, will be surprised and gratified to discover how close is the correspondence between the Discipline of 1784 and the Large Minutes of 1789. But, however interesting the task of tracing some of the most familiar language of our present Discipline to its original enactment by early English Conferences, we shall have to content ourselves in these pages with brief notices of the material legislation of 1784.

---

* Ed. of 1844, pp. 25-79.

I. Superintendents, Elders, and Deacons.

With regard to Superintendents, Elders, and Deacons the Christmas Conference passed the following regulations:

Ques. 26. What is the office of a superintendent? *Ans.* To ordain superintendents, elders, and deacons; to preside as a moderator in our Conferences; to fix the appointments of the preachers for the several circuits; and, in the intervals of the Conference, to change, receive or suspend preachers, as necessity may require; and to receive appeals from preachers and people, and decide them. N. B. No person shall be ordained a superintendent, elder, or deacon, without the consent of the majority of the Conference, and the consent and imposition of hands of a superintendent; except in the instance provided for in the 29th Minute.

Ques. 27. To whom is the superintendent amenable for his conduct? *Ans.* To the Conference: who have power to expel him for improper conduct, if they see it necessary.

Ques. 28. If the superintendent ceases from traveling at large among the people, shall he still exercise his office in any degree? *Ans.* If he ceases from traveling without the consent of the Conference, he shall not thereafter exercise any ministerial function whatsoever in our Church.

Ques. 29. If by death, expulsion or otherwise, there be no superintendent remaining in our Church, what shall we do? *Ans.* The Conference shall elect a superintendent, and the elders, or any three of them, shall ordain him according to our Liturgy.

Ques. 30. What is the office of an elder? *Ans.* To administer the sacraments of baptism and the Lord's supper, and to perform all the other rites prescribed by our Liturgy.

Ques. 31. What is the office of a deacon? *Ans.* To baptize in the absence of an elder, to assist the elder in the administration of the Lord's supper, to marry, bury the dead, and ·read the Liturgy to the people as prescribed, except what relates to the administration of the Lord's supper.

Ques. 35. How are we to proceed with those elders or deacons who cease from traveling? *Ans.* Unless they have the permission of the Conference declared under the hand of a superintendent, they are on no account to exercise any of the peculiar functions of those offices among us. And if they do, they are to be expelled immediately.

Ques. 63. Are there any further directions needful for the preservation of good order among the preachers? *Ans.* In the absence of a superintendent, a traveling preacher or three leaders shall have power to lodge a complaint against any preacher in their circuit, whether elder, assistant, deacon, or helper, before three neighboring assistants; who shall meet at an appointed time, (proper notice being given to the parties,) hear, and decide the cause. And authority is given them to change or suspend a preacher, if they see it necessary, and to appoint another in his place, during the absence of the superintendents.*

All of these regulations concerning ministers and sacra-

---

* Dr. Robert Emory's Hist. of the Discipline, ed. 1844, pp. 38–59 (extracts)

14

ments were devised and enacted at the Christmas Conference, there being, of course, nothing answering to them in the Large Minutes. Rules with regard to baptism, and particularly the liberal provision (Ques. 47) which did not refuse members of other Churches the privileges of membership with the Methodists, are worthy of notice, but need not detain us here. The duties of a superintendent are, (1) To ordain men to the three grades of the ministry; (2) to preside in the Conferences; (3) to fix the appointments; (4) to change, receive, and suspend preachers in the interval of the Conference; (4) *to entertain and decide appeals from preachers and people;* (5) to exercise, if he see fit, a suspensive veto not only upon the Conference election of deacons and elders, but also upon the election of additional Superintendents; (6) to travel at large among the people, under penalty, in the event of failure so to do, of suspension from all ministerial functions. On the other hand, for his conduct the Superintendent is amenable to the Conference "who have power to expel him for improper conduct, if they see it necessary." Thus the Conference of 1784 settled once for all the great underlying principles of episcopal administration and responsibility as they have continued with slight alteration for one hundred and ten years. The duties of Bishops have been somewhat changed from time to time: in the current Discipline their amenability to the Conference is still defined in the same terms originally employed by the fathers of the Christmas Conference. There were masters of assemblies in that body, who well knew what Israel ought to do! The regulations concerning elders and deacons are substantially the same as have since been in continuous operation. The answer to Question 63, however, reveals the fact that class-leaders were distinctly recognized as an organic part of the official pastorate of the Church, having oversight not only of the people, but in a sense also of the preachers: " In the absence of a superintendent, a traveling preacher, *or three leaders*, shall have power to lodge a complaint against any preacher," etc. The spiritual offices of the Christian ministry for edification and discipline were thus distributed among Superintendents, elders (usually presiding elders), Assistants (preachers in charge), deacons, helpers, and class-leaders. And here may be properly introduced a sketch of the origin and relations of the several grades of pastoral office in the Methodist Episcopal Church, immediately preceding and following the legislation of 1784. This sketch is taken from a hitherto unpublished manuscript of the late Joshua Soule in the possession of the writer of these lines. It is hardly necessary to remark that Joshua Soule was twice elected Bishop of the Methodist Episcopal Church (in 1820 and 1824); that he was the Senior Bishop in 1844; and that he continued in that relation to the Methodist Episcopal Church, South, until his decease in 1867. He was born in Maine in 1781; began traveling under the presiding elder in 1798; was admitted at New York in 1799; in 1804 he became presiding elder of the Maine District; in 1816, Book Agent at New York; he was a member of the General Conference of 1808, and "was author of the plan for a delegated General Conference."* This paper of Bishop Soule's is without date, but bears marks of age and is written in the steadier handwriting of his earlier years. His observations are evidently largely derived from his personal association with the fathers of the Church and from his knowledge of the workings of the Methodist system in the last decade of the eighteenth century and the first decade of this. Mr. Soule says:

The system adopted by Mr. Wesley for the execution of discipline in America was Episcopal in its nature. As he was (under God) the Father of the Methodist Societies both in Europe and America, the members and preachers united in looking up to him as such, and considered him as possessing all authority both in the temporal and spiritual concerns of the Societies. But as he could not personally take charge of the Societies in America, he appointed some to act as *General Assistants*, in maintaining the order and discipline as contained in the Minutes of Conference and his writings; to these were added *Assistants*, whose special business was to take the oversight of the circuit to which he was appointed, and when one, or

* Bishop Matthew Simpson's Cyclopædia of Methodism, p. 814.

more, was united with him as a colleague, he was denominated the *Helper*, and to these may be added the *Leaders*, in their respective classes. The Leader had the duties peculiar to his office to discharge; the Helper was authorized to attend to all the work which a Leader could perform, and when directed by those higher in office he was authorized to perform duties which a Class-leader could not. The Assistant was fully authorized to attend to all the work of the ministry and the execution of every part of the Discipline within his circuit; while the General Assistant was authorized to attend to all temporal and spiritual matters pertaining to the Societies in any and every circuit where he traveled. This was the original order of things.

In 1784 when these Societies were organized into a separate and distinct Church, there was no change in this *system*. Doctor Coke was ordained a *Superintendent* by Mr. Wesley and sent to America to act in Mr. Wesley's place, and [he] consequently vested him with ample powers to superintend and do the work of an evangelist in organizing the Church and this he did on the plan recommended by Mr. Wesley, which was on the Episcopal plan; consequently no material change was made in the system first introduced. An *Episcopacy* being recommended and appointed by Mr. Wesley, his recommendation was approved of and his appointment confirmed by the American preachers; and, in organizing the Church, they admitted of two orders in the ministry, *Elders* and *Deacons*. In the administration of the discipline of the Church, the following plan was pursued, to wit: the Bishops were to travel at large through the Connection, preside in the Conferences, fix the appointments of the preachers; in the intervals of Conference to change, receive, and suspend preachers as necessity requires and discipline directs; to perform ordinations, and, in a word, to take the general oversight of the spiritual and temporal business of the Church. To aid them in this work those who formerly attended to the business which pertained to the General Assistants were appointed to be ruling or Presiding Elders, each one having the special charge of a convenient number of circuits, denominated a District, through which he was to travel and attend to all the temporal and spiritual business of the Church within the several circuits composing his District, and that the discipline of the Church might more effectually be administered, the preacher, in general, on the several circuits who had most experience and was able to attend to the business was appointed to take charge of the circuit and, as formerly, act as Assistant to the Elder, while his colleague, as upon the old plan, was considered the Helper: these, together with the Leaders, all united in carrying the discipline into effect, so that with a well digested code of regulations, the moral discipline of the Gospel may be completely maintained and the Church preserved pure both in faith and practice. And such is the nature of an Episcopal system of government that when an *inferior* officer is deficient in discharging his duty, the *superior* is fully authorized to attend to the business. For the several grades of executive officers, whether Bishops, Presiding Elders, Assistant Preachers, or Helpers are each one authorized to do all the business which is made the *peculiar* business of the inferior. Hence a Bishop may not only preside in a General Conference; but it is his privilege and duty, when present, to preside in Annual and Quarterly Conferences, and if his time and strength is not employed in attending to higher duties, he is fully authorized to sit and preside on the trial and expulsion of private members. The Presiding Elders are equally clothed with executive power so far as it relates to their District; the Assistant and Helper as it relates to the circuit, and down to the Leader as it relates to his class.

II. The Rise of the Presiding Eldership.

We may now a little more formally than we have hitherto done notice the origin of the office of presiding elder. This office is not explicitly recognized in the Discipline of 1784. Yet this is the epoch of its virtual creation. It came with the first Superintendents, the first ordinations, the first formal provision for the administration of the sacraments, and is, therefore, coeval with the organization of the Church. Thomas Ware has already told us how the ordination of sufficient elders at the Christmas Conference "to visit the quarterly meetings and administer the ordinances" was the measure which "gave rise to the office of presiding elder among us." Bishop Soule tells us how this officer has been recognized from the beginning as the special deputy and representative of an absent Bishop, and how he stood in the same relation to Assistants which the General Assistant had formerly occupied. In the appointments of 1785, for the first time, the names of Willis, Ivy, Ellis, Reed, Matson, O'Kelly, Foster, Whatcoat, Boyer, Gill, Vasey, and Chew, some of whom were elected and ordained after the Christmas Conference, are prefixed to groups of circuits, ranging from two to eight in number, while the title *Elder* is affixed to their names. The almost invariable rule in the beginning, was that elders were assigned to districts, or, rather, to groups of circuits not yet denominated by this name. This was the origin of this office, though the title "presiding elder" does not appear regularly in the Minutes until as late as 1797. In the Discipline it occurs first in 1792. The first person to bear this title in the official records of the Church is William McKendree, whose district stands first in the appointments of 1797. Richard Whatcoat's district is the second.* The title also occurs in the Journal of the General Conference of 1796.† As early as 1786, however, the following was added to the duties of an elder, as defined above in the answer to Ques. 30, "2. To exercise within his own district, during the absence of the superintendents, all the powers vested in them for the government of our Church. Provided, that he never act contrary to an express order of the superintendents." ‡ This tallies exactly with Bishop Soule's account of the original relation existing between the Bishops and the Presiding Elders. Dr. Stevens appears to have overlooked, or to have attached little importance to, the appointment of elders to oversee groups of circuits at the very first Annual Conferences after the Christmas Conference. He similarly disregards the action recorded in the Discipline of 1786, and his statement that "the new elders, ordained at the Christmas Conference, were appointed only to administer the sacraments" § is too strong and exclusive. No doubt the administration of sacraments to the long-destitute Societies was a chief function of the new Superintendents, Elders, and Deacons; but it is not probable that the Elders (whose dignity was recognized as little inferior to that of the Superintendents themselves,) when they were assigned to the districts that we have seen were constituted at the Conference sessions of 1785, were deprived of all pastoral and disciplinary authority, save preaching and administering the sacraments. Ware expressly says the original elders "were to visit the quarterly meetings." They were placed in charge of the preachers and people of their districts, and though this official superiority was not defined in the first edition of the Discipline, as was first done a year later, Ware's testimony, as well as the usage which we know became universal very shortly afterwards, points to the fact that from the beginning the Elders who were in charge of districts presided in the Quarterly Conferences, in the absence of a Superin-

---

* Minutes, ed. of 1813, p. 193.   ‡ Emory's Hist. of the Discipline, p. 125.
† Gen. Conf. Journals, I. 16.   § Hist. M. E. Ch., II. 222.

tendent, and, as Mr. Soule says, discharged, in general, the duties which had formerly devolved on the General Assistant. One differs with diffidence from such an authority as Abel Stevens: he is quite right, however, when he adds that the Bishop, at this period, had "no 'cabinet' of presiding elders, a species of council which usage has since established, though it has no recognition in the Discipline." *

In 1789, a section "On the Constituting of Elders and their Duty" was substituted in the Discipline for the previous provisions. The Elder is "to travel through his appointed district;" "in the absence of a bishop to take charge of all the deacons," etc., showing that, as a rule, he did not have charge of other elders, and that all elders served districts; "to change, receive, or suspend preachers;" "to take care that every part of our Discipline be enforced;" "to attend *his bishop* when present," etc. These regulations stood until 1792. The Journal of the General Conference of 1792 is not extant. But Coke and Asbury in their Notes to the Discipline of 1796 have this to say:

On the principles or data above mentioned, all the episcopal Churches in the world have in some measure formed their church government. And we believe we can venture to assert, that there never has been an episcopal church of any great extent which has not had *ruling* or *presiding* elders, either expressly *by name*, as in the apostolic churches, or otherwise *in effect*. On this account it is, that all the modern episcopal churches have had their *presiding* or *ruling* elders under the names of grand vicars, archdeacons, rural deans, etc.   .   .   .   .

Mr. Wesley informs us in his Works, that the whole plan of Methodism was introduced, step by step, by the interference and openings of divine Providence. This was the case in the present instance. When Mr. Wesley drew up a plan of government for our church in America, he desired that no more elders should be ordained in the first instance than were absolutely necessary, and that the work on the continent should be divided between them, in respect to the duties of their office. The General Conference accordingly elected twelve elders for the above purposes. Bishop Asbury and the district [annual] conferences afterward found that this order of men was so necessary that they agreed to enlarge the number, and give them *the name* by which they are at present called, [of which, however, there is no trace in the Minutes: the Bishop probably acted, and the Conferences acquiesced] and which is perfectly Scriptural, though not *the word* used in our translation: and this proceeding afterward received the approbation of Mr. Wesley.

---

* Hist. M. E. Ch., II. 222, 224.

In 1792 the General Conference, equally conscious of the necessity of having such an office among us, not only confirmed everything that Bishop Asbury and the district conferences had done, but also drew up or agreed to the present section for the explanation of the nature and duties of the office. The conference clearly saw that the bishops wanted assistants; that it was impossible for one or two bishops so to superintend the vast work on this continent as to keep everything in order in the intervals of the conference, without other official men to act under them and assist them: and as these would be only the agents of the bishops in every respect, the authority of appointing them, and of changing them, ought, from the nature of things, to be in the episcopacy. If the presiding or ruling elders were not men in whom the bishops could fully confide, or on the loss of confidence, could exchange for others, the utmost confusion would ensue. This also renders the authority invested in the bishops of fixing the extent of each district, highly expedient.

From all that has been advanced, and from those other ideas which will present themselves to the reader's mind on this subject, it will appear that the presiding elders must, of course, be appointed, directed, and changed by the episcopacy. And yet their power is so considerable that it would by no means be sufficient for them to be responsible to the bishops *only* for their conduct in their office. They are as responsible in this respect, and in every other, to the *yearly* conference to which they belong, as any other preacher; and may be censured, suspended, or expelled from the connection, if the conference see it proper: nor have the bishops any authority to overrule, suspend, or meliorate in any degree the censures, suspensions, or expulsions of the conference.*

The section adopted in 1792 recognizes the duty of the Presiding Elder to preside in Annual Conferences (then called district) and first explicitly mentions quarterly meetings: " 4. In the absence of a bishop to preside in the Conference of his district. 5. To be present as far as practicable at all the quarterly meetings," etc. In two distinct questions, the bishop is empowered first to *choose*, and then to station and change the presiding elders.† This section stood unchanged until 1804.

III. *The New Term of Communion.*

The Christmas Conference imposed a new term of communion. The question, numbered 42, was asked, " What methods can we take to extirpate slavery?" and this answer was given:

---

* Emory's Hist. of the Discipline, ed. 1844, pp. 293-295. † *Ibid.*, pp. 126, 127.

We are deeply conscious of the impropriety of making new terms of communion for a religious society already established, excepting on the most pressing occasion; and such we esteem the practice of holding our fellow-creatures in slavery. We view it as contrary to the golden law of God on which hang all the law and the prophets, and the inalienable rights of mankind, as well as every principle of the Revolution, to hold in the deepest debasement, in a more abject slavery than is to be found in any part of the world except America, so many souls that are all capable of the image of God.

We therefore think it our most bounden duty to take immediately some effectual method to extirpate this abomination from among us; and for that purpose we add the following to the rules of our Society, viz.:

1. Every member of our Society who has slaves in his possession shall, within twelve months after notice given to him by the assistant (which notice the assistants are required immediately, and without delay, to give in their respective circuits), legally execute and record an instrument whereby he emancipates and sets free every slave in his possession who is between the ages of forty and forty-five immediately, or at farthest when they arrive at the age of forty-five; and every slave who is between the ages of twenty-five and forty immediately, or at farthest at the expiration of five years from the date of said instrument; and every slave who is between the ages of twenty and twenty-five immediately, or at farthest when they arrive at the age of thirty; and every slave under the age of twenty as soon as they arrive at the age of twenty-five at farthest; and every infant born in slavery after the above-mentioned rules are complied with immediately on its birth.

2. Every assistant shall keep a journal, in which he shall regularly minute down the names and ages of all the slaves belonging to all the masters in his respective circuit, and also the date of every instrument executed and recorded for the manumission of the slaves, with the name of the court, book, and folio in which the said instruments respectively shall have been recorded; which journal shall be handed down in each circuit to the succeeding assistants [pastors].

3. In consideration that these rules form a new term of communion, every person concerned who will not comply with them shall have liberty quietly to withdraw himself from our Society within the twelve months succeeding the notice given as aforesaid; otherwise the assistant shall exclude him in the Society.

4. No person so voluntarily withdrawn, or so excluded, shall ever partake of the Supper of the Lord with the Methodists, till he complies with the above requisitions.

5. No person holding slaves shall, in future, be admitted into Society or to the Lord's Supper, till he previously complies with these rules concerning slavery.

N. B.—These rules are to affect the members of our Society no farther than as they are consistent with the laws of the States in which they reside. And respecting our brethren in Virginia that are concerned, and after due consideration of their peculiar circumstances, we allow them two years from the notice given, to consider the expediency of compliance or non-compliance with these rules.

This legislation at once came to naught. It lies beyond our prescribed limits to notice the details of the excitement which followed. The general histories may be consulted for this. Thomas Ware declares, "We assumed nothing; made no new term of communion, save one on slavery, and that we could never rigidly enforce." * In less than six months the operation of these rules was suspended. The Minutes of the Annual Conferences for 1785 contain this action, "It is recommended to all our brethren to suspend the execution of the minute on slavery, till the deliberations of a future Conference; and that an equal space of time be allowed all our members for consideration, when the minute shall be put in force." † The Discipline formulated at the Christmas Conference was printed in Philadelphia in 1785, as we have seen, and bound up with the "Sunday Service" and the "Collection of Psalms and Hymns" which Mr. Wesley sent from England in sheets by the hand of Dr. Coke. As a matter of fact, this slavery legislation appeared in that first edition of the Discipline alone. The action of 1785 was, by common consent, regarded as its absolute repeal, and, in the second edition, printed in London in 1786, the above-cited legislation disappears.‡ "The suspending minute," says Dr. Sherman, "really struck out all provisions on the subject." § From this time until 1796, a period of ten years, no further mention of the subject occurs in the Discipline except in the General Rules. In 1787 however, the Minutes reveal another trend. The Annual Conferences took this decided action:

Ques. 17. What directions shall we give for the promotion of the spiritual welfare of the colored people? Ans. We conjure all our ministers and preachers, by the love of God, and the salvation of souls, and do require them, by all the authority invested in us, to leave nothing undone for the spiritual benefit and salvation of them, within their respective circuits or districts; and for this purpose to embrace every opportunity of inquiring into the state of their souls, and to unite in Society those who appear to have a real desire of fleeing from the wrath to come; to meet such in class, and to exercise the whole Methodist discipline among them. ‖

* Art. on Christmas Conf., in Meth. Mag. and Quart. Rev.. Jan. 1832, p. 100.
† Minutes, ed. 1813. p. 55.
‡ Emory's Hist. of Discipline, ed. 1844, p. 80.
§ Hist. of the Discipline, p. 116, footnote.
‖ Minutes, ed. 1813, pp. 67, 68.

BOOK IV.

—

FROM THE CHRISTMAS CONFERENCE TO THE INSTITUTION OF THE QUADRENNIAL GENERAL CONFERENCE, 1792.

(219)

CHAPTER XIII.

THE CONFERENCES FROM 1785 TO 1792.

ACCORDING to adjournment at Baltimore in the spring of 1784, notwitstanding the unexpected intervention of the Christmas Conference, three Conferences were held in the spring of 1785: the first at Green Hill's, North Carolina, April 20; the second at Mason's, Brunswick Co., Va., May 1; and the last, as usual, at Baltimore, June 1. All these slightly anticipated the appointed time.* Jesse Lee, who gives us these dates, also informs us that, in the original publications, "the business of the three Conferences was all arranged in the Minutes, as if it had all been done at one time and place," an arrangement also followed in the reprint of 1813. This continued to be the form of publication adopted for the General Minutes until 1802, when for the first time, the one traveling connection is divided into recognized Annual Conference bodies by separating and designating the appointment of the preachers as in the following Conferences: Western; South Carolina; Virginia; Baltimore; Philadelphia; New York; and New England.† The next year this improved arrangement is extended to the statistics of members in Society;‡ and in 1805 the division into Annual Conference groups is carried through the answers of all the disciplinary questions.§ Lee further says that "This year [1785] and the two succeeding years the Minutes were called ' Minutes of the General Conference of the Methodist Episcopal Church in America,' "‖ and, as he wrote in 1809, he is probably correct; but by 1813, the date of our earliest extant reprint, when the Quadrennial Dele-

---

* Minutes, ed. of 1813, p. 48.   † Minutes of 1813, pp. 275-281.
‡ Ibid., pp. 290-294.   § Ibid., pp. 325-355.
‖ Hist. of the Methodists, p. 118.

gated General Conference had already held one session, such an official heading would have been ambiguous, and then, if not in 1794, when John Dickins made the first collection of the Minutes, the change was probably made to the usual caption, " Minutes taken at the Several Annual Conferences," etc. It is probably safe to trace the conforming of the running titles of 1785, 1786, and 1787 with those of later date, to the hand of Dickins, since, when he published his General Minutes, the first General Conference of 1792 had been held. Lee gives an interesting notice of the rise of the presiding eldership, as we have outlined it in a preceding chapter, confirming our view that as early as 1785, the elder had charge of his circuit preachers. He says:

> The form of the Minutes of Conference was changed this year, and all the *elders* who were directed to take the oversight of several circuits were set to the right hand of a bracket, which inclosed all the circuits and preachers of which he was to take charge. This may be considered as the beginning of the presiding elder's office; although it was not known by that name at that time, yet, in the absence of a *superintendent*, this *elder* had the directing of all the preachers that were inclosed in the bracket against which his name was set.*

Three Conferences are appointed for 1786 and 1787, six for 1788, eleven for 1789, fourteen for 1790, extending from Georgia to New York and from Baltimore to Kentucky and Holstein; for 1792, the last year of our present period, seventeen were appointed.† We can no longer, however, follow these sessions even in the scanty detail which the extant sources afford, but must dismiss them with the remark that the Minutes cannot be depended upon for the sessions *actually held*, but only for those *appointed*. " Some, as for example, the first New York session, [1788] are unmentioned; others, like that designated in the printed list as of ' Connecticut' for 1791, did not meet." ‡

The only important business in the Conferences of 1785, as we have seen, was the suspension and virtual repeal of the slavery legislation of the Christmas Conference. Coke con-

---

* Hist. of the Methodists, pp. 119, 120.   † Minutes, 1813, pp. 55, 61, 68, 76, 85, 107.
‡ Stevens, Hist. M. E. Ch., II. 495.

tinued in America for about five months after the adjournment of that body, sailing for England June 2. Sunday, May 1, he is with Asbury at the Virginia Conference.

After mature consideration [he says] we formed a petition, a copy of which was given to every preacher, entreating the General Assembly of Virginia to pass a law for the immediate or gradual emancipation of all the slaves. It is to be signed by all the freeholders we can procure, and those I believe will not be few. There have been many debates already on the subject in the Assembly. Many of our friends, and some of the great men of the states, have been inciting us to apply for acts of incorporation, but I have discouraged it, and have prevailed. We have a better staff to lean upon than any this world can afford.

This was, doubtless, a better concerted scheme than that of emancipation by Church regulations; for, at this time, many of the statesmen and people of Virginia, as well as other parts of the South, were decidedly in favor of some method of gradual emancipation by law. By Jefferson's ordinance of 1784, though slavery then prevailed throughout much more than half the lands of Europe, it " was to be rung out with the departing century, so that in all the western territory, whether held in 1784 by Georgia, North Carolina, Virginia, or the United States, the sun of the new century might dawn on no slave." * Washington, Richard Henry Lee, Jefferson, Randolph, Madison, and Grayson desired the abolition of slavery.† The committee of eleven in the Constitutional Convention of 1787, to whom was referred the question of limiting the time of the legal toleration of the slave trade, reported in favor of the year 1800. It was moved and seconded that the time be extended to 1808. " Madison spoke earnestly against the prolongation; but, without further debate, the motion prevailed by the votes of the three New England States, Maryland, and the three southernmost States, against New Jersey, Pennsylvania, Delaware, and Virginia." ‡ At about the time when the Virginia Conference, under the lead of Coke and Asbury, was formulating and circulating its petition to the General Assembly for the immediate or gradual emancipation of the

---

* Bancroft, Hist. U. S., VI. 117. †*Ibid.*, VI. 262. ‡*Ibid.*, VI. 320.

slaves, Jefferson and Wythe, as commissioners to codify the laws of Virginia, had provided for gradual emancipation, which, however, the legislature of 1785 refused to do.* It was this movement in the civil realm, which, doubtless, the Virginia Conference in 1785 sought to foster and support. Washington's sentiments may be gathered from Coke's account of the interview, when he and Asbury dined by appointment at Mount Vernon:

> He received us [says Coke] very politely, and was very open to access. He is quite the plain country gentleman. After dinner we desired a private interview, and opened to him the grand business on which we came, presenting to him our petition for the emancipation of the negroes, and entreating his signature, if the eminence of his position did not render it inexpedient for him to sign any petition. He informed us that he was of our sentiments, and had signified his thoughts on the subject to most of the great men of the State; that he did not see it proper to sign the petition, but if the Assembly took it into consideration, would signify his sentiments to the Assembly by a letter.†

The Conferences of 1786 enacted nothing material to our history; but this year a second edition of the Sunday service was printed in London for the use of the American Methodists. Traces of the use of Mr. Wesley's prayer-book continue to be met with down to 1792: it was reprinted by order of the General Conference of the Methodist Episcopal Church, South, held in 1866, and its use made optional in the Churches. Gowns and bands were also used by the Bishops and elders for some years after the Christmas Conference. Jesse Lee attended a service conducted by Bishop Asbury in January 1785, and " to his very great surprise and no little mortification, just before the commencement of the service, Bishop Asbury came out of his room in full canonicals, gown, cassock, and band."

Mr. Asbury had evidently procured his canonicals immediately after his ordination as Bishop. Sunday, June 5,

---

* Bancroft, Hist. U. S., VI. 118.

† Drew, Life of Coke, pp. 108–113, speaks of Washington as, at this time, President of the United States which is, of course, an error. He seems to have confused this interview of the two Bishops with Washington in 1785 with an Address which they presented to the President in 1789, just after his inauguration, to which attention will be given later.

1785, he laid the corner-stone of Cokesbury College. "Attired in his long silk gown and with his flowing bands the pioneer Bishop of America took his position on the walls of the College." * To Asbury, who had been a life-long attendant on the services of the Church of England, this attire seemed no affectation in one occupying the position of a Bishop, but natural and necessary.

It was Wesley's desire that another *General* Conference, *i. e.*, an assembly of all the preachers, should be held in 1787, as may be gathered from the following letter:

LONDON, September 6, 1786.

DEAR SIR:—I desire that you would appoint a General Conference of all our preachers in the United States to meet at Baltimore on May 1, 1787, and that Mr. Richard Whatcoat may be appointed superintendent with Mr. Francis Asbury. I am, dear sir, your affectionate friend and brother.

JOHN WESLEY.

To the REV. DR. COKE.

Objections, which will presently be considered, were raised to the election of Whatcoat and he was not, at this time, made a Superintendent. Wesley also nominated Garrettson for Nova Scotia. Jesse Lee tells us that

When the business was taken under consideration, some of the preachers insisted that if he was ordained for that station, he should confine himself wholly to that place for which he was set apart. Mr. Garrettson did not feel freedom to enter into an obligation of that kind, and chose rather to continue as he was, and therefore was not ordained.†

This appears to harmonize with Garrettson's own account:

It was the desire of Mr. Wesley and others that I should be set apart for the superintendency of the work in Nova Scotia. My mind was divided. Man is a fallible creature. In the end I concluded not to leave the States, for thousands in this country are dear to me. On the whole we had a blessed Conference, and my appointment was to preside in the Peninsula. ‡

Thus the first attempt of the Methodist Episcopal Church to create a missionary bishop proved abortive. Garrettson had been ordained elder at the Christmas Conference and appointed to Nova Scotia, where his labors were extensive and successful. Wesley was so favorably impressed that

---

* Srickland's Asbury, p. 163.   † Hist. of the Methodists, p. 126.
‡ Autobiography, p. 220.

he requested his election and ordination as Superintendent for the British possessions in America, comprising the Canadas, the Northeastern provinces, and also the West Indies. Mr. Garrettson writes:

Dr. Coke, as Mr. Wesley's delegate and representative, asked me if I would accept of the appointment. I requested the liberty of deferring my answer until the next day. I think on the next day the doctor came to my room and asked me if I had made up my mind to accept of my appointment; I told him I had upon certain conditions. I observed to him that I was willing to go on a tour, and visit those parts to which I was appointed, for one year; and if there was a cordiality in the appointment among those whom I was requested to serve, I would return to the next Conference and receive ordination for the office of superintendent. His reply was, " I am perfectly satisfied," and he gave me a recommendatory letter to the brethren in the West Indies, etc. I had intended, as soon as Conference rose, to pursue my voyage to the West India Islands, to visit Newfoundland and Nova Scotia, and in the spring to return. What transpired in the Conference during my absence I know not; but I was astonished, when the appointments were read, to hear my name mentioned to preside in the Peninsula.

Thus it appears that partly through conditions imposed by the Conference, and partly through reluctance and delay on the part of the nominee, Mr. Wesley was disappointed in his desire that Garrettson should be made a Superintendent.

Dr. Coke did not escape without censure. He had sailed from the West Indies, where he had been organizing missions, for Charleston, S. C., February 10, 1787, arriving on the 28th. There he met Asbury and presided with him over the first session of the South Carolina Conference. The Baltimore Conference had been appointed the year before to meet at Abingdon, July 24, but Coke, while yet in Europe, had, according to Mr. Wesley's request, changed both the time and the place, naming Baltimore as the place and May 1 as the time. At this Conference Whatcoat's and Garrettson's nominations to the episcopacy were taken up, for final disposition. The result of the agitations was that Coke entered into an engagement with the body which, after all, amounted to little more than an agreement to refrain from the exercise of his episcopal powers while absent from the United States. It was couched in these terms:

I do solemnly engage by this instrument that I never will, by virtue of my office as Superintendent of the Methodist Episcopal Church during my absence from the United States of America, exercise any government whatever in the said Methodist Church during my absence from the United States. And I do also engage that I will exercise no privilege in the said Church when present in the United States, except that of ordaining, according to the regulations and law already existing or hereafter to be made in the said Church, and that of presiding when present in Conference, and lastly that of traveling at large. Given under my hand, the second day of May, in the year 1787. THOMAS COKE.
Witnesses: JOHN TUNNELL, JOHN HAGGERTY, NELSON REED.

Accordingly the Minutes for 1787 begin: "*Ques.* 1. Who are the superintendents of our Church for the United States? *Ans.* Thomas Coke (when present in the States) and Francis Asbury." *

The narrative of the Rev. Thomas Ware plainly points out what were the powers of which Dr. Coke deprived himself while present in the United States:

The liberty that he took in changing the time and place of holding the Conference gave serious offense to many of the preachers. But this was not all, nor even the chief matter, which caused some trouble at this Conference. Mr. Wesley had appointed Mr. Whatcoat a Superintendent, and instructed Dr. Coke to introduce a usage among us, to which, I may safely say, there was not one of the preachers inclined to submit, much as they loved and honored him. Mr. Wesley had been in the habit of calling his preachers together, not to legislate, but to confer. Many of them he found to be excellent counselors, and he heard them respectfully on the weighty matters which were brought before them; but the right to *decide* all questions he reserved to himself. This he deemed the more excellent way; and, as we had volunteered and pledged ourselves to obey, he instructed the Doctor, conformably to his own usage, to put as few questions to vote as possible, saying: "If you, Brother Asbury and Brother Whatcoat, are agreed, it is enough." To place the power of deciding all questions discussed, or nearly all, in the hands of the superintendents, was what could never be introduced among us—a fact which we thought Mr. Wesley could not but have known, had he known us as well as we ought to have been known by Dr. Coke. After all, we had none to blame as much as ourselves. In the first effusion of our zeal we had adopted a rule binding ourselves to obey Mr. Wesley; and this rule must be rescinded, or we must be content not only to receive Mr. Whatcoat as one of our superintendents, but also—as our brethren of the British Conference—with barely discussing subjects, and leaving the decision of them to two or three individuals. This was the chief cause of our rescinding the rule. All, however, did not vote to rescind it; some thought

* Ed. of 1813, p. 62.

it would be time enough to do so when our superintendents should claim to decide questions independently of the Conference, which it was confidently believed they never would do. . . . There were also suspicions entertained by some of the preachers, and perhaps by Mr. Asbury himself, that if Mr. Whatcoat were received as a superintendent, Mr. Asbury would be recalled. For this none of us were prepared.*

Jesse Lee goes a little more into detail about Whatcoat's rejection:

When this business was brought before the Conference most of the preachers objected, and would not consent to it. The reasons against it were: 1. That he was not qualified to take the charge of the Connection. 2. That they were apprehensive that if Mr. Whatcoat was ordained, Mr. Wesley would likely recall Mr. Asbury, and he would return to England. Dr. Coke contended that we were obliged to receive Mr. Whatcoat, because we had said in the minute adopted at the Christmas Conference when we were first formed into a Church in 1784, "During the life of the Rev. Mr. Wesley we acknowledge ourselves his sons in the gospel, ready in matters belonging to Church government to obey his commands." Many of the members of that Conference argued that they were not at the Conference when that engagement was entered into, and they did not consider themselves bound by it. Other preachers, who had said they were "ready to obey his commands," said they did not feel ready *now* to obey his command. The preachers at last agreed to depart from that engagement, which some of the elder brethren had formally entered into, and in the next printed Minutes that engagement was left out. They had made the engagement of their own accord, and among themselves; and they believed they had a right to depart therefrom when they pleased, seeing it was not a contract made with Mr. Wesley or any other person, but an agreement among themselves.

We have now before us the data, gathered from contemporary sources, for a proper estimate of the constitutional issues involved. The legislation of the Christmas Conference with regard to the election, duties, and amenability of a Superintendent had properly the force of constitutional law, at least until modified or repealed by the body which originated it, whether assembled at one time and place or scattered through the several sessions of the Annual Conferences. This was true of all the enactments of 1784, since they were passed by a majority vote of the entire traveling ministry. Consequently when the slavery legislation of 1784 proved impracticable, the Conferences of 1785 repealed it. It was

---

* Autobiography, pp. 129-131.

not competent for any other authority to do so. The year 1787 brought the test of the new system, which had been inaugurated in 1784. It was inevitable that sooner or later an issue would arise on some practical measure which would bring about a collision between the assumed powers of the American Conferences, where questions were decided by a majority of votes, and the supreme control of Mr. Wesley. Of the Founder, Bishop Asbury says that

He rigidly contended for a special and independent right of governing the chief minister or ministers of our order, which, in our judgment, went not only to put him out of office, but to remove him from the Continent to elsewhere, that our father saw fit; and that, notwithstanding our constitution and the right of electing every Church-officer, and more especially our Superintendent, yet we were told, "Not till after the death of Mr. Wesley our constitution could have its full operation."*

This was true so far as the operation of the Deed of Declaration was concerned in England, but had no relevancy to the enactments of the Christmas Conference for America. Asbury then cites the resolution of submission to Mr. Wesley in matters pertaining to Church government, adopted in 1784, which, he says, "we were called upon to give" and "which could not be dispensed with—it must be." † It would thus appear that this minute was exacted by Mr. Wesley by the mouth of his envoy, Dr. Coke. Unfortunately the competition of authority between Mr. Wesley and the Conference, which arose in 1787, as a consequence of the contradictory elements introduced, (apparently very innocently and almost unconsciously so far as the body of preachers was concerned,) into the constitution of 1784, has generally been treated as if the history of church government among the American Methodists began in 1784. But a series of twelve Annual Conferences had been held previously to that date, and Rankin's first Philadelphia Conference of 1773 had settled, for the time, at least, some consti-

* Letter to Rev. Joseph Benson, written Jan. 15, 1816, a little more than two months before Asbury's death. The letter is given in full in Paine's Life of McKendree, II. 293–308, Appendix.

† Paine, Life of McKendree, II. 296.

tutional questions touching the supreme authority of Mr. Wesley. All of the following events, we have minutely rehearsed and, as we have seen, troubles almost immediately arose. Bishop Asbury, in the letter to Benson cited above, throws some new light on his relations to Rankin and the correspondence with Wesley about Asbury's own recall to England:

Mr. Wesley wrote concerning Diotrephes [Rankin], honest George [Shadford], and Francis, " You three be as one; act by united counsels." But who was to do that with Diotrephes? Francis had a prior right of government, by special order and letter from Mr. Wesley, a few months after he had been in the country [when he succeeded Boardman, and before Rankin's arrival]; and if he could not exercise it in the cities, where the first missionaries that came over were located by necessity, (having no proper men to change with them,) yet Francis in the country endeavored to do the best he could. Matters did not fit well between Diotrephes and him, and poor Francis was charged with having a gloomy mind, and being very suspicious, etc. It would be presumed, because Francis was a little heady, that Diotrephes wrote to Mr. Wesley to call Francis home immediately. Be it as it might, Mr. Wesley wrote such a letter to Francis; and Francis wrote in answer, that he would prepare to return as soon as possible, whatever the sacrifice might be. Then Diotrephes said, " You cannot go; your labors are wanted here." Francis said, " Mr. Wesley has written for me; I must obey his order." Diotrephes said, " I will write to Mr. Wesley, and satisfy him." Shortly after came a letter from Mr. Wesley to Francis, in substance thus: " You have done very well to continue in America and help your brethren, when there was such a great call." *

It was doubtless with regard to the Baltimore appointment that Asbury, in extreme old age, was willing to confess frankly that he had been " a little heady." Much experience with refractory preachers had now taught him how seriously he had embarrassed Rankin's administration. But, from this time forward, there seems to have abode in Asbury's mind a constant fear, almost morbid, that, at some critical juncture, when his own views and policy clashed with Wesley's, the patriarch at home would cut short the controversy by recalling the American apostle to England. In 1783 Asbury had clearly indicated to Wesley his desire and, we may say, intention to remain at the head of the American itinerants. Wesley's letter received by Asbury, December 24,

*Paine, Life of McKendree, II. 307.

1783, was not so much an appointment as a recognition of Asbury's existing official headship in America. Coke's correspondence with Wesley before his departure on the American mission sufficiently reveals that the diplomatic foreign minister of Methodism was by no means confident of the reception he would meet with from Asbury, or that the American chief would easily consent to a sharing of his powers. Accordingly he promptly declined Dickins's proposal to make Mr. Wesley's plan public at New York before Mr. Asbury had been consulted. When the plan was first communicated to Asbury he was " shocked." Throughout the interval between Coke's arrival and the meeting of the Christmas Conference, it is evident from Asbury's Journal that his mind was troubled with many misgivings. He insisted on election by the Conference, and interposed the vote of the entire body of American itinerants between himself and the authority of Mr. Wesley. If Dr. Coke did not at first take in the full significance of this action, and the regulations concerning the Superintendents embodied in the Discipline of 1784, there can be no question that Mr. Wesley did. In a letter of October 31, 1789, published by Hammett in Charleston, Mr. Wesley alluded to the correspondence of 1783:

I was a little surprised when I received some letters from Mr. Asbury affirming that no person in Europe knew how to direct those in America. Soon after he flatly refused to receive Mr. Whatcoat in the character I sent him. He told George Shadford, "Mr. Wesley and I are like Cæsar and Pompey; he will bear no equal, and I will bear no superior." * And accordingly he quietly sat by until his friends voted my name out of the American Minutes. This completed the matter and showed that he had no connection with me.

If the preachers of the Christmas Conference innocently inserted the minute of submission, Mr. Asbury was not una-

---

* The biographers and historians who quote this letter commonly append a footnote to the effect that Mr. Wesley was mistaken in attributing this language to Asbury. It was doubtless an imprudence which Asbury sincerely regretted, but I know of no evidence that he ever denied it, though he had abundant opportunity to do so. Shadford was his bosom friend and stood also very close to Mr. Wesley; if Asbury ever used the language it was a private confidence to Shadford.

ware of its purpose and meaning. Wesley was, by common consent, a man of the keenest penetration, of unexampled common sense, and of the first abilities as an ecclesiastical statesman, likened, by competent authorities, to the greatest rulers in Church and State the world has ever produced. He had seen the growing tendency to independence in Asbury and the Americans. His heart was set on a perpetual, world-wide union of Methodists. He had been cut off from all control of the American Methodists during the Revolution. Their independence was inevitable, or Wesley would have arrested the tendency, if anybody could have done so. Asbury was a man of the same practical, and scarcely inferior, talents. He is the real founder of American Methodism. "I did not think it practical expediency," he says, "to obey Mr. Wesley at three thousand miles distance." But Mr. Wesley did; and here the issue was joined. The resolution of submission in 1784, which, Asbury says, "could not be dispensed with—it must be," was Wesley's measure, submitted according to his instructions by his representative, Dr. Coke, for destroying the centrifugal movement in America, and bringing all into subordination to himself. Asbury alone, among the Americans, comprehended the full import and bearing of the minute. Some dross of human infirmity may have mingled with his motives, but his heart was true to the cause of American autonomy. "I never approved of that binding minute," he says, under date of November 28, 1796, "at the first General Conference I was mute and modest when it passed; and I was mute when it was expunged."

In 1787, the underlying issue was, after all, not so much between Wesley and the Conference, or between Coke and the Conference, as between the Wesleyan and Asburyan policies for the government and development of American Methodism. Coke, no doubt, undertook honestly and zealously to carry out the wishes and instructions of Mr. Wesley. In so doing, he came into collision with the Conference and, for a time, forfeited the sympathies of Bishop Asbury. Coke says in his Journal that when he arrived in the country, in the latter part of February, 1787, on his way, according to Mr. Wesley's instructions, to hold a "General Conference," he was "very coolly" received by Asbury. Nevertheless, Asbury acquiesced in Wesley's nomination of Whatcoat for the superintendency, and at the first South Carolina Conference, held in Charleston, with both the Superintendents present, the nomination was confirmed. At the Virginia Conference, however, serious opposition was made by James O'Kelly, who declared that he did not consider Whatcoat "adequate to the task on account of his age, and also that he was a stranger in the wilderness of America." The era of the modern palace-car Bishop had not yet dawned; and O'Kelly may have entertained a sneaking notion that he was better qualified for the office than Whatcoat. It was, however, agreed in Virginia that the matter should be finally disposed of at the Baltimore Conference, "on condition," as Nicholas Snethen says, "that the Virginia Conference might send a deputy to explain their sentiments." According to Snethen, "a vote was taken that Richard Whatcoat should not be ordained Superintendent, and that Mr. Wesley's name should for the future be left off the American Minutes. Mr. Asbury neither made the motion nor advocated it; the whole case was constitutionally carried through the Conference and voted by a fair majority. Mr. Asbury, indeed, foresaw the consequence when the question was in contemplation, and informed the patrons of it that he expected all the blame would be imputed to him, if it should be carried." *

It is evident from the letter in which Mr. Wesley directed Dr. Coke to call a General Conference at Baltimore, May 1, 1787, that he understood the contradictory principles which the Christmas Conference had bound up together in the constitution of the Church. The resolution of submission, literally interpreted, empowered him to appoint superintendents. But the resolution was general, and the directions for electing a superintendent, placed in the Discipline of 1784,

---

* Reply to Mr. O'Kelly's Apology.

particular. Wesley himself saw that the resolution, practically, must be interpreted in the light of the law, especially as Asbury had been elected in 1784. Consequently he did not venture beyond nomination in the case of Whatcoat and Garrettson, submitting their election to the voice of a General Conference to be called for the purpose. But here loomed up the ancient spectre of Asbury's removal:

Early in 1787 [says Mr. Morrell], Mr. Wesley intimated a design of removing Mr. Asbury from America to Europe, and of sending us a Superintendent of his own nomination. When the Conference assembled, some of the eldest and most sensible of the elders observed that Mr. Wesley had no authority to remove Mr. Asbury, much less could he impose a Superintendent on us without our choice; for it was written in our constitution that "no person should be ordained a Superintendent over us without the consent of the majority of the Conference;" that no such consent had been given; that though they highly venerated Mr. Wesley, and were willing to receive his advice, and preserve and promote our union with him, and our Methodist brethren in Europe, as far as the political interest of our country would authorize us; yet they could not give up their rights to any man on earth. And after a number of arguments to show the impropriety and impolicy of any man having the power to exercise such an uncontrollable and unlimited authority over us, as Mr. Wesley wished to do, and to prevent him from exercising this power in the present case, by virtue of his name standing at the head of the Minutes, they moved that it should be struck off. The vote was carried and his name was omitted. Mr. Wesley complained that we were ungrateful. We felt ourselves grieved that the good old man was hurt, and determined to give him every satisfaction in our power, consistent with our rights, and in 1789 the Conference consented that his name should be restored on the Minutes, in testimony of our union with and respect for him; but inserted in such a manner as to preclude him from exercising an unconstitutional power over us. *

Dr. Coke, though at first disposed to indulge in public complaint, submitted with a good grace. Many thought that the shepherd of the Methodist flock had received a heavy blow in the house of his friends, and fears were entertained of a schism among the American Methodists. Later O'Kelly publicly charged that " after these things Francis took with him a few chosen men, and in a clandestine manner expelled John whose surname was Wesley from the Methodist Episcopal Church." But Snethen amply vindicated Asbury against this attack. In his Journal, Coke says:

---

*Rev. Thomas Morrell, in " Truth Discovered."

Our painful contests, I trust, have produced the most indissoluble union between my brethren and me. We thoroughly perceived the mutual purity of each other's intentions in respect to the points in dispute. We mutually yielded and mutually submitted, and the silken cords of love and affection were tied to the horns of the altar forever and ever.

It is now easy to grasp the import of the certificate which Dr. Coke gave to this Conference. The embassador fell with his chief, the agent with his principal, the servant with his master. There is no evidence, known to the writer, that the Conference formally demanded this instrument: Coke, in a revulsion of feeling and exuberance of zeal, brought about by the Conference atmosphere in which he moved, probably made a voluntary tender of it, which the Conference did not decline. The language of the document is that of personal surrender of privileges, hitherto exercised, rather than that of enforced restraint by a controlling tribunal. Coke's language in his Journal, "We mutually yielded and mutually submitted" lends support to this view. When abroad he was to exercise no episcopal functions, since he could not have the latest advices as to the state of affairs in America and would be more or less subjected to alien influences. But when in America he was (1) to preside in the Conferences, (2) to ordain, and (3) to travel at large. But these embrace all the duties and privileges of a General Superintendent. He agreed to "use no other power," says Stevens, "when in the country than that of his Episcopal functions." * The Minutes placed him on a perfect parity with Asbury when in the United States. "Who are the Superintendents of our Church for the United States?" the first question reads in 1787. "Thomas Coke (when present in the States) and Francis Asbury" is the answer.† Why then did Coke engage that he would exercise no other privilege when present in the United States? What privilege can be referred to? Evidently the privilege of being the proposer, patron, and special champion of such measures as Mr. Wesley might seek to introduce under cover of the resolution of submission, together with the de-

* Hist. M. E. Ch., II. 496. † Minutes, ed. 1813, p. 62.

cision of questions before the Conference by the Superintendents, as Wesley wished, instead of by a majority vote of
the body.* Ware's testimony, cited above, is decisive on
this latter point. That binding minute was rescinded, and
Coke, to guarantee his loyalty, surrendered all functions he
had been accustomed to exercise as Mr. Wesley's special
envoy and personal representative. The Conference protected itself by incorporating in the Minutes, as we have
seen, the limitation springing out of Coke's agreement, and
there can be no question that the year 1787 marks a great
forward stride in home government for the American
Church. The principle for which Asbury and the Conference stood triumphed over that represented by Coke and
Wesley: the binding minute was expunged never to be restored, and the Founder's name was temporarily left off the
Minutes. Much has been written about the curtailment of
Coke's "episcopal powers," by vote of the Conference,
which is wide of the mark. Coke was as much a Bishop,
when in America, after the adjournment at Baltimore in
1787, as he had been before that Conference met. Both
before and after he was as much a Bishop as Asbury. His
name always appears first in the Minutes. "It was also
my pleasure, when present," writes Asbury to Benson in
1816, "always to give Dr. Coke the president's chair." †
It is not in evidence that any vote of the Conference was
taken in Coke's case. Jesse Lee says, "He acknowledged
his faults, begged pardon, and promised not to meddle with
our affairs again when he was out of the United States."
Lee was not an admirer of Coke's and his testimony may be
relied upon as none too favorable. He adds, "He then
gave in writing a certificate to the same purpose" and cites
the certificate in full. From him, so far as we are aware,
all other writers have taken their copy of this document. It

---

* As late as 1806, however, according to William Watters (Life. p. 105),
in case of an equal division in the Conference, the Bishop exercised the
right of giving the casting vote; and until 1808 the Bishops offered resolutions in the General Conference and discussed them.

† Paine's Life of McKendree, II. 294.

must not be forgotten, finally, that Coke's position was peculiar and anomalous. There has never been another like it and, in the nature of the case, cannot be. Originally appointed and ordained a Superintendent by Wesley, and continuing to hold official relations to the British Conference as well as to the American, the position of Mr. Wesley's representative and vehicle of personal communication in America was unique, and cannot be brought under any general rule. To undertake to do so is to ignore history and lose sight of material particulars amid the glitter of confusing generalities. Coke's relations to American Conferences will come up again, however, and a candid discussion and correct interpretation of later facts must not be anticipated.

It remains to determine the character of this Conference of 1787. In view of Wesley's letter of instructions to Coke, the business transacted, and some other considerations, it is not surprising that the claim has been set up that this was a General Conference. "It is singular how plausible the argument for the affirmative appears," remarks Stevens, "and yet how decisive that of the negative really is." We present a brief summary of the evidence for and against. Those who contend that the Baltimore session of 1787 was a General Conference bring forward the following proofs:

(1) Mr. Wesley wrote to Dr. Coke, "I desire that you would appoint a General Conference of all our preachers in the United States, to meet at Baltimore on May 1, 1787."

(2) The business to be transacted was the election of Superintendents, and, as a matter of fact, this Conference did canvass the names of Mr. Wesley's two nominees and reject them both.

(3) Coke did invite the preachers by correspondence to attend a General Conference.

(4) The Baltimore Conference, which had been appointed the year before for Abingdon, Md., July 24, 1787, did, in fact, meet in Baltimore, May 1, the place and time proposed by Wesley.

In the absence of evidence to the contrary, these statements of facts would have to be accepted as decisive proofs. But the contrary evidence is conclusive. Let us consider it.

(1) The facts of Wesley's requesting and Coke's calling a General Conference and his changing the time and place of the Baltimore session are not denied. But, though Coke did these things, Asbury and the preachers dissented. Asbury received Coke "very coolly" on his arrival in Charleston, and the Conference itself rebuked him for his presumption. Moreover, Wesley's name was dropped from the Minutes, and the resolution of submission was expunged.

(2) Neither Whatcoat nor Garrettson was elected.

(3) "That many of the measures of the sessions of 1787–88 were of a general character," says Stevens, "appropriate only to the general action of the ministry, cannot be denied, but this fact can be easily explained. The first General Conference (of 1784) assembled for the organization of the Church, and having accomplished its business, adjourned witnout providing for any subsequent session. General as well as local business went on as before. Measures of a general character were submitted to the successive Annual Conferences, and, at the final session of the year, were considered to be determined by the majority of votes in all; the Minutes of all appeared still, in print, as the records of but one conference; and their enactments were from time to time inserted in the Discipline without reference to where or how they were enacted. Now it so happened that the Baltimore session for 1787 was the last session for that year, and therefore its reported doings were given as the results of all the sessions of the year; that is to say, not of a General Conference, but of the Conferences generally. I am also of the opinion, from scattered allusions in contemporary books, that not a few important measures, applying to the whole Church, were decided by one or two of the principal Conferences, without reference to the remoter sessions."

(4) Jesse Lee, the earliest historian of the Church, was present in 1787 and stationed in Baltimore; yet he does not speak of the session as a General Conference, but numbers it among the other annual sessions.

(5) Lee does distinctly name the session of 1792 as "the first regular General Conference."

(6) James O'Kelly, when he withdrew from the Church, five years later, in his pamphlet against Asbury accused him of excessive "sharpness" toward Coke at Charleston. About fourteen years after the alleged General Conference, Asbury writes: "There was no sharpness at all upon my side with Dr. Coke, at Charleston, respecting the *proposed* General Conference, (*which was afterward held* in 1792.) I was fully convinced that nothing *else* would finish the un-happy business with O'Kelly, and that did finish it."

Coke says, in his letter to the General Conference of 1808,

> There are few of you who can possibly recollect anything of what I am next going to add. Many of you were then only little children. We had at that time [1791] no regular General Conference. One only had been held in the year 1784. I had indeed, with great labor and fatigue, a few months before I wrote this letter to Bishop White, prevailed on James O'Kelly to submit to the decision of a General Conference. This Conference was to be held in about a year and a half after my departure from the States. And at this Conference, held, I think, the latter end of 1792, I proposed and ob-tained that great blessing to the American connection, a permanency for General Conferences, which were to be held at stated times. Previously to the holding of this Conference (except the general one held in 1784) there were only small district meetings, excepting the council which was held at Cokesbury College either in 1791 or 1792.

And here the case may be rested: the Baltimore Confer-ence of 1787 was *not* a General Conference, nor did one meet until 1792.*

In 1787 the Discipline underwent a complete revision. For the first time it was arranged in sections under appro-priate heads. This was done by Bishop Asbury, with the aid, chiefly clerical, of John Dickins. As early as Nov. 27, 1785, he says in his Journal, "For some time past, I had not been quite satisfied with the order and arrangement of our Form of Discipline; and, persuaded that it might be im-proved without difficulty, we accordingly set about it, and, during my confinement [with a disabled foot] in James' City, completed the work, arranging the subject matter thereof

---

*The preceding arguments have been mainly condensed from Stevens.

under their proper heads, divisions, and sections." April
5, 1786, he writes, "Read our Form of Discipline in manuscript, which brother Dickins has been preparing for the
press." The publication was delayed, however, until May,
1787, "probably with a view of obtaining the concurrence
of Dr. Coke;" * but there is no evidence that it was submitted to the Baltimore Conference which met at that time. In
this Discipline the superintendents were first called Bishops,
and from it the second question of the former Discipline,
embracing the resolution of submission to Mr. Wesley, was
omitted. This omission is proof that this Discipline was not
published until after the Baltimore Conference of May, 1787,
which took this action: the introduction of the title "bishop,"
without the sanction of this Conference, but for which Conference confirmation was subsequently asked, is proof that
this edition of the Discipline, newly revised and arranged as
it was, was not submitted to the inspection or approval of
the Conference, but was published by authority of the Bishops. Asbury and Coke were hardly shorn of all espiscopal
prerogatives, and an unfastidious Church, in whose memory
the powers long exercised by General Assistants were still
fresh, did not deny them these privileges. Jesse Lee says:

The third question in the second section, and the answer, read thus:
Ques. Is there any other business to be done in Conference? *Ans.* The
electing and ordaining of bishops, elders, and deacons. This was the first
time that our superintendents ever gave themselves the title of bishops in
the Minutes. They changed the title themselves, without the consent of
the Conference; and at the next Conference they asked the preachers if the
word *bishop* might stand in the Minutes—seeing that it was a Scripture name,
and the meaning of the word *bishop* was the same with that of *superintendent.* Some of the preachers opposed the alteration, and wished to retain the
former title; but a majority of the preachers agreed to let the word *bishop*
remain; and in the Annual Minutes for the next year the first question is,
Who are the bishops of our Church for the United States? In the third
section of this Form of Discipline, and in the sixth page, it is said: We have
constituted ourselves into an *Episcopal Church* under the direction of *bishops,
elders, deacons,* and *preachers,* according to the form of ordination annexed to
our prayer-book, and the regulations laid down in this Form of Discipline.
From that time the name of bishop has been in common use among us,
both in conversation and in writing.†

° Emory, History of Discipline, p. 81. † History of the Methodists, pp. 128, 129.

The Minutes of 1787 retain the title "Superintendents;"* in 1788, the question is first asked, "Who are the Bishops of our Church for the United States?" The answer is, "Thomas Coke, Francis Asbury," the qualifying clause with regard to Coke, "when present in the States," being omitted.† This is fresh proof that the Discipline of 1787 was published after the Conference of that year: the "next Conference," referred to by Lee, which confirmed the change made by the Bishops in the Discipline, was the Conference of 1788.

Referring to the eleven Conferences appointed for 1789, Lee says that "several of these Conferences were within thirty or forty miles of each other, which was pretty generally disliked; but at that time the bishop had the right of appointing as many Conferences as he thought proper, and at such times and places as he judged best." ‡ He gives us, also, the best account of the manner of the formal restoration of Mr. Wesley's name to the Minutes, in 1789, without the reënactment of the resolution of submission.

As some persons had complained of our receding from a former engagement made by some of our preachers, that "during the life of Mr. Wesley, in matters belonging to Church government, they would obey his commands," and as others had thought that we did not pay as much respect to Mr. Wesley as we ought, the bishops introduced a question in the Annual Minutes, which was as follows: *Ques.* Who are the persons that exercise the episcopal office in the Methodist Church in Europe and America? *Ans.* John Wesley, Thomas Coke, and Francis Asbury, by regular order and succession. The next question was asked differently from what it had ever been in any of the former Minutes, which stands thus: *Ques.* Who had been elected by the unanimous suffrages of the General Conference to superintend the Methodist Connection in America? *Ans.* Thomas Coke and Francis Asbury. §

Both Lee, as above, and Bangs give the clause, "by regular order and succession," though it is not contained in

---

* Ed. of 1813, p. 62.

† Minutes, p. 69. Lee also says, "When the Minutes of this year were printed, the condition of Dr. Coke's being a bishop when in the United States," was left out.

‡ History of the Methodists, p. 140.

§ *Ibid.*, p. 142.

16

the reprint of the Minutes in 1813. Mr. Tyerman follows them as noted above.* The Bishops doubtless framed the two questions, as Lee says, by which Mr. Wesley's name was restored, and his powers discriminated from their own, but the substance of them was passed upon by all the Annual Conferences. Coke's testimony is decisive on this point:

> On the 9th of March [he says] we began our Conference in Georgia. Here we agreed (as we have ever since in each of the Conferences) that Mr. Wesley's name should be inserted at the head of our Small Annual Minutes and also in the Form of Discpline,—in Small Minutes, as the fountain of our episcopal office; and in the Form of Discipline, as the father of the whole work, under the divine guidance. To this all the Conferences have cheerfully and unanimously agreed.

So Mr. Wesley's name stood in the American Minutes of 1789 and 1790:† before those of 1791 were issued the Founder of Methodism had joined the general assembly and church of the firstborn.

The New York Conference of 1789 voted an address to President Washington, in recognition of the new federal constitution, and the first chief magistrate elected under it. Dickins and Morrell waited on Washington, and he designated May 29 for the reception of the Bishops and the presentation of the Address. He had previously entertained them, as we have seen, under his own roof at Mount Vernon. Asbury "with great self-possession," says Morrell, "read the address in an impressive manner. The President read his reply with fluency and animation. They interchanged their respective addresses; and, after sitting a few minutes, we departed." In a few days, the other denominations followed this Methodist lead.

There is nothing else in the action of the Annual Conferences down to the assembling of the first General Conference in 1792 that affects the constitution or government of the Church sufficiently to demand notice in our history.

---

* Page 16. † Ed. 1813, pp. 77, 90.

CHAPTER XIV.

THE COUNCIL.

THE need of a General Conference, equally with the difficulties, apparently insuperable, in the way of convening such an assembly, began to press heavily upon the Church. "*If* the early custom of carrying general measures from one conference to another, till all had acted upon them, still continued," remarks Stevens, "it had now become exceedingly inconvenient." * Well may this judicious historian express this doubt: it is highly probable that measures of prime importance or pressing urgency were sometimes determined upon by leading Conferences, occasionally by one such body, especially if the last of the year, or by the Superintendents themselves, acting on their own responsibility. The general usage, however, was still to pass legislation through all the Conferences.

To meet the demands of the hour, the bishops—Bishop Asbury, in particular—devised the plan of " The Council," and laid it before the Conferences of 1789. This plan, after some debate and opposition, was adopted by a majority of the preachers,† as follows:

1. Our bishops and presiding elders shall be the members of this Council; provided, that the members who form the Council be never fewer than nine. And if any unavoidable circumstance prevent the attendance of a presiding elder at the Council, he shall have authority to send another elder out of his own district to represent him; but the elder so sent by the absenting elder shall have no seat in the Council without the approbation of the bishop, or bishops, and presiding elders present. And if, after the above-mentioned provisions are complied with, any unavoidable circumstance or any contingencies reduce the number to less than nine, the bishop shall immediately summon such elders as do not preside, to complete the number.

2. These shall have authority to mature everything that they shall judge expedient: (1) To preserve the general union. (2) To render and preserve

---

* Hist. M. E. Ch., III. 12.   † Lee, Hist. of the Methodists, p. 149.

the external form of worship similar in all our societies through the continent. (3) To preserve the essentials of the Methodist doctrines and discipline pure and uncorrupted. (4) To correct all abuses and disorders; and, lastly, they are authorized to mature everything they may see necessary for the good of the Church, and for the promoting and improving our colleges and plan of education.

3. Provided, nevertheless, that nothing shall be received as the resolution of the Council, unless it be assented to unanimously by the Council; and nothing so assented to by the Council shall be binding in any district till it has been agreed upon by a majority of the Conference which is held for that district.

4. The bishops shall have authority to summon the Council to meet at such times and places as they shall judge expedient.

5. The first Council shall be held at Cokesbury, on the first day of next December [1789].

In this plan the title "presiding elder" occurs for the first time in the official records of our Church. It is used, also, in the Minutes of 1789,* doubtless to conform them to the language of the plan: the title then disappears from the Minutes until 1797, as previously noticed.

There were several capital and, as the event proved, fatal defects, in this scheme. The passage of such a measure through the Conferences is proof of Asbury's commanding influence in those bodies, rather than of his wisdom in devising the plan. Its cardinal faults are these: (1) the requirement of unanimous assent in the Council virtually gave Bishop Asbury—for Bishop Coke was not present at either of the sessions held—an absolute veto on all proposed legislation for the Church; (2) the presiding elders, being the appointees of the bishops, removable from office at their pleasure, were not representatives of the Conferences or of the Church, but the delegates of the episcopacy: the composition of the Council was thus, for the most part, in the hands of Bishop Asbury alone; (3) the provision that the enactments of the Council should have the force of law only in those districts whose Conferences confirmed them, threatened the Connexion with speedy disunion and disintegration, for, said Jesse Lee, who stoutly opposed the plan from the beginning, "if one district should agree to any impor-

---

* Ed. of 1813, pp. 81–84.

tant point, and another district should reject it, the union between the two districts would be broken, and in process of time our United Societies would be thrown into disorder and confusion." Thus the Council, though apparently clothed with large powers, for so small a body, in reality could exercise but little, and that little for the destruction rather than the edification of the infant Church. Nullification was incorporated in the constitution, and even a useful measure could be rendered hurtful by the rejection of a single District—*i. e.*, Annual—Conference, which would thereby create a difference of administration, if not positive schism, in the body ecclesiastic. The plan was as if each Annual Conference, at the present day, were empowered to confirm the legislation of our General Conference, before it could have legal force within the bounds of that Conference.

Lee has preserved entire the Minutes of the first session, of which the chief points follow:

The proceedings of the Bishop and Presiding Elders of the Methodist Episcopal Church, in Council assembled at Baltimore, on the first day of December, 1789.

The following members which formed the Council were present: Francis Asbury, Bishop; Elders: Richard Ivey, Reuben Ellis, Edward Morris, James O'Kelly, Philip Bruce, Lemuel Green, Nelson Reid, Joseph Everett, John Dickins, James O. Cromwell, Freeborn Garrettson.

After having spent one hour in prayer to Almighty God for his direction and blessing, they then unanimously agreed, that a General Conference of the bishops, ministers, and preachers of the Methodist Episcopal Church, on the Continent of America, would be attended with a variety of difficulties, with great expense and loss of time, as well as many inconveniencies to the work of God. And, as it is almost the unanimous judgment of the ministers and preachers that it is highly expedient there should be a general Council formed of the most experienced elders in the connection, who, for the future, being elected by ballot in every Conference, at the request of the bishop, shall be able to represent the several Conferences and districts in the United States of America, they therefore concluded that such a Council should be so appointed, and convened. The Council then proceeded to form the following constitution, to wit:

The aforesaid Council, when assembled at the time and place appointed by the bishop, shall have power to mature and resolve on all things relative to the spiritual and temporal interests of the Church, viz.:

1. To render the time and form of public worship as similar as possible through all their congregations.

2. To preserve the general union of the ministers, preachers, and people in the Methodist doctrine and discipline. . . . . . .

6. In the intervals of the Council, the bishop shall have power to act in all contingent occurrences relative to the printing business, or the education and economy of the college.

7. Nine members, and no less, shall be competent to form a Council, which may proceed to business.

8. No resolution shall be formed in such a Council without the consent of the bishop and two-thirds of the members present.

After the Council had completed its own constitution, it unanimously proposed eight resolutions, of which the only one of sufficient importance to engage our attention is the first:

Every resolution of the first Council shall be put to vote in each Conference, and shall not be adopted unless it obtains a majority of the different Conferences. But every resolution which is received by a majority of the several Conferences shall be received by every member of each Conference.

Here is a serious attempt to relieve the obvious difficulties and objections to which the original plan was exposed. The resolution, cited above, was doubtless intended to submit the items of the new constitution, adopted by the Council itself, to the confirmation of the District, or Annual, Conferences, since the " resolutions of the *first* Council " are specially mentioned.

Whether this resolution itself was submitted to the Conferences, under the condition of the original plan, that nothing " shall be binding in any district till it has been agreed upon by a majority of the Conference " for that district, is more than doubtful. This was a source of additional trouble, for Lee complains:

When the Council was first proposed, the preachers in each district were to have the power to reject or retain the measures which had been adopted by the Council. But when the proceedings of the Council came out, they had changed the plan, and determined that if a majority of the preachers in the different districts should approve of the proceedings of the Council, it should then be binding on every preacher in each district.

Thus the Council had made an alteration for the better, but the Conferences doubted its power to do so. The Bishop's veto is expressly retained; but the requirement of unanimous action in the Council is altered to a two-thirds majority. Moreover, the composition of the body is made dependent on election by the Conferences. These were vital concessions and improvements, necessary even to an experimental working of the plan. They indicate the purity of Bishop Asbury's motives and his willingness to reach any accommodation with the Conferences and preachers, which would secure the benefits of a general and uniform government for the Connexion. He regarded the Council as in part a device for relieving his responsibilities, increasing his amenability, and curtailing his powers.

Can you think it right that the Bishops or Bishop—as the chief lies upon myself—should have the sole government of our college and schools, [he writes to Morrell, soon after the adjournment of the first Council,] unaided by the counsel of the wisest and most able of our brethren, whom I hope the wisdom of the Conferences will elect? Ought he not to try to be guarded better and have a Council, as so many witnesses to his probity and transactions, and a security that he may not run headlong to make the community insolvent? The profits arising from printing, if that work is prudently conducted, will, ere long, make one thousand per year. We have told the public how these profits shall be applied, and they expect that we not only mean, but will do, what we promise. Now as the train of this was laid by me, it ought not to be and cannot be taken out of my hands altogether as the Bishop of the Church—as in some sense to many the father of the Connection, unless it can be proved I have done wickedly. As to acting weakly, I may have done so. Therefore I want good and frequent counsel. I can ask the Conferences, but I cannot drag the business twelve or thirteen times through Conferences; that is enough to tire the spirit of Moses and Job.

From his Journal we learn that in this first session, Ivey represented the Georgia District or Conference; Ellis, the South Carolina; Morris, the North Carolina; Bruce, the North Virginia; O'Kelly, the South Virginia; Green, the Ohio; Reid, the Western Shore of Maryland; Everett, the Eastern Shore; Dickins, Pennsylvania; Cromwell, Jersey; and Garrettson, New York. Thus the Council was truly representative and connexional, and Asbury adds, "A spirit of union pervaded the whole body; producing blessed effects and fruits." *

Jesse Lee, unaware of these proposed reforms, emanating

---

* Journal, II. 59: Dec. 4, 1789.

from the Council itself, addressed a letter to the body pointing out the errors and evils of the plan. He received an official reply, dated "In Council, Baltimore, December 7, 1789:"

VERY DEAR BROTHER: We are both grieved and surprised to find that you make so many objections to the very fundamentals of Methodism. But we consider *your want of experience* in many things, and therefore put the best construction on your intention. You are acquainted with the discipline of the Methodist Church: if you can *quietly* labor among us under our discipline and rules, we cheerfully retain you as our brother and fellow-laborer, and remain yours in sincere affection.*

Attached to this epistle was the signature of James O'Kelly, as one of the members of the Council. Scarcely had he returned from the session, however, before he began a course of determined and systematic opposition to Asbury and the Council. He had been ordained elder at the Christmas Conference, and from that time had continued without interruption on the South Virginia District: as a leader his position and influence were hardly inferior to that of Asbury himself. He charged, "That Francis refused two worthy ministers a seat in Council in his absolute manner, without rendering any reason for such conduct;" to which Nicholas Snethen replied, "Mr. Asbury asked leave of the District Conferences to meet all the presiding elders in Council at Baltimore. Two preachers, it appears, who were not presiding elders, asked leave to sit in the Council, but Mr. A. had no authority to grant them their request." January 12, 1790, Asbury writes:

I received a letter from the presiding elder of this district, James O'Kelly: he makes heavy complaints of my power, and bids me stop for one year, or he must use his influence against me—power! power! there is not a vote given in a Conference in which the presiding elder has not greatly the advantage of me. . . . But who has the power to lay an embargo on me, and to make of none effect the decision of all the Conferences of the union? †

The Council and its legislation came before the Conferences of 1790. February 15, Asbury is at the South Carolina Conference, and records, "The business of the Coun-

---

* Dr. L. M. Lee, Life and Times of Jesse Lee, p. 282. † Journal, II. 62.

cil came before us; and it was determined that the concerns
of the college and the printing should be left with the Council to act decisively upon; but that no new canons should be
made, nor the old altered, without the consent of the Conference." *   June 1, he is holding the North Carolina Conference, and says, " Our business was much matured, the
critical concern of the Council understood, and the plan,
with its amendments [proposed by the Council] adopted." †
At the Virginia Conference, June 16, the Bishop records,
"All was peace until the Council was mentioned. The
young men appear to be entirely under the influence of the
elders, and turned it out of doors. I was weary and felt
but little freedom to speak on the subject. The business is
to be explained to every preacher; and then it must be carried through the Conferences twenty-four times; *i. e.*,
through all the Conferences for two years." ‡   August 26,
he says, "To conciliate the minds of our brethren in the
south district of Virginia, who are restless about the Council, I wrote their leader [O'Kelly] informing him, 'that I
would take my seat in council as another member;' and, in
that point, at least, waive the claims of Episcopacy;—yea, I
would lie down and be trodden upon, rather than knowingly
injure one soul." §   September 14, " We held our Conference for the eastern shore of Maryland and Delaware. One
or two of our brethren felt the Virginia fire about the question of the Council, but all things came into order and the
Council obtained." ǁ   September 23, "The Conference
began in poor Pennsylvania district. . . . I am weak
and have been busy, and am not animated by the hope of
doing good here; I have therefore been silent the whole
week." ¶   He did not have the heart even to mention the
Council. But at the New Jersey Conference, at Burlington, September 28, " Harmony has prevailed and the Council has been unanimously adopted." **

---

* Journal, II. 65.   † *Ibid.*, II. 76.   ‡ *Ibid.*, II. 76.   § *Ibid.*, II. 82.   ǁ *Ibid.*, II. 83.
¶ *Ibid.*, II. 83.   ** *Ibid.*, II. 84.

In O'Kelly's district was a young preacher, William Mc-Kendree by name. September 27, 1790, his presiding elder held his quarterly meeting. "We had a melting time at sacrament," says McKendree, in his diary, "and then the poor miserable Council took up all our time until ten o'clock at night."* Early in November, nearly a month before the second session of the Council, which he did not attend, O'Kelly called an irregular meeting of the preachers of his district. "On Thursday, Nov. 4," says McKendree, "met the preachers in conference at Brother Young's; twenty-two preachers present, and by nine o'clock agreed to send no member to Council, but stand as we are until next Conference." This Conference session had been convened by "proclamation of Mr. O'Kelly, inviting the preachers to meet in Mecklenburg." On the second day of this called Conference, a document was approved and directed to be forwarded to the Council, "thus placing the Virginia Conference," adds Bishop Paine, "almost in the position of seceders." †

Lee has carefully preserved the Minutes of the second session of the Council, also, from which a brief extract may embody the important points:

Minutes, taken at a Council of the Bishop, and Delegated Elders of the Methodist Episcopal Church, held at Baltimore, in the State of Maryland, December 1, 1790.

Q. What members are present? A. Francis Asbury, bishop: Freeborn Garrettson, Francis Poythress, Nelson Reid, John Dickins, Philip Bruce, Isaac Smith, Thomas Bowen, James O. Cromwell, Joseph Everett, and Charles Connaway.

Q. What power do the Council consider themselves invested with by their electors? A. First they unanimously consider themselves invested with full power to act decisively in all temporal matters. And secondly, to recommend to the several Conferences any new canons, or alterations to be made in any old ones.

Q. When and where shall the next Council be held? A. At Cokesbury College or Baltimore, on the 1st day of December, 1792.

"But," continues Lee, "their proceedings gave such dissatisfaction to our Connexion in general, and to some of the traveling preachers in particular, that they were forced to

---

* Paine, Life of McKendree, I. 113. † *Ibid.*, I. 128.

abandon the plan; and there has never since been a meeting of the kind." *

Lee tells us that in his letter to the Council at its first session he " contended for a General Conference, which plan was disapproved of by all the Council." His biographer says, " Notwithstanding the unceremonious rejection of his letter and himself, by the Council of 1789, he maintained his position and his principles; and in July, 1791, submitted a plan for a delegated General Conference in 1792 to Bishop Asbury. . . . There may have been an earlier advocate of such a measure, but we have not discovered it." † " This day," writes Asbury, July 7, 1791, " Jesse Lee put a paper into my hand proposing the election of not less than two, nor more than four preachers from each Conference, to form a General Conference in Baltimore, in December, 1792, to be continued annually." ‡ Stevens concedes that Lee is " entitled to the credit of being the author of the change, which, though resisted for sixteen years, was at last forced upon the body in 1808 by irresistible necessity." § At that time, however, Lee's persistent opposition on minor points endangered the passage of the whole measure.

But Mr. O'Kelly also contributed, in his way, towards securing a General Conference, as the only sufficient remedy for the ills that were then afflicting the Church. He had written to Dr. Coke in England, and had created a temporary alienation, once more, between the two Superintendents. " It is nothing strange," says Snethen, " that Dr. Coke should be affected by Mr. O'Kelly's representation of Mr. Asbury's conduct; and finding Mr. Asbury averse to a General Conference, it is not surprising that the Doctor should insist upon Mr. O'Kelly's request being granted. A few sharp words passed between the two Bishops on this

---

* For Lee's entire account, embracing full minutes of both sessions, see Hist. of Meth., pp. 150–159.

† Dr. L. M. Lee, Life of Jesse Lee, pp. 270, 271.

‡ Journal, II. 110.

§ Hist. M. E. Ch., III. 15.

occasion, but the heat was over in a moment." * Snethen adds, " Mr. Asbury submitted to a General Conference for fear of a division in the Connexion. Like the true mother, he could not bear the idea of dividing the living child." Asbury's own account harmonizes with Snethen's. February 23, 1791, he says: " Long-looked-for Doctor Coke came to town [Charleston]. He had been shipwrecked off Edisto. I found the Doctor's sentiments with regard to the Council quite changed. James O'Kelly's letters had reached London. I felt perfectly calm, and acceded to a General Conference for the sake of peace." † Although it was expected that some would attempt to revive the Council at the General Conference, it was not so much as mentioned. All "showed a disposition," says Lee, " to drop the Council, and all things belonging thereto." Indeed Bishop Asbury " requested that the name of the Council might not be mentioned in the Conference." It was dead, and Jesse Lee, who had done so much to kill it, was present at its burial. " His triumph had come; and it was complete. He enjoyed it in silence." ‡

One act, commonly attributed to the Council, has long survived it. The General Rules, as framed by Mr. Wesley, contained nothing with regard to slavery. The Discipline of 1789 contains, for the first time, a general rule on this subject, in this language: " The buying or selling the bodies and souls of men, women, or children, with an intention to enslave them." § Of this interpolation, a competent authority says: " No Conference put it there, and no editor or printer ever confessed doing it. It happened in the time of the Council, the limit of whose powers was not well defined, in its own estimation." ||

* Reply to O'Kelly.

† Journal, II. 95.

‡ Dr. L. M. Lee's Life of Jesse Lee, p. 271.

§ Emory, Hist. of the Discipline, pp. 180, 181; Sherman, Hist. of the Discipline, p. 114.

|| McTyeire, History of Methodism, pp. 403, 404. Bishop Harris (Powers of the General Conference, p. 64, ed. 1860) mistakenly asserts that this General Rule was enacted in 1784 by the Christmas Conference.

The last question in the Minutes of 1792 is this, "When and where shall the next Conferences be held?" Twenty Annual Conferences are appointed; but before the announcement of their times and places, this entry is made: "General Conference, November 1, 1792." * Thus this General Conference was appointed by authority of the Annual Conferences.

In his communication to the General Conference of 1808, explanatory of his letter to Bishop White in 1791, Bishop Coke expresses his alarm for the unity and stability of the Methodist Episcopal Church, caused by O'Kelly's schismatic Conference and the widespread disaffection at this time on account of the Council and its doings, and urges these facts in extenuation of his confidential overture to Bishop White. He says:

> I had indeed, with great labor and fatigue, a few months before I wrote this letter to Bishop White, prevailed on James O'Kelly, and the thirty-six traveling preachers who had withdrawn with him from all connection with Bishop Asbury, to submit to the decision of a General Conference. This Conference was to be held in about a year and a half after my departure from the States. And at this Conference, held I think the latter end of 1792, I proposed and obtained that great blessing to the American Connection—a permanency for General Conferences, which were to be held at stated times. . . . The society as such, taken as an aggregate, was almost like a rope of sand. I longed to see matters on a footing likely to be permanent. Bishop Asbury did the same; and it was that view of things, I doubt not, which led Bishop Asbury, the year before, to call and endeavor to establish a regular Council, who were to meet him annually at Cokesbury. For this point I differed in sentiment from my venerable brother.

In truth, Coke, O'Kelly, and Lee, may fairly claim the honors of securing the session of the first Quadrennial General Conference. It is evident that the Conference and the Council were competing solutions of the existing legislative difficulties of the Church. Snethen declares that "the instant a General Conference was acceded to, the Council was superseded." Asbury was the author and patron of the latter. Lee and O'Kelly—the former, loyally and legitimately, and the latter, schismatically and insidiously—became its

---

* Minutes, ed. of 1813, p. 119.

chief opponents. O'Kelly enlisted the coöperation of Coke, and he, by becoming the champion of a General Conference, must be allowed to have been the agent who brought about at once the destruction of the Council and the inauguration of the Conference. At the General Conference of 1792, he was the father of the measure which incorporated the General Conference permanently in the government of the Church. Asbury had been, indeed, in 1784, the proposer of the Christmas Conference. Then, and again in 1787, he successfully interposed the authority of the American itinerants between himself and Mr. Wesley. But he does not seem, at this juncture, to have been favorable to a permanency of General Conferences, or even to a repetition in 1792 of the experiment of 1784. The Council was his personal measure, to which he appears to have been ardently attached. In this, we need not asperse his motives. But the inherent weaknesses and evils of the scheme doomed it from the beginning. As a consequence, Coke, Lee, and O'Kelly secured a General Conference.

BOOK V.

—

THE QUADRENNIAL GENERAL CONFERENCES TO THE INSTITUTION OF THE DELEGATED GENERAL CONFERENCE.

(255)

CHAPTER XV.

THE GENERAL CONFERENCE OF 1792.

N O official Minutes of this Conference are extant. " The Minutes of the General Conference for 1792," says Dr. McClintock, "were never printed to my knowledge, nor can I find the original copy." * This is confirmed by Jesse Lee, who says in his History: " The proceedings of that Conference were not published in separate Minutes, but the alterations were entered at their proper places, and published in the next edition of the Form of Discipline." † The title of this eighth edition is, " The Doctrine and Discipline of the Methodist Episcopal Church in America, revised and approved at the General Conference held at Baltimore, in the State of Maryland, in November, 1792: in which Thomas Coke and Francis Asbury presided. ‡ This Discipline, Lee's History, Coke's and Asbury's Journals, together with the reminiscences of Ware, Garrettson, and Colbert, are our sole, but sufficient, sources, for the transactions of this First Quadrennial General Conference.

The attendance was large. Lee says that

Our preachers who had been received into full connection came together from all parts of the United States where we had any circuits formed, with an expectation that something of great importance would take place in the Connection in consequence of that Conference. The preachers generally thought that in all probability there would never be another Conference of that kind, at which all the preachers in connection might attend. The work was spreading through all the United States and the different Territories, and was likely to increase more and more, so that it was generally thought that this Conference would adopt some permanent regulations which would prevent the preachers in future from coming together in a General Conference.

---

* Gen. Conf. Journals, I. 4.

† In reply to some inquiries of Bishop Morris, in the *Christian Advocate and Journal*, in 1858, F. S. De Hass says, " We are happy to say that the Minutes are not entirely lost, and at some future day we may give the Minutes of these two important Conferences in full." So far as known, he has never done so, and as one of the "two important Conferences" is an alleged General Conference in 1788, we may despair of Mr. De Hass's possessing any Minutes of 1792.

‡ Emory, Hist. of Discipline, p. 88.

Bishop Coke was just in time. He arrived in Baltimore at 9 P.M., Wednesday, October 31: the next morning the General Conference convened. Mr. Asbury and the preachers "had almost given me up," he writes. "Whilst we were sitting in the room at Mr. Rogers', " says Asbury, " in came Dr. Coke, of whose arrival we had not heard, and whom we embraced in great love." *

The first day was consumed in the adoption of rules of order, a precedent faithfully followed ever since. One of the regulations was, " It shall take two thirds of all the members of the Conference to make a new rule [of Discipline], or abolish an old one; but a majority may alter or amend any rule." A business committee was appointed to mature and bring forward measures for the action of the Conference, with the idea of saving time, but, as its debates were repeated on the floor of the House, it was found useless, and first enlarged, and then dismissed; when " any preacher," says Lee, " was at liberty to bring forward any motion." A rule of debate was, " That each person, if he choose, shall have liberty to speak three times on each motion."

On the second day, Friday, O'Kelly introduced his historic resolution, radically modifying the appointing power of the Bishops, and indirectly reflecting on Asbury's administration. It was framed in these words:

> After the bishop appoints the preachers at Conference to their several circuits, if any one think himself injured by the appointment, he shall have liberty to appeal to the Conference and state his objections; and if the Conference approve his objections, the bishop shall appoint him to another circuit.†

" I felt awful at the General Conference," writes Asbury, " my power to station the preachers without an appeal, was much debated, but finally carried by a very large majority. Perhaps a new bishop, new Conference, and new laws, would have better pleased some. . . . Some individuals among the preachers having their jealousies about my influence in the Conference, I gave the matter wholly up to them,

---

* Journal, II. 146: Oct. 31 1792.	† Lee, Hist. of the Methodists, p. 178.

and to Dr. Coke, who presided: meantime I sent them the following letter:

"My Dear Brethren: Let my absence give you no pain—Dr. Coke presides. I am happily excused from assisting to make laws by which myself am to be governed: I have only to obey and execute. I am happy in the consideration that I never stationed a preacher through enmity or as a punishment. I have acted for the glory of God, the good of the people, and to promote the usefulness of the preachers. Are you sure that, if you please yourselves, the people will be as fully satisfied? They often say, 'Let us have such a preacher;' and sometimes, 'We will not have such a preacher—we will sooner pay him to stay at home.' Perhaps I must say, 'His appeal forced him upon you.' I am one—ye are many. I am as willing to serve you as ever. I want not to sit in any man's way. I scorn to solicit votes: I am a very trembling poor creature to bear praise or dispraise. Speak your minds freely; but remember, you are only making laws for the present time: it may be, that as in some other things, so in this, a future day may give you further light.

"I am yours, etc., Francis Asbury."*

Under the presidency of Coke, therefore, with Asbury delicately retiring from the Conference room, and ill at his lodgings, the first great General Conference debate, on a point vital to episcopacy and itinerancy, proceeded. It was led by O'Kelly, Ivey, Hull, Garrettson, and Swift, speaking for the adoption of the resolution, and by Willis, Lee, Morrell, Everett, and Reed in opposition.† Lee declares, "the arguments, for and against the proposal, were weighty and handled in a masterly manner. There never had been a subject before us that so fully called forth all the strength of the preachers." He gives our only outline of the parliamentary proceedings:

A large majority appeared at first to be in favor of the motion. But at last John Dickins moved to divide the question thus: 1. Shall the bishop appoint the preachers to the circuits? 2. Shall a preacher be allowed an appeal? After some debate the dividing of the question was carried. The first question being put, it was carried without a dissenting voice. But when we came to the second question, "Shall a preacher be allowed an appeal?" there was a difficulty started, whether this was to be considered as a new rule, or only an amendment of an old one. If it was a new rule, it would take two-thirds of the votes to carry it. After a considerable debate it was agreed by vote that it was only an amendment of an old rule. Of course after all these lengthy debates we were just where we began, and

* Journal, II. 146, 147. † Colbert's Journal

had to take up the question as it was proposed at first. By dividing the question, and then coming back to where we were at first, we were kept on the subject, called the *Appeal,* for two or three days. On Monday we began the debate afresh, and continued it through the day; and at night we went to Otterbein's church, and again continued it till near bedtime, when the vote was taken, and the motion was lost by a large majority.

The Sunday intervening was a high day. In the morning Coke preached a " delightful sermon " on the Witness of the Spirit; in the afternoon O'Kelly discoursed on "Lord, increase our faith;" Henry Willis closed at night with an appropriate text from the Psalms.*

As Lee supplies us with the parliamentary details of the debate, so Thomas Ware, who was a member of the Conference, furnishes us with a *résumé* of the arguments employed:

Had O'Kelly's proposition been differently managed it might possibly have been carried. For myself, at first I did not see anything very objectionable in it; but when it came to be debated, I very much disliked the spirit of those who advocated it, and wondered at the severity in which the movers, and others who spoke in favor of it, indulged in the course of their remarks. Some of them said that it was a shame for a man to *accept* of such a lordship, much more to *claim* it; and that they who would submit to this absolute dominion must forfeit all claims to freedom, and ought to have their ears bored through with an awl, and to be fastened to their master's door and become slaves for life. One said that to be denied such an appeal was an insult to his understanding, and a species of tyranny to which others might submit if they chose, but for his part he must be excused for saying he could not. The advocates of the other side were more dispassionate and argumentative. They urged that Wesley, the father of the Methodist family, had devised the plan, and deemed it essential for the preservation of the itinerancy. They said that, according to the showing of O'Kelly, Wesley, if he were alive, ought to blush, for he claimed the right to station the preachers to the day of his death. The appeal, it was argued, was rendered impracticable on account of the many serious difficulties with which it was encumbered. Should one preacher appeal, and the conference say his appointment should be altered, the bishop must remove some other one to make him room; in which case the other might complain and appeal in his turn; and then again the first might appeal from the new appointment, or others whose appointments these successive alterations might interrupt.

O'Kelly, on the defeat of his measure, at once abandoned his seat in the Conference and his place among the Methodists. Garrettson, who had been with O'Kelly in the pro-

---

* Colbert's Journal.

posed reform, was appointed on a committee to wait on him and a few other recalcitrants, to urge them to resume their seats. "O'Kelly's distress was so great," he says, "on account of the late decision, that he informed us by letter that he no longer considered himself one of us. This gave great grief to the whole Conference." But the committee's labors were unavailing. Lee says:

> I stood and looked after them as they went off, and observed to one of the preachers that I was sorry to see the old man go off in that way, for I was persuaded he would not be quiet long, but would try to be head of some party. . . . So it was, James O'Kelly never more united with the Methodists.

Among those who left with him was William McKendree, who "obtained liberty of the Conference to return home." His whole ministerial life had been passed in O'Kelly's district; they were traveling companions to the General Conference; they lodged together there, and "their room became the place for the meeting of Mr. O'Kelly's discontented friends." Many confused consultations occurred among the travelers by the way, until the old gentleman and his youthful *protégé* pursued their journey homewards alone. O'Kelly then fully unfolded his scheme to have "a republican, no-slavery, glorious Church! Bishop Asbury was a pope; the General Conference was a revolutionary body; the Bishop and his creatures were working the ruin of the Church to gratify their pride and ambition." *

Bishop Asbury met the Virginia Conference at Manchester, November 26, eleven days after the adjournment of the General Conference. Christmas day, 1791, he had ordained William McKendree, elder:† at the Manchester Conference, the young man "sent him his resignation in writing," ‡ respectfully declining appointment as a Methodist preacher. He soon afterward, however, accepted an invitation to travel with Bishop Asbury. They calmly and

---

* Paine, Life of McKendree, I. 138, 139.

† The parchment to this effect is in the possession of the writer, together with those of his ordination as deacon and bishop.

‡ Journal, II. 148.

fully discussed the recent upheavals, and the better influence ended in McKendree's reclamation.

It was only a month's suspension of an itinerant ministry which ended only with his useful and holy life. This shaking up, this honest doubt, led him to study the whole subject closely, and McKendree became the constitutional expounder of Methodism. He mastered the philosophy as well as the details of its government, and was prepared, at a future crisis, to stand in the breach and save it against a host of strong men.*

Of O'Kelly, Bishop Asbury writes to Morrell, after the adjournment of the General Conference:

I believe now nothing short of being an episcopos was his first aim. His second was to make the Council independent of the Bishop and General Conference, if they would canonize his writings. This could not be done. His next step was with the authority of a pope to forbid me, by letter, to go one step farther with the Council, after carrying it once around the continent and through the first Council, which ordered me to go round and know the minds of the brethren. His following step was to write against me to Mr. Wesley, who he knew was disaffected to me, because I did not merely force the American Conference to accede to Mr. Wesley's appointment of Brother Whatcoat, which I did submit to Dr. Coke only for peace with our old father.† How moved he then to make himself independent of me and the general Connection, and dragged in the little doctor, whom, a little before, he would have banished from the continent. Then he stipulated with me through the doctor to let him stay in that station, and consented to leave the decision to a General Conference, and when the decision went against him, went away.

In the eight years since the Christmas Conference, the "Form of Discipline had been changed and altered in so many particulars," remarks Lee, "and the business of the Council had thrown the Connection into such confusion that we thought proper at this Conference to take under consideration the greater part of the Form of Discipline, and either abolish, establish, or change the rules." ‡ The sections were distributed into three chapters: the first, including twenty-six sections, related to the ministry; the second,

---

* McTyeire, Hist. of Methodism, p. 413.

† Coke testifies: "When T. Coke and Mr. Asbury met in Charleston, T. Coke informed him that Mr. Wesley had appointed Richard Whatcoat as a joint Superintendent, and Mr. Asbury acquiesced in the appointment. T. Coke proposed the appointment to the Virginia Conference, and, to his great pain and disappointment, James O'Kelly most strenuously opposed it."

‡ Cf. Asbury's Journal, II. 147.

including eight sections, to the membership; and the third, including ten sections, to temporal economy, with the doctrinal tracts and Offices.* In their address, the Bishops say, " We think ourselves obliged frequently to view and review the whole order of our Church, always aiming at perfection, standing on the shoulders of those who have lived before us, and taking advantage of our former selves."

The revision of the Discipline began Tuesday morning, November 6,† immediately after the decisive vote on O'Kelly's resolution at Otterbein's Church the preceding evening. It was determined that another General Conference should be held four years later, and thus this body became the permament organ of connexional government in American Methodism. As a mass convention of the entire traveling ministry its powers were general, supreme, and final. The Conference of 1796 was to be composed of " all the traveling preachers who shall be in full connection at the time of holding the Conference." Thus an itinerant of two years' standing was eligible to a seat. But it was found necessary gradually to decrease the membership by successive restrictions. In 1800, each member must " have traveled four years;" and in 1804 it was provided that these four years should date from the time of reception on trial by an Annual Conference, thus cutting off any antecedent years of employment as a " supply" under the elder. ‡ In 1808 the Delegated General Conference was determined upon.

The District Conferences are appointed to be held annually, the time to be fixed by the bishop, and the Conference to include " not fewer than three, nor more than twelve " circuits. The germ of the Annual Conference, composed of many districts, appears, however, in this, that the bishop is " authorized to unite two or more districts together," provided the resulting Conference does not exceed the prescribed number of circuits. The order of business includes eighteen questions. These Annual Conferences are called

---

* Emory, Hist. of Discipline, p. 84.   † Colbert's Journal.
‡ Emory, Hist. of Discipline, p. 111.

District Conferences throughout the Discipline of 1792, but never afterward. From 1820 to 1836, however, this name was applied to the conferences of local preachers for each presiding elder's district. In 1796, the "yearly conferences" were reduced to six, each including several districts, and their boundaries were fixed for the first time by the General Conference.

It is expressly determined that, in future, a bishop shall be constituted "by the election of the General Conference, and the laying on of hands," etc. Thus this business is removed permanently from the province of the yearly conferences, and the difficulties of 1787, when some Conferences concurred, and others refused concurrence, in Whatcoat's nomination, are provided against. The Bishops are made amenable to the General Conference for their conduct, and provision is also made for the trial of an immoral bishop in the interval of the General Conference.

In 1792 the office and title of presiding elder appear for the first time in the Discipline. "Such an order of elders," says Lee, "had never been regularly established before. They had been appointed by the bishop for several years; but it was a doubt in the mind of the preachers whether such power belonged to him. The General Conference now determined that there should be presiding elders, and that they should be chosen, stationed, and changed by the bishop," provided no elder should preside in the same district more than four years successively.* The solemnity and dignity of their ordination, together with the smallness ot their number and the commanding influence which, in most instances, they speedily acquired in their districts, gave rise to a doubt of the bishop's power to control or remove them. O'Kelly's case probably influenced the General Conference decisively in its present action. He had moved "to make himself independent of Asbury and the general Connection" and had "stipulated" with Asbury, through Dr. Coke, "to let him stay in that station;" but had "con-

* See, also, Emory, Hist. of Discipline, pp. 126, 127.

sented to leave the decision to a General Conference."
He had traveled the same district ever since his ordination
in 1784, and had been stationed in that region for some
years before. The disadvantages in his case doubtless led
the General Conference to place the presiding elder, like
other preachers, at the disposal of the bishops, to constitute
him, in a special sense, the bishop's deputy and representative, and to limit his term of office in a given district. The
duties of this officer have been before enumerated. "If the
episcopate has been the right arm," says Stevens, "the presiding eldership has been the left arm of the Church's disciplinary administration."

Provision was made for the trial of preachers for immorality, improper conduct, and heresy, for arbitration between
members, and for the expulsion of members convicted of
sowing dissensions, by inveighing against doctrines or discipline. The right and order of appeal from a lower to a
higher court were, also, secured. The order of public worship was prescribed, without any reference to Wesley's Liturgy, which had now fallen into disuse.

The Conference adjourned after a two weeks' session on
Thursday, November 15. William Colbert and James
Thomas were solemnly ordained elders the day before.
After the conclusion of business on Thursday, Coke
preached on "pure religion and undefiled." "A solemn
awe rested upon the congregation," writes Coke, "the
meeting was continued till about midnight." He departed
with the highest estimate of the abilities and consecration of
the American itinerants:

We continued our Conference [he says] for fifteen days. I had always
entertained very high ideas of the piety and zeal of the American preachers, and of the considerable abilities of many; but I had no expectation, I
confess, that the debates would be carried on in so very masterly a manner;
so that on every question of importance the subject seemed to be considered
in every possible light. Throughout the whole of the debates they considered themselves as the servants of the people, and therefore never lost sight
of them on any question. Indeed, the single eye, and the spirit of humility,
which were manifested by the preachers throughout the whole of the Conference, were extremely pleasing.

CHAPTER XVI.

THE GENERAL CONFERENCE OF 1796.

THE Second Quadrennial General Conference met in Baltimore, Thursday, October 20, 1796; though the preceding Conference had inserted in the Discipline that this session should begin November 1.* The change of date was, however, authorized by the Annual Conferences.† Bishop Coke arrived from Europe two days before the opening and Bishop Asbury joined him the next day. "About a hundred preachers," he says, " were met for General Conference. . . The Conference rose on Thursday, the 3d of November: what we have done is printed." ‡ "We present to you in a separate tract from our form of discipline the result of our deliberations,"§ say the Bishops in an address to the Church on behalf of the General Conference, thus, once more, affording an intimation that the Minutes of 1792 had not been published apart from the Discipline. The sole legislative prerogative of the General Conference, in contrast with the ordinary executive business of the Yearly Conferences, under the laws prescribed for them, is, in this same prefatory address, brought out clearly: "We have, therefore, on a former occasion [1792] confined solely to the General Conference the work of revising our form of discipline, reserving for the Yearly Conferences the common business of the connexion, as directed by the form." ‖

According to Lee, the number present increased to a hundred and twenty. The district bodies disappear, and the General Conference for the first time defines the boundaries of the Annual Conferences, ordaining six at this session:

---

* Emory, Hist. of Discipline, p. 111.   † Minutes, ed. 1813, p. 162.
‡ Journal, II. 267.   § Gen. Conf. Journals, I. 7.
‖ *Ibid.*, I. 7.

New England, Philadelphia, Baltimore, Virginia, South Carolina, and Western. The Bishops, however, were empowered to create others if necessary.* The "chartered fund" is established.† There had been nothing on the subject of slavery in the Discipline of the Church for more than ten years, since the Conferences of 1785 annulled the legislation of the Christmas Conference, except the General Rule, of uncertain parentage, inserted (some say "interpolated") in 1789. This General Conference asked " What regulations shall be made for the extirpation of the crying evil of African slavery?" and enacted the following elaborate legislation:

1. We declare that we are more than ever convinced of the great evil of the African slavery which still exists in these United States, and do most earnestly recommend to the yearly Conferences, quarterly meetings, and to those who have the oversight of districts and circuits, to be exceedingly cautious what persons they admit to official stations in our Church; and, in the case of future admission to official stations, to require such security of those who hold slaves, for the emancipation of them, immediately or gradually, as the laws of the states respectively and the circumstances of the case will admit. And we do fully authorize all the yearly Conferences to make whatever regulations they judge proper, in the present case, respecting the admission of persons to official stations in our Church.

2. No slaveholder shall be received into our society till the preacher who has the oversight of the circuit has spoken to him freely and faithfully on the subject of slavery.

3. Every member of the society who sells a slave shall immediately, after full proof, be excluded the society. And if any member of our society purchase a slave, the ensuing quarterly meeting shall determine on the number of years in which the slave so purchased would work out the price of his purchase. And the person so purchasing shall, immediately after such determination, execute a legal instrument for the manumission of such slave at the expiration of the term determined by the quarterly meeting. And in default of his executing such instrument of manumission, or on his refusal to submit his case to the judgment of the quarterly meeting, such member shall be excluded the society. Provided, also, that in the case of a female slave, it shall be.inserted in the aforesaid instrument of manumission, that all her children who shall be born during the years of her servitude, shall be free at the following times, namely: every female child at the age of twenty-one, and every male child at the age of twenty-five. *Nevertheless,* if the member of our society, executing the said instrument of manumission, judge it proper, he may fix the times of manumission of the children of the

female slaves before mentioned, at an earlier age than that which is pre-scribed above.

4. The preachers and other members of our society are requested to con-sider the subject of negro slavery with deep attention till the ensuing Gen-eral Conference: and that they impart to the General Conference, through the medium of the yearly conferences, or otherwise, any important thoughts upon the subject, that the Conference may have full light, in order to take further steps toward the eradicating this enormous evil from that part of the church of God to which they are united.*

At the request of the General Conference, Coke and As-bury appended their "Notes on the Discipline," to the edi-tion of 1796. "It may be worthy of remark," says Emory, "that this is almost the only section upon which the bishops make no notes." †

On temperance this Conference was also decided:

If any member of our society retail or give spirituous liquors, and any-thing disorderly be transacted under his roof on this account, the preacher who has the oversight of the circuit shall proceed againt him as in the case of other immoralities. ‡

Asbury says, "At the Conference, there was a stroke aimed at the president eldership," § but nothing of its nature can be gathered from the official Journal or contemporary sources. The election of presiding elders by the Annual Conferences became a subject of debate in the General Conference of 1800 and continued a burning question until 1828, when it was finally put to rest.

But aborted measures are not recorded. The Journal says nothing of "strengthening the episcopacy" at this Conference, yet this question furnished matter for earnest and protracted debate. At first, a committee was raised, to which the subject was referred; but objections were urged, and it was dissolved. "They agreed to a committee," says Asbury, "and then complained; upon which we dis-solved ourselves." ‖ Pending the discussion, Asbury stated to the Conference his fears of an imprudent selection and

---

* Gen. Conf. Journals, I. 22, 23; Emory, Hist. of Discipline, pp. 275, 276.
† Hist. of Discipline, p. 276, footnote.
‡ Gen. Conf. Journal, I. 28.
§ Journal, II. 267.
‖ *Ibid.*, II. 267.

expressed a desire for a colleague established in the doctrines and discipline of Methodism. '' This threw a damper on all present, and seemed to paralyze the whole business.'' The resolution before the Conference was then amended, '' to strengthen the episcopacy in a way which should be agreeable to Mr. Asbury.'' It was then almost unanimously requested of Mr. Asbury to make the selection himself, which he appeared very unwilling to do. At this juncture, Coke, who occupied the chair, '' begged that the business might be laid over till the afternoon.'' '' When we met in the afternoon,'' continues Jesse Lee, '' the doctor offered himself to us, if we saw cause to take him; and promised to serve us in the best manner he could, and to be entirely at the disposal of his American brethren, and to live and die among them.'' *

Of the debate which followed, the Rev. John Kobler, who was present, gives an account, in a letter to Dr. L. M. Lee, written, however, as late as 1843:

This unexpected offer, and to many an unwelcome one, opened the way to a large and spirited debate. A number present were warmly in favor of accepting the offer, and as many were against it. Mr. Lee was decidedly against and he warmly opposed it. In fact, I believe he never liked the Doctor anyway, from his first entering among us in 1784, to the last. He could not endure the absolute spirit and overbearing disposition of Dr. Coke, as a high officer in the Church. Mr. Lee was a candid man, and in no wise disposed to give flattering titles to any, and, as such, he opposed the offer with great zeal and eloquence from first to last. He was a man of great penetration, and could see through circumstances and read men well. He was the best speaker in the Conference. He first showed that there were several members in our Connection who were well qualified to fill the office, having been long and well proved; who were natives of the country, one of ourselves, and were well acquainted with the rules by which our civil and religious privileges were regulated. But his most powerful argument, I well remember, was this: '' That the doctor was a thoroughbred Englishman; and an entire stranger abroad in the country (*out* of the Church); that the deep-rooted prejudices against British oppression, which by our arduous Revolutionary struggle we had so recently thrown off, still hung heavily, and was operating powerfully upon the public mind; and that to select a high officer to govern our Church from that distant and tyrannizing nation, whose spirit and practice were held in abhorrence by the American people, would, in his judgment, be a very impolitic step, and would tend to raise the

* Hist. of Methodists, pp. 247, 248; cf. Dr. L. M. Lee, Life of Jesse Lee, pp. 325-330.

suspicions and prejudices of the public against us as a Church. He further said he had frequently heard the same objections made against us as an American Church for having a native of England (Bishop Asbury) at our head; and now to add another, who, in many respects, had not the experience, prudence, nor skill in government that Bishop Asbury had, would operate very materially against the best interests of the Church."

The debate lasted two days, and was incessant; and during the time the Doctor was secluded from the Conference room. Mr. Lee and his party evidently had the better of the cause in debate, and were gaining confidence continually. In one of his speeches, Mr. Lee said he was confident the Doctor would not fill the high office, and perform the vast amount of labor attached to it; that England was his home, his friends and best interests were there, and without doubt he would spend most of his time in going to and fro between England and America, and leave the Episcopacy and the Connection as void of help as they were before. When Bishop Asbury saw how the matter was likely to go, he rose from the chair, and with much apparent feeling said: " If we reject him it will be his ruin, for the British Conference will certainly know of it, and it will sink him vastly in their estimation." Here the debate ended. I well remember during the debate, the Doctor came into Conference and made a speech. Among other things, he said, " he never was cast upon such a sea of uncertainty before." This, I expect, made Bishop Asbury say, "*If we reject him, it will be his ruin.*" The discussion was now stopped, and the whole matter submitted (though by many with reluctance) to Bishop Asbury's judgment—for they had, previously to the Doctor's offer, urged him to make his own selection. I have often wondered at Bishop Asbury's implicit confidence in Dr. Coke. Whether he felt himself bound, in conscience, to submit to one who ordained him to the office of Superintendent, or whether it was because he was Mr. Wesley's representative, I am at a loss to say. But the Doctor's conduct, in a short time, fully proved that Mr. Lee's opinions of his course were founded in a wise discrimination of character—for in a few months he went to England, and never appeared among us till four years afterwards.[*]

Jesse Lee says, however, that " the Conference at length agreed to the Doctor's proposal " and concluded that they could do with two bishops. The Doctor then gave the following paper to the Conference:

I offer myself to my American brethren entirely to their service, all I am and have, with my talents and labors in every respect, without any mental reservation whatsoever, to labor among them, and to assist Bishop Asbury; not to station the preachers at any time when he is present, but to exercise all episcopal duties, when I hold a Conference in his absence, and by his consent, and to visit the West Indies and France when there is an opening, and I can be spared.

(Signed)   THOMAS COKE.

Conference Room, Baltimore, October 27, 1796.[†]

---

[*] Letter in Life of Jesse Lee, pp. 327, 328.   [†] Lee, Hist. of the Methodists, p. 248.

"Bishop Coke was cordially received," writes Asbury, "as my friend and colleague, to be wholly for America, unless a way should be opened to France." *

Let us unravel, if we may, this somewhat tangled skein. Coke had left America in May 1791, on hearing the news of Wesley's death. After an absence of eighteen months, he returns barely in time for the General Conference of 1792, in the appointment of which he had exercised a decisive influence. In December following he sails for the West Indies, and does not again reach America until the eve of the General Conference of 1796. Throughout the quadrennium he had been absent in the West Indies, England, Ireland, and Holland. He had been of no assistance to Bishop Asbury in the labors of the general superintendency, though the work was extending and Asbury's health failing. Yet throughout this period, in the Minutes of 1792, 1793, 1794, and 1795, the question and answer are uniform, " Ques. 6. Who have been elected by the unanimous suffrages of the General Conference to snperintend the Methodist Episcopal Church in America? *Ans.* Thomas Coke, Francis Asbury." † So, indeed, the question and answer had stood, without qualification, since 1788, except that in this year the question read, " Who are the Bishops of our Church for the United States?" ‡ So this question and answer continued to stand until 1800 § when it is changed to " Who are the Bishops?" and the name of Richard Whatcoat is added.‖ Thus the Minutes read until 1806.¶ In 1807, Richard Whatcoat having died, his name is dropped, and the question is changed to, " Who are the Superintendents and Bishops?" and, as in the beginning, the answer is, " Thomas Coke, Francis Asbury." ** In 1808, the answer is, " Francis Asbury, William McKendree," and this note is appended, " Dr. Coke, at the request of the British Confer-

---

* Journal, II. 267.   † Minutes, Ed. of 1813, pp. 112, 124, 137, 152.
‡ *Ibid.*, pp. 60, 77, 89, 100.   § *Ibid.*, pp. 169, 188, 204, 220.
‖ *Ibid.*, p. 236.   ¶ *Ibid.*, pp. 253, 271, 288, 308, 332, 361.
** *Ibid.*, p. 385.

ence, and by consent of our General Conference, resides in Europe: he is not to exercise the office of Superintendent among us in the United States, until he be recalled by the General Conference, or by all the Annual Conferences respectively." * This question, answer, and note continued unchanged in the Minutes of 1809, 1810, 1811, 1812, and 1813, until Bishop Coke's death in 1814.† This completes the official record of Coke's episcopate, so far as the Minutes give information.

Let us turn, now, to the proceedings of the General Conference. When Coke returned to the General Conference of 1796, after an absence of nearly four years, he was accorded, apparently without question, his place in the chair as one of the presidents of the Conference, and was presiding when the question of strengthening the episcopacy was raised. His name precedes Asbury's in the signatures attached to the address prefixed to the Journal.‡ His name alone is signed to the Journal of 1800 as President of the Conference.§ The action of this Conference with regard to Dr. Coke will presently come under review. In 1804, his name is appended to the Journal, with those of Asbury and Whatcoat, but stands last.‖ This was the last General Conference at which Bishop Coke was present: by an almost unanimous vote, as we shall see hereafter, the Americans maintained their claim upon him. In 1808 the General Conference ordered the note, before noticed, to be inserted in the Minutes: this stood, as we have seen, until the Doctor's death.

After this epitome of the official history of Dr. Coke's episcopate, we return to the circumstances of 1796. Before leaving England to attend this General Conference, an African mission, projected by the Doctor, in Sierra Leone, had proved unsuccessful, and " rendered his last attendance at the English Conference far from being pleasing. These

---

* Minutes, ed. of 1813, p. 411.   † *Ibid.,* pp. 442, 471, 504, 540, 575.
‡ Gen. Conf. Journals, I. 8.   § *Ibid.,* I. 46.
‖ *Ibid.,* I. 69.

circumstances, connected with a hope of being more extensively useful in America, than he could be in England, rendered it somewhat doubtful on his departure, whether he should not take up his final abode with his friends on the continent." *   These were the circumstances, so far as his British connections and obligations were concerned, under which Coke made a tender of himself to the General Conference, and "was cordially received," as Asbury records.

But why were a tender of his services and an acceptance of them by the Conference necessary? Was not Coke a bishop, entitled, without challenge, to exercise the duties and privileges of his office? Undoubtedly he was. At this very juncture, he was occupying the president's chair in a General Conference, though he had been absent from the United States the four years preceding. From 1784 to 1804 he presided in every General Conference of the Methodist Episcopal Church. We know of no instance from 1787, when some of his acts were first called in question, to 1796, when he did not exercise all the powers of a bishop at any Annual Conference at which he was present. Asbury tells us expressly in his letter to Benson, that, on such occasions, he was accustomed to yield the chair to Coke whenever he was present. But, in answer to such questions as those suggested above, tacitly if not expressly raised, it is usual with not a few writers to plunge into an abstract discussion of the mutual relations of the General Conference and the Episcopacy, and to generalize on Coke's case until the supremacy of the General Conference and the dependence of the bishops upon its authority are established to their satisfaction. Upon the merits of this discussion there is nothing in Coke's situation at this juncture, or in the action of the General Conference of 1796, that calls us to enter. To allay the sensitiveness of any critical or doubting reader, however, it may be conceded, once for all, without debate, that the General Conference, as then constituted, had unlimited

---

* Drew, Life of Coke, p. 273.

18

power to govern the Methodist Episcopal Church. It could amend or annul the Articles of Religion or the General Rules; leave the place hitherto occupied by them vacant, or substitute others in their stead. It could abolish episcopacy or the presiding eldership and ordain government by presbytery or on the congregational plan. It could terminate its own existence, and organize a Council or any other organ of administration which its wisdom might suggest. It could accept the rule and supremacy of the British Conference, as there is evidence that Asbury feared might be done, in the event of his own death before the election of another bishop. It is difficult to see why it could not have divided the Church, substituting two or more General Conferences, with mutually exclusive jurisdictions, in its own room, had that course been deemed expedient, since the body was composed of the traveling ministry of the Church, with supreme and unlimited powers, and there was nowhere lodged any authority to offer any legal check to the execution of its decisions, which must have been carried out, unless the laity had refused compliance. It was a mass convention of the entire ministry of the Church in full connexion. There are no terms too broad or too high to express the unlimited powers which belonged to this body, and which continued to belong to it until 1808. But it is not writing history to canvass Dr. Coke's case at length, as a recent distinguished historian has done, and then declare unexpectedly, " This power [of deposition of a General Superintendent without trial] was asserted by the General Conference of ——," naming a Delegated Conference which assembled nearly half a century later. It is a question whether the General Conference alluded to exercised any such power; but that is not the present issue. It is freely allowed that the General Conference of 1796 possessed all the powers enumerated above; but it will become manifest, beyond contradiction, that, as a matter of fact, it exercised none of them.

In their notes to the Discipline ordained by this very General Conference, Bishops Coke and Asbury say, " they [the Bishops] are perfectly dependent; that their power, their usefulness, themselves, are entirely at the mercy of the General Conference."* The principle of the absolute supremacy of the Quadrennial General Conferences from 1792 to 1808, in the government of the Methodist Episcopal Church, is undisputed and indisputable. The Bishops were foremost in the acknowledgment of this supremacy in terms the most unqualified.

Having unreservedly conceded this point, let us now continue our inquiry as to what was actually done in Bishop Coke's case by the General Conference of 1796. The unquestioned recognition of his episcopal character at this time has already been noticed. In view of Dr. Coke's relations to his brethren in Europe, there can be no doubt that his tender of himself to the General Conference was both natural and sincere. In view of his relations to his brethren in America, this tender, if he found it possible at length to give his entire services to this continent, was highly expedient. It was, indeed, necessary to the intelligent action of the General Conference on the question of strengthening the episcopacy, then before the body. Dr. Coke had never been able to pledge his entire time to the Americans since his first acceptance as one of their bishops in 1784. During the five years and a half since his departure in the spring of 1791, he had been able to spend but two months in America. Notwithstanding these numerous interruptions and these protracted absences, his episcopal character was still recognized. He had now come, as he did four years before, to attend the General Conference. The natural supposition of the Americans was that he intended to return to Europe, as before, shortly after the adjournment of the Conference. They knew nothing of the temporary embarrassment of his relations with the English Conference, growing out of the failure of his African mission. There was no way of their knowing that his entire services were available, and at their disposal, unless he informed them of

---

* Emory, Hist. of the Discipline, p. 291; Sherman, p. 351.

it. The question under discussion, let it be borne in mind, was not Coke's episcopal character, but the strengthening of the episcopacy, in view of Asbury's increasing infirmities and the enlarging Church, and, particularly, as Bishop Coke was nearly continuously absent from the country, and thus unable to render aid. During these five and a half years of absence, Coke's position in the Methodist Episcopal Church had not been for a moment forgotten or ignored. In all the official publications of the Church, it was formally and constantly recognized, equally with Asbury's. On his return, he assumes a rightful presidency in the General Conference. Instead of treating him with any shade of discourtesy, inquiring why he should not surrender an office whose duties were imperative but which he was unable to discharge, or handling him in any other way, as this autocratic assembly might have done, the Conference uniformly bestowed upon him the most distinguished consideration. He was permitted liberties with respect to absence and foreign service, on account of his unique relation to Ecumenical Methodism, that would not be tolerated in a General Superintendent of the present day, who, " if he cease from traveling without the consent of the General Conference, shall not thereafter exercise the Episcopal office in our Church."

We have cited Mr. Kobler's letter in full, but writing nearly half a century after the events he describes, his testimony is of low evidential value, and he is clearly mistaken in some of his recollections. This can be shown, in some points, from general history; while contemporary sources are uniform as to the unanimity and cheerfulness with which the Conference accepted Bishop Coke's services. Mr. Kobler says the Doctor " went to England and never appeared among us till four years afterward." When the General Conference adjourned, Coke remained in America until Feb. 6, 1797, performing episcopal labors according to his agreement with the General Conference and much to the relief of Asbury. The two bishops attended together the Virginia and South Carolina Conferences, and Coke, doing

much preaching by the way, was in his happiest mood until
the day he sailed from Charleston. August 28, following,
he again left Liverpool for America, in the meantime having
presided over the English Conference. In November 1797
he was once more with Asbury at the Virginia Conference,
and performed his episcopal duties throughout the autumn
and winter, returning to Europe in the spring of 1798.
Meantime an affectionate contest had sprung up between
the English and the Americans as to the possession of the
little Doctor and his services. It had been supposed at the
General Conference of 1796 that he would have to return to
England for the settlement of his affairs, personal and ecclesiastical, before his permanent residence in America
could begin. Indeed it is evident from the document itself,
and from Asbury's account, that the engagement into which
Coke entered with the General Conference was not absolute, but contemplated various interruptions of his American
labors, especially by the affairs of the French and West Indian missions. The written engagement itself, it is highly
probable, Coke impetuously tendered, after the debate on
the matter, without demand from the Conference, which
takes no official notice of it in Journal or Minutes. Indeed
Dr. Coke, on various occasions, exhibits a decided *penchant*
for papers of this description, which involved him in some
troubles from which a little reserve and diplomacy would
have saved him. After his long absence from America,
and considering Asbury's growing experience and entire familiarity with the preachers and the work, in the continental
proportions to which it had now attained, the generous and
impulsive Coke, to anticipate objections, or to fend off Lee's
insinuations in debate, modestly represents his province
as "to assist Bishop Asbury," which would doubtless have
been the attitude of the new bishop, had one been elected.

In March, 1797, Dr. Coke was in Ireland. "Keeping in
view," says his biographer, "his engagements to return to
America, his farewell admonitions had a powerful effect
upon his audiences." Many sorrowed for the words he

spoke, that they should see his face no more. At the succeeding Irish Conference, he found himself firmly riveted in
the affections of preachers and people. "At the English
Conference, which speedily followed, the preachers who assembled intimated one to another the prevailing report, that
Dr. Coke intended quitting them forever, and taking up his
abode for life in the United States. . . The affairs of Conference being ended, and an address prepared for the brethren
in America, requesting them to cancel Dr. Coke's engagements to continue among them," he sailed from Liverpool,
Aug. 28, 1797, as previously noticed. "He was again
brought into a dilemma, but it was of the pleasing kind. He
was importuned on each side of the Atlantic." *

Mr. Kobler's presentation of Jesse Lee's argument against
the acceptance of Dr. Coke by the American Conference
deserves a moment's consideration, though we cannot depend upon its verbal accuracy. Its substance being accepted
as sufficiently correct, the argument amounts to this, that it
was impolitic for the Americans to have another English
bishop. Evidently this view did not impress the General
Conference, then or afterwards. Bishop Asbury continued
in the successful prosecution of his superintendency until
1816; Bishop Coke was cordially and almost unanimously
accepted at this time and, besides much episcopal labor in
the Annual Conferences and throughout the Church, presided in the General Conferences of 1800 and 1804; in 1800,
Bishop Whatcoat, another Englishman, was elected to the
episcopal office, after a tie vote between him and brother
Jesse Lee. Lee was a great and good man who brought
things to pass; a giant of the itinerancy who deserves recognition among the very ablest and best Methodist preachers,
produced in either England or America. Those who knew
him best thought he ought to have been a bishop, and this is
almost certainly true. He stood deservedly high in the esteem of Asbury, who, in 1797, nominated him, with Poythress
and Whatcoat, for the episcopacy, under circumstances

* Drew, Life of Coke, pp. 275, 276.

which will presently pass under review. If Asbury had now consented to make a nomination as requested, or if Coke had not made this tender of himself, or if the General Conference had rejected him, it is by no means improbable that Lee would have been chosen a bishop in 1796. It is not necessary or allowable to impeach his motives with respect to the position he took in debate before the Conference. It is enough to remember that he was neither more nor less than human, and that he was not ignorant of the importance of his achievements for American Methodism, or of the esteem in which he was held by his brethren, north and south, from Asbury down. As to Asbury's alleged language, "If we reject him, it will be his ruin," if he used the expression at all, it was a piece of rhetorical exaggeration, which Coke's subsequent reception in Ireland and England, and the demands of his English brethren, proved to have no foundation in fact. Kobler testified to Asbury's "implicit confidence in Dr. Coke," and though Bishop Coke had doubtless confidentially communicated to his colleague the recent events in England, connected with the failure of his African mission, and the "sea of uncertainty" on which he was cast, in his wounded feelings, the event demonstrated that both of them estimated too lightly the esteem in which Dr Coke was held by the English Conference. At the very next Conference, at Leeds, in 1797, he was elected President of the Conference, the highest honor in British Methodism, and again at Sheffield in 1805 he was elevated to the same distinguished office. Of the English Conference he was almost continuously Secretary from 1799 to 1813; but it is useless to adduce further proof of the supreme regard in which he was held by the English Methodists until his death.

The Rev. William Phoebus has left us an account of the transactions of 1796 connected with "strengthening the episcopacy," which makes quite a different impression from Mr. Kobler's, and by which we may correct or supplement the latter:

The question before the house was, "If Francis Asbury's seat as Superintendent be vacated by death, or otherwise, was Dr. Coke considered, from the authority he had in the Church, as having a right to take the Superintendency in the same manner as it was exercised by Francis Asbury?" Dr. Coke was then asked, if he would be ready to come to the United States and reside there, if he were called to take the charge as Superintendent, so that there might be a succession from Wesley. He agreed, as soon as he should be able to settle his charge in Europe, with all pleasure and possible dispatch to come and spend his days in America. The Rev. Superintendent Asbury then reached out his right hand in a pathetic speech, the purport of which was: " Our enemies said we were divided, but all past grievances were buried, and friends at first, are friends at last, and I hope never to be divided." The doctor took his right hand in token of submission, while many present were in tears of joy to see the happy union in the heads of department, and from a prospect of the Wesleyan Episcopacy being likely to continue in regular order and succession. *

Some pretty high churchmanship, for Methodists, was floating about in that General Conference, despite the anxiety of a few later scribes to impress upon us that Bishop Coke was a nondescript, upon whom neither the General Conference nor its members bestowed any special regard. He was hardly a football or a plaything. Of the episcopal election of 1800, the same authority says:

At a General Conference in 1800 a resolution passed to strengthen the episcopacy by adding a third. There were two principal candidates in nomination. But such as thought correctly perceived that it could not be strengthened if one should be joined to it who was not convinced that such an order was apostolic. He would see no necessity to submit to such an ordination, nor to defend it if he thought it not divine, any more than he would pray fervently and devoutly for the dead, while he did not think purgatory a doctrine of the Bible. A man who did not believe in three orders in the ministry would weaken the episcopacy. Such was one of the nominated, as may be seen by the memoirs of the Rev. Jesse Lee. Richard Whatcoat had thought it an honor to be ordained a deacon, as St. Stephen was; and an elder, as the Seventy; and had magnified both orders, and was a warm advocate for the third; esteeming it not an office taken at pleasure, but an order of God.

If these were some of the considerations which determined that election—and such they doubtless were, judging from the tenor of the vindication of Methodist Episcopacy, which Bishops Coke and Asbury insert in their Notes on the Discipline of 1796, in which they refer to Timothy and Titus

* Memoirs of Bishop Whatcoat, p. 84.

as " traveling bishops,"—a General Conference of unlimited powers gave rather strong endorsement to the "three order" doctrine, which seems to have been generally accepted among the earliest Methodist Episcopalians. But on this point we shall not linger. Rather may we contemplate the pleasing scene before the General Conference when Coke and Asbury, the "heads of department," were publicly reconciled. They had not met in four years, else the alienation had perhaps been more speedily removed. In 1787, they had been unhappily opposed, and Asbury's policy was adopted. In 1792 Asbury had been the champion of the Council and Coke of the Conference, and Coke's plan had triumphed. Coke had also fallen, Asbury thought, too much under O'Kelley's influence. In 1796 " all past grievances were buried," and "friends at first" were "friends at last." When Coke died, Asbury, who survived him two years, wrote, " He was a minister of Christ in zeal and labors, and in services, the greatest man of the last century."

Colbert confirms Asbury's and Phoebus's account of the cordiality and unanimity of Coke's reception:

Friday, [Oct.] 28. There was much talk about another Bishop, and in the afternoon Dr. Coke made an offer of himself. It was not determined whether they would receive him; but to-day I suppose there were not a dozen out of a hundred that rejected him by their votes. This gave me satisfaction. The afternoon was spent debating whether the local deacons should be made eligible to the office of elder, and it went against them.*

When Coke returned to America in 1797 with the epistle of the English Conference requesting that his obligations to the American Conference should be canceled, of course there was no General Conference in session. But this address was laid before the Virginia Conference then in session, and Asbury assumed the responsibility of a reply, dated from the Virginia Conference, November 29, 1797:

Respected Fathers and Brethren: You, in your brotherly kindness, were pleased to address a letter to us, your brethren and friends in America, expressing your difficulties and desires concerning our beloved brother, Dr. Coke, that he might return to Europe to heal the breach which designing men have been making among you, or prevent its threatened overflow.

---

* Colbert's Journal.

We have but one grand responsive body, which is our General Conference, and it was in and to this body the doctor entered his obligations to serve his brethren in America. No yearly conference, no official character dare assume to answer for that grand federal body. By the advice of the yearly conference now sitting in Virginia, and the respect I bear to you, I write to inform you that in our own persons and order we consent to his return, and *partial* continuance with you, and earnestly pray that you may have much peace, union, and happiness together. May you find that your divisions end in a greater union, order, and harmony of the body, so that the threatened cloud may blow over, and your devisive party may be of as little consequence to you, as ours is to us. With respect to the doctor's returning to us, I leave your enlarged understandings and good sense to judge. You will see the number of souls upon our annual Minutes, and as men of reading, you may judge over what a vast continent these societies are scattered. I refer you to a large letter I wrote our beloved brother Bradburn on the subject. . . . From Charleston, South Carolina, where the conference was held, to the province of Maine, where another conference is to be held, there is a space of about 1,300 miles; and we have only one worn-out superintendent, who was this day advised by the yearly conference to desist from preaching till next spring, on account of his debilitated state of body. But the situation of our affairs requires that he should travel about 5,000 miles a year, through many parts unsettled, and other thinly peopled countries. I have now with me an assistant, who does everything for me he constitutionally can; but the ordaining and stationing the preachers can only be performed by myself in the doctor's absence. We have to lament that our superintendency is so weak, and that it cannot constitutionally be strengthened till the ensuing General Conference.*

And so Dr. Coke remained in suspense between the importunities of the English and American Conferences until the General Conference of 1800, and the election of his fellow Englishman, Whatcoat, to the joint superintendency with Asbury. But previous to his return and before the meeting of the Virginia Conference, there were some important occurrences which cannot be overlooked.

In the summer of 1797, during Dr. Coke's absence, Asbury began to despair of meeting his episcopal engagements. He accordingly wrote to Jesse Lee requesting him to be in readiness to accompany him from the approaching session of the New England Conference to Charleston and the Southern Conferencs, at which, however, as the event proved, Bishop Coke was present, and assisted in the discharge of the episcopal labor. September 12, Asbury

---

* Drew, *Life of Coke*, pp. 280, 281.

again writes, appointing Lee president of the New England Conference, and indicating his further intentions:

My Very Dear Brother: I am convinced that I ought not to attempt to come to the Conference at Wilbraham. Riding thirteen miles yesterday threw me into more fever than I have had for a week past. It will be with difficulty I shall get back. The burden lieth on thee; act with a wise and tender hand, especially on the stations. I hope it will force the Connexion to do something, and turn their attention for one to assist or substitute me. I cannot express the distress I have had in all my afflictions, for the state of the Connexion. We say the Lord will provide. True; but we must look out for men and means. Your brethren in Virginia wish you to come forth. I think the most general and impartial election may take place in the Yearly Conferences; every one may vote; and in General Conference, perhaps one-fifth or one-sixth part would be absent. I wish you to come and keep as close to me and my directions as you can. I wish you to go, after the Conference, to Georgia, Holston, and to Kentucky; and perhaps come to Baltimore in June, if the ordination should take place, and so come on to the Eastern Conference.

The reference to ordination is explained by the fact that Asbury had sent a communication to the New England Conference, nominating Lee, Poythress, and Whatcoat for "assistant bishops." But the Conference wisely declined to act, in view of the requirements of the Discipline, and his proposal appears not to have been laid before any other Conference. At the time of writing to Lee, Asbury was sick with "swelling in the face, bowels, and feet" at New Rochelle, N. Y. Afterward he attempted to reach the Conference, but returned and went to bed with a high fever, "distressed at the thought of a useless and idle life." The New England Conference, while refusing to act on Asbury's nominations, gave Lee written instructions to "travel with the bishop, and fill his appointments when the latter could not be present." In his Journal, under date of September 21, 1797, Asbury says:

It is a doubt if the Doctor cometh to America until spring, if at all until the General Conference. I am more than ever convinced of the propriety of the attempts I have made to bring forward Episcopal men: First, from the uncertain state of my health; secondly, from a regard to the union and good order of the American body, and the state of the European connexion. I am sensibly assured the Americans ought to act as if they expected to lose me every day, and had no dependence upon Dr. Coke, taking prudent care not to place themselves at all under the controlling influence of British Methodists.*

Asbury clearly perceived the value of Wesley's episcopacy to the American connexion, and the divisions and disasters which were threatening the English from the lack of it. He feared the lapse of that episcopate in America, and consequent amalgamation with the English, and the possible supremacy of the British Conference in America as well as at home. But in a few weeks his episcopal colleague was by his side, and in 1800 the General Conference legally chose a new bishop. "That he meant well, and nominated wisely in this," remarks a recent author, " none can doubt. If not an abusive procedure, it was liable to abuse." † It must not be forgotten, however, that, notwithstanding the unlimited powers of the General Conference, and the subordinate position of the Yearly bodies, no hard and fast line had yet been drawn in the mind of the Church between the action of the ministry assembled in General Conference, and the action of the ministry generally in the Annual Conferences. Indeed as the action would be taken in either case by the same persons, it is difficult to see how any conflict of authority could arise. As a matter of fact, the Annual Conferences took it upon themselves to alter the time of meeting appointed for both the General Conference of 1796 and that of 1800. And even General Conferences of unlimited powers governed themselves accordingly, for the very persons who composed them, acting in a scarcely distinguishable capacity, had authorized the change. Asbury was destined to be left alone in the episcopacy once more, on the death of Whatcoat in 1806. And, at that late date, when four General Conferences had sat, a measure much more radical, dangerous, and indefensible was initiated in the Annual Conferences, to anticipate the election of a bishop by the General Conference of 1808. But this transaction will be examined at the proper point in our history.

---

* Journal, II. 292, 293.   † McTyeire, Hist. of Meth., p. 470.

CHAPTER XVII.

THE GENERAL CONFERENCES OF 1800 AND 1804.

I. The General Conference of 1800.

THE Conference assembled Tuesday, May 6, and continued in session fifteen days, adjourning Tuesday evening, May 20.* The Journal is attested by the signatures of T. Coke, *President*, and Nicholas Snethen, *Secretary*. It is probable that Asbury, on account of his health and the usual precedence he accorded to Coke, surrendered to the latter the presidency of the body. Since that time all the General Conferences of both Episcopal Methodisms have been held in the spring, usually in May.

Asbury records a brief summary of proceedings:

> We had much talk, but little work: two days were spent in considering about Dr. Coke's return to Europe, part of two days on Richard Whatcoat for a bishop, and one day in raising the salary of the itinerant preachers from sixty-four to eighty dollars per year. We had one hundred and sixteen members present. It was still desired that I should continue in my station. On the 18th of May, 1800, elder Whatcoat was ordained to the office of a bishop, after being elected by a majority of four votes more than Jesse Lee.†

Jesse Lee, Philip Bruce, George Roberts, John Bloodgood, William P. Chandler, John McClaskey, Ezekiel Cooper, Nicholas Snethen, Thomas Morrell, Joseph Totten, Lawrence McCombs, Thomas F. Sargent, William Burke, and William McKendree, were among the members—" representative men, who laid the broad foundations of Methodism, east, west, north, and south." ‡

The second day of the session, Snethen introduced a resolution, whose preamble recited that though the preceding General Conference had appointed Oct. 20, 1800, for the

---

* Gen. Conf. Journals, I. 31, 46; Asbury's Journal, II. 375.   † Journal, II. 375.
‡ Boehm's Reminiscences, p. 35.

present session, the prevalence of a " very malignant epidemic disorder, called yellow fever " in Baltimore and other seaports, made it doubtful whether the Conference could safely assemble at that season, and " Mr. Asbury did, by the advice of certain judicious friends, lay the case before the yearly conferences," which appointed May 6. And the body adopted his resolution, " that this General Conference, now met according to the above alteration and appointment, do unanimously approve of the said alteration, and ratify it accordingly." *

The question of prospective episcopal supervision had many complications. Dr. Coke's case, and the request of the English Conference, were to be disposed of. Mr. Asbury's suggestion of superannuation and retirement must be considered. If a new bishop should be chosen, it remained to be determined whether his powers should be coördinate with those of Bishop Asbury or subordinate to them. Let us consider these matters in order, and first the case of Dr. Coke.

The first day, as soon as Conference opened, Dr. Coke presented the address from the British Conference, explaining the parts relating to himself and his return to Europe, and adding that the address was not his own and that he was not consulted about it. He then placed the decision of the case entirely with the General Conference, as he viewed himself as their servant.† Three things are evident: (1) the British Conference " clearly perceived that the Methodism of England needed such a man, and sought to reclaim him;" ‡ (2) Coke now saw the necessity of his services in England, especially in connection with the missions, and was willing to give them, but considered himself bound to the Americans, and meant to observe his compact, unless honorably released; (3) the Americans yielded their claim, but partially and with reluctance.

Wednesday morning, May 7, McClaskey moved, " that

---

* Gen. Conf. 'ournals, I. 32.   † Gen. Conf. Journals, I. 31.
‡ Smith, Hist. of Meth., II. 306. .

in compliance with the address of the British Conference, and request to us to let Dr. Coke return to Europe, this General Conference consent and agree to his return, upon condition that he come back to America as soon as his business will allow, but certainly by the next General Conference." This motion was made the order of the day for the afternoon session, when the subject was warmly debated, and postponed until Thursday morning. The Conference was evidently not yet prepared to grant the request from England. Thursday morning, "the business of the address was called up, and debated all the forenoon." Thursday afternoon, "the vote being called for on brother Mc-Claskey's motion, a large majority arose in favor of it. Dr. Coke is to return to Europe accordingly." * "We have lent the Doctor to you," they wrote in response to the English Conference, " for a season."

Bishop Asbury's relation to the work also came under review. Lee says:

Some time previous to the meeting of the preachers in that Conference Mr. Asbury had said that when they met he would resign his office as Superintendent of the Methodist Connection, and would take his seat in the Conference on a level with the elders. He wrote to several of the preachers in different parts of the Connection, and informed them of his intention; and engaged other preachers to write to their brethren in the ministry, and to inform them of his intention to resign. Withal, he wrote his resignation with an intention to deliver it into the Conference as soon as they met, and to have it read in their first meeting. He said he was so weak and feeble both in body and mind that he was not able to go through the fatigues of his office.†

The Journal of the General Conference reads:

A request being made that Mr. Asbury should let the Conference know what he had determined to do in future, he intimated that he did not know whether this General Conference were satisfied with his former services. A member proposed that a vote should be taken. The vote was objected to until a reason should be assigned for such suspicion. Mr. Asbury then rose, he said, to speak in his own behalf. His affliction, since the last General Conference, had been such that he had been under the necessity of having a colleague to travel with him; that his great debility had obliged him to locate several times, and that he could only travel in a carriage; and he did not know whether this General Conference, as a body, were satisfied

*Gen. Conf. Journals, I. 32-34. † Hist. of Methodists, p. 265.

with such parts of his conduct. Whereupon a motion was made by brother Ezek. Cooper, That this General Conference do resolve that they consider themselves under many and great obligations to Mr. Asbury, for the many and great services he has rendered to this connexion.

Secondly, That this General Conference do earnestly entreat a continuation of Mr. Asbury's services as one of the general superintendents of the Methodist Episcopal Church, as far as his strength will permit.*

This action was "agreed to, *nem. con.*" This was the first case of partial cessation from traveling, by permission of the General Conference. The law then stood, if a bishop should cease from traveling, "without the consent of the General Conference, he shall not thereafter exercise any ministerial function whatsoever in our Church." Bishop Asbury was now a superannuated man. He delicately desired to give the General Conference an opportunity to express dissatisfaction with his services, if any existed. The result was as recorded above.

The same day Burke moved the election and ordination of two bishops. Tolleson offered an amendment, that the Conference inquire, "whether any help ought to be afforded Mr. Asbury, and if any, what that help shall be." The next afternoon, this motion was called up and divided into two parts, "Shall any assistance be given?" which was answered, "Yes;" and "What shall that assistance be?" when a large majority appeared in favor of one bishop. Mr. Asbury was also authorized to take with him an elder as a traveling companion. The following Monday, May 12, was appointed for the episcopal election. Meantime many projects were brought forward. Dr. Coke moved that the new bishop, whenever presiding in a Conference in the absence of Bishop Asbury, should bring the stations of the preachers into the Conference and read them, that he might hear what the Conference had to say about the appointments—"withdrawn next day." This was the English plan, but the Americans did not care even to vote upon it. Wells moved that the new bishop, in stationing the preachers, be aided by a committee of not less than three, or

* I. 33.

more than four preachers, chosen by the Conference—
"voted out next day." McClaskey moved that the Conference determine, before the election, the powers of the new
bishop, whether he shall be equal to Bishop Asbury, or subordinate to him—"withdrawn by consent." Buxton moved
that the yearly conferences have liberty to appoint a committee of four to aid the bishops in stationing the preachers,
a majority determining, thus extending the principle to Asbury as well as the new bishop, and settling the appointments by a majority vote of this assembly of five, including
the bishop. "A dispute arising, whether the motion would
go to abolish an old rule, the Conference were of opinion
it would. Upon a division of the house the motion was
negatived. In the afternoon of the same day, Mansfield
moved the election by the Annual Conferences of the cabinet of four, "the bishops still having the ultimate decision"
—"negatived." Thus, by prompt rejection of all these
proposed modifications, the Conference left the appointing
power as it was, and placed the new bishop on an equal
footing with the old. Methodist episcopacy is a joint, general, itinerant superintendency. Finally, on Saturday afternoon before the election on Monday, Mansfield moved
"that the bishops shall have full and equal jurisdiction in all
and every respect whatsoever; that each and every bishop
shall attend each and every Conference, and then and there
mutually preside, and station the preachers: *provided*, that
in case they should unavoidably be prevented from attending, the bishop or bishops then present shall be competent
to discharge the duties of the office as fully and effectually,
in every respect, as if they were all present; that at each
and every Conference the bishops present shall mutually
determine and agree upon their several different routes to
the ensuing Conference." This resolution was too minute
and complex to be imposed as law upon men having to meet
the exigencies of Methodist bishops, and was promptly negatived. The equal jurisdiction was sufficiently guaranteed
by the refusal of the Conference to modify the *status quo* in

19

any way; the details of administration were wisely left to the arrangement of the bishops among themselves, and so continue until this day.*

The Journal thus records the episcopal election which followed:

The Conference proceeded to the election of a bishop; the first poll being a tie, and supposed delective. Upon the second, there were fifty-nine votes for Brother Richard Whatcoat, fifty-five for Brother Jesse Lee, and one blank—the whole number of votes being one hundred and fifteen; whereupon Brother Richard Whatcoat was declared duly elected.†

This agrees with Lee's own account, except that according to him there were three ballots taken, the first yielding no election, and the second and third being the same as the first and second as recorded in the Journal. Lee's account is probably correct, the Secretary omitting the first ballot from his record. All authorities agree as to the tie vote and the final majority of four.

Bishop Asbury is the author of the law for the inspection of Annual Conference journals by the General Conference. On the last day of the session he moved "that a general book of records be kept of the proceedings of the Annual Conferences by a secretary, and a copy of the said record be sent to the General Conference." On the second day Ormond moved that the Annual Conferences be permitted "to nominate and elect their own president elders," and thus introduced a question into the councils of the Church which proved a disturbing influence for a quarter of a century. When his motion was called up for final action, it was negatived, apparently promptly and by a general vote, without debate. Tolleson introduced a resolution for a delegated General Conference, which was defeated "by a great majority." Jesse Lee is the author of the motion, which prevailed, that no preacher should be eligible to a seat in the General Conference until he had traveled four years. Motions to make local preachers eligible to elder's orders were defeated, but this became an absorbing question for years afterward. The bishops were granted leave to

* For all the preceding, see Gen. Conf. Journals, I. 35, 36. † *Ibid.*, I. 36, 37.

admit colored preachers to local deacon's orders, though the law was never inserted in the Discipline. Richard Allen was the first deacon ordained according to these provisions. He led the first secession of colored people from the Church in 1816, and became the first bishop of the African Methodist Episcopal Church.[*]

This Conference was one of the earliest of those conservative bodies, notable rather for what it did not do, than for what it did. Just after the episcopal election, Ormond introduced the subject of slavery in an elaborate preamble and resolution, upon which no action was taken. Friday, May 16, Snethen moved, " that from this time forth no slaveholder shall be admitted into the Methodist Episcopal Church." —" Negatived." Brother Bloodgood moved " that all negro children belonging to the members of the Methodist Society, who shall be born in slavery after the fourth day of July, 1800, shall be emancipated, males at — years, and females at — years."—" Negatived." Brother Lathomus moved that every member of the Church holding slaves shall, within one year, emancipate — negatived. Cooper moved an address to the Societies on the evils of slavery, which was carried. Timmons and McKendree offered the only measures which were incorporated in the Discipline of the Church,[†] as follows:

2. When any traveling preacher becomes an owner of a slave or slaves, by any means, he shall forfeit his ministerial character in our Church, unless he execute, if it be practicable, a legal emancipation of such slaves, conformably to the laws of the state in which he lives.

6. The annual conferences are directed to draw up addresses for the gradual emancipation of the slaves, to the legislature of those states in which no general laws have been passed for that purpose. These addresses shall urge, in the most respectful, but pointed manner, the necessity of a law for the gradual emancipation of the slaves; proper committees shall be appointed, by the annual conferences, out of the most respectable of our friends, for the conducting of the business; and the presiding elders, elders, deacons, and traveling preachers, shall procure as many proper signatures as possible to the addresses, and give all the assistance in their power in every respect to aid the committees, and to further this blessed undertaking. Let this be continued from year to year, till the desired end be accomplished.[‡]

II. The General Conference of 1804.

The General Conference of 1804 assembled in Baltimore, May 7, 1804. The preceding body had appointed May 6 for the session, but this day was Sunday. It adjourned Wednesday, May 23, after a session of seventeen days. Coke, " as senior bishop," presided,* and John Wilson was chosen Secretary.

Under date of Monday, May 7, 1804, Asbury says, " Our General Conference began. What was done, the Revised Form of Discipline will show. There were attempts made upon the ruling eldership. We had a great talk. I talked little upon any subject; and was kept in peace." †

There were one hundred and twelve members, though five were denied seats. The Philadelphia Conference had forty one representatives; Baltimore, twenty nine; Virginia, seventeen; and New York, twelve: while the New England had but four; the Western, four, and South Carolina, five. The Philadelphia and Baltimore Conferences had together seventy representatives, nearly two-thirds of the whole Conference. Four of those who were refused seats, however, came from the Philadelphia Conference, while an additional member was added later to the Baltimore delegation.

The Discipline was revised section by section, Coke reading the items from the chair and the Conference debating and deciding. The results were incorporated in the Discipline, and no separate minutes were published. ‡

On motion of Ezekiel Cooper, the twenty-third Article of Religion was changed into its present form, "Constitution of the United States " being substituted for " General Act of Confederation," and the words, " are a sovereign and independent nation," inserted. The case of the five brethren who were denied seats led to the adoption of the resolution that " the preachers who shall have traveled four years from the time they were received on trial by an Annual Conference, and are in full connection, shall compose the Gener-

---

*Quinn's Life, p. 82. (Q. was present.)   † Journal, III. 137.
‡ Lee, Hist. of Meth., p. 298.

al Conference." On Snethen's motion the bishops were required to allow the Annual Conferences to sit a week at least; hitherto they had adjourned them when they regarded the business finished. The Annual Conferences were empowered to appoint the places of their sessions. Thursday morning, May 10, Thomas Lyell moved " the abolition of the whole fifth section, concerning presiding elders. This was afterward altered by the mover, that there be no presiding elders." In the afternoon, after a long debate, the motion of Lyell was lost. On Cooper's motion, provision was made for the election of a presiding elder to preside in an Annual Conference in the absence of a bishop. On motion of George Daugherty it was agreed to limit the appointing power of the bishop as follows: " Provided, he shall not allow any to remain in the same station more than two years successively, excepting the presiding elders," etc.*

When the letters from the European Conferences were read, Cooper moved that " Dr. Coke shall have leave from this General Conference to return to Europe, agreeably to the request of the European Conferences, provided he shall hold himself subject to the call of three of our Annual Conferences, to return to us when he shall be requested; but at furthest, that he shall return, if he lives, to the next General Conference." When called up, a week later, this resolution " by a vote very general, if not unanimous, was carried."†

On the question, " Shall there be an ordination of local elders? " there was a tie vote of 44 to 44, whereupon Dr. Coke moved " that it lie over, as unfinished business, till the next General Conference," and the motion prevailed.‡

Slavery legislation was considerably modified. The question was altered to, " What shall be done for the extirpation of the evil of slavery?" "A variety of motions were proposed on the subject," says the Journal, " and, after a long conversation, Freeborn Garrettson moved, that the subject

---

* For the whole of the above, see Gen. Conf. Journal, 1804, *passim*.
† Gen. Conf. Journals, I. 57, 64.
‡ *Ibid.*, I. 62.

of slavery be left to the three bishops, to form a section to suit the Southern and Northern states, as they in their wisdom may think best, to be submitted to this Conference." This measure prevailed, but Bishop Asbury declined to serve. The next day, on motion of Cooper, a committee of seven, one from each Conference, composed of Daugherty, Bruce, Burke, Willis, Cooper, Garrettson, and Lyell, was appointed " to take the different motions and report concerning slavery." This committee reported an elaborate statute considerably qualifying the provisions of previous legislation. The provision for the expulsion of a member for selling a slave was modified by the proviso, " except at the request of the slave, in cases of mercy and humanity, agreeably to the judgment of a committee of the male members of the society appointed by the preacher in charge." It was further ordained that " if a member of our society shall buy a slave with a certificate of future emancipation, the terms of emancipation shall, notwithstanding, be subject to the decision of the quarterly-meeting Conference." The Methodists in North and South Carolina, Georgia, and Tennessee were " exempted from the operation " of all the rules on slavery. The directions to the Annual Conferences to prepare petitions for emancipation to the state legislatures were annulled, and the whole concluded with this rule, " Let our preachers from time to time, as occasion serves, admonish and exhort all slaves to render due respect and obedience to the commands and interests of their respective masters." *

On Coke's motion the Discipline had been ordered to be divided into two parts, " The Doctrines and Discipline of the Methodist Episcopal Church," and " The Temporal Economy of the Methodist Episcopal Church." It was ordered " that a number of the first or spiritual part of our Discipline be printed as a separate part, for the benefit of the Christian slaves belonging to our Society in the South." This part did not contain the laws on slavery, and the next day, on motion of Daugherty, it was ordered " that two

---

* Gen. Conf. Journals, I. 60-63.

thousand copies of the first or spiritual part of our Discipline be printed off and bound, for the use of the South."

We refrain, as usual, from any comment on this slavery legislation, leaving the reader to draw his own conclusions: he has a right to expect, however, a complete history of the legislation of the Church on this subject in these pages, and this demand we shall continue to meet.

Coke, Asbury, and Whatcoat were to meet no more in General Conference. This was the last visit Coke made to America; before the meeting of the next General Conference, Whatcoat departed this life: Asbury came to the General Conference of 1808 once more alone in the episcopacy.

After the death of Bishop Whatcoat in 1806, and in view of the failing health of Bishop Asbury, a sense of insecurity with regard to the episcopacy and the stability of the Church itself seemed to pervade the Connexion. Under these circumstances, " a plan agreed upon by the New York Conference, to organize and establish a permanent Superintendency over the Methodist Episcopal Church in the United States, and recommended to the other six Conferences for their concurrence " was laid before the several Conferences by Bishop Asbury. The plan proposed that forty nine delegated electors, seven from each Conference, should convene in Baltimore, July 4, 1807, " for the express purpose, and with full powers, to elect, organize, and establish a permanent Superintendency, and for no other purpose." The document from which the quotations above are cited was " signed by order and in behalf of the unanimous voice of the Conference " by Freeborn Garrettson, Ezekiel Cooper, and Samuel Coate, attested by Francis Ward, Secretary, and dated New York, May 22, 1806. Appended to this circular are the following subscriptions:

The New England Conference concur with the proposal made by the New York Conference, for calling a delegated General Conference on July 4, 1807, for the express purpose of strengthening the Superintendency. Yeas, 28; nays, 15. THO. BRANCH, *Sec'y.*

The Western Conference concur with the proposal made by the—etc., etc. Unanimity. WM. BURKE, *Sec'y.*

The South Carolina Conference concur—etc. Two members only excepted. LEWIS MYERS, *Sec'y.*

Virginia Conference, Newbern, Feb. 6, 1807.—The New York Conference having written a circular letter to the several Annual Conferences, proposing a plan to strengthen the Superintendency, the letter was read in this Conference yesterday, and a vote taken—"Shall we consider the subject?" Only seven were in favor of the motion. The subject was called up again to-day, and a second vote was taken; fourteen were in favor of it. It is therefore the decision of Conference not to be concerned in it.

Signed in and by order of the Conference.

P. BRUCE,
JESSE LEE,
THOS. L. DOUGLASS, *Sec'y*.*

Jesse Lee's account in his History agrees in every particular with Bishop Paine's original document:

In the course of the year 1806 there was a plan laid which would have overset and destroyed the rules and regulations of the Methodists respecting the election and ordination of bishops. It was said that the plan originated in the New York Conference, which was as follows: " To call a delegated Conference of seven members from each Conference, chosen by the Conferences, to meet in Baltimore, to meet on the 4th of July, 1807, to choose superintendents, etc." This plan was adopted by four of the Conferences; viz., New York, New England, the Western, and South Carolina Conferences; and delegates were accordingly chosen. But when it was proposed to the Virginia Conference, which met in Newbern in February, 1807, they refused to take it under consideration, and rejected it as being pointedly in opposition to all the rules of our Church. The bishop labored hard to carry the point, but he labored in vain; and the whole business of that dangerous plan was overset by the Virginia Conference. The inventors and defenders of that project might have meant well; but they certainly erred in judgment.†

And so Jesse Lee, despite the influence of Bishop Asbury, brought these very doubtful proceedings to an end in the Virginia Conference. It was not the least of the services which he rendered the Church.

---

* Paine's Life of McKendree, I. 184–186. The original document was in possession of Bishop Paine, and was probably the identical paper which Bishop Asbury took from the New York to the other Conferences. This appears from the official entry of their endorsements upon it by the Secretaries. When the plans failed at the Virginia Conference, Bishop A. doubtless retained the paper. From him it passed to Bishop McK., and thence to Bishop Paine.

† Hist. of the Methodists, pp. 344, 345.

CHAPTER XVIII

THE GENERAL CONFERENCE OF 1808.

THE Fifth Quadrennial General Conference assembled, like all of its predecessors, in Baltimore, Friday, May 6, and adjourned Thursday, May 26, 1808, after a three weeks' session. Jesse Lee alludes to it as " our· fifth and last General Conference," *i. e.*, the last mass convention of the traveling preachers of four years' standing, with unlimited powers. Until the election of McKendree, Asbury was the only bishop present. One hundred and twenty nine members took their seats, among whom were five future bishops of the Church—William McKendree, of the Western Conference, elected at this time; Enoch George and Robert R. Roberts, of the Baltimore Conference, elected in 1816; and Joshua Soule and Elijah Hedding, of the New England Conference, elected in 1824. The Baltimore Conference had thirty one representatives, and the Philadelphia, thirty two, these two Conferences together having nearly a majority of the body. The conditions had been similar in 1804, and it was this apparently permanent preponderance of the central over the border Conferences, giving the former control of legislation and elections, that brought about the demand of the latter for a Delegated General Conference, in which all the Annual Conferences should have proportionate representation. In 1804 the necessity for a delegated, representative body had been generally acknowledged, but as preparatory steps had not been taken, and it was desirable for the Annual Conferences to act with mature deliberation, by common consent the measure was deferred until 1808. " It was therefore understood throughout the whole Church," remarks Bishop Paine, " that at this Conference the organization of the Church should be completed by some general measures which should effect a cen-

(297)

tralization of power in a delegated body having supreme legislative jurisdiction." *

This was, indeed, the completion of the organization of the Church. The Christmas Conference, as we have seen, was, in no proper sense, a General Conference. No attempt was made in that meeting to provide for any successor in the way of a permanent legislative assembly. It was an extraordinary convention of the ministry for initiating ministerial orders and for the episcopal organization of the Church, and when these ends were accomplished, the convention dissolved. It had no successor. The Annual Conferences and Superintendents resumed, in general, the functions and powers which they had exercised before the meeting of the Christmas Conference, modified by the legislation of that body. These conditions continued until the disastrous experiment of the Council in 1789 and 1790. The disabilities under which the infant Church labored, for the lack of a supreme legislative assembly, compelled the convening of the General Conference of 1792, which Jesse Lee and Dr. Nathan Bangs, the earliest historians of the Church, agree in designating the *first*. Five of these assemblies were held from 1792 to 1808; but, in addition to the growing inequalities of representation, the wisest and most prudent ministers of the Church felt that such a General Conference, in which a majority vote might at any time overthrow the Articles of Religion, the General Rules, or the Episcopal government of the Church, was no safe centre of power or bond of union for the rapidly expanding Methodism of America. Hence the General Conference of 1808 completed the organization of the Church by creating the Delegated General Conference, and giving to that body a constitution, under which the operations of Episcopal Methodism have ever since been conducted.

The business was brought before the Conference, Monday afternoon, May 9, by a memorial from the New York, the New England, the Western, and the South Carolina Con-

* Life of McKendree, I. 184.

ferences—the same bodies which the year before had been defeated in their effort for an episcopal electoral college. As before, the measure had originated in the New York Conference, and had received the endorsement of the others. Its material part reads as follows:

When we take a serious and impartial view of this important subject, and consider the extent of our Connection, the number of our preachers, the great inconvenience, expense, and loss of time that must necessarily result from our present regulations relative to our General Conference, we are deeply impressed with a thorough conviction that a representative or delegated General Conference, composed of a specific number on principles of equal representation from the several Annual Conferences, would be much more conducive to the prosperity and general unity of the whole body, than the present indefinite and numerous body of ministers, collected together unequally from the various Conferences, to the great inconvenience of the ministry and injury of the work of God. We therefore present unto you this memorial, requesting that you will adopt the principle of an equal representation from the Annual Conferences, to form, in future, a delegated General Conference, and that you will establish such rules and regulations as are necessary to carry the same into effect.

As we are persuaded that our brethren in general, from a view of the situation and circumstances of the connection, must be convinced, upon mature and impartial reflection, of the propriety and necessity of the measure, we forbear to enumerate the various reasons and arguments which might be urged in support of it. But we do hereby instruct, advise, and request every member who shall go from our Conference to the General Conference to urge, if necessary, every reason and argument in favor of the principle, and to use all their Christian influence to have the same adopted and carried into effect. And we also shall, and do, invite and request our brethren in the several Annual Conferences, which are to sit between this and the General Conference, to join and unite with us in the subject matter of this memorial.

Appended to this memorial were the following official certificates:

The Eastern Conference unanimously voted to concur with the New-York Conference in the subject-matter of the above memorial.

Boston Conference, June 3, 1807. THOMAS BRANCH, *Secretary.*

The Western Conference unanimously voted to concur with the New-York Conference in the subject-matter of the above memorial.

Chillicothe, O., Sept. 16, 1807. WILLIAM BURKE, *Secretary.*

The South Carolina Conference, with the exception of five members, concur with the New York Conference in the above memorial.

Jan. 2, 1808. LEWIS MYERS, *Secretary.*

* Gen. Conf. Journals, I. 76-78.

The three great central Conferences, Baltimore, Philadelphia, and Virginia, had all held their sessions for 1807 before this memorial originated in the New York Conference, in May 1807, as had also the Western and South Carolina Conferences, in the autumn and winter of 1806.[*] The New England was the only Conference which met later than the New York, and here the memorial was promptly and unanimously adopted within a month. The Western and South Carolina Conferences concurred at their sessions of the following year.[†] There is no reason to suppose that the memorial was not laid before the Baltimore, Philadelphia, and Virginia Conferences at their spring sessions in 1808. But, whatever may have been the general expectation of the Church, these strong central bodies did not concur.[‡] Either they were suspicious of the Conferences which had unitedly originated the scheme of an electoral commission, to strengthen the episcopacy contrary to existing law, in 1807, or they were satisfied with the General Conference as it was, since their

[*] Minutes, ed. of 1813, pp. 377, 378.

[†] Compare dates, Gen. Conf. Journals, I. 78, and in Minutes, p. 404, Stevens, Hist. M. E. Ch., IV. 440, confuses the memorials of 1806 and 1807.

[‡] Dr. L. M. Lee says expressly that the New York memorial was brought before the Virginia Conference of 1808, and that, partly through Jesse Lee's influence, it was adopted with great unanimity. That Jesse Lee was personally favorable to a Delegated General Conference is not open to question. But it is quite certain that his biographer is mistaken in supposing that the Virginia Conference adopted the memorial, though it doubtless came before the body. He adds, "It is believed all the Conferences adopted this memorial," but in this he is clearly wrong, as it is not credible that when the memorial was read in General Conference, with the official certificates of the concurrence of the New England, Western, and South Carolina Conferences attached, the delegates of the other three Conferences should have failed to inquire why the official endorsement of their own bodies was omitted. The same objection applies of course to the alleged endorsement by the Virginia Conference alone. It is a case of Dr. Lee's memory against the General Conference Journal, where a very precise and important document, with its several official endorsements, is recorded *verbatim*. The decision must be against the Doctor and Abel Stevens, who follows him. Moreover Jesse Lee's persistent opposition to the plan for a delegated body as reported in the General Conference of 1808 renders it more than doubtful whether he favored the memorial when laid before his Annual Conference. See Life of Jesse Lee, p. 429.

permanent control of legislation and elections was assured. Thus the memorial came before the General Conference with the endorsement of four Annual Conferences out of seven; but these four Conferences had but forty eight representatives on the floor of the General Conference, while the three non-concurring Conferences had eighty one. Despite the general feeling of the Church that something would be done, the prospects of the memorial were not brilliant.

The day following the presentation of the memorial, Bishop Asbury, at the opening of the session, " called for the mind of the Conference, whether any further regulation in the order of the General Conference" was necessary. This question was carried in the affirmative. So far all was well for the memorial. Stephen G. Roszel, of the Baltimore Conference, seconded by William Burke, of the Western, now moved for a committee " to draw up such regulations as they may think best, to regulate the General Conferences," which motion prevailed. The parentage of this motion was auspicious. But here Bishop Asbury, who was, for many reasons, a hearty supporter of the proposed Delegated Conference, interposed with a motion, " that the committee be formed from an equal number from each of the Annual Conferences." This was excellent parliamentary tactics, for it insured to the memorialists a majority of the committee that was to frame the measure for which they asked. Had the committee been a miscellaneously selected one of five, nine, or fifteen, the character of the plan brought into the Conference for its action would have been very doubtful. The Bishop's motion carried, no one objecting; and, after the defeat of a motion that the committee be composed of three from each Conference, Roszel and Burke moved for two, and their motion prevailed. Ezekiel Cooper and John Wilson, from the New York; George Pickering and Joshua Soule, from the New England; William McKendree and William Burke, from the Western; William Phoebus and Josias Randle, from the South Carolina; Philip Bruce and Jesse Lee, from the Virginia; Stephen G. Roszel and Nelson Reed, from the Baltimore; and John McClaskey and Thomas Ware, from the Philadelphia Conference, were elected.* An abler committee could hardly have been formed from the Conference. Seldom has a committee had a more important work committed to its hands. The memorialists had a clear majority of two, and thus, by the old bishop's timely help, had won the skirmish for position.

So far the official record has been our guide. It here deserts us, until the report of the committee is brought in nearly a week later. Of the private work in committee Dr. Charles Elliott gives an account in his Life of Bishop Roberts:

> On the first meeting of the Committee, they conversed largely on the provisions which their report to the Conference should contain. After considerable deliberation, they agreed to appoint a sub-committee of three to draft a report to be submitted to Conference—subject, however, to such additions or modifications as a future meeting of the whole Committee might see fit to make. The sub-committee consisted of *Ezekiel Cooper*, *Joshua Soule*, and *Philip Bruce*. When the sub-committee met, it was agreed, after a full exchange of sentiments, that each should draw up a separate paper comprising the necessary restrictions or regulations in the best way he could, and that each should present his form in writing, and they would then adopt the one deemed best, with such amendments as might be agreed upon. When the sub-committee met to examine their plans, Mr. Cooper had his regularly drawn up, Mr. Soule also had one, but Mr. Bruce had nothing committed to writing. On comparing the two papers, Mr. Bruce fell in with the main points of the one brought forward by Mr. Soule. Mr. Cooper pleaded for his own with his usual ability, but he finally agreed to Mr. Soule's plan, with some slight additions or amendments suggested by the others. At the next meeting of the whole Committee, although the plans of Messrs. Cooper and Soule were both before them, Mr. Soule's was adopted by all the members, with some slight modifications.†

Cooper differed from Soule, chiefly if not exclusively, on the point which the latter embodied in the third restrictive rule concerning the itinerant general superintendency. Cooper was an ardent advocate, at this very Conference,

---

* Gen. Conf. Journals, I. 78, 79.

† Compare, Dr. L. M. Lee's Life and Times of Jesse Lee, p. 441. I have preferred to insert Dr. Elliott's testimony, favorable to Bishop Soule, in the text. They were for some years neighbors in Ohio.

for the election of seven bishops, one for each Annual Conference, thus creating a species of diocesan episcopacy,
with Asbury, for the time being, as a sort of Archbishop.
Cooper's restriction accordingly ran in these words, " They
[the General Conference] shall not do away Episcopacy,
nor reduce our ministry to a presbyterial parity." Had his
view prevailed, it might have been urged with some show of
truth that " Our Church constitution recognizes the Episcopacy as an abstraction " and leaves the General Conference
free " to work it into a concrete form in any hundred or
more ways we may be able to invent," as Mr. Hamline, of
Ohio, maintained in debate on the floor of a subsequent
General Conference, which was working under this " constitution." * But Mr. Soule's restrictive rule was quite a
different thing. According to its provisions, the General
Conference "*shall not change or alter any part or rule of
our government,* so as to do away episcopacy, or *destroy the
plan of our itinerant general superintendency.*" The particular, concrete " plan," with all the vitally related parts or
rules of our government, described then in the Discipline of
the Church, and familiar to all the members of the Conference, (which plan for the last quarter of a century had been
operated by three bishops, and which, for the next quarter
of a century was to be operated by five other bishops, all of
whom had seats in the General Conference of 1808, and one
of whom, not the least distinguished of their number, was
the author of the restrictive rule which protected them in the
exercise of their constitutional powers)—this plan, and no
other, so far as the rules and regulations enacted by the
Delegated General Conference were concerned, was to be
perpetuated in the Methodist Episcopal Church. The
snapping of the mainspring in a watch destroys its plan and
its value as a timekeeper: it is not necessary to crush the
whole into atoms with a trip-hammer. So the rule has
stood, in Mr. Soule's language, in the Disciplines of both

---

* Gen. Conf. Journals, II., Debates, pp. 131, 132; Hibbard's Life of Hamline, p. 460.

Episcopal Methodisms from the time of its enactment in 1808 to this year of grace 1894. By it every Delegated General Conference that has ever sat, before or since the division of the Church, has been bound. The issue between Soule and Cooper was joined on this point. Finally Bruce sided with Soule; Soule's plan was submitted to the whole committee of fourteen and adopted, with slight changes which did not touch this rule, and so came before the Conference.*

> Thus [says Dr. Elliott] to a very considerable extent we owe to Bishop Soule the restrictive regulations—or, rather, the Constitution of the Methodist Episcopal Church—which exhibits a degree of wisdom and prudent foresight that characterizes men of the first mental powers. In fact, those who know Bishop Soule would expect from him the wise deliberation necessary to produce such a measure as the Constitutional Restrictions of the Methodist Episcopal Church.†

Monday morning, May 16, the report of the committee " relative to regulating and perpetuating General Conferences," was presented to the Conference as follows:

Section III.—Of the General Conference.

1st. The General Conference shall be composed of delegates from the Annual Conferences.

2d. The delegates shall be chosen by ballot, without debate, in the Annual Conferences respectively, in the last meeting of Conference previous to the meeting of the General Conference.

3d. Each Annual Conference respectively shall have a right to send seven elders, members of their Conference, as delegates to the General Conference.

4th. Each Annual Conference shall have a right to send one delegate, in addition to the seven, for every ten members belonging to such Conference over and above fifty—so that if there be sixty members, they shall send eight; if seventy, they shall send nine; and so on, in proportion.

5th. The General Conference shall meet on the first day of May, in the year of our Lord eighteen hundred and twelve, and thenceforward on the first day of May, once in four years perpetually, at such place or places as shall be fixed on by the General Conference from time to time.

---

* The biographer of Jesse Lee (Life, p. 443) cites from the Gen. Conf. Journal, Mr. Lee's motion for the final adoption of this rule, and is thus misled into claiming his authorship of it. " But Bishop Soule *undoubtedly originated* it," says Bishop Paine, " the above explanations [including the statement of differences between Soule and Cooper] are from the lips of Bishop Soule himself."—Paine's McKendree, I. 191.

† Life of Bishop Roberts, p. 159.

6th. At all times, when the General Conference is met, it shall take two-thirds of the whole number of delegates to form a quorum.

7th. One of the *original** superintendents shall preside in the General Conference; but in case no general superintendent be present, the General Conference shall choose a president *pro tem.*

8th. The General Conference shall have full powers to make rules, regulations, and canons for our Church, under the following limitations and restrictions, viz.:

The General Conference shall not revoke, alter, or change our Articles of Religion, nor establish any new standards of doctrine.

They shall not lessen the number of seven delegates from each Annual Conference, nor allow of a greater number from any Annual Conference than is provided in the fourth paragraph of this section.

They shall not change or alter any part or rule of our government so as to do away episcopacy. or to destroy the plan of our itinerant general superintendency.

They shall not revoke or change the General Rules of the United Societies.

They shall not do away the privileges of our ministers or preachers of trial by a committee, and of an appeal; neither shall they do away the privileges of our members of trial before the society, or by a committee, [and] of an appeal.

They shall not appropriate the produce of the Book Concern or of the Charter Fund to any purpose other than for the benefit of the traveling, superannuated, supernumerary, and worn-out preachers, their wives, widows, and children.

Provided, nevertheless, that upon the joint recommendation of all the Annual Conferences, then a majority of two-thirds of the General Conference succeeding shall suffice to alter any of the above restrictions.

The Conference proceeded at once to the consideration of the report, and continued the debate at the afternoon session. Bangs says the debate continued for "one whole day," and this is confirmed by the Journal. All the evidence points to Jesse Lee, though he had been the earliest and most persistent advocate of a Delegated Conference, as the "most prominent opponent" of the report, both in committee and on the floor of the Conference. "Mr. Lee is understood to have opposed the whole thing on the plea of 'Conference rights,'" says Bishop Paine, "and to have defeated it temporarily by advocating *seniority* in preference to the *election* of delegates." "Others joined him in this

---

* This word is probably a clerical error or misprint for *general:* it disappears in the final action.

opposition, and the debate was animated and protracted,"
says Lee's biographer, "but this was the strong point, and
Mr. Lee led the van of the attack." *   At this juncture of
the debate, late in the afternoon, when the report had been
before the Conference since the opening of the morning
session, Ezekiel Cooper, seconded by Joshua Wells, carried
a motion "to postpone the present question to make room for
the consideration of a new resolution, as preparatory to the
minds of the brethren to determine on the present subject;"
whereupon he and Wells introduced the following resolution, "That in the fifth section of Discipline, after the question, 'By whom shall the presiding elders be chosen?' the
answer shall be, '*Ans.* 1st. Each annual conference respectively, without debate, shall annually choose, by ballot, its
own presiding elders.' " †

At this point, a few observations will explain this sudden
turn of Cooper's, who was a masterly strategist in debate.
(1) The motion of McClaskey and Cooper for seven additional bishops had been defeated.   Seeing its hopelessness,
they had sought to withdraw it, but Pickering and Soule had
forced a vote upon it, that diocesan episcopacy might be
killed by formal vote of the Conference.   This action was
in line with the differences, developed between Cooper and
Soule in committee, whose report was yet to be presented.
The Conference decided on the election of one additional
bishop, and Thursday afternoon, May 12, McKendree received ninety-five out of one hundred and twenty-eight votes
on the first ballot.‡   (2) As the next best thing to a diocesan episcopacy, Cooper and others desired an elective presiding eldership, and this opportunity was considered a good
one for carrying a measure that had been frequently defeated, chiefly by those who now sought a Delegated General Conference.   (3) The Conference recognized the pertinency of this resolution to the measure under consideration, and so turned aside to settle first the fate of this motion

---

* Life of Lee, p. 442.   † Gen. Conf. Journals, I. 83.
‡ Gen. Conf. Journals, I. 80, 81.

for an elective presiding eldership. It had no vital relation, however, to any part of the report of the committee except the third restrictive rule. An elective presiding eldership would be a "rule of our government" entering into the "plan of our itinerant general superintendency," and, by deciding this question before the adoption of the report of the committee, and "as preparatory to the minds of the brethren to determine" on that report, this last General Conference of unlimited and supreme powers, would more narrowly and concretely define the powers of the Delegated General Conference, which it was about to create; just as the defeat of Cooper's proposed restrictive rule in committee, and of his plan for a bishop of each Annual Conference on the floor of the General Conference, had also contributed to the better determination of the kind of superintendency which the Delegated General Conference must continue in the Church. The final adoption of Soule's restrictive rule fixed the character of this superintendency in the most comprehensive, ("any part or rule of our government,") and yet the most concrete, ("itinerant general superintendency,") form conceivable.

The step from the facts to these statements is so short as hardly to deserve the name of inference; it is little more than interpretation. Yet short as it is, we are not left to it to establish the conclusion. Mr. McKendree says:

When the report of the Committee which was appointed to draw up a constitution was before the General Conference, a member moved the postponement of that subject for the express purpose of bringing in a motion to authorize the Annual Conferences to elect the Presiding Elders. It was done; and that body, who had as much right to introduce the proposed alteration as they had to form the constitution, took up the proposition, amply discussed the subject, and *rejected* it. The friends of the proposed alteration thought the constitution would put it out of the power of the Delegated Conference to effect the desired change, and therefore proposed to make the alteration before the constitution was ratified. But the preachers preferred the old plan, and therefore rejected the motion. After twenty years' experience, and with the constitution fully before them, they refused to invest the Annual Conferences with power to elect Presiding Elders, and at the moment of constituting the Delegated Conference, deliberately confirmed it, and continued it 'in the General Superintendents, with whom it had been intrusted from the beginning. The Presiding Elders never were elected by the preachers, either in their Annual or General Conference capacity, but were from their commencement chosen by the General Superintendents, with the consent of the preachers collectively; and this rule was ratified and confirmed by the same authority that constituted the Delegated Conference.*

We may now return to the course of affairs on the floor of the General Conference. Tuesday morning was spent in debate on Cooper's motion for electing presiding elders, and at the close of the session Soule, seconded by Beale, moved what we should now call the previous question, which was lost by a vote of 61 to 33. The debate was continued the whole of Tuesday afternoon, during which time the previous question was moved twice, once by Soule, and postponement once; but all three motions were lost. Wednesday morning dawned, and thus far the whole week had been spent, Monday on the report of the committee on a Delegated General Conference, and Tuesday on the cognate matter of the election of presiding elders. The fathers were not destitute of a keen sense of humor, and the first gun of the third day's battle was fired by Thomas F. Sargent and Francis Ward, who moved, "that the motion for electing presiding elders be postponed until the fifteenth day of August next," which motion was lost. Sabin and Soule then moved the previous question once more and this time it carried. Garrettson and Sparks secured the passage of an order that the vote should be taken by ballot, and when the tickets were counted, there were 52 votes for the election of presiding elders, 73 against. Thus in a full house of 125 members, the motion to elect presiding elders was defeated by a majority of twenty-one.†

Immediately after taking this ballot, Wednesday morning, May 18, 1808, William McKendree was ordained a bishop of the Methodist Episcopal Church—its first native American General Superintendent. His episcopal parchment, with the signatures of Francis Asbury, Jesse Lee, Freeborn Garrettson, Thomas Ware, and Philip Bruce, all clearly legible, and dated as above, now lies before the writer of these

---

* Paine's McKendree, II. 367, 368.   † Gen. Conf. Journals, I. 83, 84.

lines. His ordination took place at the close of the exhaustive debate on the presiding elder question, and immediately after its decision. We shall not anticipate the course of our history; but, at a later date, this bishop, supported by Joshua Soule, then a bishop-elect but declining ordination, felt it his duty to take a stand against the constitutionality of a measure providing for the election of presiding elders, he and Soule alike basing their objection on the third restrictive rule. Is it probable that McKendree, ordained under these circumstances, and Soule, the author of the third restrictive rule, should have been mistaken as to the purport of its terms?

Wednesday afternoon, it was " moved by John McClaskey, and seconded by Daniel Ostrander, that the vote on the first resolution of the report of the committee of fourteen be taken by ballot," and the motion prevailed. When the ballot was counted " there were yeas 57, nays 64," and the first resolution of the report was lost. This carried with it the defeat of the whole measure, for the first resolution read, " The General Conference shall be composed of delegates from the Annual Conferences." The memorialists had won in committee: they were now defeated in the General Conference.

Great excitement ensued, for the measure was lost, it was believed, principally by the votes of the Philadelphia and Baltimore Conferences. " This defeat," says Dr. Lee, " was a source of surprise and sorrow." * "Asbury and other chief advocates of the measure," says Stevens, " were profoundly afflicted." † " The New England delegates asked leave of absence," says McTyeire, " stating that they were not disposed to make any faction, but they considered their presence useless. The Western delegates were in no pleasant mood. 'Burke's brow gathered a solemn frown; Sale and others looked sad; as for poor Lakin, he wept like a child.' " ‡ " When the vote announcing the

---

* Life of Jesse Lee, p. 442.   † Hist. M. E. Ch., IV. 440.
‡ Hist. of Meth., p. 512.

failure of the plan was declared," says Bishop Clark, "great dissatisfaction was manifested; and fears were at one time entertained that the Conference would break up without establishing any general bond of union among the widely-scattered portions of the work. Many of the preachers from the remote Conferences resolved to leave immediately, and return home. It was a crisis in the affairs of the Church, then in the infancy of its organization. 'Had they left at this crisis,' says Mr. Hedding, 'it would probably have been the last General Conference ever held.' All the members from the New England Conference, except himself, were making arrangements to depart. In this emergency he entreated them to remain." * "Six members from New England and two from the West retired in a body," says Bishop Paine, "and began to make preparations for their journey. But Bishop Asbury and Mr. McKendree sought an interview with them . . . and, aided by the wise and prudent Elijah Hedding, prevailed upon them to wait a day and see if a reconsideration of the question could not be effected, leading to a different result." † The central Conferences now saw the necessity of action if the unity of the Church was to be assured.

Thus matters stood from Wednesday afternoon, when the adverse vote was taken, until the following Monday morning, May 23. The subject of the time and place of the next General Conference being before the house, Leonard Cassell and Stephen G. Roszel moved, what was in fact but not in form, a reconsideration of the vote by which the report of the committee of fourteen had been rejected, namely, "that the motion for considering when and where the next General Conference shall be, lie over until it be determined who shall compose the General Conference." This motion prevailed, whereupon Enoch George, seconded by Roszel, moved "that the General Conference shall be composed of one member for every five members of each Annual Conference," which was "carried by a large majority." This was

---

* Life of Bishop Hedding, pp. 172, 173.   † Life of McKendree, I. 191.

a simple substitute for the somewhat complex recommendation of the committee, contained in the third and fourth
items of their report. The question now recurred on the
method of appointment of these delegates and, according to
the Journal, Joshua Soule, seconded by George Pickering,
moved that "each Annual Conference shall have the power
of sending their proportionate number of members to the
General Conference, either by seniority or choice, as they
shall think best." This was Soule's method of closing the
mouth of Jesse Lee, whose biographer gives us a precise
and interesting account of the adoption of this measure,
which substituted the second item of the committee's report:

> At a pause in the discussion, Mr. Soule moved to amend the article so as
> to read, "to be appointed by seniority or choice, at the discretion of such
> Annual Conference." This motion, if it did not put him [Lee] in a dilem-
> ma, neutralized his opposition, and he was speechless. Mr. Soule knew Mr.
> Lee was as inveterate an advocate of the independent rights of the Confer-
> ences, as he was of the condition of seniority in constituting the General
> Conference; and, with a sagacity that has not yet failed him, he placed his
> strongest adversary between the cross-fires of his own favorite doctrines. As
> amended, it maintained the independence of the Conferences, and commit-
> ted to the custody of that independence the very condition he defended as
> the proper basis of representation. His point was gained; but he felt that
> he had lost a victory. But he submitted; and, walking up to his friend, poked
> him in the side with his finger and whispered, "Brother Soule, you've
> played me a Yankee trick!"*

Soule's motion was carried at the afternoon session. It
was then decided that the next General Conference should
meet in New York, May 1, 1812. All the general assemblies of the Church had, thus far, been held in Baltimore:
the First Delegated General Conference assembled in New
York. At the same session, on the motion of Roszel, seconded by Lee, it was determined that "two thirds of the representatives of all the Annual Conferences" shall be necessary for a quorum in the General Conference. Tuesday
morning, May 24, the business concerning the Delegated
General Conference was rapidly completed, as follows:

> Moved by Jesse Lee, and seconded by William Burke, that the next † Gen-

---

* Life of Jesse Lee, pp. 442, 443.

† By this word Lee means the Delegated as distinct from the old General Conference. In
his history he speaks of 1808 as " the last General Conference."

eral Conference shall not change or alter any part or rule of our government, so as to do away episcopacy, or to destroy the plan of our itinerant general superintendency. Carried.

Moved by Steven G. Roszel, and seconded by George Pickering, that one of the superintendents preside in the General Conference; but in case of the absence of a superintendent the Conference shall elect a president *pro tem*. Carried.

Moved by Stephen G. Roszel, and seconded by Nelson Reed, that the General Conference shall have full powers to make rules and regulations for our Church, under the following restrictions, viz.:—

1. The General Conference shall not revoke, alter, or change our Articles of Religion, nor establish any new standards or rules of doctrine, contrary to our present existing and established standards of doctrine. Carried.

2. They shall not allow of more than one representative, for every five members of the Annual Conference, nor allow of a less number than one for every seven. Carried.

Moved by Daniel Hitt, and seconded by Samuel Coate, that a committee of three be appointed to modify certain exceptionable expressions in the General Rules. Lost.

3. They shall not revoke or change the " General Rules of the United Societies." Carried.

4. They shall not do away with the privileges of our ministers or preachers of trial by a committee, and of an appeal; neither shall they do away with the privileges of our members of trial before the society, or by a committee, and of an appeal. Carried.

5. They shall not appropriate the produce of the Book Concern or of the Charter Fund to any purpose other than for the benefit of the traveling, supernumerary, superannuated, and worn-out preachers, their wives, widows, and children. Carried.

6. *Provided*, nevertheless, that upon the joint recommendation of all the Annual Conferences, then a majority of two-thirds of the General Conference succeeding shall suffice to alter any of the above restrictions. Carried.[*]

In the afternoon of the same day, on motion of Ostrander, seconded by Cooper, it was agreed " that the general superintendents, with or by the advice of all the Annual Conferences, or, if there be no general superintendent, all the Annual Conferences, respectively, shall have power to call a General Conference, if they judge it necessary, at any time." It was then " moved from the chair," *i. e.*, by Bishop Asbury, " that the General Conference shall meet on the first day of May once in four years, perpetually, at such place or places as shall be fixed on by the General Conference from time to time."[†]   Finally, late on Thursday afternoon,

---

[*] Gen. Conf. Journals, I. 89.   [†] *Ibid.*, I. 90.

just before the final adjournment of the General Conference, on motion of Totten, seconded by Roszel, it was decided " that no preacher shall be sent as a representative to the General Conference, until he has traveled at least four full calendar years from the time that he was received on trial by an Annual Conference, and is in full connexion at the time of holding the Conference." *

Thus has been presented to the reader, in chronological order, the entire history of the legislation of 1808 concerning a Delegated General Conference. The skillful hand of the editor or editors of the Discipline of 1808 effected a logical combination of the whole in a section which does not deviate from the action of the Conference by a hair's breadth, as follows:

Ques. 2. Who shall compose the General Conference, and what are the regulations and powers belonging to it?

Ans. 1. The General Conference shall be composed of one member for every five members of each Annual Conference, to be appointed either by seniority or choice, at the discretion of such Annual Conference; yet so that such representatives shall have traveled at least four full calendar years from the time that they are received on trial by an Annual Conference, and are in full connection at the time of holding the Conference.

2. The General Conference shall meet on the first day of May, in the year of our Lord 1812, in the city of New York, and thenceforward on the first day of May once in four years, perpetually, in such place or places as shall be fixed on by the General Conference from time to time. But the general superintendents, with or by the advice of all the Annual Conferences, or, if there be no general superintendent, all the Annual Conferences respectively, shall have power to call a General Conference, if they judge it necessary, at any time.

3. At all times when the General Conferences meet, it shall take two-thirds of the representatives of all the Annual Conferences to make a quorum for transacting business.

4. One of the general superintendents shall preside in the General Conference; but in case no general superintendent be present, the General Conference shall choose a president *pro tempore.*

5. The General Conference shall have full powers to make rules and regulations for our Church, under the following limitations and restrictions, viz.:

1. The General Conference shall not revoke, alter, or change our Articles of Religion, nor establish any new standards or rules of doctrine contrary to our present existing and established standards of doctrine.

* Gen. Conf. Journals, I. 95.

2. They shall not allow of more than one representative for every five members of the Annual Conference, nor allow of a less number than one for every seven.

3. They shall not change or alter any part or rule of our government, so as to do away episcopacy or destroy the plan of our itinerant general superintendency.

4. They shall not revoke or change the General Rules of the United Societies.

5. They shall not do away the privileges of our ministers or preachers of trial by a committee, and of an appeal. Neither shall they do away the privileges of our members of trial before the society or by a committee, and of an appeal.

6. They shall not appropriate the produce of the Book Concern, nor of the Chartered Fund, to any purpose other than for the benefit of the traveling, supernumerary, superannuated, and worn-out preachers, their wives, widows, and children.

Provided, nevertheless, that upon the joint recommendation of all the Annual Conferences, then a majority of two-thirds of the General Conference succeeding shall suffice to alter any of the above restrictions.*

The Twenty-first Delegated General Conference of the Methodist Episcopal Church, which met at Omaha, Neb., in May, 1892, adopted, in lieu of the first part of the report of its able Constitutional Commission, appointed four years before, what is known as the Goucher substitute, the material part of which follows:

The section on the General Conference in the Discipline of 1808 [namely, the entire instrument cited above in full], as adopted by the General Conference of 1808, has the nature and force of a Constitution.

That section, together with such modifications as have been adopted since that time in accordance with the provisions for amendment in that section, is the present Constitution, etc.†

The writer of these lines had the pleasure of listening to the very able debate, which closed with the adoption of Dr. Goucher's substitute and Dr. Buckley's motion for the indefinite postponement of the remainder of the report of the Commission. That report recommended that under the heading of "The Organic Law of the Methodist Episcopal Church," the Discipline should contain, "Part I. Articles of Religion;" "Part II. The General Rules;" and "Part

---

* Emory, Hist. of the Discipline, ed. of 1844, pp. 111–114.
† Gen. Conf. Journal, XII., 1892, pp. 206, 228.

III. Constitution and Powers of the General Conference." *
The Constitution of the General Conference, as reported by
the Commission, contained somewhat more, however, than
that defined in Dr. Goucher's substitute, which, by the action of the General Conference, has become the *authoritative definition* of the Constitution, as accepted by the Methodist Episcopal Church.   That the Articles of Religion, the
General Rules (which embrace the only terms of membership and communion in Methodism), and the Constitution of
the General Conference make up the organic law of American Episcopal Methodism, there is no question.   There is
also universal agreement that the whole of the fifth answer
to Question 2, as established by the General Conference of
1808, and cited above, including the enacting clause, " The
General Conference shall have full powers to make rules
and regulations for our Church," and the six restrictive
rules, with the proviso for their amendment, generally
known as the " constitutional " or " restrictive rule " process, together with such alterations as have been introduced
by this process,—*i. e.*, by the concurrent action of General
and Annual Conferences by the constitutional majorities,—
is included in the Constitution of the General Conference.
Whether the four preceding answers to Question 2, enacted
likewise by the last General Conference of unlimited authority, by which (1) the composition, (2) the quadrennial
and extra sessions, (3) the quorum, and (4) the presidency
of the Delegated General Conference, are defined, are likewise a part of the Constitution, is a question about which
there is difference of opinion.   Dr. Goucher's substitute,
adopted by the General Conference of 1892, authoritatively
commits the Methodist Episcopal Church to the inclusion of
these four answers in the Constitution of the Delegated
General Conference.   There is much to be said in favor of
this view; but in this history, we are not called upon to enter upon the merits of this controversy as an abstract question.
It will be brought before us in concrete form by the action of

*Gen. Conf. Journal, XII., 1892, p. 394.

Delegated General Conferences of both the Methodist Episcopal Churches in modifying this portion of the Discipline.*

It remains, in pursuance of our plan, to notice the action
of the General Conference of 1808 with regard to Bishop
Coke, and also its action on the subject of slavery. This
was the first time the Doctor had been absent from a General Conference. In 1804 his recall to America had been
made subject to the action of any three Annual Conferences.
The Doctor in April, 1805, had married Miss Penelope
Goulding Smith, a lady of ample fortune, who proposed to
devote it to the advancement of the cause of missions, which
lay so near her husband's heart and her own. In June,
1805, Dr. Coke addressed a circular to the American preachers, saying: "As long as he [Asbury] can regularly visit
the seven Annual Conferences, you do not want me. But
if he was so debilitated that he could not attend the seven
Conferences, I should be willing to come over to you for
life, on the express condition that the seven Conferences
should be divided betwixt us [Asbury and himself], three
and four, and four and three, each of us changing our divisions annually; and that this plan, at all events, should continue permanent and unalterable during both our lives." †
This proposal, which strangely and unpardonably overlooked the position of Bishop Whatcoat, who was then engaged in the active discharge of his episcopal duties, and
which took the plan of superintendency out of the hands of
the General Conference as long as Coke and Asbury were
both alive, the Conferences very properly declined. Bishop
Coke addressed two letters to the General Conference of
1808, one with regard to his relations to American Methodism, dated Nov. 26, 1807, and the other, dated Jan. 29,
1808, explanatory of his negotiations with Bishop White, in
1791, which, in 1804, and afterwards, through a breach of

* For details, see Gen. Conf. Journal, XII., 1892, pp. 94, 132, 170, 206, 227,
228, 390–400. For the debates, see *Daily Christian Advocate*, 1892, for May
11, 12, and 13.

† An original copy of this circular, which Dr. Coke printed, addressed to
Martin Ruter, lies before me.

confidence, had become public and had excited much "un-circumcised rejoicing " in the Protestant Episcopal body. These two letters, together with an address from the British Conference, were referred to two committees, one to report on the case of Dr. Coke, and one on correspondence.*

In his second letter, Coke briefly recapitulates the contents of the first, " that if you judged that my being with you would help to preserve your union, and if I was allowed to give my opinion or judgment on every station of the preachers as far as I chose, and upon everything else that could come under the inspection of the bishops, or superintendents, you might call me, and we would settle our affairs in Europe as soon as possible and sail for America and be with you for life. Without your compliance in the latter point—namely, in respect to a full right in giving my judgment—I should be so far from being useful in preserving union that I should *merely* fill the place of a preacher." He explains at length his proposals for union with the Protestant Episcopal Church. In simple justice to Dr. Coke we must remember (1) that his office as a Methodist bishop did not deprive him of his position as a presbyter in the Church of England, which character he maintained, like Wesley, to the day of his death; (2) that the disastrous experiment of the Council had just failed; (3) that the O'Kelly and Hammett schisms were threatening the unity of American Methodism; (4) that no General Conference had yet been established; (5) that there was alienation between Asbury and Coke; and (6) that before his departure from the continent, Coke learned of Wesley's death, and was alarmed for the stability of English, no less than of American, Methodism. After mentioning most of these points, Coke, in his letter to the General Conference of 1808, continues:

I did verily believe then that, under God, the Connection would be more likely to be saved from convulsions by a union with the old Episcopal Church than any other way—not by a dereliction of ordination, sacraments, and the Methodist Discipline, but by a junction on proper terms. Bishop White, in two interviews I had with him in Philadelphia, gave me reason to believe

---

*Gen. Conf. Journals, I. 73.

that this junction might be accomplished with ease. Dr. Magaw was perfectly sure of it. Indeed (if Mr. Ogden, of New Jersey, did not mistake in the information he gave me), a canon passed the House of Bishops of the old Episcopal Church in favor of it. Bishop Madison, according to the same information, took the canon to the lower house. "But it was there thrown out," said Mr. Ogden, to whom I explained the whole business, "because they did not understand the full meaning of it." Mr. Ogden added that he spoke against it because he did not understand it, but that it would have met with his warm support had he understood the full intention of it.

I had provided in the fullest manner in my indispensable, necessary conditions for the security and, I may say, for the independence of our discipline and places of worship. But I thought (perhaps erroneously, and I *believe so now*) that our field of action would have been exceedingly enlarged by that junction, and that myriads would have attended our ministry in consequence of it who were at that time much prejudiced against us. All things unitedly considered led me to write the letter and meet Bishop White and Dr. Magaw on the subject in Philadelphia. . . . Therefore, I have no doubt but my consecration of Bishop Asbury was perfectly valid, and would have been so even if he had been reconsecrated. I never did apply to the general convention or any other convention for reconsecration. I never intended that either Bishop Asbury or myself should give up our episcopal office if the junction were to take place.

Bishop Coke's letter to Dr. White had closed with the request, "that if you have no thoughts of improving this proposal, you will burn this letter and take no more notice of it." On the contrary, in later years it was published by representatives of the Protestant Episcopal Church, in a diocesan controversy. In his Memoirs,* Bishop White says, "Dr. Coke's letter was answered by the author with the reserve which seemed incumbent on one who was incompetent to decide with effect on the proposal made." No doubt the good Bishop of Pennsylvania, in later years, regarded this as a fair account of his share in a correspondence which issued in nothing. But in his reply to Bishop Coke, he said, "I can say of the one and the other [of two difficulties mentioned by Coke] that I do not think them insuperable, provided there be a conciliatory disposition on both sides," and again, "In this situation, it is rather to be expected that distinct Churches, agreeing in fundamentals, should make mutual sacrifices for a union than that any Church should divide into two bodies without a difference

* Page 197.

beingeven alleged to exist in any leading point. For the preventing of this the measures which you may propose *cannot failo f success, unless there be on one side, or on both, a most lam entable deficiency of Christian temper."* As a matter of fact, Bishop Madison's proposals for union passed the House of Bishops—consisting then of four persons, Seabury, White, Provoost, and Madison—in the General Convention of 1792; but were thrown out in the House of Clerical and Lay Deputies.*

Commenting on this transaction a judicious authority says:

It was to be a *union*, where both parties made concessions and got advantages, but neither was absorbed. . . He [Coke] verily thought each Church could bring to the other some element of strength in their day of weakness. . . . The worst, the inexcusable part of this pragmatism is that Asbury was at his side when Coke wrote the letter, and was not taken into his confidence.†

Coke's letter to White bore date, April 24, 1791. April 25, Asbury records in his Journal, "I found the Doctor had much changed his sentiments since his last visit to this continent, and that these impressions still continued. I hope to be enabled to give up all I dare for peace sake, and to please all men for their good to edification." Thus Asbury was in an approachable mood, and Coke missed his opportunity. He declares, however, in his letter to the General Conference, that at Newcastle, Del., before sailing for England, he laid the matter before Asbury, "who, with that caution which peculiarly characterizes him, gave me no decisive opinion on the subject."

The final form of the action of the General Conference of 1808 in Bishop Coke's case was:

That the General Conference do agree and consent that Dr. Coke may continue in Europe till he be called to the United States by the General Conference, or by all the Annual Conferences, respectively; that we retain a grateful remembrance of the services and labors of Dr. Coke among us, and the thanks of this Conference are hereby acknowledged to him, and to God, for all his labors of love toward us, from the time he first left his native country to serve us; that Dr. Coke's name shall be retained on our Minutes after the name of the Bishops in a N. B.—"Dr. Coke, at the request of the British Conference, and by the consent of General Conference, resides in Eu-

* Bishop White's Memoirs, pp. 195-199. † McTyeire, Hist. of Meth., p. 516.

rope;" he is not to exercise the office of superintendent or bishop among us in the United States until he be recalled by the General Conference, or by all the annual conferences respectively; that the committee of correspondence be and are hereby directed to draft two letters, one to the British Conference, the other to Dr. Coke, in answer to their respective letters to us, and therein communicating to them respectively the contents of the above resolutions.*

In his earlier letter to the General Conference Dr. Coke had suggested an "N. B. Dr. Coke (or Bishop Coke, as you please) resides in Europe till he be called to the States by the General Conference or by the Annual Conferences," and thus the final action in 1808 was conformed very closely to his wishes. In their reply to Dr. Coke, the committee of correspondence say, among other things:

Your two letters were respectfully received and had a salutary effect upon our minds. . . . You may be assured that we feel an affectionate regard for you; that we gratefully remember your repeated labors of love toward us; and that we sensibly feel our obligations for the services you have rendered us. . . . In full Conference, of near one hundred and thirty members, we entered into a very long conversation, and very serious and solemn debate upon sundry resolutions which were laid before us relative to your case. Probably on no former occasion, in any Conference in America, was so much said in defense of your character and to your honor as a ministerial servant of God and his Church. Your worth, your labors, your disinterested services, fatigues, dangers, and difficulties to serve your American brethren were set forth pathetically, and urged with the force of reason and truth in an argumentative manner; and our candid and impartial judgments were constrained to yield to the conclusion that we were bound by the ties of moral and religious obligations to treat you most respectfully, and to retain a grateful remembrance of all your labors of love toward us.†

Thus amicably ended, as the event proved, relations which dated back to 1784. That Bishop Coke's prudence was not equal to his zeal, and that he more than once needlessly strained his relations with the American Conference, must be allowed by all, For the purposes of our history, these relations, as reviewed in detail in our pages for a quarter of a century from 1784 to 1808, may be summed up in the following paragraphs:

1. During the whole period of Bishop Coke's visits to

* Gen. Conf. Journals, I. 75, 76.   † See Bang's Hist. M. E. Ch., II. 196-226.

America, from 1784 to 1804, his episcopal character was never impeached, nor was he for a single day disqualified for the performance of any episcopal duty: he presided in every general assembly of the preachers from the Christmas Conference of 1784 to the General Conference of 1804, inclusive; and in the Annual Conferences where he was present exercised his episcopal functions of presidency and ordination.

2. Bishop Coke's affairs came under review in General Conferences of the original unlimited and supreme order only, working under no constitution, and confessedly competent to the entire abolition of both the doctrines and the government of the Church; consequently, had such a General Conference deprived Bishop Coke, even temporarily, of his episcopal character or functions, when he was present on the ground to exercise them—which no Conference ever did —no precedent or parallel would be thereby created with regard to the prerogatives of a General Conference exercising delegated and constitutionally limited powers.

3. Bishop Coke was never more than a visitor to America. His relations to Ecumenical Methodism were unique, and have had no parallel, at the time, before, or since. Almost all, if not all, of the actions of General Conferences in his case were taken *on his own initiative*, and concerning questions which he himself raised, growing out of his relations to both Methodisms. Most of these questions would have been settled tacitly and by common consent in a manner to meet his approval, as many of them were by express action, had not the Bishop's imprudence hurried him into formal demands at inopportune times, when his relations were complicated with other questions before the Conference, such as the election and powers of new bishops, etc.

4. From the beginning of General Conferences in 1792, the law has been that a bishop might cease from traveling by the consent of the General Conference. Coke's circumstances were such that it was simply impossible for him to travel at large as Asbury did. His service could not be

21

continuous. The successive permissions given to him, therefore, to render a limited service, with which the Conference and the Connexion would be content, were legally of the nature of " consent by the General Conference " for a bishop to " cease from traveling at large among the people." * The action is thus of a piece with that which takes place at nearly every General Conference when our aged and worn out bishops make formal application for permission to cease from traveling. The law has never made sickness and infirmity the sole ground upon which this permission may be granted. In Coke's case, it was given on the ground of necessary foreign residence. In every case, the General Conference is the sole judge of the sufficiency of the ground.

5. Notwithstanding the frequent imprudences of Bishop Coke, and the uncertainties which attached to our episcopacy and the whole government of the Methodist Episcopal Church, until the adoption of the Constitution of 1808, the successive General Conferences, of unlimited powers, treated Bishop Coke, not with severity, but with the utmost kindness and consideration, frequently seeking to obtain or to retain his permanent services, which, with the best intentions, he was never able to give. Finally, when satisfied after repeated experiment that such continuous service could not be rendered by Bishop Coke in America, notwithstanding his willing engagements to that end, and when his standing was greatly prejudiced and complicated by the discovery of his ill-advised and most unfortunate negotiations with Dr. White, the General Conference respectfully and affectionately consented to Bishop Coke's foreign residence and service, adding an official proviso, which contemplated the contingency of his recall to episcopal duty and station in America.

With regard to slavery, on motion of Roszel and Ware, it was determined " that the first two paragraphs of the section on slavery be retained in our Discipline; and that the General Conference authorize each Annual Conference to form

---

* Discipline of 1792.

their own regulations relative to buying and selling slaves." *
This action was taken apparently without debate or division.
Thus all that related to slaveholding among private members
was struck out, and the action recorded above became paragraph 3. It was also " moved from the chair," that is, by
Bishop Asbury, " that there be one thousand forms of Discipline prepared for the use of the South Carolina Conference,
in which the section and rule on slavery be left out," and
this motion, too, was carried, as it seems, unanimously and
without debate.† Dictated by the experience and prudence
of Bishop Asbury, though this measure was,

Here were two codes of Discipline, put forth as law by the same ecclesiastical legislature, and intended to operate for the promotion of unity and
uniformity among the same people! . . . In 1808 the Discipline itself
was expurgated [of both the " general rule" and the section of statutory
law]; and, by special enactment, exempted from conveying the laws of the
Church to a select circle of its members. Doubtless there was benevolence
intended by this measure; but it presents such an anomaly in legislation, as
tempts us to blush at every aspect in which it presents the legislative acumen
of our fathers. Was it from this feeling, or from unwillingness to circulate
this great disparaging fact of their pro-slavery affinities after all, that Dr.
Bangs omits all reference to the subject in his account of the General Conference of 1808?‡

This dangerous and unjustifiable act of 1808 was one of
the entering wedges that ultimately split the Church in twain.
Thursday afternoon, May 26, 1808, adjournment without a
day was reached: thus ended the Fifth and last unlimited
and supreme Quadrennial General Conference of the Methodist Episcopal Church.

The term " Delegated " is chosen to mark the altered and
distinct character of all subsequent General Conferences.
This word indicates, not only that the members of these
later bodies are elected representatives, or delegates, but
that the Conference itself exercises delegated powers. It is
an agent, not a principal. It is a dependent body, with derived powers. These powers are defined in a Constitution
issuing from the body that ordained the Delegated Confer-

---

* Gen. Conf. Journals, I. 93. † *Ibid.*, I. 93.
‡ Dr. L. M. Lee's Life of Jesse Lee, pp. 444, 445.

ence. Historically the fountain of authority in Episcopal Methodism is the body of traveling elders. They created the existing General Conference, ordained its Constitution, and finally admitted laymen to their seats in the body. That body of traveling elders saw fit to place (1) the doctrines, (2) the General Rules, (3) the Episcopacy, or itinerant general superintendency, according to the "plan" then existing in the Church, (4) the rights of ministers and members to formal trial and appeal, (5) the produce of funds and plants originating with and sustained by the traveling preachers, and (6) the ratio of representation in the delegated body, beyond the reach of the new General Conference. Of these six restrictive rules, one only protects an integral part of the government of the Church—the Episcopacy—which the Church had tested for a quarter of a century, from modification by the Delegated Conference. This branch of the government is best described as " executive," since here is lodged the duty of administering the " rules and regulations " enacted by the General Conference in the exercise of its constitutional powers. If sometimes it is said that the Episcopacy and the General Conference are coördinate departments of our government, it is not meant to raise the question of their relative importance, or even to stress the analogies of civil government, but only to express the fact that the Episcopacy holds a charter from the same body of elders that created the present General Conference. By law existing then and ever since, the Episcopacy is responsible to the General Conference for the execution of all statutes enacted according to its constitutionally delegated powers. Should a difference of view arise as to the construction of these powers, the appeal would lie in equity to the body of elders from whom the Episcopacy holds its charter and the General Conference its constitution. How this problem has been wrought out in the later history of the Church our next Book will show.

BOOK VI.

—

THE DELEGATED GENERAL CONFERENCES OF THE UNDIVIDED METHODIST EPISCOPAL CHURCH.

(325)

CHAPTER XIX.

THE FIRST AND SECOND DELEGATED GENERAL CONFERENCES, 1812 AND 1816.

THE First Delegated General Conference of the Methodist Episcopal Church met, according to appointment, in John Street Church, in the city of New York, May 1, 1812, and adjourned May 22. It was composed of ninety delegates from eight Conferences, of whom the Philadelphia and Baltimore Conferences had less than one third. The Genesee Conference had been created by the two Bishops in 1809, without warrant from the General Conference of 1808; though in 1796 it had been provided, " that the Bishops shall have authority to appoint other Yearly Conferences in the interval of the General Conference." This grant of power, however, appears never to have been inserted in the Discipline; and a great outcry was raised against this exercise of episcopal authority, but Bishop Asbury declares it " was one of the most judicious acts of our Episcopacy." The question of the constitutionality of this proceeding of the Bishops was expressly raised in the Virginia Conference, however, and Bishop Asbury passed the matter around to all the Annual Conferences for decision, and the course of the Bishops was approved. The General Conference of 1812 also passed a resolution, " that the Genesee Annual Conference is a legally constituted and organized Conference;" but it was the last time an Annual Conference was organized in this way.

Alternate or reserve delegates had been elected by the New England Conference, and these were recognized and seated in the place of absent principals: this precedent has been received as sufficient legal warrant for the continuance of the practice in both Episcopal Methodisms to this day.

This was the first Conference under the Constitution; but, just as the government of 1784 was first tested in 1787, so the Constitution of 1808 received its first strain in 1820, when the election of presiding elders was carried affirmatively. Jesse Lee was defeated in an effort to have the delegates to the General Conference appointed by seniority, and to change the ratio of representation from five to six. Local deacons were admitted to elders' orders, provided "no slaveholder shall be eligible to the office," etc. The election of presiding elders, after animated and protracted debate, and an amendment that the bishops should continue to nominate until an election was effected, was defeated in both the amended and the original forms.

Bishop McKendree presented the first, formal, episcopal address to the Conference, a precedent which the bishops have ever since uniformly followed. Among other things, he said that the extent of the work might "make it proper for you to inquire if the work is sufficiently under the oversight of the Superintendency, and to make such arrangements and provisions as your wisdom may approve;" but the Conference declined "to strengthen the episcopacy" at this time. He invited inspection of his episcopal administration by the Conference; saying,

> I consider myself justly accountable, not for the system of government, but for my administration, and ought therefore to be ready to answer in General Conference for my past conduct, and be willing to receive information and advice to perfect future operations. I wish this body to exercise their rights in these respects.*

This address had been submitted privately to a "committee of the most respectable and influential members" of the Conference, from which some of Bishop McKendree's confidential friends were designedly omitted, and "men of talents of different sentiments as to the polity of the Church" selected. Moreover, an amendment suggested by these brethren had been adopted,† but when the address was read in Conference,

---

* See the whole address in Paine's McKendree, I. 265-270.

† *Ibid.*, MoKendree's *memorandum*, pp. 270, 271.

As it was a new thing, the aged Bishop (Asbury) rose to his feet immediately after the paper was read, and addressed the junior Bishop to the following effect: " I have something to say to you before the Conference." The junior also rose to his feet, and they stood face to face. Bishop Asbury went on to say, " This is a new thing. I never did business in this way, and why is this new thing introduced?" The junior Bishop promptly replied, " You are our *father*, we are your sons; you never have had need of it. I am only a *brother*, and have need of it." Bishop Asbury said no more, but sat down with a smile on his face.*

With reference to the addresses of Bishops before the Conference, we find several entries in the Journal. Friday, May 8: "After calling the list, Bishop Asbury addressed himself to Bishop McKendree, or to the Conference through him, in a kind of historical account of the work in past years, the present state, and what probably may be the future state of the work on the continent. Bishop McKendree rose and replied, expressive of his approbation." Saturday, May 9: "After calling the list, Bishop Asbury rose and addressed himself to Bishop McKendree on the subject of defining the bounds of the Annual Conferences." Friday, May 15: "After calling the list, Bishop Asbury rose and requested leave of the Conference to address Bishop McKendree in the presence of the Conference. Leave was granted. Bishop Asbury then proceeded to address himself to Bishop McKendree and the Conference conjointly. Bishop McKendree then rose and addressed himself to Bishop Asbury and the Conference." † In each case, Bishop McKendree appears to have been in the chair. To this extent—once by formal leave, asked and granted—a bishop who was not presiding participated in the business of the Conference. There is no record of either bishop's offering a motion or resolution, or taking part in debate. The Constitution of the Delegated General Conference did not formally exclude the bishops from the privileges they had hitherto exercised in the Conference; but when the body became delegated, representative, elective, and acted

---

* Rev. Henry Smith's letter to Bishop Paine, Feb. 6, 1855: Smith was a member and present.

† Gen. Conf. Journals, I. 104, 106, 110.

under a Constitution, the bishops ceased to claim the rights of the floor.   But the bishops seem occasionally to have given the casting vote in a tie until 1840, when Bishop Hedding from the chair expressly declined to do so.*   At this Conference, however, Bishops Soule and Morris introduced resolutions.

In addition to Bishop McKendree's written address, Bishop Asbury made a verbal communication; and so much of it as related to " his thoughts of going to Europe on a visit " and to " regulations, providing for the locating, or supernumerary, or superannuated relation of a bishop," was, with similar portions of Bishop McKendree's address referred to the committee on episcopacy, consisting of eight members, one from each Annual Conference, who had been previously elected.   Other standing committees, such as those on revisal, boundaries, and book concern, were raised at this General Conference, and have ever since been a part of the working machinery of the body.   The committee on boundaries reported in favor of dividing the Western Conference into the Ohio and Tennessee, which was concurred in, and in favor of a Mississippi Conference, which the bishops were authorized to form during the quadrennium if necessary.

The committee on episcopacy reported on Bishop Asbury's suggestions as follows:

1. That it is our sincere request and desire that Bishop Asbury would relinquish his thoughts of visiting Europe, and confine his labors to the American connexion so long as God preserves him a blessing to the Church.

2. As it respects the instituting of a rule to fix the relation of our bishops other than that in which they now stand to the Church of God, we do not see our way clear to recommend such a measure: this much we would observe, that we conceive it to be a case in which our bishops should exercise their own discretion, and, should circumstances make it necessary for them to curtail their labors, it will be for the succeeding General Conference to approve of the same.†

This action was reported and adopted May 9.   Previously the committee had requested the opinion of the bishops as to the propriety of electing another bishop, and, as Bishop Asbury had been invited to England by the British Conference, the episcopal committee wished to know if he contem-

---

*Clark's Life of Hedding, pp. 556–558.   † Gen. Conf. Journals, I. 115.

plated the visit. It seems that action similar to that which
had been taken in the case of Bishop Coke had been regarded as necessary or desirable. This appears from the first
item of the committee's report, cited above, and also from
Bishop Asbury's reply to the inquiries of the committee,
dated New York, May 9, 1812:

My Dear Brethren: Whatever I may have thought or spoken in former
times upon strengthening the Episcopacy, I am not at liberty to say to you
at this time, Do this, or that. I am bound in duty to serve the Connection
with all my power of body and mind, as long and as largely as I can; and,
while I am persuaded that my services are needed and acceptable, to give
up all thoughts of visits out of the American Continent. I feel myself in-
dispensably bound to the Conference and my colleague, never to leave them
nor forsake them upon the above conditions.   F. ASBURY.*

When McKendree first entered on his episcopal duties,
Asbury proposed that they should both attend in company
all the Annual Conferences, as Asbury and Coke had done
when the latter was in the country, and as Asbury and
Whatcoat had continued to do, as long as Bishop Whatcoat
lived. The junior bishop readily acceded to this proposal
of his senior colleague, and such was their custom until the
death of Asbury in 1816. Of their first episcopal tour, Asbury says, " We are riding in a poor thirty-dollar chaise, in
partnership, two Bishops of us; but it must be confessed
that it tallies well with our purses." They often, however,
pursued different routes from the seat of one Annual Conference to that of the next, that they might preach and more
extensively oversee the work. In 1811 Bishop Asbury attended all the Conferences, and found time to visit Canada.
At first both the bishops shared in the public presidency of
the Conferences, but gradually, as the senior became convinced of the exceptional abilities of the junior bishop, and
his own infirmities increased, he relinquished to him the
presidential chair, and confined himself to the duty of stationing the preachers and assisting in the ordinations. The
last Conference Asbury attended was the Tennessee, at

---

* Paine's McKendree, I. 275. The original was in Bishop Paine's possession, endorsed by Roszel, a member of the committee.

Bethlehem, Wilson county, Oct. 20, 1815. Here he says, "My *eyes* fail: I will resign the *stations* to Bishop McKendree." Both the bishops were unalterably opposed to the plan of an elective presiding eldership; Asbury always refused their aid in stationing the preachers. He was perfectly familiar with the preachers and the work and preferred to make the appointments solely on his own judgment and responsibility. This plan of Asbury's, McKendree refused to adopt, and to him we owe the " cabinet" of presiding elders, who regularly assist the bishops in making the appointments. As is well known, there is no provision for such a meeting in the Discipline: it has simply become universal usage, and its introduction we owe to Bishop McKendree. When urged by Bishop Asbury to adopt his plan of stationing the preachers without consulting the elders, Bishop McKendree addressed to him the following letter, which, as a kind of *Magna Charta* of the cabinet meeting, is here cited.

CINCINNATI, Oct. 8, 1811.

Brother Asbury: I am fully convinced of the utility and necessity of the council of the Presiding Elders in stationing the preachers, but you fear individuals will make it difficult, if not impracticable, for you to proceed on this plan. I am willing to assist you in the best way I can; and, as I am in duty bound, so I hold myself in readiness to render the most effectual service to the Church. Consequently, I am still willing to accede to the proposition which you made at the Genesee Conference, if it may be qualified. If it is still your wish, I will take the plan of stations, after you have matured it—call the Elders to my assistance, and, after deliberate council, report in favor, or dictate such alterations as may be thought necessary. But I still refuse to take the *whole* responsibility upon myself, not that I am afraid of proper accountability, but because I conceive the proposition included one highly improper.

Yours, in the bonds of a yoke-fellow, W. McKENDREE.*

The Second Delegated General Conference assembled in Baltimore, May 1, 1816, and adjourned May 24. A valedictory address of the deceased Asbury to the General Conference was read. Bishop McKendree's episcopal message was presented by Thomas L. Douglass. Both addresses were referred to a committee to distribute the distinct topics contained in them to appropriate committees. As a result

---

* Paine's McKendree, I. 260, 261.

six standing committees were ordered: on Episcopacy; on the Book Concern; on Ways and Means; on Review and Revision; on Safety; and on Temporal Economy.

Tuesday, May 7, Samuel Merwin moved that in answer to the question, "How shall the presiding elders be chosen and appointed?" the Discipline should read, "At an early period in each Annual Conference the bishop shall nominate a person for each district that is to be supplied, and the Conference shall, without debate, proceed in the choice, the person nominated being absent; and if the person nominated be not chosen according to nomination, the bishop shall nominate two others, one of whom it shall be the duty of Conference to choose;" and in answer to the question, "By whom shall the preachers be appointed to their stations?" Merwin moved, "By the bishop with the advice and counsel of the presiding elders." * The motion was ordered to lie on the table. Wednesday afternoon the subject was taken up, and the Conference resolved itself into a committee of the whole. Bishop McKendree called Garrettson to the chair and retired. The committee rose, reported progress, asked leave to sit again, and the Bishop resumed the chair. Thursday afternoon the committee of the whole sat again on the same business, Bishop McKendree calling Philip Bruce to the chair. Friday the same process was gone through with once more, George Pickering being in the chair. Saturday morning, in committee of the whole, with Philip Bruce in the chair, Nathan Bangs offered the following amendment, which was accepted by the original mover:

The bishop, at an early period of the Annual Conference, shall nominate an elder for each district, and the Conference shall, without debate, either confirm or reject such nomination. If the person or persons so nominated be not elected by the Conference, the bishop shall nominate two others for each of the vacant districts, one of whom shall be chosen. And the presiding elder so elected and appointed shall remain in office four years, unless dismissed by the mutual consent of the Bishop and Conference, or elected to some other office by the General Conference. But no presiding elder shall be removed from office during the term of four years without his consent, unless the reasons for such removal be stated to him in presence of the Conference, which shall decide, without debate, on his case.†

---

* Gen. Conf. Journals, I. 135. † *Ibid.*, I. 140.

"After considerable debate the committee rose, reported progress, and begged leave to sit again. Bishop McKendree resumed the chair." Saturday afternoon, the vote on the measure was taken in committee of the whole, "and it was lost, 42 in favor and 60 against it." Philip Bruce, chairman, so reported to the Conference. Monday morning, May 13, the vote was "taken on the first part of the main question— 38 in favor of the motion and 63 against it." In the afternoon, the vote was "taken on the second part of the motion and it was lost." * Thus after being before the Conference for a week, and having been thoroughly analyzed and debated, the measure was defeated by an overwhelming majority. At a later date, a resolution, " that the motion relative to the election and appointment of presiding elders is not contrary to the constitution of our Church," was lost.†

The Committee on Episcopacy formally approved the administration of the bishops, and recommended the election of two additional bishops. Enoch George obtained 57 out of 106 votes on the first ballot, and Robert Richford Roberts, 55 on the second. After their election, but before their ordination, McKendree several times retired and called William Phœbus to the chair. Friday, May 17, was appointed for the ordinations, and Saturday morning Bishop Roberts occupied the chair, as he did frequently during the remainder of the session. From the Journal, which is signed by McKendree only, it appears that Bishop George was not in the chair during the session. " His feeling of self-distrust was such as to make the duties of public intercourse, which his office drew upon him, embarrassing and painful. For constitutional questions he had no taste." ‡

The select committee on slavery reported, " that the evil appears to be past remedy," and that " they are constrained to admit that to bring about such a change in the civil code as would favor the cause of liberty is not in the power of the General Conference." They find that some of the Annual

* Gen. Conf. Journals, I. 135–141.   † *Ibid.*, p. 164.
‡ McTyeire, Hist. of Meth., p. 537.

Conferences have made no efficient rules on the subject, and recommend

That all the recommendatory part of the second division, ninth section, and first answer of our form of Discipline, after the word "slavery" be stricken out, and the following words inserted: "Therefore no slaveholder shall be eligible to any official station in our Church hereafter where the laws of the state in which he lives will admit of emancipation, and permit the liberated slave to enjoy freedom."

The report was adopted.*

It was made "the duty of the bishops, or of a committee which they may appoint at each Annual Conference, to point out a course of reading and study to be pursued by candidates for the ministry," and ordered that "before any such candidate is received into full connexion he shall give satisfactory evidence of his knowledge of those particular subjects." This is the first legislation of the kind in the history of the Church.

As appears from the Journal of Bishop McKendree, at the close of the General Conference of 1816, the three bishops divided the work among themselves, "mutually agreeing to attend the Conferences alternately, thus changing their work every year; and for the Bishop, whose turn it might be to attend a Conference, to be the responsible president of it; and the other Bishops, if present, to be his counselors."

"Thus," remarks Bishop Paine, "was begun the practice of dividing the work of superintending the Conferences by the Bishops themselves, and also of alternating." † It was, however, proposed by the senior bishop, that they should all attend the first three Conferences in company, "to adjust their views and mode of presiding, so that they might administer harmoniously when separated," as neither of the juniors "was acquainted with the general state of the Church, nor with the peculiarities and difficulties of the episcopal duties." To this proposal Bishop Roberts acceded, but Bishop George could not see it "necessary for three men to go and do one man's work." Accordingly McKendree and Roberts set out together, and all three of the bishops met at the

---

* Gen. Conf. Journals, I. 169, 170.   † Paine's McKendree, I. 361, 362.

session of the Ohio Conference, at Louisville, Ky., Sept. 3.
" From that point they were to commence their general plan
of operation. According to this arrangement, there was an
ideal division of the work into three parts—the senior Bishop taking the first, Bishop George the second, and Bishop
Roberts the third. Each was bound to attend his allotted
part; not, however, to the exclusion of the other two, who
were at liberty to attend officially." *

In addition to the address to the General Conference of
1816, Bishop Asbury left, "A Valedictory Address to William McKendree, Bishop of the Methodist Episcopal
Church." The paper is dated Lancaster Co., Penn., Aug.
5, 1813, and fills thirty five pages of Bishop Paine's Life of
McKendree. Only a sentiment or two from it can be given
here:

Guard particularly against two orders of preachers—the one for the
country, the other for the cities. . . . You know, my brother, that the
present ministerial cant is, that we cannot now, as in former apostolical
days, have such doctrines, such discipline, such convictions, such conver-
sions, such witnesses of sanctification, and such holy men. But I say that
we can; I say we must; yea, I say we have. . . . Should we go to Pres-
byterians to be ordained Episcopal Methodists? or to Episcopalians, who at
that time had no Bishop, or power of ordination in the United States? . . .
Here let it be observed, that the Methodist was the first Church organized after the establishment of peace in 1783, and that the Protestant Episcopalians
were not organized as a Church until after there was a law passed by the
British Parliament. . . . And suppose this excellent [Methodist] constitution and order of things should be broken, what shall the present or future
Bishops do? Let them do as your noble countryman [George Washington]
did—resign and retire into private life. It is a serious thing for a Bishop to
be stripped of any constitutional rights chartered to him at his ordination,
without which he could not, and would not, have entered into that sacred
office—he being conscious at the same time he had never violated those sacred rights. . . . Thus I have traced regular order and succession in
John Wesley, Thomas Coke, Francis Asbury, Richard Whatcoat, and William McKendree. Let any other Church trace its succession as direct and
as pure if they can. . . . Should there be at any time failure in any department, such as you cannot cure nor restore, appeal to the General Conference. . . . Never be afraid to trust young men. . . . It is my
confirmed opinion that the apostles acted both as bishops and traveling superintendents in planting and watering, ruling and ordering the whole Connection; and that they did not ordain any local bishops, but that they or-

---

* Paine's McKendree, I. 361-363.

dained local deacons and elders. . . . Mark! it was in the *second* visit that Paul and Barnabas established order: and why was Timothy or Titus sent if elders could ordain elders? And why had the apostle to go or send, if it was not held as the divine right of the apostles to ordain? . . . You know that for four years past I have, with pleasure, resigned to you the presidency of the nine Annual Conferences. .. . . Our government being spiritual, one election to office is sufficient during life, unless in cases of debility, a voluntary resignation of the office, corruption in principle, or immorality in practice. . . . My dear Bishop! it is the traveling apostolic order and ministry that is found in our very constitution.*

Such were the mature opinions and the parting counsels of the Apostle of American Methodism, expressed to his colleague in the episcopacy. We are not concerned to establish the correctness of the opinions, or, in every case, the wisdom of the counsels; but it is the province of history to ascertain what, as a matter of fact, were the tenets cherished by a man like Asbury, and, particularly, his life-long views with regard to Methodist government and its Episcopacy. He was not a Presbyterian: on the contrary, he was a staunch Episcopalian, of the once common moderate type, to the last. In this he was the representative of many. The modern writers who would reduce our ministry to a " presbyterial parity," and ascribe their doctrine to the founders of our Church, do the fathers and themselves a gross injustice, when they hang their arguments on the chance employment of a word. The early literature of American Methodism is filled with express statements and arguments, as well as passing references, which decisively prove the contrary.

---

* Paine's Life and Times of William McKendree, I. 310–345.

22

CHAPTER XX.

THE THIRD DELEGATED GENERAL CONFERENCE, AND MR. SOULE'S FIRST ELECTION TO THE EPISCOPACY, 1820.

THE Conference met in Baltimore, May 1, 1820, and was composed of eighty nine delegates, from eleven Conferences. Bishop McKendree presented, as usual, a written address, cited in full by Bishop Paine,[*] and Bishops George and Roberts made verbal communications, all of which were referred to appropriate committees. The Missionary Society was organized; the educational interests of the Church set forward; District Conferences for local preachers created; slavery legislation resumed; the Canada question considered; and the election of presiding elders agitated amid much excitement which did not soon abate.

Saturday morning, May 13, after prayer by Freeborn Garrettson, Joshua Soule was elected the seventh bishop of the Methodist Episcopal Church, receiving 47 out of 88 votes on the first ballot. Nathan Bangs, who favored at that time the election of presiding elders, received 38 votes.

Three days later, " the resolution that had been laid on the table relating to the choice of presiding elders " was called up. The Journal is evidently defective, for this is the first mention of the subject in the official record. From a memorandum of William Capers, (a member of the Conference and of the committee which reported the " suspended " resolutions,) prepared at the time for the information of Bishop McKendree, who had retired into the country, we learn that Messrs. Merritt and Waugh had previously introduced the motion for the election of presiding elders. Their resolution, as the Journal shows, was debated, when called up,

---

* Life of McKendree, I. 397–404.

almost continuously for two days, when Cooper and Emory offered their substitute, " that the Bishops should nominate three times the number of presiding elders wanted," out of which the Conference should elect by ballot without debate.* Emory and Capers, who were on opposite sides of the question at issue, agree that Bishop George was the real author of this measure, as well as of the proposal for a committee of conciliation, brought in later by Messrs. Bangs and Capers.† This committee, appointed by Bishop George, consisted of Cooper, Emory, and Bangs, who favored the proposed change, and of Roszel, Wells, and Capers, who approved the existing plan. Their duty was to confer with the Bishops, and thus mature a report which should " conciliate the wishes of the brethren upon this subject."

Of the consultations which followed, we have three accounts, by McKendree, Capers, and Emory, respectively, all participants, and all agreeing in essentials.‡ McKendree disapproved of the proposed change; the other two Bishops were favorable to some alteration. On the adjournment of Conference, Friday morning, May 19, Bishop George invited the committee to meet him in the gallery of the Church. He, it appears, had stated in a note to Mr. Merritt, the author of the original resolution, that the views of the two parties could not be harmonized; but explanations were now made on this point, and the Bishop set forth his "accommodating plan" to the satisfaction of Roszel; the committee then united on a report written by John Emory, which the Conference passed that afternoon, without debate, by a majority of 61 to 25. It included the nomination by the Bishops of three times the number of presiding elders wanted, from which the Conference should elect, and declared " that the presiding elders be, and they hereby are,

* Capers's *Mem.* in Paine's McKendree, I. 409; Gen. Conf. Journals, I. 211–213.

† Capers, as above; Dr. Emory's Life of Bishop Emory, p. 146.

‡ McKendree's Journal and Capers's *Mem.* in Paine's McKendree, I. 409, 410, 415; Dr. Emory's Life of Bishop Emory, p. 146.

made the advisory council of the bishop or president of the Conference in stationing the preachers." *

Immediately upon the adoption of this report, the Journal shows that Joshua Soule obtained leave of absence for the afternoon. He at once prepared the following letter, addressed to Bishops George and Roberts:

Dear Bishops:—In consequence of an act of the General Conference, passed this day, in which I conceive the constitution of the Methodist Episcopal Church is violated, and that Episcopal government which has heretofore distinguished her greatly enervated, by a transfer of executive power from the Episcopacy to the several Annual Conferences, it becomes my duty to notify you, from the imposition of whose hands only I can be qualified for the office of Superintendent, that under the existing state of things *I cannot, consistently with my convictions of propriety and obligation, enter upon the work of an itinerant General Superintendent.*

I was elected under the *constitution and government of the Methodist Episcopal Church* UNIMPAIRED. On no other consideration but that of their *continuance* would I have consented to be considered a candidate for a relation in which were incorporated such arduous labors and awful responsibilities.

I do not feel myself at liberty to wrest myself from your hands, as the act of the General Conference has placed me in them; but *I solemnly declare, and could appeal to the Searcher of hearts for the sincerity of my intention, that I cannot act as Superintendent under the rules this day made and established by the General Conference.*

With this open and undisguised declaration before you, your wisdom will dictate the course proper to be pursued.

I ardently desire peace, and if it will tend to promote it, am willing, perfectly willing, that my name should rest in forgetfulness.†

This act of the Bishop-elect was prompt and decisive. The question was not new to him; and on the very afternoon when the General Conference passed the measure of whose unconstitutionality he was satisfied, he penned and delivered to the bishops this clear, straightforward, manly document. The candid reader will keep in mind (1) that Joshua Soule was himself the author of the Constitution of the Methodist Episcopal Church; (2) that, in particular, he had insisted, against Cooper, on the exact phraseology of the third restrictive rule, which forbade the General Conference to "*change or alter any part or rule of our government,* so as to do away episcopacy, or *destroy the plan* of our itiner-

---

* Gen. Conf. Journals, I. 221.   † Paine's McKendree, I. 420, 421.

ant general superintendency;'' (3) that the adoption of the report which embodied this Constitution was expressly postponed until this very question of the election of presiding elders could first be settled; (4) that twice in his letter to the Bishops, Mr. Soule declares that he '' cannot enter upon the work of,'' that he '' cannot act as,'' a General Superintendent; and, while leaving the final disposition of the matter to the joint wisdom of the Bishops, professes perfect willingness that his ''name should rest in forgetfulness;'' (5) that such prompt declination of the high office to which the General Conference had elected him, can leave no doubt as to the purity of Mr. Soule's motives and the strength and clearness of his conviction of the unconstitutionality of the act, which, rather than obligate himself to execute, he would surrender his election to the General Superintendency.

When Bishop Roberts brought this letter to the notice of Bishop McKendree, Monday, May 22, he (Roberts) expressed the opinion that the Bishop-elect did not seem disposed to submit to the authority of the General Conference. McKendree thought this would constitute a serious objection to Mr. Soule's ordination; but doubted whether such a sentiment was expressed in the letter. '' It was agreed,'' continues McKendree, in his Journal, '' that Bishop Roberts should see Brother Soule, and report at a meeting of the Bishops to be held next morning. Soule disavowed the sentiment which the letter was supposed to contain, and stated his views on the back of the letter in terms too plain to be misunderstood.''

Bishop McKendree has left on record a full account of the private consultations of the Bishops:

The Bishops met early next morning [Tuesday, May 23] and the communication was attentively considered. It appeared that the difficulties of the Bishop-elect rested entirely upon the question of the constitutionality of the resolutions; and it was proposed for the Bishops to express their opinions on their constitutionality. Bishop Roberts was of the opinion that the resolutions of the Conference were an infringement of the constitution. Bishop George chose to be silent. The senior Bishop considered them unconstitutional. The next question was the propriety of ordaining the Bishop-elect under existing circumstances. It was unanimously agreed that he should be ordained. The time was agreed upon, and Bishop George was appointed to prepare the credentials, and to preach the ordination-sermon. The senior Bishop then suggested the propriety of informing the Conference of the state of things. It was approved, and he was requested to make the communication, and the Bishop-elect, having been informed of the design, approved of the course. When the president—Bishop Roberts—had called the attention of the Conference, the senior Bishop laid the case before them. The letter of the Bishop-elect to the Bishops was read; the conclusion of the council of the Bishops, and their resolution to ordain Brother Soule were stated, as well as an intimation of their opinions respecting the constitutional difficulty.*

Thus far McKendree's record: from the Journal of the Conference, we gather, that, on Tuesday morning, May 23, Bishop Roberts being in the chair, " the debate on the subject under consideration was suspended, to allow Bishop McKendree to make a communication to the General Conference." † This communication embraced not only the matters agreed upon at the Bishops' meeting in the early morning of the same day, but also what McKendree euphemistically styles above " an intimation of his opinions respecting the constitutional difficulty." His letter had been prepared the day before and runs as follows:

BALTIMORE, May 22, 1820.

To the Bishops and General Conference, now in session:

On Saturday evening I received a copy of the resolution which passed on the 19th instant, which, contrary to the established order of our Church, authorizes the Annual Conference to elect the Presiding Elders, and thereby transfers the executive authority from the General Superintendents to the Annual Conferences, and leaves the Bishops divested of their power to oversee the business under the full responsibility of General Superintendents. I extremely regret that you have, by this measure, reduced me to the painful necessity of pronouncing the resolution *unconstitutional, and therefore destitute of the proper authority of the Church.*

While I am firmly bound, by virtue of my office, to see that all the rules are properly enforced, I am equally bound to prevent the imposition of that which is not properly rule. Under the influence of this sentiment, and considering the importance of the subject, I enter this *protest.*

If the delegated Conference has a right in one case to impose rules contrary to the constitution which binds hundreds of preachers and thousands of members in Christian fellowship, and on which their own existence and the validity of their acts depend, why may not the same right exist in another? why not in all cases? If the right of infringing the constitution is ad-

---

* Paine's McKendree, I. 422-424. † Gen. Conf. Journals, I. 229.

mitted, what will secure the rights and privileges of preachers and people, together with the friends of the Church? If the constitution cannot protect the executive authority, in vain may the moneyed institution and individual rights call for help from that source.

Believing, as I do, that this resolution is unauthorized by the constitution, and therefore not to be regarded as a rule of the Methodist Episcopal Church, I consider myself under no obligation to enforce or to enjoin it on others to do so.

I present this as the expression of my attachment to the constitution and government of the Church, and of my sincere desire to preserve the rights and privileges of the whole body.

Your worn-down and afflicted friend,   W. McKENDREE.*

That this letter was presented at the same time with the one from the Bishop-elect, is evident, not only from its date, but from the memorandum of Mr. Capers, who says, " Bishop McKendree came forward and stated his objections to the rule adopted, and had read in the Conference a letter from Joshua Soule." " This was followed," says Mr. Emory, " by a formal protest against the resolutions, by one of the bishops." †

Bishop McKendree's views, as more fully expressed later, are thus summarized by Bishop McTyeire:

It is the duty of the Bishops, as general superintendents, to carry into effect the laws made by the General Conference; therefore, they are elected by that body, and amenable to it for their moral and official conduct. In this way uniformity may be preserved throughout the Annual Conferences, and errors in the administration corrected; while the administration, even from the very extremities of the work, through the responsibility of the General Superintendents, is brought under the inspection and control of the General Conference.

The presiding elder, ever since the office was created in 1792, is the agent or assistant of a Bishop; is part of the executive government; and in his district is authorized to discharge all the duties of the absent Bishop, except ordination. The authority by which the Bishop is enabled "to oversee the business of the Church" consists largely, therefore, in the power of appointing the presiding elders. In case they should neglect or refuse to do their duty, as laid down in the Discipline, it becomes the duty of the General Superintendent to remove such from office, and supply their places with others who will carry out the law. But if the presiding elders are elected by the various Annual Conferences, they may counteract the General Superintendent, or clash with each other, administering law differently in different places. How could the General Conference then hold the Bishop responsible for the perversion or contempt of its laws? One Annual Confer-

* Paine's McKendree, I. 418, 419.   † Dr. Emory's Life of Bishop Emory, p. 147.

ence may sustain a presiding elder in an administration for which another Annual Conference would condemn him. The General Conference, in thus transferring executive power from the General Superintendents to the Annual Conferences, effectually destroys its own power of regulating the general administration; and the connection between making laws and executing them ceases.*

The ordination of Mr. Soule had been appointed for 11 A.M., Wednesday, May 24. "To the sentiments of Bishop McKendree and Mr. Soule," says Mr. Capers, "those in favor of a change took exceptions, held a caucus without consulting those not in favor of the change, and agreed to arrest the ordination of J. Soule."† Accordingly on Tuesday afternoon, after the communications of Bishop McKendree on the morning of the same day, and with the announcement of the ordination for the next morning published, D. Ostrander and J. Smith submitted the following:

Whereas brother Joshua Soule, bishop-elect, has signified in his letter to the episcopacy, which letter was read in open Conference, that if he be ordained bishop he will not hold himself bound by a certain resolution of the General Conference, relative to the nomination and election of presiding elders; wherefore,

Resolved, That the bishops be earnestly requested by this Conference to defer or postpone the ordination of the said Joshua Soule until he gives satisfactory explanations to this Conference.‡

Mr. Soule had not said, however, that "if he be ordained bishop, he will not hold himself bound," etc.; but, on the contrary, he had declined to "enter upon the work of an itinerant General Superintendent," at the same time leaving the final disposition of his case in the hands of the Bishops, at whose disposal the General Conference had placed him. Thereupon, after further inquiry, the Bishops "unanimously agreed that he should be ordained," and so announced to the Conference, with all the related information in their possession. This action of the Bishops, it must be allowed, if it had been carried into execution, would have placed Mr. Soule, after his ordination, in the same category with Bishop McKendree, who declared, "I consider myself under no obligation to enforce," etc. But Mr. Os-

---

* Hist. of Meth., p. 570, footnote.   † Paine's McKendree, I. 412.
‡ Gen. Conf. Journals, I. 230.

trander's resolution did Mr. Soule a great injustice in attributing to him what was the consequence of the unanimous decision of the bishops, after his candid communication had been laid before them. "After some debate," says the Journal, " brother Soule made some remarks," and perhaps called attention to the false light in which the resolution before the Conference placed himself. After a motion for indefinite postponement, and before the question was taken, the resolution was withdrawn. Immediately, a reconsideration of the presiding-elder question was moved; for those who were opposed to the election of presiding elders considered themselves no longer tied to the compromise. Wednesday morning, a postponement of the reconsideration was moved, but the motion was lost. The motion for reconsideration " being under debate, it was suggested by brother Reed that if we go into the ordination of brother Soule, it was now time to rise for that object;" but at this critical juncture the manly dignity * of Mr. Soule again came to the rescue, and at " five minutes before 11 o'clock," he "rose and expressed a wish that the General Conference should, by vote, request the episcopacy to delay his ordination for some time;" but " no order was taken on the subject." The debate on reconsideration went on, and at seven minutes before twelve o'clock, it was discovered that the Conference was without a quorum. The Discipline required two-thirds of the members to make a quorum, and it looks a little as if the opponents of reconsideration resorted to dilatory tactics. Bishop George stated that the episcopacy had deferred the ordination, and the Conference adjourned.†

At roll-call, Wednesday afternoon, all but four members were present, and Bishop Roberts took the chair. The vote on the motion for reconsideration was finally taken by ballot, and resulted in a tie—43 to 43. The chair properly pronounced it lost. During Thursday morning's session,

---

* Dr. Stevens speaks of Bishop Soule's dignified carriage as at times verging on majesty.

† Gen. Conf. Journals, I. 231.

"Bishop George informed the Conference that the ordination of brother Soule would take place at 12 o'clock to-day in this house." Thus the Bishops persisted; but promptly "brother Joshua Soule presented a communication in which he stated his resignation of the office of a bishop in the Methodist Episcopal Church, to which he had been elected." His letter was laid on the table. At the opening of the afternoon session, Mr. Soule "expressed a wish that the Conference would come to a decision on his letter of resignation." It was moved and seconded that he be requested to withdraw his letter, but this motion was itself withdrawn, and the Conference postponed consideration of the subject until the next morning.*

Friday morning, May 26, a resolution was introduced, "that the rule passed at this Conference respecting the nomination and election of presiding elders be suspended until the next General Conference, and that the Superintendents be, and they are hereby directed to act under the old rule respecting the appointment of presiding elders." This resolution, if passed, would give relief to Bishop McKendree, clear the way for the ordination of Mr. Soule, and perhaps calm the dangerous excitement that had now arisen. After a protracted debate, in which Griffith, Hedding, and Bangs took part, the measure of suspension was passed, late in the afternoon, by a vote of 45 to 35. Meantime, at an earlier hour of the afternoon session, "the letter of brother Soule," "in which he tendered his resignation," being read, it was moved to accept it; but the motion was at once withdrawn; whereupon Roszel and Hodges offered a resolution, "that brother Soule be, and hereby is requested to withdraw his resignation, and comply with the wishes of his brethren in submitting to be ordained." "Carried," says the Journal; "forty-nine voting for it," says Mr. Capers; "he was requested to withdraw his petition," deposes Bishop McKendree, "by a larger majority than that by which he had been elected." Mr. Soule's path to ordination seemed

* Gen. Conf. Journals, I. 232, 233.

now open and smooth, the bishops and the General Conference agreeing in demanding it, especially as at the same session, the presiding elder resolutions were suspended. But "the bishop-elect" had been "attacked in different ways, and sorely pressed;" the tide of excited feeling had been running high for two weeks, and it had become impossible for a man of Mr. Soule's delicate and high sense of honor to submit to ordination. "Having come into Conference," he "again stated his purpose to resign," and, adds the Journal, "his resignation was accepted." This appears to have been done, however, not by a reconsideration of the former refusal to accept it, nor even by formal vote of the Conference, but by tacit submission to the peremptory decision of the Bishop-elect that he could not be ordained. The Journal does not name, as it usually does, the authors of a resolution of acceptance, nor does it state the majority by which the measure prevailed. When the refusal of the Conference to accept his resignation, "was stated by Bishop George to J. Soule," says Mr. Capers, "he still stated his wish to resign: upon which James Quinn remarked 'We cannot accept or receive his resignation,'" meaning, doubtless, that it was not possible to reverse the increased majority, by which the resignation had just been refused. "No vote was taken on it," continues Mr. Capers, "permission, therefore, was not given him by vote of the Conference to resign." "It was announced from the chair that it was accepted," says Bishop McKendree, "but that it was accepted by a vote of the Conference was not ascertained." * Many of Mr. Soule's best friends opposed the resignation. They entreated him by his love of the Church and of constitutional Methodism, and in view of the increased majority which persisted in demanding his ordination, to submit. But he was conscientiously convinced that he could never perform the duties of a Bishop under the new plan, and that in administering the law, "fealty to the Delegated General Con-

---

* Gen. Conf. Journals, I. 235-237; Paine's McKendree, Capers's *Mem.*, I. 413; McKendree's Journal, I. 424.

ference would be treason to the Church." To avoid conflict with the Conference, and an apparently arrogant assumption of power, he believed himself obliged to reject the counsels of friends and to place the responsibility again upon the Conference. "It is difficult to conceive," says Bishop Paine, "the mental agony which such a train of circumstances would produce in an intelligent, conscientious, and sensitive mind." Mr. Soule, it seems, was unaware of the determination of the Bishops to ordain him at 12 M., Thursday, May 25, and was taken by surprise when Bishop George made the second announcement of such an appointment in the Conference. He hastily presented his resignation, and on the same day made an explanation to the Bishops:

Bishops McKendree, George, and Roberts.

Dear Bishops: The course which I have pursued, in presenting my resignation to the Conference, may savor of disrespect to you, and therefore needs apology. I spent the night in a sleepless manner, and could not prepare the communications, which I designed to make to you and to the Conference, in time to see you until after Conference hours. Not having the least intimation or idea of the appointment for ordination this morning, my intention was to have seen you together, immediately after the morning session, and to communicate to you first my resignation, and to the Conference at the opening of the afternoon session. But on coming to the Conference, I learned that the ordination was notified for *this morning;* and in order to prevent improper excitement as to the time appointed for ordination, I presented my resignation to the Conference when I did. I hope you will not pass a severe censure on me until you shall hear the reasons which have led to this measure.

Yours most respectfully, JOSHUA SOULE.

May 25, 1820.

At an earlier time, or, as the tenor and tenses of the letter (which is without date,) would indicate, when the Bishops first had his case under consideration, Mr. Soule addressed himself to Bishop McKendree:

Dear Bishop McKendree: I cannot doubt *you* will think me sincere when I assure you that the labor of my mind, in the extraordinary situation in which I am placed, has weighed down my spirits, and in some measure, broken down that firmness of resolution which dignifies the human character, and of which, I trust, I have not been altogether destitute while I have encountered that portion of adversity which, in the administrations of Providence, has fallen to my lot.

I entered the Methodist Episcopal Church when I was but a child. I have grown up in her bosom, and my attachment to her institutions has increased with my increasing years. My happiness has been ingrafted on her communion, and I have contemplated her apostolic order with admiration and delight. The constitution which secures her government, and guards the *powers* and *privileges* of her ministers and members, I have ever held sacred. To touch it *in any other way than that which is provided in the constitution itself*, awakens my sensibility and gives me indescribable pain. In this state of things the important question is, *How shall I act?* O that wisdom from above might guide my decision!

I was *elected* to the office of a Superintendent when the *constitution* and *government* were *untouched;* but, by an extraordinary train of occurrences, between my election and consecration to office, a law has been passed with special reference to the Episcopacy, which, in my judgment, transfers an important executive prerogative from the Episcopacy to the Annual Conferences, and which law I cannot conscientiously administer, *because* I firmly believe it to be unconstitutional, and therefore doubt my *right* to administer it. If I receive the imposition of hands, under these circumstances, without an open and honest declaration to the body which elected me, how shall I sustain the character of INTEGRITY? What shall I answer when, in the course of my administration, I am placed at issue with the law? I have seriously reflected on the subject of a *partial* (sectional) visitation of the Conferences. I have attempted to analyze this in relation to our plan of itinerant General Superintendency, and I perceive a dissonance which I cannot harmonize. I apprehend that my path, should I proceed, would inevitably lead me to a point where I should be at issue with my predecessors and seniors in office. I declare to you, my dear sir, that these considerations, connected with the train of consequences which must follow, drink up my spirit and involve me in a torrent of difficulties and responsibilities which that portion of fortitude which Providence has imparted to me is not sufficient to sustain. *If this is weakness, I am weak.*

Had I been ordained previously to the passing of that resolution, my path would have been marked with sunbeams; it is now quite otherwise.

By many I shall be considered an enthusiast, and shall, probably, *sink* in the estimation of all; but my conscious integrity I hope to retain as long as I live. And, rather than practice the *least deception*, I will cheerfully suffer the loss of all I hold dear on earth.

From these considerations, the final decision of my mind (not unaccompanied with prayers and tears) is, that *I cannot receive the imposition of hands without a full and undisguised development of my situation to the General Conference.**

To every man who spoke to me on the subject, previous to my election, I *unequivocally* declared my *entire* adherence to the *old-established plan*, and

---

* Sept. 1, 1820, Mr. Soule wrote to Bishop McKendree, " With this conviction [of unconstitutionality] I might have gone *silently* and perhaps without opposition to the altar of consecration. But how should I have stood in the judgment of my own mind? or how should I be able to an_ swer for this silence to that great religious body to which the voice of the Conference had placed me in the most responsible relation?"

that I *stood or fell with the constitution and the government*. I believe no one can say, with a knowledge of my sentiments, that I have *deceived* any man. I have *betrayed* no trust.

I cannot say that I feel no sensibility at the thought of losing the confidence of those friends to whom I have been bound by the most sacred ties for a succession of years; and if I am doomed to sink in *your* estimation, suffer me to entreat you to consider fully the difficulties of my situation, and ascribe to the frailty of human nature that which, I most solemnly assure you, is dictated neither by *perverseness of will nor impurity of motive*. And whatever loss I may sustain in your confidence, permit me to beg that I may *live* in your *prayers*.   JOSHUA SOULE.

Thus the original communication of the Bishops to the General Conference of their intention to ordain Mr. Soule was not only " approved " by the bishop-elect, as Bishop McKendree says, but was apparently suggested by him, and certainly made a *conditio sine qua non* of his ordination: " I cannot receive the ordination of hands without a full and undisguised development of my situation to the General Conference."

A biography of Bishop Soule is still a *desideratum*. The facts are Mr. Soule's vindication; but so far as I am aware, they have not hitherto, in the literature of the Church, been presented in such completeness and order as indisputably to answer this end. In this narrative, I have sought to combine, mainly in chronological order, all the data derivable from contemporary documents, that this critical chapter in Bishop Soule's life may be presented to the last detail. This minute treatment of a transaction, concerning which, at home as well as abroad, accurate information has seemed lamentably lacking, is demanded no less by the duty of the Methodist Episcopal Church, South, to Bishop Soule's memory than by the constitutional aims of this history. An orderly array of the facts constitutes a sufficient vindication of Mr. Soule; to which it is hardly necessary to add this statement of Bishop McKendree's:

The Conference, by the vote of a respectable majority, had put him into the hands of the Bishops for ordination. In this situation he certainly had a right to address a letter to the Bishops, and when he was involved in difficulties by a subsequent act of the Conference, he certainly acted an honorable part to inform them of his difficulties prior to his ordination, and thereby put it in their power to guard against future difficulties. For this letter and its contents Brother Soule was accountable to the Bishops, not to the Conference. Had the Bishops judged his conduct unworthy of the trust confided to him by his election, they would have returned him to the Conference with their objections to his ordination. This would have brought him under the jurisdiction of the Conference, so far as to reconsider and rescind their vote, or confirm it, and order his consecration. But instead of this, after a formal examination of the subject, they [*i. e.,* the Bishops] had admitted his principle, resolved on his ordination; and that nothing might be done in the dark, they previously informed the Conference of their design. The General Conference had a right to take exceptions, but they should have been directed against the Bishops, and not against the Bishop-elect, who was not accountable to them for this act, and was then under the protection of the Bishops, who were amenable to the Conference for their official acts. For the Conference to undertake to convince the Bishops of an error in their determination to ordain the Bishop-elect under existing circumstances, would have been proper; and as the Bishops had resolved to ordain him, it would have been better for the President to arrest proceedings against Brother Soule, and invite the attack upon themselves.*

Saturday, May 27, Messrs. Wells and Capers moved that "we immediately proceed to elect a general superintendent." After a motion to lay it on the table was lost, the motion was withdrawn. This withdrawal was probably occasioned by information given out by the Bishops; for, on that day, a protest was sent to them, against entering into another election, written by Nathan Bangs, and signed by thirty members of the New York, New England, Genesee, Philadelphia, and other Conferences.† The fact was that a new election could have led to but one result, the reëlection of Mr. Soule, and this would have been embarrassing and irritating to all concerned. Bishops George and Roberts, assisted by the Senior Bishop, agreed to do the work of the quadrennium, and so the question was disposed of.

The only slavery legislation was the repeal of the law permitting the Annual Conferences "to form their own regulations about buying and selling slaves." The Canada question also claimed a share of attention. Messrs. Bennett and Black, missionaries of the British Conference in Canada, attended the General Conference of 1816, with a proposal that the Americans should confine their operations to Upper, and

* Paine's McKendree, I. 424, 425. † *Ibid.,* I. 436, 437.

the British to Lower, Canada.   But this division of territory
and relinquishment of members was declined, the General
Conference declaring, "that we cannot consistently with
our duty to the societies of our charge in the Canadas, give
up any part of them, or any of our chapels in those provinces, to the superintendency of the British Connexion."
In 1820, however, many and urgent memorials were received from the Canadian societies, and the General Conference empowered the Bishops "to negotiate with the British Conference respecting Lower Canada, in the way and
manner they shall see fit," and, if possible, to send a delegate to England for this purpose.   The Rev. John Emory
was appointed, and, in their letter of official instructions to
him, the Bishops say, "We are of opinion that the most effectual means to prevent collisions in future will be to establish a specific line by which our field of labors shall be
bounded on one side, and the British missionaries on the
other.   With this view you are at liberty to stipulate that our
preachers shall confine their labors in Canada to the upper
province, provided the British missionaries will confine
theirs to the lower." *   Mr. Emory succeeded in effecting
this arrangement with the British Conference, and, accordingly, Bishop McKendree addressed to "the private and
official members, trustees," etc., in Lower Canada, a circular letter dated October 16, 1820:

It has been agreed that our British brethren shall supply the Lower
Provinces, and our preachers the Upper. It becomes our duty, therefore,
to inform you of this agreement, and to advise you, in the most affectionate
and earnest manner, to put yourselves and your chapels under the care of
our British brethren, as their Societies and chapels in the Upper Province
will be put under our care. . . .   This communication, we confess, is not
made without pain. . . .   But necessity is laid upon us. . . .   It is a
peace-offering. . . .   Forgive, therefore, our seeming to give you up.

Accordingly a committee of three preachers from each
Connexion met at Montreal, Feb. 15, 1821, and fixed the
time and manner for delivering up the several charges
which were to be relinquished on both sides.

---

* Dr. Emory's Life of Bishop Emory, pp. 93, 94.

Thus the General Conference empowered the Bishops, and the Bishops empowered Mr. Emory, and Mr. Emory contracted with the British Conference, to surrender to that ecclesiastical jurisdiction a portion of the membership of the Methodist Episcopal Church in return for a like cession from that body. The contract was faithfully executed. The constitutional question involved is a delicate and important one, upon which a later General Conference (1848) pronounced judgment: hence we postpone its consideration.

On the last day of the session, however, a measure of vital importance was passed. In 1820 the Constitution of 1808 was subjected to its first severe strain, and a grave defect in its provisions was revealed. No tribunal had been provided to pass upon the constitutionality of the acts of the General Conference. There were many parties in interest, the Church, the General Conference, the Bishops, and the Connexion of itinerant preachers, distributed in the several Annual Conferences. " This want of a constitutional test," remarks a high authority, " must be supplied sooner or later by the civil, if not by the Church, courts." Face to face with the practical difficulty in an alarming form, the General Conference of 1820 adopted the following measure of relief:

Whereas a difference has arisen in the General Conference about the constitutionality of a certain resolution passed concerning the appointment of presiding elders; and whereas there does not appear to be any proper tribunal to judge of and determine such a question; and whereas it appears important to us that some course should be taken to determine this business, therefore,

Resolved, &c., That we will advise, and hereby do advise the several annual conferences to pass such resolutions as will enable the next General Conference so to alter the constitution that whenever a resolution or motion which goes to alter any part of our Discipline is passed by the General Conference it shall be examined by the superintendent or superintendents; and if they, or a majority of them, shall judge it unconstitutional, they shall, within three days after its passage, return it to the conference with their objections to it in writing. And whenever a resolution is so returned, the conference shall reconsider it, and if it pass by a majority of two-thirds it shall be constitutional and pass into a law, notwithstanding the objections of

23

the superintendents; and if it be not returned within three days, it shall be considered as not objected to and become a law.*

Thus, by a majority vote, the General Conference of 1820 agreed to the principle of a veto power to be exercised by the Bishops over all enactments of the General Conference, which in the preamble was acknowledged to be no " proper tribunal to judge of and determine such a question." This measure provided, not merely a method by which the Bishops might carry an appeal from the decisions of a General Conference to the tribunal of the Annual Conferences—which really lodges the veto power in the body of the traveling ministry—but, in the strictest sense, clothed the episcopacy with a veto power, which required a two-thirds majority of the General Conference to overcome it. We may here sacrifice chronological order to topical completeness, and finish the history of such action in our Church. There is no record in the Journal of 1824 of the action of the Annual Conferences on this measure; but, instead, a forward step is taken in the evolution of this species of constitutional legislation. Tuesday, May 18, Lovick Pierce and William Winans gave notice of intention to introduce the following resolution:

Resolved, by the delegates of the annual conferences in General Conference assembled, That it be and is hereby recommended to the several annual conferences to adopt the following article as a provision to be annexed to the sixth article of the " limitations and restrictions " adopted by the General Conference in 1808, viz.:—

Provided, also, that whenever the delegated General ·Conference shall pass any rule or rules which, in the judgment of the bishops, or a majority of them, are contrary to or an infringement upon the above " limitations and restrictions," or any one of them, such rule or rules being returned to the conference within three days after their passage, together with the objections of the bishops to them, in writing, the conference shall reconsider such rule or rules, and if, upon reconsideration, they shall pass by a majority of two-thirds of the members present, they shall be considered as rules, and go into immediate effect; but in case a less majority shall differ from the opinion of the bishops, and they continue to sustain their objections, the rule or rules objected to shall be laid before the annual conferences, in which case the decision of a majority of all the members of the annual conference present when the vote shall be taken shall be final. In taking the vote in all such cases in the annual conferences, the secretaries shall give a certificate

---

*Gen. Conf. Journals, I. 238.

of the number of votes, both in the affirmative and negative, and such certificates shall be forwarded to the editor and general book-steward, who, with one or more of the bishops, who may be present, shall be a committee to canvass the votes and certify the result.*

Friday afternoon, May 21, a motion of Cooper and Bangs to take the vote on this resolution by ballot was lost, and, the vote being taken in the usual manner, the measure of Pierce and Winans was adopted by a majority of 64 to 58.† Previously an amendment had been accepted that the vote on constitutional questions in both General and Annual Conferences should be taken by ballot. Curiously enough, there seems to be no record, in the Journal of 1828, of the action of the Annual Conferences on this proposal sent down to them; but since the proviso then required the joint recommendation of *all* the Annual Conferences to secure a constitutional amendment, there can be no doubt of its failure: the adverse decision of a single Annual Conference would defeat it.

Twice, however, in 1820 and 1824 did the General Conferences of the undivided Methodist Episcopal Church endorse the principle of the incompetency of the General Conference to pass finally upon the constitutionality of its own acts, and of a suspensive veto to be exercised by the Bishops or by the Annual Conferences. It will be noticed that the measure of Messrs. Pierce and Winans adopted in 1824 was a distinct advance upon the action of 1820. It still permitted a two-thirds majority of the General Conference to pass a measure over the veto of the Bishops. But in case the measure should obtain a smaller majority than two-thirds, when returned to the General Conference with the constitutional objections of the Bishops, if the Bishops persisted in their objections, the proposed legislation was to be submitted to the Annual Conferences, whose decision by a majority vote should be final. Thus was the proper tribunal for an appeal at last partially recognized. Two-thirds of the General Conference, or a majority in the Annual Conferences, could thus overrule the Bishops. For the Bishops, being a party whose interests the legislation of the General Conference

*Gen. Conf. Journals, I. 267.   † *Ibid.*, I. 277.

may directly and materially affect, ought not to be allowed an absolute and final veto. This would be but little improvement upon the plan of allowing the General Conference to be the final judge of the constitutionality of its own acts. But the Annual Conferences, though like the Bishops a party in interest, affected by the legislation of the General Conference, are also made up of the body of traveling preachers, who originated both the Delegated General Conference and its constitution. They, therefore, are rightfully the ultimate judges of any infringement of the grant of power which they have made to their agent, the Delegated General Conference. But the Bishops are the easy and natural executive agents for the temporary arrest of legislation until an appeal can be taken to the Annual Conferences, to which a veto power, in the proper sense, alone belongs. Accordingly, in the Methodist Episcopal Church, South, this want was supplied in 1870, when the following amendment was made to the constitution by the General Conference voting 160 yeas to 4 nays, and the Annual Conferences concurring by 2,024 yeas to 9 nays:

When any rule or regulation is adopted by the General Conference which, in the opinion of the Bishops, is unconstitutional, the Bishops may present to the Conference which passed said rule or regulation their objections thereto, with their reasons, in writing, and if the General Conference shall, by a two-thirds vote, adhere to its action on said rule or regulation, it shall then take the course prescribed for altering a Restrictive Rule.

The action of 1824, though introduced by Messrs. Pierce and Winans, did not originate with them. Bishop Paine— who was the youngest member of the General Conference of 1824—has preserved a document, which is in nearly *verbatim* agreement with the actual measure passed, and which is signed by W. McKendree, Enoch George, R. R. Roberts, Thomas L. Douglass, and Wm. Capers. Bishop Paine wrote from his notes, made at the time, without access to the Journals of the General Conference.* His memoranda and the official Journal agree in essentials. He says:

* The General Conference Journals were ordered published by the General Conference of 1852; the oldest edition of which I am aware has the

Friday, May 20th [21st], another question of importance came up, called the "constitutional test," the object of which was to prevent hasty action, violative of the constitution, by giving the Bishops a qualified veto, with an ultimate reference of the question to the Annual Conferences. It involved constitutional questions only. The Bishops, anticipating some action of the kind, had agreed to unite, and, if desired, present to the Conference the following amendment to the sixth Article of the " limitations and restrictions," adopted by the General Conference in 1808, signed by their own hands and two others.

Then follows, with few and unimportant verbal variations, a copy of the measure which the General Conference actually passed, signed by the three bishops. The names of Douglass and Capers were doubtless added to anticipate the objection that the Bishops had no constitutional right to introduce measures into the General Conference, but it was found inexpedient or unnecessary to attach the signatures of the bishops to the measure as presented to the Conference; and Pierce and Winans, for some reason now undiscoverable, were selected to introduce it instead of Douglass and Capers. " Whether the subject was brought into Conference," continues Bishop Paine, " by the presentation of this document, or by another series of resolutions, the writer cannot say; but the discussion of the subject was upon substantially a similar, if not an identical, presentation of the question." That this was the case we know from the published Journal of the Conference. Mr. Paine ·preserved notes of Mr. Soule's speech in the debate which followed, which he cites, and thus concludes his account:

" L. McCombs and James Smith opposed the resolution at considerable length, and W. Winans replied in one of the strongest, most analytical, and effective speeches ever delivered on the floor of the General Conference. The question was carried by a vote of 64 to 58. [The Journal, as we have seen, gives the same figures.] A heavy load was lifted from the heart of the senior Bishop. His face put on a subdued smile, and he breathed freer." *

---

date 1855 on its title page. The General Conference of 1854 appointed Bishop Paine Bishop McKendree's biographer.

* Paine's McKendree, II. 35-38.

Toward the close of the General Conference, the Senior Superintendent delivered an address, which was stenographically reported by Mr. Paine and the Rev. John Summerfield. On this point Bishop McKendree said:

At the commencement of the present General Conference, your Bishops consulted together, to devise some way to harmonize the brethren and the connection at large. . . . They thought they saw a plan open and they entered in. The plan was to invite the brethren on both sides to vote a *peace measure* which should meet the wishes of all. In order to guard against a recurrence of like disagreements, they agreed to recommend to the General Conference a *constitutional test* which should forever settle these things. I was pleased with an adjustment which is calculated to heal the past by the peace measure proposed, and to guard against a recurrence by the constitutional test.*

Thus Bishops McKendree, George, and Roberts—and, of course, Bishop Soule and, probably, Bishop Hedding, both of whom were elected and ordained at this time—agreed with the General Conference of 1824 that the General Conference itself is not the proper tribunal to pass final judgment on the constitutionality of its own proceedings, but that this function shoul be exercised, primarily and for purposes of temporary arrest, by the Bishops, and ultimately, in a given contingency, by the Annual Conferences themselves. In an able article on the "Rights of a General Conference President," Bishop S. M. Merrill announces and advocates principles, which would seem to fall but little short of those of Bishop McKendree, and which, if followed to their results, must lead to something like the veto law of the Methodist Episcopal Church, South. Bishop Merrill says:

There are, however, some laws in the Church which the General Conference did not make, and which it cannot unmake or modify. When these are involved, what is the duty of the Bishop? The rule which inhibits him as president of the law-making body from deciding questions of law cannot apply where a proposed action appears to him to be an infringement of the constitution. Is he powerless to arrest such proposed action? Must he become a party to a violation of the fundamental law? Has he no right to interpose his own judgment, so far, at least, as to stay proceedings till the question of constitutionality is decided? Suppose he is not the final authority in determining the question, may he not demand a formal investigation and decision before he is required to submit the matter to a vote in the

* Paine's McKendree, II. 44, 45.

General Conference? . . . . How else can the proper distinction be made between the action of a Bishop in determining the constitutionality of a proposed measure and determining a point of order under the rules? In the latter case the General Conference is supreme. Its dictum is final. In the former case it exercises a power given to it tacitly and by usage, or taken in the absence of any contrary provision—a power which may be invoked to touch things most vital in Methodism, and which should never be exercised except in the most formal and deliberate manner. It is the highest judicial power with which the body is invested, if indeed it be invested with such power at all, which it is not except by implication. It decides appeals from the decision of the chair on questions of order by a majority vote, without debate. Is it seemly that it should, or will it claim the right to, pass upon the gravest constitutional problems in the same way? . . . Suppose a motion is made which plainly contravenes a restrictive rule. In the hurry or excitement of the hour the members of the body do not catch the bearing of the motion in that respect, and no point of order is raised. Must the president entertain the motion, knowing it to be unlawful? He would be derelict of duty if he saw that it was in conflict with the rules of order and did not promptly refuse to entertain it. Must he be less watchful in guarding the constitution than in upholding the rules of order? Is his power complete in the less important case, and utterly wanting in the more important? But suppose he does not rule the motion out on constitutional grounds, but simply hesitates, and calls the attention of the General Conference to his conviction, and waits for the motion to be withdrawn; is not this debating the subject, and throwing the weight of his influence on one side as against the other, and has he any more right to debate than he has to rule? Turn the matter over and look at it on every side, and each additional view will strengthen the conviction that a motion to do an unlawful thing is never in order in the General Conference, and that the president, who is bound to maintain the rules of order, is also bound, by the nature of his office as a Bishop in the Church, to protect the constitution from infraction by refusing to entertain a motion that he believes to be unlawful under that instrument. His obligation in this regard is as high as his obligation to preside and enforce the rules of order.*

It would be wrong to attribute to Bishop Merrill any sentiments which he does not distinctly avow, but it hardly requires reading between the lines, to see that he has very grave doubts about the power of the General Conference to pass finally upon the constitutionality of its own acts, if not a reasoned conviction that it has no such prerogative. He describes it as " a power given to it tacitly and by usage;" as "*taken* in the absence of any contrary provision;" as " the highest judicial power with which the body is invested,

*Art. in New York *Christian Advocate*, (supplement) March 24, 1892.

if indeed it be invested with such power at all, which it is
not except by implication.'' Here is a clear and robust legal intellect, which surely in 1820 and 1824 must have planted itself on the ground occupied by McKendree and Soule.
Must a bishop '' become a party to a violation of the fundamental law?'' asks Bishop Merrill, and answers his own
question: '' The president, who is bound to maintain the
rules of order, is also bound, by the nature of his office as a
Bishop in the Church, to protect the constitution from infraction by refusing to entertain a motion that he believes to
be unlawful under that instrument.'' Rather than '' become
a party to a violation of the fundamental law,'' as he believed
the act of the General Conference to be, Joshua Soule, in
1820, after election, and the refusal of his resignation, declined to be ordained a bishop. '' While I am firmly bound,
by virtue of my office, to see that all the rules are properly
enforced,'' said William McKendree, '' I am equally bound
to prevent the imposition of that which is not properly rule.''
Bishop McKendree and Bishop Merrill are one in the principle they adopt, but differ in the degree of its application.
Bishop Merrill believes it to be the duty of a General Conference President to arrest legislation judged to be unconstitutional and to appeal formally to the Judiciary Committee
as now constituted in the General Conference of the Methodist Episcopal Church. But the Committee can possess no
power which does not inhere in the body which institutes it,
and we already know Bishop Merrill's opinion of the powers of the General Conference in this regard. Bishop Mc-
Kendree, in the light of the origin of the General Conference and its Constitution, and sustained by express precedent
in Bishop Asbury's time, believed it to be the duty of a Superintendent to carry his appeal to the tribunal of the Annual Conferences.

But if it be the duty of the Bishop who happens to be in
the chair on a given day of the General Conference session
to arrest temporarily any measure which he believes to be
unconstitutional, how much more is it the duty of the whole

College of Bishops, or a majority of them, to signify to the General Conference their objections to pending legislation which they are convinced is an infringement of the Constitution? And, if it be allowed that the General Conference is not the proper tribunal to pass finally upon such a protest of the Bishops, to what tribunal can it go for decision, save that of the Annual Conferences? Thus the constitutional provision of the Methodist Episcopal Church, South, on this point, is seen to be the legal, logical, and necessary result of the mutual relations of the Delegated General Conference, the Bishops, and the Annual Conferences. This is after all no Episcopal veto power, in the proper sense, but a simple and natural arrangement by which the executive officers of the Church may take the sense of the Annual Conferences on an alleged unconstitutional exercise of powers by their agent, the Delegated General Conference.

Thus, in the General Conference of the Methodist Episcopal Church, South, the Bishops are present to guard the constitution against infraction in any concrete instance of specific legislation. The principle of the procedure by which a delegated body of limited powers is assumed to be competent in any final way to fix the limits and meaning of a grant of power made to it by others—in this case the body of traveling preachers—is dangerous, anomalous, and, in civil affairs, without precedent. This power of definition and interpretation belongs alone to the Annual Conferences which, in a very vital sense, created the General Conference to act as their agent, with instructions. If any doubt arises as to the purport of these instructions, the principal, not the agent, must decide their meaning. Moreover, among other purposes, constitutions are constructed for the protection of minorities. But, if a majority of the General Conference may both define and interpret the constitution, then are not only the absent body of elders, but also the minority of representatives present, helpless. Much less could the principle be admitted that one General Conference, of equal powers, and of presumably equal intelligence, could sit in judgment upon the constitutionality of the acts of a preceding General Conference; for in that case, since each constitutional decision could be opened afresh every four years, certainty and finality would never be reached.

All these dangers and evils are avoided by the constitutional provision inserted in the Discipline of the Methodist Episcopal Church, South, by the joint authority of the General and Annual Conferences. When the General Conference of 1808 adjourned, it left in existence the body of traveling preachers, distributed in the several Annual Conferences; the Bishops, constitutionally protected in the enjoyment of all the powers they had hitherto exercised "according to the plan of our itinerant general superintendency;" and the plan for a Delegated General Conference, ordained by the body of traveling preachers in General Conference assembled, as a charter or constitution for their agent, the Delegated General Conference. These three things, the first Delegated General Conference of 1812 found in existence when it assembled. The Bishops, being a distinct branch of the government, coeval with the existence of the Church, antedating the Delegated General Conference and its constitution by a quarter of a century, and in that constitution protected by a restrictive rule emanating from the body of elders and giving permanency and independence to their office as it existed from the beginning, are the natural and only efficient guardians of the rights of the Annual Conferences against General Conference encroachment.

If it be objected that this power lodged in the bishops is unwise or unsafe, the reply is: (1) this provision is the legitimate if not the necessary development of the earliest principles manifest in the working of our Church government, and corresponds with the best analogies of civil government, which separates legislative and judicial functions; (2) while our state and national Constitutions usually lodge a veto power in one man, the chief executive, this provision lodges it in a body of picked men larger than the Supreme Court of the United States; (3) while our state and national executives can use the veto power on any grounds satisfactory to themselves, the bishops can veto only upon the sole ground of constitutional invalidity; (4) since the General Conference of the Methodist Episcopal Church, South, is composed of equal numbers of ministers and laymen, who may vote separately upon a proper call, this veto power, which gives the bishops to this extent participation in legislation, makes it necessary for a proposed enactment whose constitutionality is open to question to be subjected to the rigid scrutiny of three distinct houses, to say nothing of the final tribunal of the Annual Conferences, and (5) this provision is, strictly, not an absolute episcopal veto power, but a proper arrangement for carrying an appeal to the court of last resort. the tribunal of the Annual Conferences.

CHAPTER XXI.

THE QUADRENNIUM, 1820–1824: THE CONTRASTED GOVERN-
MENTS OF THE TWO EPISCOPAL METHODISMS.

B ISHOP McKendree continued firm in his purpose to lay his address on the constitutionality of the suspended resolutions before the Annual Conferences. He justified his course in part by the following precedent:

> The Bishops formed the Genesee Conference in 1809. In the Virginia Conference there was an objection to this act, being, as it was supposed, unconstitutional. The Bishops [Asbury and McKendree] submitted the question to the Annual Conferences. They acted upon it as a proper subject of their decision, and confirmed the act of the Bishops. By this act, the Bishops and the Annual Conferences tacitly declared the Annual Conferences to be the proper judges of constitutional questions; and the senior Bishop is fully persuaded that, conformably to the genius of our government, all such cases as cannot be otherwise adjusted ought to be submitted to their decision until otherwise provided for by the same authority on which the present General Conference depends for its existence.*

The General Conference of 1812 approved the administration of the Bishops in approving the legality of the organization of the Genesee Conference, for which the previous General Conference had not provided. Of his motives and intentions in preparing and submitting the address to the Annual Conferences, Bishop McKendree has left a simple statement:

> I am fully persuaded that confidence, peace, and harmony among the preachers and people, and the perpetuity of our itinerant system now in successful operation, very much depend upon the confidence reposed in the delegated General Conference as to their intention to preserve the constitution inviolate, and regard it as their rule of conduct. My opposition to the "peace-measure resolutions," as they were called, arose from a conviction that they were a violation of the constitution, and contravened a principle destructive of the "limitations and restrictions" imposed on the delegated Conference; and as these restrictions were imposed by the traveling preachers collectively, and from whom the delegated body derived its being and all its powers, I considered them the proper judges of the constitutionality

---

* McKendree's Journal, cited by Paine, I. 426.

of their acts. Influenced by these views, and a hope of adjusting our difficulties and harmonizing the traveling preachers, an address to the Annual Conferences was drawn up, in which I gave my reasons for believing the suspended resolutions to be unconstitutional; intending, if a majority of the Annual Conferences were of a different opinion, to submit to their judgment as a legal decision, and upon that authority admit, recommend, and act according to the provisions of those resolutions; but in the event that my opinion should be confirmed, to advise the Conferences to recommend their adoption by the ensuing General Conference, and thereby introduce them conformably to the constitution.*

Nevertheless Mr. Soule entertained fears as to the results of the course adopted by Bishop McKendree, and expressed his views to the Senior Bishop. His letter lies before me, and as it has not heretofore been published, I shall here insert it. It is dated " New York, 6 May, 1821." After acknowledging the receipt of letters from the Bishop, and explaining his delay, Mr. Soule continues:

On proposing and recommending to the Annual Conferences the adoption of the suspended resolutions of the General Conference, I have my *doubts* and *fears.* I am decidedly of your opinion that, although the resolutions are no improvement of our system, but rather tend to enfeeble its energies, yet, *if no further encroachments are made upon the executive authority,* the government may be administered, under the provisions of those resolutions. And if I had any sufficient security, that the adoption of those resolutions, *in constitutional order,* would be the means of reconciliation, and lay the foundation for a permanent peace, I would cordially recommend them for *such* adoption. But it is impossible for me to conceive that those brethren who, for so many years, have contested the radical principles of the government, will rest satisfied while the essential features of Episcopacy remain. And I am fully persuaded, that one change will be urged as a ground, plead as a precedent, and used as an auxiliary, to promote another. If the course which you propose is pursued, it follows that each Conference must act, in recommending the adoption of the resolutions, upon the ground that they are *unconstitutional.* I think it is a fair presumption that some of the Conferences will not act on this ground. But my principal fears are the effect which the measure may have on the membership. The measures of the last General Conference have given many of our people great alarm. From the time the Constitution was formed, in which the character of the government was fixed, and the rights of the members, private and official, secured, all seem to have settled down in peace and quietude and confidence. It seemed like the return of a calm after a storm; and general joy prevailed under the conviction that we had arrived to that permanent state of things in which all might rest. No alteration of the government was expected or desired, nor did an apprehension prevail that any new burdens would be imposed, or

*McKendree's Journal, cited by Paine, I. 439, 440.

terms of communion established. Under these assurances, what must have been the surprise when the proceedings of the General Conference were made public? A transfer of important and long established prerogatives from one official department to another, and even doubts suggested as to the validity of the Constitution itself! From this view of the subject, I am fully convinced that the resolutions can never go into operation with safety to the peace of the Church on any other ground but that which you propose; and, all things considered, I am inclined to think that your course is the best and safest which can be pursued. If I do not see you in New York, I will avail myself of the earliest opportunity, after our Conference, to communicate more fully on the subject.*

Accordingly "To the Annual Conferences of the Methodist Episcopal Church, commencing with the Ohio Conference, to be held in Lebanon, September 6, 1821," the senior Bishop took his appeal. After a brief, but pertinent, historical introduction, he states his constitutional objections in three propositions:

1. It would effectually transfer the executive authority from the Bishops to the Annual Conferences, and thereby do away that form of Episcopacy and itinerant General Superintendency which is recognized in our Form of Discipline, and confirmed in the third Article of the Constitution.

2. By doing away the present effective General Superintendency, our itinerant plan of preaching the gospel would be greatly injured, if not entirely destroyed.

3. In point of law, it would effectually divest the members of our Church of all constitutional security for their rights, and reduce them to the necessity of depending entirely on the wisdom and goodness of the General Conference for those inestimable blessings.

A summary of Bishop McKendree's argument on the first head has been previously presented.† On the second point he says in part:

Could all our traveling preachers attend one Annual Conference, to account for their administration, and receive their appointments and instructions, the itinerant plan might go on and prosper in America as it does in England, without either General Conference or General Superintendency. But our situation is widely different from theirs. Our work extends over more than twenty States, and has to encounter difficulties arising from the civil regulations of different State and Territorial governments. We are divided into twelve Annual Conferences. These are all equal in power, and independent of each other, no one having power to impose laws on another.

___

* Extract from original letter in the author's possession. The reply to Mr. Soule's letter, as well as the one to which it was a reply, may be seen in Paine's McKendree, II. 372–376. The italics in this and preceding letters of Mr. Soule's are his own.

† See above, pp. 343, 344.

The jurisdiction of each Annual Conference is restricted to its own bounds, and each Presiding Elder to his own District. Out of this state of things arises the necessity of a General Conference to make rules or laws for the united Annual Conferences, and of a General Superintendency to enforce those rules; to preserve a uniform administration of discipline; to preserve the union of the several Annual Conferences; and by removing preachers from District to District, and from Conference to Conference, (which no Annual Conference nor Presiding Elder can do,) perpetuate and extend missionary labors for the benefit of increasing thousands, who look unto us as teachers sent of God. Such is our situation in this country that our itinerant system can no more do without an effective General Superintendency, sufficiently under the control of the General Conference, than they can without the General Conference itself. It [the General Superintendency] was, therefore, ratified by the constitution, after twenty-four years' experience in proof of its utility and necessity.

Under the third proposition, is included this argument:

For it requires no more power to change our articles of religion, erect new standards of doctrine, and do away the rights of preachers and members, than to do away our General Superintendency; and, if the delegated General Conference is not bound by these restrictions, then their power is undefined and unlimited—they may make what changes they please, and there can be no legal redress—no constitutional guarantee for our rights and privileges. Your Superintendent most cordially disapproves of such a state of things, and will do nothing which he believes will produce it, because he conceives it would go to deprive both preachers and members of *constitutional security*, and reduce them to the necessity of relying solely on the General Conference for all their rights and privileges. . . . Since that memorable era [1808] in Methodism, your Superintendent conceives the General Conference to be bound as sacredly to observe all those restrictions, (as the laws by which their proceedings are to be tested,) as each member of the Church is *bound* to *submit* to the examination of his conduct, according to the legitimate rules enacted by said Conference, because the restrictions arise from the same *source*, and are supported by the same authority, which gave existence to the delegated General Conference, and validity to their rules and regulations; consequently, they must both stand or fall together.

This notable address, one of the most important documents of our Constitutional history, concludes with this language:

From the preachers *collectively* both the General Conference and General Superintendents derive their powers; and to the Annual Conferences, jointly, is reserved the power of recommending a change in our constitution. To you, therefore, your Superintendent not only submits the case, but he would advise you to adopt such measures as you in your judgment may deem most prudent, by which to recognize the adoption of the change proposed in the resolutions, conformably to the provision in the sixth Article of

the Constitution. Not that he believes the change would be an improvement of our system of government, or that it would fully answer the expec-
tations of its advocates, but as an accommodating measure, on the utility of
which men equally wise and good may, in some degree, differ in opinion.
Your Superintendent is, therefore, disposed to submit his opinion for the
harmony of the body, as far as is consistent with his duty and obligations to
the Church. And, as a majority of more than two-thirds of the last General Conference, after having received assurances that it would be satisfactory,
and put the controverted subject to rest, voted in favor of the resolutions,
they tacitly say, all things considered, the change is at least prudentially
necessary. To this decision all due deference is paid. In the opinion of
your Superintendent, no sacrifice for peace and harmony, which can be
made consistently with the constitution and preservation of our general itinerant plan of preaching the gospel, is too great. With your recommendations and instructions, your representatives in General Conference may act
as they may judge most for the glory of God and the good of his Church.
Thus introduced, the case would commend and establish the constitution,
and form an effectual barrier against any future infringement of that bulwark of our rights and liberties.*

Of the twelve Annual Conferences into which the Church
was then divided, seven " judged the suspended resolutions
unconstitutional " and yet " authorized the ensuing General
Conference, as far as they could do so, to adopt them without alteration."   This statement of Bishop McKendree's is
sufficiently exact: six of the Conferences which pronounced
the resolutions unconstitutional, nevertheless recommended
their adoption; the seventh, the South Carolina, while declining to recommend, did not pronounce against their adoption. " But the five other Conferences," continues the
Bishop, " in which the steady friends and most powerfnl
advocates of the proposed change were found, refused to
act on the address, and thereby prevented its adoption [*i. e.*,
the adoption of the recommendation for the proposed change,
which required the assent of all the Conferences] in a constitutional way, and, of course, set in for another vigorous
contest at the next General Conference.   In this way my
hope of a safe and peaceable adjustment of our difficulties,
and the prevention of a dangerous, probable schism in the
Church was frustrated, and the way for the spread of the
schism already commenced was made more easy."

---

* The entire address is given in Paine's McKendree, I. 444-458.

The seven Conferences which pronounced the proposed change unconstitutional, but, on the recommendation of Bishop McKendree, interposed no barrier, if made in a constitutional way, were the southern and western bodies, namely, the Ohio, Kentucky, Missouri, Tennessee, Mississippi, South Carolina, and Virginia Conferences. The five Conferences which, in effect, refused to accept their own measure as a constitutional change, were the New England, New York, Genesee, Philadelphia, and Baltimore. They declined to acknowledge the powerlessness of the General Conference to act alone in the premises, and tacitly avowed their determination to accept the change, if at all, only on their own terms, despite the constitutional scruples of the Senior Bishop and a majority of the Conferences. Thus the issue was joined on the naked constitutional principle alone. Heavy and bitter attacks were delivered upon Bishop Mc-Kendree—that " he would not submit to the authority of the General Conference," etc. He had been willing, however, though he regarded the measure as impolitic, unconstitutional, and revolutionary, to recommend its adoption, provided that adoption was reached in a constitutional way. He did this (1) to harmonize the episcopacy, (2) to save the constitution, and secure a fresh committal to the inviolability of that instrument, and (3) to pacify the sadly divided Church. Bishop Roberts admitted the " infringement of the constitution," but was willing for the measure to go into effect as an act of the General Conference. Bishop George, while withholding his opinion on the constitutional point, evidently desired the adoption of the change. " To secure harmony in the episcopacy, maintain the authority of the constitution, and, by yielding his preference as to the mode of administering the polity of the Church, obtain a fresh indorsement of the Constitution, and thus restore peace without the sacrifice of a vital principle," concludes McKendree's biographer, " were certainly his objects." In the collection of unpublished papers, described in the preface of this work, I find an official transcript from the Journal of the Philadelphia Con-

24

ference, made by the Secretary " for Bishop McKendree," and endorsed in the Bishop's handwriting, " Resolutions of the Philadelphia Conference on the Address." As it happens that the action of the South Carolina Conference is also among these unpublished documents, I shall insert the two as instructive examples of the radically opposed views of the Northeastern and Southwestern Conferences on this question. The Philadelphia action was as follows:

Ezekiel Cooper moved and Joseph Osborne seconded, the following resolutions:

Whereas Bishop McKendree, in his communication to this Conference has pronounced that the resolutions of the last General Conference relative to the election of presiding elders, are, in his belief, an infringement on the constitution of the Methodist Episcopal Church, wherefore

Resolved, 1. That in the opinion and full conviction of this Conference, there is nothing in the said resolutions that makes any infringement on the constitution or restrictive regulations of our Church. Carried unanimously.

Resolved, [2.] That the restrictive resolutions do not in our opinion prohibit or restrict any changes, alterations or new modifications of the episcopal powers or duties, provided such changes do not do away episcopacy or destroy the plan of our itinerant general superintendency. Carried unanimously.

True copy from the Journal.   L. LAWRENSON, *Secretary*.

May 16, 1822.*

Thus Ezekiel Cooper, the champion of a diocesan episcopacy and of an elective presiding eldership in 1808, whose proposed restrictive rule on this subject was at the time rejected for Joshua Soule's, carried the Philadelphia Conference unanimously in 1822 for the constitutionality of an elective presiding eldership.

Lewis Myers, writing to Joshua Soule, from Charleston, March 7, 1822, says:

The last General Conference's two resolutions are taking the rounds. Bishop M. has delivered us his address on the subject. We have acted on it. The identical words, *verbatim*, I cannot rehearse. The substance is as follows:

Resolved, 1. That in our judgment the two resolutions relative to Presiding elders, etc., passed at the last General Conference and suspended to the next, are contrary to the constitution of the Methodist Episcopal Church, established by the General Conference of 1808.

2. That this Conference views with sentiments of gratitude, the firm and prudent stand which our Senior Bishop made to maintain inviolate the said constitution.

---

*Original document in possession of the author.

3. That much ought to be yielded for the sake of peace; but our minds are not yet prepared to decide on this all-important point.

4. That Bishop M. be respectfully requested to grant a copy of his address to be entered into our Journals.

"The second and third," continues Mr. Myers, "appeared seriously to affect our good old Bishop George's mind. He appeared depressed. He met several of us and proposed that we should make some alterations, so as to recommend such a change in the constitution as would embrace the resolutions: we remained as we were. I could wish he had left us with a more satisfied mind. As to the first resolution, as far as I can judge, the minds of the Conference are united." *

Thus, nearly a quarter of a century before the division of the Church, the Northeast and Southwest were solidly and determinedly arrayed against each other on a question purely constitutional, affecting the principles of ecclesiastical government alone. That sectional differences, particularly the contrast between the civil institutions of the northern and southern portions of the Union, afterwards largely entered, directly and indirectly, into the estrangement of the two wings of Episcopal Methodism, must be allowed, as a matter of course, by any one enjoying a tolerable acquaintance with the principles of human nature and the events recorded on the broad page of history. But this fact must not blind us to an antecedent difference, which radically divided the northern and southern sections of the Church on the nature of our ecclesiastical government, and particularly on the powers which the Delegated General Conference was entitled to exercise under the constitution which had been given to it. In our Church, as in our nation, the division was along the line of strict construction of the powers delegated by the constitution, on the one hand, and a loose and broad interpretation of those powers, on the other. These differ-

---

* Original letter in possession of the author. The action of the Kentucky and Ohio Conferences, which, though pronouncing them unconstitutional, recommend the adoption of the resolutions, may be seen in Paine's McKendree, II. 332.

ences in the Church, instead of fading away with the lapse
of time, have been accentuated at critical junctures, before,
at, and since the division of Episcopal Methodism, until distinct and opposed conceptions of our Church government,
particularly of the powers and relations of the General
Conference, the Annual Conferences, and the Episcopacy,
have been crystallized in the Methodist Episcopal Church
and the Methodist Episcopal Church, South. That the
organic union of these congenetic Churches is a consum-
mation devoutly to be wished for, is an abstract proposition, which it would be equally devoid of practical result to
support or to oppose, and which, as lying beyond the province of these pages, we may be pardoned for passing without
raising.   A union—not absorption—on terms equally honorable and satisfactory to both (if there is any reasonable
hope that the Churches can satisfy the conditions of this
easily recited but hitherto imaginary formula) is, it may be
allowed, an adjourned question, which neither party should
hastily or peremptorily close.   Certainly we have no desire
to prejudice its decision here.   But it would be folly to shut
our eyes to these historic, fundamental differences of three
quarters of a century's standing, and attempt to bring the
severed parts by external pressure into a mechanical and superficial union.   Bishop Asbury exercised the episcopal
office for thirty two years—twenty four before the adoption
of the constitution, and eight under its operation.   His conception of the important organic functions of his office, and
of its unique position in the government of Methodism, is
sufficiently obvious from the preceding pages.   Bishop Mc-
Kendree was chosen a bishop by the General Conference
which created the delegated body and ordained its constitution.   During the eight closing years of Asbury's episcopate
and life, the two Bishops, alone in the discharge of their
high duties, were inseparable in their official characters and
functions, and most intimate in their personal associations.
They attended the Conferences in company, and, when the
constitutionality of their episcopal administration in the crea-

tion of the Genesee Conference was challenged in the Virginia Conference, Asbury took his appeal to the Annual Conferences which, like the General Conference which followed, approved the administration of the Bishops. That McKendree, in these long tours, became, in no servile but yet in a very vital sense, the depositary and custodian of the primitive Asburyan views and practices, there can be no doubt. Joshua Soule was an itinerant preacher for seventeen years under the administration of Asbury. The whole of his itinerant life, with the exception of two years in Baltimore, just before he accepted the episcopal office, was passed in the New England and New York Conferences. He thus had no sectional affiliations with the Southern wing of the Church. He was the author of the Constitution of the Church, acquainted with every detail of its history from its inception to its adoption. In 1820, after a double election—for the refusal to accept his resignation was equivalent to a second election, and that by an increased majority—he refused, under circumstances most creditable to himself, to be ordained to the high office of a Bishop in the Methodist Episcopal Church. In 1824, with no change or concealment of his views, and after a quadrennium of (at that time) unparalleled excitement in the history of the Church, during which time his sympathy and coöperation with the Senior Bishop, in the heroic remedies which he sought to administer to the body ecclesiastic, were universally known, he was the first man elected to the episcopal office by a General Conference which had been chosen with express reference to the decision of the controversies that were then rending the Church. This was high endorsement, but no higher than such a man deserved. The same General Conference passed a measure, which, as we have seen, settled, so far as that body could, the method by which constitutional issues might be appealed to the tribunal of the Annual Conferences, in accordance with the views and practice of Bishop McKendree. Twenty years roll by. McKendree and George and Roberts have joined the celestial ranks. Soule is the Senior Bishop of a yet undivided but irreconcilably discordant Episcopal Methodism. By his side stand Hedding and Andrew and Waugh and Morris—good men and true, all of them, whom the Church honored in their lives, and whom devout men carried to their burial with great lamentation. If Emory and Fisk had been there, another result might possibly have been reached. But an All-wise Providence did not so permit. There is again a sharp conflict between the Episcopacy and the General Conference, before which that of 1820 pales into insignificance. Into its merits and changing phases it would be premature to enter at this stage of our history. Nor is it necessary. The tall New England Senior is found standing where he stood a quarter of a century before—once more, and on an intenser issue, against his own New England people. His place of residence was not in the Southland; and the difference between the civil institutions of the North and the South was not the primary issue in his mind. Doubtless on that question he was one with his colleague, Bishop Hedding, both of them, in their administration, having taken the same stand. But he planted himself, as aforetime, on the Constitution. A gentleman of keen intellect and unblemished Christian character, whose subsequent official career, though brief, was highly useful and honorable, arose in his seat one Monday morning to address the General Conference. He had been reared among influences foreign to Methodism, and, though finally adopting the law as a profession, had, in earlier life, intended entering the ministry in the Congregational Church, and, indeed, though at times suffering from temporary mental aberration, had begun to preach in Congregational and Presbyterian pulpits. He had been a Methodist about sixteen years, and it had been less than twelve years since his admission on trial, at the age of thirty five, into an Annual Conference.* In polished periods, he had somewhat to say about *mandamus* proceedings, a tortious *seizin*, the episcopacy as an " abstraction " and a " gallery of disa-

---

* Hibbard's Hamline, pp. 16, 17, 20, 21, 43, 54.

bilities," and finally advanced, " as a mere logical formula," (to use his own words) an ingenious and novel theory of the government of the Methodist Episcopal Church—the celebrated " Croton River " view of the universal supremacy of the General Conference, legislative, judicial, and executive. " If it err, which is not a legal presumption," said Mr. Hamline, " its unwholesome error is incurable, except by the *vis medicatrix*—the medicinal virtue—of its own judicial energies." It was such a speech as for originality, analytical power, and literary finish, the General Conference had not heard for many a day. It made its author a Bishop, for the majority had at last found a man who had laid a platform broad enough for them to stand upon. We have said the theory was novel: the Senior Bishop declared to the General Conference he had never before heard its doctrines so much as hinted.* It would be difficult to find a trace of them in the literature of the Church before 1844. But the Conference not only adopted them, but proceeded at once to act upon them, and Mr. Hamline's views have since become canonical in the Methodist Episcopal Church. The constitutional party—for such the minority were, whatever else they may have been—withdrew. A separate and distinct Methodist Episcopal Church was organized. As the law book of this Church, the existing Discipline of the Methodist Episcopal Church was adopted, without the change of a doctrine or provision, constitutional or statutory.† Bishop

---

* Bishop Soule said: " I wish to say explicitly that if the Superintendents are only to be regarded as the officers of the General Conference, liable to be deposed at will by a simple majority of this body without a form of trial, no obligation existing, growing out of the constitution and laws of the Church, even to assign cause wherefore—everything I have to say hereafter is powerless and falls to the ground. But, strange as it may seem, although I have had the privilege to be a member of the General Conference of the Methodist Episcopal Church ever since its present organization; though I was honored with a seat in the convention of ministers which organized it, I have heard for the first time, either on the floor of this Conference, in an Annual Conference, or through the whole of the private membership of the Church, this doctrine advanced; this is the first time I ever heard it."

†Said Annual Conferences, "are hereby constituted a separate ecclesiastical connexion," " based upon the Discipline of the Methodist Episcopal

Soule, the last Senior Bishop of the undivided Methodist Episcopal Church, became the first Senior Bishop of the Church thus established, abandoning his section and his exalted station, alienating many old friends and making many new enemies, to cast in his lot, amid much obloquy, with the new and untried organization, which had naught to commend it to the first officer of the Methodist Episcopal Church, save its adherence to the constitutional principles which he had always embraced and championed. This man's life is all of a piece—in 1808, in 1820, in 1844. That he should have taken this course, under these circumstances, is a vindication of the claim of the Methodist Episcopal Church, South, that, back of all sectional differences, however disruptive and uncontrollable, lay this constitutional difference. It was as marked when seven Southern Conferences took their stand in 1821–2 by the side of McKendree and Soule, and five Northern Conferences ranged themselves over against them, as it was at any later period. To-day, the Constitution framed by Joshua Soule, with his interpretation of it, is still the corner-stone of the government of the Methodist Episcopal Church, South.

Since the separation, each Church has moved along its own chosen course. The Bishops of the Methodist Episcopal Church are commonly said to be " officers of the General Conference " and no more. The General Conference is both the primary and final judge of the constitutionality of its own acts. One of the Bishops ably and conclusively argues in an official journal, his right to refuse to put a motion which, in his judgment, is an infraction of the constitution; but, if he should reduce his principles to practice, it is not doubtful that he would be rather severely handled by the General Conference. Should the General Conference at any time, however innocently, exceed its constitutional powers, the Annual Conferences have no protection and no

Church," and "comprehending the doctrines and entire moral, ecclesiastical, and economical rules and regulations of said Discipline, except only in so far as verbal alterations may be necessary to a distinct organization."
—*Action of Louisville Convention.*

redress; the Bishops can only submit or resign; the Church
itself, should the guaranteed rights of the membership be
invaded, has no remedy save that of revolution. There is
no power but of—the General Conference. If a proposed
amendment fails of the constitutional majority in the Annual
Conferences, the General Conference may and does return
the same proposition in reversed statement, so as to require
the constitutional majority in order to maintain the government as it is.* Should a Bishop decline to submit, or an Annual Conference refuse to vote, upon this new statement of
a proposition already constitutionally rejected, it is difficult
to see why either would not be guilty of contumacy and a
disorderly rejection of the General Conference supremacy.
The Bishops, in formal communications to the General Conferences, ask that body to decide questions of law or to interpret the language of the Discipline. Their communication is referred to the Judiciary Committee, and when the
General Conference acts on their report, the decision is final, and the Bishops govern themselves accordingly. Thus
the functions of a legislature and a supreme court are combined in the same body. An appeal from the decision of the
President of an Annual Conference on a point of law,
likewise, lies to the ensuing General Conference. The
" Croton River " conception of the government has been
universally accepted, and its principles are applied without
question.

On the other hand, in the Methodist Episcopal Church,
South, the constitutional origin and protection of the episcopacy is accepted as a maxim. The College of Bishops is
the supreme court of appeals in legal decisions. An appeal
from the decision of a President of an Annual Conference
on a law point lies to the whole College of Bishops, whose
decision is final. Their interpretation of the law is authoritative, and governs the administration until the General Con-

---

* See Report No. II. of the Committee on Judiciary, the Moore substitute,
and the Hamilton amendment, on the seating of women in the General Conference. Gen. Conf. Journals, XII. 1892, pp. 358, 359, 486.

ference changes the statute.* Moreover the Bishops are constitutionally the primary judges of the constitutionality of the acts of the General Conference. Their functions as the law-officers of the Church are never suspended, during the session of the General Conference, which creates no judiciary committee, or at any other time. Not that they possess a "veto power" in the proper sense, but that they are empowered to carry the appeal to the tribunal of the Annual Conferences, that the Bishops, the Annual Conferences, and the Church itself, may be protected from that most dangerous of all tyrannies—the tyranny of an oligarchy, which proclaims its own supremacy and irresponsibility—whose errors, even though they be undesigned and unconscious, are not the less dangerous, and are incurable by any independent or constitutional or coördinate agency.

The merits of these two contrasted systems of government in Episcopal Methodism, it does not become us to argue in these pages. If we have inadvertently fallen into the smallest error as to matter of fact in the preceding statements, no one could be more grateful for a prompt correction. Thus the differences which date back to 1820 have been crystallized in two Churches, which, bearing the same generic name, and to the superficial observer having the same episcopal government, are as widely separated as the poles. According to the precedents and genius of the government of the Methodist Episcopal Church, with its broad construction of the constitution, and its universally supreme General Conference, there is no reason why this body should not, by a majority vote, alter the tenure of the episcopal office from life to a term of years; confine the administration of a Bishop

---

* "An Annual Conference shall have the right to appeal from such decision to the College of Bishops, whose decision in such cases shall be final. . . . And each Bishop shall report in writing to the Episcopal College, at an annual meeting to be held by them, such decisions as he has made subsequently to the last preceding meeting; and all such decisions, when approved by the College of Bishops, shall be recorded in a permanent form, and published in such manner as the Bishops shall agree to adopt, and when so approved, recorded, and published, they shall be authoritative interpretations or constructions of the law."—Discipline, 1890.

by law to a given episcopal district; or enervate the episcopacy by a refusal to elect additional Bishops as their ranks
are thinned by death.* Similarly the presiding eldership
might, by a majority vote, be essentially modified or abolished.
If any of these measures were determined upon, it might be
that the conservatives could prevail upon their advocates to
consent to effect them by the constitutional process; but this
would be an abandonment of the principles generally accepted by the Church since they were first set forth by Mr.
Hamline, and the Annual Conferences would speak purely
by the concession and grace of the General Conference. If
the General Conference in its supreme judicial capacity
should decide against the submission of any of these measures, or others like them, to the Annual Conferences, and
should pass any of them simply by a majority vote, the
Bishops, the Annual Conferences, and the Church would
all be alike helpless, unless they resorted to the inalienable
right of revolution. On the other hand, in the Methodist
Episcopal Church, South, if any of these changes become
desirable, there would be no question that they must be effected by the constitutional process. The episcopal office
might be held by a quadrennial tenure, or the presiding eldership become elective or cease to exist; but such changes
could not be effected by a majority vote of the General Conference. Hence waiving, as before, or conceding, if the
reader choose, the abstract question of the desirability of the

---

*In his celebrated speech, Mr. Hamline said: "Our Church constitution
recognizes the Epicopacy as an abstraction, and leaves this body to work it
into a concrete form in any hundred or more ways we may be able to invent. We may make one, five, or twenty bishops; and if we please, one for
each Conference. We may refuse to elect another until all die or resign;
and then, to maintain the Episcopacy, which we are bound to do, we must elect
one, at least. As to his term, we may limit it at pleasure, or leave it unde-
termined. But in this case is it *undeterminable?* Certainly not. The power
which elected may then displace. In all civil constitutions, as far as I know,
not to fix an officer's term, is to suspend it on the will of the appointing power.
Cabinet ministers and secretaries are examples. No officer as such can
claim incumbency for life, unless such a term be authoritatively and expressly fixed upon."

reunion, on broad Christian principles, of the two Methodist Episcopal Churches, there confronts us the problem, of whose easy solution only one ignorant of the history of the Church could be sanguine, of a formal, explicit, and mutually satisfactory adjustment and reconciliation of the fundamentally opposed schemes of government in the two Churches.

Between the General Conferences of 1820 and 1824, Bishop McKendree's health was infirm and his trials great; but, says he,

I pursued my course as well as I could until the fall preceding the General Conference of 1824, when, observing the method adopted by some, and thinking that I could not attend the Annual Conferences without interfering with their measures, or at least seeming to interfere in the election of delegates to the ensuing General Conference, which I deemed derogatory to my station, therefore, notwithstanding the fate of our controversy depended on the representatives to be chosen at the three following Conferences, I committed the cause to God, and went no farther than the Tennessee Conference. Great were the efforts to secure a majority in favor of the suspended resolutions, but they proved unsuccessful.

CHAPTER XXII.

THE FOURTH AND FIFTH DELEGATED GENERAL CONFERENCES, AND THE INTERVENING QUADRENNIUM, 1824–1828.

THE Fourth Delegated General Conference met in Baltimore, Saturday, May 1, 1824, with the three bishops and about one hundred and twenty five delegates present at the opening. Memorials poured in declaring that " the people were the source of legislative authority;" that " the power of the Bishops was to be found nowhere else but in popes;" that " we have no constitution;" that " the restrictive parts of the Discipline are not binding on succeeding General Conferences after 1808;" nor " upon the laity, as they were made by a legislative body, without the design or authority to adopt a constitution," etc.*

The question on the suspended resolutions was introduced by Peter Cartwright, who gave notice, May 19, that the next day he would offer the following:

Whereas the resolutions which were suspended at the last General Conference are null and void, inasmuch as a majority of the Annual Conferences have judged them unconstitutional, and whereas six of the Annual Conferences have recommended their adoption; therefore

Resolved, etc., That said resolutions go into effect as soon as their adoption shall be recommended by those Annual Conferences which have not recommended them, they being approved by two thirds of the present General Conference.

Mr. Cartwright represented the Kentucky Conference, which had both pronounced the suspended resolutions unconstitutional and recommended their constitutional adoption by the consent of all the Conferences. His preamble recites the facts correctly: seven Conferences, including South Carolina, had pronounced them unconstitutional; but

---

* Paine's McKendree, II. 33.

(381)

the South Carolina had refused to recommend their adoption, as we have seen from original evidence, leaving but six
which had taken the positive action recommended by Bishop McKendree for the sake of peace.

Bishop McKendree's address submitted two questions:
(1) Are the suspended resolutions constitutional? (2) If
unconstitutional, shall they be adopted in a constitutional
way, by the suspension of the restrictive rule? Mr. Cartwright's resolution formally recognizes the principle, which
seems to have been universally admitted at the time, that a
majority of the Conferences, acting in a judicial capacity,
might determine the question of constitutionality, for or
against. If a majority decided the resolutions to be constitutional, that ended the controversy, adversely to Bishop
McKendree and the constitutionalists, and the resolutions
were to go into effect. But, if the majority decided them to
be unconstitutional, there was still the constitutional method
of making them effective, namely, by the recommendation
of *all* the Annual Conferences, required for the alteration or
suspension of the restrictive rule. If we are mistaken in the
statement that the principle was generally accepted that a
majority of the Conferences might decide the primary question of constitutionality, it is true that Bishop McKendree,
at least, assumed and acted upon it, and that Mr. Cartwright, a member of the constitutional party, by formally
embodying it in his resolution, sought to commit the General Conference to this view by its own express action.
As the measure which the General Conference finally passed
contained an equally clear and express statement of the principle, the General Conference of 1824 placed the formal
stamp of its official approval upon the course which Bishop
McKendree had pursued, and recognized the binding, legal
force of the decision which he had procured from the Annual Conferences. Mr. Cartwright designed, however, to give
the Northern Conferences one more opportunity to secure
the adoption of their favorite measure in a constitutional way.

The next day Mr. Cartwright failed to call up his measure;

but, May 21, David Young, of the Ohio Conference, gave
notice that he would offer a resolution on the "suspended
resolutions." In the afternoon, the withdrawal of a resolution of Mr. Cartwright's is recorded: it appears to have
been the one cited above. The constitutionalists were gaining confidence and were rather forcing the fighting. Mr.
Cartwright's measure had been thrown out to develop the
position and strength of the opposing parties. The result
proving satisfactory to those who had introduced it, it was
probably understood privately that Mr. Young's measure,
which was stronger, should substitute Mr. Cartwright's.
Accordingly, May 22, Mr. Young submitted the following:

> Whereas a majority of the Annual Conferences have judged the resolu-
> tions making presiding elders elective, and which were passed and then sus-
> pended at the last General Conference, unconstitutional; therefore
>
> *Resolved*, etc., That the said resolutions are not of authority and shall not
> be carried into effect.

The delay, after the introduction of Mr. Cartwright's resolution, had probably enabled the constitutionalists to satisfy
themselves of one or both of two things, (1) that a fresh reference to the Annual Conferences would only increase the
agitation, with no prospect that the Northern Conferences
would accept the measure on a constitutional basis, and (2)
that the constitutional party was strong enough to pass the
decisive measure of Mr. Young in the General Conference.
Mr. Young's resolution had the great advantage of joining
the issue on the constitutional question, pure and simple,
without reference to the merits of the presiding elder controversy. Accordingly Monday morning, May 24, his measure
was called up; a motion to lay it on the table was defeated;
the Journals of the last General Conference, and of the
Ohio, Kentucky, Mississippi, Tennessee, Missouri, Philadelphia, New York, and South Carolina Conferences, were
read, so far as they bore on this subject; and, in the afternoon, the vote being taken by ballot, Mr. Young's resolution was sustained, and the constitutionalists triumphed by
the narrow margin of 63 to 61.*

---

*Gen. Conf. Journals, I. 270, 276, 277, 278, 281.

By this action the General Conference formally recognized the validity and finality of a decision of the majority of the Annual Conferences against the constitutionality of the suspended resolutions, since the decision was recited in the preamble of Mr. Young's measure as the sole and sufficient ground of the declaration that the suspended resolutions "are not of authority" and "shall not be carried into effect." The Senior Bishop had prosecuted to a successful issue his appeal from the action of a General Conference to the tribunal of the Annual Conferences; and the Delegated General Conference, acting under a constitution, formally recognized the supremacy of the primary bodies which had called it into existence.

But the constitutionalists triumphed—always by a narrow majority—all along the line. By a vote of 64 to 58, as we have seen in a preceding chapter, they sent to the Annual Conferences for adoption the constitutional amendment, providing for an episcopal veto power and, in a defined contingency, for an appeal to the Annual Conferences.* A majority, no doubt, favored this plan, but that it was defeated need not excite surprise, as the constitution then required the consent of all the Annual Conferences to such a change. The lines were closely drawn in the episcopal election. Two bishops were to be elected, and Joshua Soule and William Beauchamp were the representatives of the constitutionalists, and Elijah Hedding and John Emory of their opponents. On the first ballot the constitutional "candidates" —the word is freely employed by contemporaries—led the poll, Soule having 64, Beauchamp 62, Hedding 61, and Emory 59; but, 128 ballots having been cast, there was no election. On the second ballot, Mr. Soule received 65 votes and was elected, no other receiving a majority.´ But before the third ballot was taken, Mr. Emory arose and withdrew his name. This is commonly regarded as the modest act of the youngest man whose name was before the Conference. Undoubtedly it was such an act, and Mr. Emory

* See above, pp. 354-357.

could well afford to wait. But it was more than this. The fathers were not quite so innocent in such matters as is usually supposed. There was now no possibility of the election of more than one of the candidates of the anti-constitutionalists, and the younger man withdrew in favor of the senior and leading name. Moreover, but one name was to go on the ballots this third time, since Mr. Soule had been elected, and if Messrs. Hedding and Emory divided the votes of their party, it was almost certain to elect Mr. Beauchamp. Consequently Mr. Emory withdrew, and on the third ballot Mr. Hedding received 66 votes to Mr. Beauchamp's 60, and was elected.[*] There was an element of danger in the fact that each Bishop had been chosen by a sectional and party vote; but it was well for the unity of the Church, divided on a constitutional issue, but by a sectional line, that each party secured a Bishop. No fracture took place but, if a severe strain should come, the plane of cleavage was painfully evident.

Mr. Young's measure made a final disposition of the suspended resolutions. Nevertheless, it was agreed, on motion of Robert Paine and William Capers, both of whom were elected Bishops at the first General Conference of the Methodist Episcopal Church, South, that

> It is the sense of this General Conference that the suspended resolutions, making the presiding elder elective, etc., are considered as unfinished business, and are neither to be inserted in the revised form of the Discipline, nor to be carried into operation, before the next General Conference.[†]

So high did the tide of party feeling run that twice, while this resolution was pending, Bishop Roberts in the chair, the

---

[*] Gen. Conf. Journals, I. 285.

[†] *Ibid.*, I. 297. Bishop McKendree takes this view of the intention of this resolution. He says: "On the commencement of the late General Conference [1824], the Bishops took the subject into consideration, and unanimously agreed to recommend the introduction of the suspended resolutions so soon as they should be recommended by those Annual Conferences which had not already authorized the change. This the old side—the majority—I understand, are willing to do. But this our reformers refused to do. The majority, still desirous of an amicable adjustment of differences, would not destroy the resolutions, but perpetuated their suspension. This is my view

quorum was broken, and only under the remonstrances of the chairman and the venerable Freeborn Garrettson was it restored, and the measure finally passed.*

We have seen how it was the custom first of Coke and Asbury, then of Asbury and Whatcoat, and finally of Asbury and McKendree, to attend all the Conferences in company whenever practicable. The new arrangement in 1816, when George and Roberts were added to the espiscopal college, has also been noticed.† When the General Conference of 1824 adjourned, there were seventeen Annual Conferences and five Bishops, four of whom were effective. It was necessary that the plan of episcopal supervision should be somewhat further developed and, to meet the new situation, which to the fathers seemed a little complex, the Committee on Episcopacy recommended, and the Conference passed, the following:

Resolved, &c., 4. That it is highly expedient for the general superintendents, at every session of the General Conference, and as far as to them may appear practicable, in the intervals of the sessions, annually, to meet in council to form their plan of traveling through their charge, whether in a circuit after each other or by dividing the connexion into several episcopal departments, with one bishop or more in each department, as to them may appear proper and most conducive to the general good, and the better to enable them fully to perform the great work of their administration in the general superintendency, and to exchange and unite their views upon all affairs connected with the general interests of the Church.‡

This, so far as appears, was the origin of the "Bishops' Meeting." It was now both impossible and unnecessary for all the Bishops to be present at every Conference. The form of the General Conference action, it will be noticed, is advisory only; and leaves to the discretion of the Bishops

of the matter. Hence the change in our government, which was dictated by the reformers is defeated by the reformers. It is said by authority to be relied upon, that nothing short of investing the Annual Conferences with authority to constitute the presiding elders, independently of the Bishops, and to make the presiding elders thus appointed a committee to station the preachers, in which the Bishop shall have only the casting vote, will satisfy the Northern brethren."

* Paine's McKendree, II. 40.
† See above, pp. 335, 336.
‡ Gen. Conf. Journals, I. 301, 302.

the plan of Episcopal visitation. Under the Constitution of
the Church, a Methodist Bishop remains in the enjoyment
of all his Episcopal powers at all times and in every part of
the Church. His administration cannot be constitutionally
restrained, either as to time or place, by any statute of the
General Conference. Any such limitation arises from the
comity of his agreements with his colleagues, in the administration of a *joint, itinerant, general,* superintendency. In
the present complex administration, certain violations of this
comity might and would result in disaster; but any proper
episcopal act of any Bishop at any time, in any part of the
Church, would be valid. Violations of this comity would be
primarily canvassed in the College of Bishops, not in the
General Conference. If the difference could not be settled there, the final resort would be to the General Conference, to which the Bishops are *jointly* responsible for the
whole administration. In a conceivable state of affairs, a
constitutional measure might become necessary for the permanent settlement of such issues. In the General Conference of 1824, it was contended by some that the body had
authority to divide the Church into episcopal districts for the
quadrennium; but Winans triumphantly vindicated the constitutional view, in a speech which Bishop Paine, who heard
it, describes as "thrilling;" and the report of the committee was adopted as recited above. Accordingly, the Bishops agreed among themselves that Roberts and Soule were
to attend the western and southern Conferences, and
George and Hedding the eastern and northern. The Senior Bishop sometimes attended more Conferences in a year
than either of his colleagues, as he traveled throughout the
Church. For many years following it was not unusual for
two Bishops, and frequently three, to be present at the sessions of the Annual Conferences.

The legislation in 1824 on the subject of slavery is embraced in the following paragraphs inserted in the Discipline:

3. All our preachers shall prudently enforce upon our members the necessity of teaching their slaves to read the word of God; and to allow them

time to attend upon the public worship of God on our regular days of divine service.

4. Our colored preachers and official members shall have all the privileges which are usual to others in the district and quarterly conferences, where the usages of the country do not forbid it. And the presiding elder may hold for them a separate district conference, where the number of colored local preachers will justify it.

5. The annual conferences may employ colored preachers to travel and preach where their services are judged necessary; provided that no one shall be so employed without having been recommended according to the Form of Discipline.*

The quadrennium from 1824 to 1828 was the era of radicalism. The discussion of the " rights " of the itinerants in the election of presiding elders, had aroused the local preachers to an assertion of their " rights " in the government of the Church. The laity in turn took up the agitation for "rights," in the election of class-leaders and in making changes in the economy of the Church. All the discontented found a vehicle of communication in a vigorous organ, "*The Mutual Rights.*" Baltimore was the center of the maelstrom, and here a convention of the reformers was held in 1827. Large *demands* were made upon the General Conference of 1828.

But by this time the conservative elements had rallied against the destructive rush of threatened revolution. Even lay delegation, the last plank and the most popular one in the new platform, could not then be considered with the favor which it received at a later day. The temper on both sides, in the greatly widened controversy, was unfavorable to concession. The reformers were aggressive and hopeful, for several reasons. They believed their cause just; it was favored by the political tendency of the country; an envious element of sectarianism which once existed in other denominations, and was ever ready to humble Methodism, was forward and loud to encourage disaffection; but chiefly they miscalculated as to the final adhesion of men who had, at one time or other, expressed views in sympathy with their own. Even Bascom uttered some sentiments, in the heyday of his blood, which were not in harmony with his maturer life as one of the strongest, steadiest, and most trusted leaders of Episcopal Methodism the Church has ever had. Hedding leaned that way once,† on the original question, and Bangs and Waugh. Emory criticised and antagonized Bishop McKendree and Joshua Soule for the prompt, resolute means they used to save the constitution. Bishop George, in judicial weakness, and Bishop Roberts, by

---

* Gen. Conf. Journals, I. 294; Emory's Hist. of the Discipline, p. 279.
† That Hedding completely reversed his opinion on the presiding elder question, see his life by Bishop Clark, pp. 217–220.

amiable irresolution, in the primary movement let the ship drive. But now, when the radical tendencies of these things were seen, the conservatives closed ranks and stood firm. The report of the General Conference, made by John Emory, was kind, strong, and conclusive, and put an end to the hopes of the reformers, who proceeded to the organization of the Methodist Protestant Church. . . . Thoughtful men must not be counted on to join in a theoretical and destructive reform because every pin and screw in the tabernacle that has sheltered them is not exactly to their notion.*

Before me lies the original copy of what may, not improperly, be styled the official minutes of the first Bishops' meeting ever held in the Methodist Episcopal Church. It is in the handwriting of Bishop McKendree, who made a small, neat, unbound blank book, in which he wrote his notes. About this, with the letters which passed between the Bishops at the time, he placed a paper band, whose ends are fastened together with sealing wax, and inscribed the packet: "The official interviews of the Bishops in Philadelphia, April, 1826." The General Conference of 1824 had recommended, as we have seen, such an annual meeting. Before that time, there had never been more than three contemporary Bishops, and their interviews were more or less irregular and informal. As they were frequently all present together at Annual Conferences, set times for the transaction of business of a general nature were unnecessary. During the two years since the General Conference, Bishops George and Hedding had been laboring in the North, and Bishops Roberts and Soule in the South. That no meeting of this character had been held in 1825 appears certain from a letter which Bishop McKendree addressed to Bishop George, dated Philadelphia, April 22, 1826, in which he says, "Almost two years have elapsed since we saw each other." This, therefore, was the first official meeting of the Bishops, the main business which called them together being to appoint a fraternal delegate to England, according to the direction of the General Conference, and to discuss the plan of episcopal visitation. Two sessions were held, both in Bishop McKendree's room, one on the afternoon of

* Bishop McTyeire, History of Methodism, pp. 572, 573.

April 13, and the other at six o'clock in the morning of April 18—an hour long since abandoned for such episcopal interviews. Bishops George and Hedding were holding the Philadelphia Conference, and Bishops McKendree and Soule came from the South. Bishop Roberts was absent.

These *memoranda* have not hitherto been published: the thoughtful reader will see in the sequel how their insertion here subserves the ends of this history. Says Bishop Mc-Kendree:

Bishop Soule and myself arrived at Dr. Sargent's, in Philadelphia, in the evening of the 12th of April, and waited in expectation of seeing Bp. George, who put up within about one square of our lodging. When the morning of the 13th was far spent, I addressed a note to Bp. George requesting an interview as soon as practicable, and proposed to [wait] on him at the place and hour which he would appoint. On account of business he deferred it until the afternoon and promised to wait on us at my room. Accordingly Bishops George and Hedding came. Bp. Soule was present, and our business was introduced.

The appointment of a messenger to the British Conference was proposed. Bp. G. thought that appointment was discretionary with the bishops,—that we had no business of material consequence,—that the expense would be considerable; and, therefore, he was opposed to appointing a man. Bishop Soule produced the resolutions of the General Conference,* and a letter from the preachers in Canada, proposing instructions to the contemplated messenger; they were read. And Wm. Capers, who had been fixed on by Roberts and Soule, was nominated by McKendree and objected to by George and Hedding, because he was the owner of slaves. George nominated W. Fisk or E. Cooper. A little desultory conversation passed. Bp. George said his business pushed—he must retire—but take business into consideration. Bp. McK. then proposed another subject for their consideration, which was for the bishops, George and Hedding, to change with Roberts and Soule next year, in order for each bishop to visit all the Annual Conferences before the next General Conference.

There were several other subjects of great importance to the Church to be discussed, but the bishop was in a great hurry, and they were reserved for the next meeting. This interview took up about three quarters of an hour, and we parted.

While sitting in Conference, Monday, 17, a note from Bishop George was handed to me by Hedding, proposing an interview at six o'clock next morning, if advisable. Bp. Soule consenting to the proposal, the note was immediately answered in the affirmative: and about the appointed time on the 18th the bishops came to my room.

---

* "*Resolved*, that the general superintendents be, and are hereby authorized and requested to appoint a delegate to the British Conference, to visit them in 1826, under the same regulations that were adopted in 1820."—Gen. Conf. Journals, I. 294.

The business was introduced by Bp. George. He professed to be pressed with business—to be in a great hurry—introduced the subject of appointing a delegate to England—supposed Bp. Soule and myself had not altered our opinions—that he could not approve of the man of our choice—that he still thought we were not obliged to appoint a representative to England at this time. The resolution of the General Conference, he said, was advisory. There was not business of sufficient importance to make it necessary and the expense would be very considerable. He was therefore opposed to the appointment of a delegate at this time. After a few remarks on the resolution of the General Conference, Bp. Hedding thought the resolution required the appointment of a minister to England; but such were his apprehensions of consequences from the North if a slave-holder should be appointed, that he would join with Bp. George to send no one, and risk the consequences. To all of which, Bps. McKendree and Soule made no reply. They said nothing for or against either of the persons in nomination; but let the subject drop, in consequence of a determination on the part of the other bishops to have matters conducted as they pleased—or do nothing. Further conversation on this subject ceased of course.

Bp. George then mentioned the subject of the Bishops changing their ground for the next year, and proceeded to show difficulties, impracticability, etc. An attempt was made to answer them, and to show the practicability and propriety of the measure. But the Bishop pronounced it inadmissible! Said he was hurried by a press of business and must go! On this occasion the bishops were together about an hour.

Thus ended our official interviews, on various business of the Church, which, by McKendree, Roberts, and Soule, was judged to be of sufficient magnitude to call all the bishops together to consult and arrange their business. Bp. Roberts, whose situation exposed him to the most serious inconveniences, concluded, for the sake of the case, to make the sacrifice, and the time was appointed for them to meet in Baltimore, to perform this duty of a jointly responsible general superintendency, and labor of love to the Church. But, alas! for the accomplishment of the laudable design.

The relations of Bishops McKendree and George had been somewhat strained since 1820. But with this we have nothing to do here: the good men have long since seen eye to eye in their Father's house. The material point is that at this early date, the College of Bishops, no less than the General Conference, and the Annual Conferences, was divided, not only on the issue of the appointment of a delegate to England, but upon a proper rotation of the Bishops, who, as itinerant general superintendents, should have been equally known in every part of the Church. Of the two questions discussed at the first Bishops' meeting, (1) the appointment of the delegate, and (2) the fixing of a *general* itinerary of the superintendents, the latter was of incomparably greater importance to the peace and unity of the Church. As a matter of fact, Bishop Hedding in twenty years, from 1824 to 1844, made but a single tour of the Southern Conferences, and that in 1831, seven years after he became a Bishop: in the same year Bishop Soule made his first episcopal visitation in the North! The Bishops were localized. Again and again Roberts and Soule advanced as far north as the Baltimore Conference and returned again on their southern track; again and again George and Hedding came as far south as the Philadelphia Conference, and retreated into New York, New England, and Canada; many a time since have the Bishops of two Episcopal Methodisms carried their oversight to the same limits and retired into the North or the South! Let us look a little more closely into this. The day after the adjournment of the " Bishops' meeting," Bishop McKendree penned this letter:

Philadelphia, April 19, 1826.

To Bishops George and Hedding:

In our interviews in this city, I have advised you and the other Bishops to change, in order for each to visit all the Annual Conferences before the next General Conference.

The harmony of the episcopacy and the prosperity of the Church influence me to give this advice; but I claim no anthority over my colleagues. If, therefore, the change involves insurmountable difficulties, on your part, it is your right to decline such a course. But, in either event, it is my earnest request, that our next round of Conferences may commence in Philadelphia, May 3, 1827, or, if more convenient to you, on the 26th of April, and conclude in Ohio, October 11, and proceed as near the following dates as the distance from one to another will admit: New York, May 24; New England, June 14; Maine, July 5; Genesee, Aug. 2; Canada, Aug. 23; Pittsburg, Sept. 21

The object of this request is to enable me to attend those Conferences next year, which I hope to do if health and strength are preserved; and conformably to the above plan I am persuaded it may be done.

Most respectfully yours, etc.   W. McKendree.*

The proper supervision of the work is weighing on the Senior Bishop's mind. To this epistle, the Bishops addressed returned the following reply:

---

* Unpublished letter: original in the author's possession.

Philadelphia, April 20, 1826.

To Bishop McKendree:

We have received yours of yesterday, and are of opinion that the plan will be impracticable. For, instead of the Philadelphia Conference being fixed at a later date, we shall have, by degrees, to bring it earlier, in order to have it meet in 1828 before the time of the General Conference, and give time to get to Pittsburg. As it respects the other Conferences it is impossible for us to determine at what time they can be held till we know where they will be, on account of the distances; but we think the time at which you have fixed some of them would be too short for the distance; and with due respect we would suggest the opinion that in your state of debility it would be impossible for you to reach them all. Again the change of time, in some of the Conferences, would be so great we fear it would give them serious dissatisfaction. The New York Conference, in 1828, will probably have to be about the 1st of April; because the superintendents and delegates cannot return from Pittsburg till too late in the summer for that Conference.

Respecting a change, so as to enable us to visit all the southern and western Conferences before the General Conference, it seems to us to be impossible that our health would admit of it.

With respect to the delegate, though we cannot agree to your nomination, nor you to ours, we shall be glad to meet you and Bp. Soule as soon as our business will admit of it, and see if we can fix on some other man in whom we can all be agreed. Or, if this cannot be done, we would suggest the propriety of writing to the British Conference.

Affectionately yours, etc., ENOCH GEORGE,
E. HEDDING.*

Thus, however valid these objections to Bishop McKendree's proposal may have been in detail, the infirm Senior received little encouragement to visit the Northern Conferences, under the supervision of his junior colleagues; and as for the exchange with Roberts and Soule, it was impossible that the health of George and Hedding would admit of it. It may have been their misfortune, and not their fault, but in either case Bishop McKendree's plan for such an episcopal itinerancy as would make the superintendency truly general, failed, and great hurt came to the Church thereby. A letter of inquiry which the two Bishops addressed to the Senior in New York, serves to show that their testimony about the "Bishops' meeting" agrees with his, and, for that reason, it is presented here:

---

* Original letter (unpublished) in author's possession.

May 12, 1826.

To Bishop McKendree,

Dear Sir: We desire respectfully to inquire if you recollect the following particulars in our interviews at Philadelphia on the subject of a delegate for England.

First, That you proposed Brother Capers, we objected on account of his holding slaves. Then we proposed Brothers Fisk and Cooper.

Secondly, But in another conversation, when it was asked in what sense the vote of the General Conference was to be understood, E. George stated that he did not understand the vote to be *imperative;* E. Hedding stated that he supposed the vote laid the Superintendents under an obligation to send one, but that he, for his part, would rather risk the responsibility of sending none, than that of sending any brother who held slaves.

Thirdly, That in our note addressed to you, in answer to one we received of you, we proposed another meeting to see if you could nominate some other brother in whom we could all agree.

An answer to these inquiries will much oblige, dear sir,

Yours affectionately,

E. HEDDING,

E. GEORGE.*

Bishop McKendree's answer may be seen in the pages of his biographer. It is a somewhat fuller reproduction of his original notes of the Bishops' meeting; but adds that Bishop Soule had returned to Baltimore after the last episcopal interview, and that, from the tenor of their note, the Senior had expected to be informed when their "business would admit" of another meeting, but that he had received no further information on the subject. He concludes, "I judge it most prudent for me to decline any further agency in the case, not with a design to prevent the appointment, but for you to manage the business as you may think best." †

Our authorities commonly locate this "Bishops' meeting" in Baltimore.‡ From Bishop McKendree's notes it appears that this was the place appointed, and that McKendree, Roberts, and Soule came together there. Bishop Roberts' engagements did not permit him to go to Philadelphia, but he concurred in the nomination of Capers, and Bishops McKendree and Soule agreed to go on to Philadelphia, where it was known they would fall in with Bishops George and

---

*The original is in Bishop Hedding's handwriting.

†Paine's McKendree, II. 387-390.

‡So Clark, Life of Hedding, p. 324; McTyeire, History, p. 575.

Hedding at the session of the Philadelphia Conference. The business of the Annual Conference seems to have taken precedence with Bishop George, and the interviews were unsatisfactory and void of result. The next year (1827) all the Bishops met; four of them retained their opinions of a year before; Bishop Roberts amiably refused to decide the question; and the appointment of a delegate to England went over to the General Conference of 1828.

The biographers, concerned with the doings of single Bishops only, have generally failed to state accurately the plan of episcopal visitation actually pursued, and have apparently not apprehended how dangerous it was to the unity of the Church. Thus Bishop Paine declares that at the close of the General Conference of 1824, it was agreed that " for the first two years Bishops Roberts and Soule were to attend the Western and Southern Conferences, and Bishops George and Hedding the Eastern and Northern, and to exchange their fields of labor for the ensuing two years—thus enabling each of them to attend every Conference before the next General Conference." * Well had it been for the future of Methodism had such an exchange taken place, and had such exchanges become the permanent policy of the Bishops. We have seen how earnestly and persistently the Senior Bishop strove to effect it, foreseeing the evils which must afflict the Church from such a sectionalizing of the Bishops. These evils began to appear at Philadelphia, in the hopeless division of the Bishops over the appointment of a delegate. Roberts and Soule, apparently, acquiesced in the plan of McKendree; at least there is no evidence of opposition on their part, while George and Hedding pointedly declined to concur. In a private letter to Bishop McKendree, written at New York, May 18, 1826, Bishop George thus construes the action of the General Conference of 1824 with regard to the visitation of the Bishops:

As to visiting all the Conferences and becoming jointly responsible, it is to me a new thought; I did believe that the General Conference gave liberty to the Episcopacy to make such arrangements as would meet the increase

* Life and Times of McKendree, II. 48.

of labor without its becoming insupportable.   I am sincere when I say that I did think such arrangements were made at the time the Episcopal commit-tee met at Baltimore, and that they were made for four years; and being thus impressed at the time, I made all arrangements to meet that plan. . . . And I do sincerely think that I have neither strength of body or mind, at present, to undertake a continental superintendency.*

Thus Bishop George regarded the resolution of the Epis-copal committee, adopted in 1824 by the General Conference, as decisive, and had not so much as contemplated any other work for the quadrennium than the northern circuit of Con-ferences: the new conditions, in his judgment, necessitated a localized episcopacy, a *quasi* diocese, and he decided to act accordingly.

Bishop Clark says of the division of episcopal labor in 1824 that it " was agreed upon *for the year:* Bishops Rob-erts and Soule were to take the supervision of the Baltimore and Kentucky Conferences, and all the Conferences south and southwest of them; while Bishops George and Hedding were to take the Philadelphia and Pittsburg Conferences, and all the Conferences north and northeast of them."[†] What a division of the work, when it became practically permanent! With the exception of a single year, when Bishop Hedding took the southern circuit, as we have seen, it became altogether permanent, so far as the subject of Dr. Clark's biography is concerned; yet year after year he re-cords the treadmill round of his hero—Philadelphia, New York, New England, Genesee, (until 1828, Canada,) Pitts-burg, Ohio, with small variations, as new Conferences were created in these regions—without detecting any thing re-markable in this sectionalizing of a Methodist Bishop, or noting its bearings on the future of the Church.[‡]

After attending the Baltimore and Philadelphia Confer-ences, Bishop McKendree took the southern circuit with Roberts and Soule in the autumn of 1824, attending the Ken-

_____

* Original letter in possession of the author.

† Life and Times of Hedding, p. 306.

‡ I have carefully traced all of Bishop Hedding's tours in Dr. Clark's biog-raphy, pp. 305-586, and the above is a sufficiently accurate generalization of the facts

tucky, Missouri, and Tennessee Conferences. At last the superannuated senior, weighed down by increasing infirmities, is compelled to relinquish work, in a letter, written at Nashville, Dec. 12, 1824, and addressed to Bishops Roberts and Soule. But in 1825 he is at it again, attending the Kentucky Conference with Bishop Roberts, September 22; thence he crosses the Cumberland and Alleghany mountains, and attends a quarterly meeting at Lynchburg, Va., with Hezekiah G. Leigh; from there he goes to the Baltimore, Philadelphia, and Genesee Conferences; comes back to the Baltimore and Philadelphia Conferences * in the spring of 1826, and attempts to impress upon the other Bishops his views of a "continental superintendency," illustrated by such an example! In the winter and spring of 1826-7, he attends the South Carolina, Virginia, Baltimore, and Philadelphia Conferences. In May he returns westward, visiting for the third time his beloved Wyandotte missions in Ohio, and again reaching the session of the Kentucky Conference at Versailles, in October, 1827. In March, 1828, he sets out for the General Conference at Pittsburg. Thus throughout the quadrennium, 1824-1828, the irrepressible and indefatigable Senior, presumably superannuated, was the only episcopal link binding together the North and the South: the health of George and Hedding did not admit of their coming south, and Roberts and Soule could not exchange without their consent. It was bad enough that the General Conference and the Annual Conferences should be split into two nearly equal parts on a constitutional issue and by a sectional line; it had its dangers that Soule and Hedding should have been put into office by opposed sectional votes; it was too bad that the episcopacy could not harmonize in their first formal conference; it was perhaps worst of all, in its effects on the

---

* Bishop Paine adds the New York (II. 82); but in this he is probably mistaken. Bishop McKendree wrote Bishop George in the spring of 1826 that he had not seen him for two years. George and Hedding presided alternately at the New York Conference; but Hedding was alone at Philadelphia and Genesee, except as Bishop McKendree aided him. See Clark's Hedding, pp. 320-322.

mind of the Church, that the effective Bishops should have been permanently sectionalized in their superintendency. Perhaps better things were designed at the General Conference of 1828. The report of the Committee on Episcopacy, adopted· by the Conference, recommended that " each of our bishops should, if practicable, be known in each of the Annual Conferences once in four years." But Bishop George died in the autumn of that year, on his way south to hold the Holston Conference. As late as 1831, when Hedding took the southern circuit for the first and only time, Soule first appeared in his native New England in his episcopal character. By common consent, each section was entitled to a bishop in 1832, and Andrew and Emory were chosen by handsome majorities on the first ballot. This indicated a spirit of mutual conciliation; but at the same time it perpetuated the sectional balance and division. But to this election little importance is to be attached. The work of division was accomplished in the years 1820–1828. During that period it came to pass, perhaps before many of the active participants were awake to it, that the line of division, constitutional and sectional, had been run through the Church, separating it, in all but name, into two sharply contrasted Episcopal Methodisms. He who hangs his theory of the division of the Church upon the slender thread of the accidents of an episcopal matrimonial alliance, or even upon the difference of civil institutions, North and South, *alone*, may satisfy himself. But his proceeding is unhistorical. The preceding pages have been written to little purpose, if the conviction is not forced upon the mind of the impartial reader, that in this troublous period of 1820–1828 the work of division was really accomplished. The line, like a thread of scarlet, ran clearly and discernibly through the General Conference. It ran, openly and undisguisedly, through the Annual Conferences. It ran with decent concealment, but no less certainly and fatally, through the College of Bishops, and was intensified, if not rendered indelible, by their sectional administration. The line ran through the Church, and it was only an accident of time, when the strain should come which should cause the already severed sections visibly to fall apart.

Bishop McKendree did all he could to make the superintendency general. In his person it was general, notwithstanding his knowledge of his own unpopularity in the Northern Conferences. Neither this, nor the discouragement of his episcopal colleagues at the North, could deter the venerable man, tottering under the weight of seventy years,* from the exercise of the *general* superintendency prescribed by the constitution of the Church. Upon his colleagues he sought to enforce the same; but in this he failed. No doubt Bishops George and Hedding were sincere—entirely so—in their expressed objection to the appointment of Dr. Capers, as the fraternal delegate to England. But the embarrassments —the ecclesiastical politics, if the phrase be admissible—of years were behind it all. Hedding had never itinerated in the South, and knew nothing of the pedestal of preëminence upon which Capers stood by universal acclaim. He knew that Capers belonged to the constitutional party; he knew how he voted in 1824. Soule's relations to Fisk might be described in similar terms. What more natural than that the sectionalized episcopacy—Roberts and Soule on the one hand, and George and Hedding on the other—should have fastened on these eminent men, in their respective sections of the Church, for this honorable and responsible post? The issue once joined could not be settled.

The Fifth Delegated General Conference met for the first time west of the Alleghanies, at Pittsburg, Penn., May 1, 1828. Bishops McKendree, George, Roberts, Soule, and Hedding were all present: the Senior Bishop opened the session, as he had done in every case since the death of Asbury. It was composed of 177 delegates elect, of whom 125 were present at the opening session.† In the episcopal

---

* He was seventy in the summer of 1827, and lived to be seventy-eight.

† Paine's McKendree, II. 106. The Journal (I. 342, 343) if I have counted correctly, gives 176 delegates elect. Clark's figures are approximate.

address, the Bishops regretted their failure to appoint a delegate to England, and, without stating the cause or the names which had been canvassed, all of which, it would appear from the election which followed, was sufficiently well known, they suggested that the General Conference should elect such a fraternal messenger. Accordingly an election was held for this purpose. On the first ballot William Capers had 75 and Wilbur Fisk, 67; but scattering votes defeated a choice. On the second ballot there were 138 votes, making 80 necessary to a choice; Fisk had 72 and Capers 82, and was elected. He discharged the duties of his mission with distinguished success.*

The presiding elder controversy which had so long and so dangerously agitated the Church was finally disposed of in the following manner:

John Early moved, and it was seconded, that the report of the Committee on Revisal and Unfinished Business, in relation to the suspended resolutions and the election of presiding elders, be taken up and considered. The motion prevailed.

William Winans moved, William Capers seconded, that the subject of the report be disposed of by adopting the following resolution, as a substitute for the resolution which was laid over as unfinished business, viz.:—

Resolved, etc., That the resolutions commonly called the suspended resolutions, rendering the presiding elders elective, etc., and which were referred to this conference by the last General Conference as unfinished business, and reported to us at this conference, be, and the same are hereby rescinded and made void. Carried.†

Nevertheless on the next day, D. Ostrander and T. Merritt bravely brought forward the old measure; but it was promptly tabled, apparently without debate.‡

At this General Conference the first formal amendment of the Constitution by the process prescribed in the Constitution itself, was initiated. On the afternoon of May 15, Wilbur Fisk submitted the following:

Resolved, etc., 1. That this General Conference respectfully suggest to the several annual conferences the propriety of recommending to the next General Conference so to alter and amend the rules of our Discipline, by which the General Conference is restricted and limited in its legislative powers, commonly called the Restrictive Rules, number six, as to read

---

*Gen. Conf. Journals, I. 339. † *Ibid.*, I. 332. ‡ *Ibid.*, I. 335.

thus: *Provided*, nevertheless, that upon the joint recommendation of three-fourths of all the annual conferences, then a majority of two-thirds of the General Conference succeeding shall suffice to alter any of the above restrictions; or whenever such alterations shall have been first recommended by two-thirds of the General Conference, then, so soon as three-fourths of said annual conferences shall have concurred with such recommendations, such alteration or alterations shall take effect.

Resolved, etc., 2. That it is hereby made the duty of the several bishops in their tours to the different annual conferences, to carry around and lay before any such annual conference which they may visit respectively any address or resolution, or other papers of a decent character, which this General Conference or any annual conference may request them so to carry around to obtain the opinion or decision of said annual conferences thereon. Signed, Wilbur Fisk, Joseph A. Merrill.*

May 21, Fisk's resolutions were called up on motion of William Winans. A division of the matter was called for, and the first resolution was adopted, with some alterations which had probably been made by the original movers, with consent, to obviate objections that had come to their knowledge while the measure was awaiting action. It now read as follows:

That this General Conference respectfully suggest to the several Annual Conferences the propriety of recommending to the next General Conference so to alter and amend the rules of our Discipline, by which the General Conference is restricted and limited in its powers to make rules and regulations for our Church, commonly called the Restrictive Rules, as to make the proviso at the close of said Restrictive Rules, No. 6, read thus: *Provided*, nevertheless, that upon the joint recommendations of three-fourths of all the Annual Conferences, then a majority of two-thirds of the General Conference succeeding shall suffice to alter any of the above restrictions except the first "Article."

This is an improvement in some particulars: for Fisk's phrase "legislative powers," the practically synonymous language of the Constitution, "powers to make rules and regulations for our Church," is substituted; the capital exception of the first restrictive rule, which protects the standards of doctrine, is added; but Fisk's provision for the initiation of constitutional changes in the General as well as in the Annual Conferences is omitted. The General Conference of 1828, though really initiating such a change, care-

---

* Gen. Conf. Journals, I. 331, 332.

fully respected, in the phraseology of its action, the exclusive constitutional prerogative of the Annual Conferences: "This General Conference respectfully suggests to the several Annual Conferences the propriety of recommending to the next General Conference," etc. There was evidently dissatisfaction with the shape into which the measure had gotten; the vote by which it had been adopted was reconsidered, and it was referred to a select committee of three, of which Fisk was chairman.* May 22, Fisk made his report and it was adopted as follows:

Resolved, That this General Conference respectfully suggest to the several Annual Conferences the propriety of recommending to the next General Conference so to alter and amend the rules of our Discipline, by which the General Conference is restricted in its powers to make rules and regulations for the Church, commonly called the Restrictive Rules, as to make the proviso at the close of said Restrictive Rules, No. 6, read thus:

Provided, nevertheless, that upon the concurrent recommendation of three-fourths of all the members of the several Annual Conferences who shall be present and vote on such recommendation, then a majority of two-thirds of the General Conference succeeding shall suffice to alter any of such regulations, excepting the first article.

And, also, whenever such alteration or alterations shall have first been recommended by two-thirds of the General Conference, so soon as three-fourths of the members of the Annual Conferences shall have concurred, as aforesaid, with such recommendation, such alteration or alterations shall take effect.*

This final form well illustrates how an important measure may be perfected by passing without haste through the several stages to which a deliberative assembly may subject it: (1) the first restrictive rule, which protects the doctrines of the Church, is excepted from the operation of the new method of constitutional amendment; (2) Fisk's original provision for initiation of constitutional changes in the General Conference is restored; and, most important of all, (3) the language "three fourths of all the Annual Conferences" is altered to "three fourths of all the members of the several Annual Conferences who shall be present and vote." The original provision in the Constitution of 1808 put it in the power of a single small Annual Conference to

---

* Gen. Conf. Journals, I. 346.   † *Ibid.*, I. 353, 354.

defeat the will of the remainder of the Church; and Fisk's original proposition put it in the power of any group of Annual Conferences, greater than one fourth of the whole number, however small and however feeble their minority, to defeat a constitutional change. This feature of the Constitution of 1808 was evidently borrowed from the Constitution of the United States; and Fisk, at first, inadvertently retained the same principle. The truth is that the several Annual Conferences bear no such relation to the Connexion as the several states bear to the general government of the Union. The number and extent of the Annual Conferences is a mere accident, mutable at the will of any General Conference. The Church was not formed by their amalgamation; but they were hewn out of the territory and the ministry of the Church. The one unbroken traveling Connexion; the undivided body of itinerant preachers—this, and this only, was the original or primary constituency which gave existence to the Delegated General Conference, and prescribed the Constitution which defines its powers. Afterwards, in both Episcopal Methodisms, this primal body admitted the laity to a share of the government. It follows that whether the majority of those favoring a constitutional change be concentrated in one Annual Conference or be scattered through them all, their will should prevail. And for this the measure of 1828, as adopted, provided. The Annual Conference rightfully ceased to be in any sense a constitutional unit.

Accordingly in the General Conference of 1832 the Committee on Itinerancy reported that the measure submitted in 1828 had been approved as the Constitution required by all the Annual Conferences, " in full and due form, with the exception of the Illinois, where we find some want in the formality; not sufficient, however, in the judgment of your committee to alter or set aside the principle." The entire Illinois delegation joined in a written assurance to the General Conference that " the informality arose from the want of information, and not with any intention to embarrass the true

design of the said resolution." Thereupon the General
Conference unanimously concurred.* The amendment
then adopted stands unaltered in the Discipline of the Methodist Episcopal Church to this day; so it stands, *verbatim*,
in the Discipline of the Methodist Episcopal Church, South:
to it was added, by the constitutional process, in 1870, the
provision for the so-called veto power of the Bishops.

The question is often asked, Are the doctrinal statements
and standards of Methodism unchangeable? It is true that
the Discipline nowhere contains any express provision for
their change; but it is also true that the original provision
of 1808 has never been abrogated by the joint action of the
General and Annual Conferences. The new method of
constitutional amendment is applicable to all the restrictions
"excepting the first article." While the legislators of 1828–
1832 did not think it wise to suggest the mutability of the
doctrines of the Church by incorporating in the Discipline a
prescribed constitutional process for their alteration, the General Conference of 1828 did not ask the Annual Conferences
to vote upon the abrogation of the existing constitutional
method provided for the change of the restrictive rule which
guarded the doctrines or doctrinal standards of the Church:
consequently, the original method of constitutional change,
prescribed in 1808 for all the restrictive rules, by which such
changes depend upon the joint recommendation of all the
Annual Conferences, confirmed by a majority of two-thirds
in the succeeding General Conference, is still applicable
to the first restrictive rule, and could be constitutionally
used to open the way to doctrinal changes. Other methods
have been suggested, such as eliminating by the constitutional process, from the present provision for amendment,
the words, "excepting the first article;" and then, by a
second use of the constitutional method, suspending or altering the first restrictive rule. But this is of doubtful validity. It is true it requires the General and Annual Conferences to give the constitutional majorities twice over, be-

*Gen. Conf. Journals, I. 377, 378, 382, 383.

fore the doctrines can be touched, and thus appears doubly
to guard them. But, in reality, could these majorities be
once obtained, it would hardly be difficult to have them repeated by the same constituencies. The facts are clear and
indisputable. The General Conference of 1808 ordained a
given method of constitutional amendment for all the restrictive rules. In 1828 the General Conference asked the
Annual Conferences to alter this, for all the restrictions except the first. It was done. The General Conference did
not ask for any change in the method prescribed for constitutionally amending the first restriction. The Annual
Conferences did not have any such proposition before
them. Hence the original prescription of 1808 remains in
force.

Four years after the division of territory with the British
Conference, and the mutual exchange of members, Upper
Canada, in 1824, was constituted an Annual Conference.
And in 1828 the five delegates of the Canada Conference
were in their seats at Pittsburg, representing nearly 10,000
members. But a petition from the body was presented by
William Ryerson, praying that it might " be separated from
the jurisdiction of the General Conference of the Methodist
Episcopal Church in the United States." The petition
was referred to a special committee consisting of Messrs.
Bangs, Bonney, Pitman, Paddock, Bigelow, and Leach.
May 12, the committee reported; but " after considerable
discussion, Wm. Capers moved and R. Paine seconded,
that the motion for adopting the report be laid on the table,
and that the report be made the order of the day for Friday
next;" and this motion prevailed. Friday, May 16, the report of the committee was taken up as ordered: constitutional difficulties appear to have been started by the committee, whose report does not appear in the Journal. Capers, seconded by Hodges, moved to amend the first resolution of the report by striking out the words, " it is unconstitutional to grant," and inserting in lieu, " as well as that
the expediency of the measure does not certainly appear,

we decline granting." The Conference adjourned with the
Capers amendment pending. The next day Luckey moved
to amend the Capers amendment so as to read, " it is expedient to grant," etc.; but the Chair ruled that this motion
could not then be acted on; and the original resolution of
the committee was taken up. Ostrander moved " to strike
out the first clause of the resolution, which says that the several Annual Conferences have not recommended it to the
General Conference," which motion was lost. The Conference finally adjourned without action on the report.
This report of the first select committee seems to have been
an unmanageable document, and as the Conference, after
two trials, could do nothing with it, it is not recorded in the
Journal. Dr. Bangs says that " it was contended, and the
committee to whom it was first referred so reported, which
report was approved of by the General Conference, that we
had no constitutional right to set off the brethren in Upper
Canada as an independent body," etc.* The Doctor, who
was the chairman of the committee, is no doubt correct as
to the nature of the report; but it does not appear from the
Journal that the General Conference approved it, or finally
disposed of it in any way. Up to this time it had not occurred to any one that the Canada Conference, though situated in a foreign country, sustained any different relation to
the General Conference and the Connexion, from that occupied by the other Annual Conferences. It had been constituted in the same way; it exercised its prerogatives under
the same rules and regulations which defined the province
and duties of the remaining Annual Conferences; and its
delegates represented it in the General Conference, elected
like those of other Conferences. But this Annual Conference was before the General Conference with a petition to
be erected into a distinct ecclesiastical Connexion, which,
for various reasons, not necessary to canvass here, it was
highly desirable to grant. At this juncture, it was, apparently, that Mr. Emory proposed his theory of a voluntary

* Hist. M. E. Church, III. 390, 391.

compact between the Canadians and the Americans—" we had offered them our services, and *they* had accepted them —and therefore, as the time had arrived when they were no longer willing to receive or accept of our labors and superintendence, they had a perfect right to request us to withdraw our services, and we the same right to withhold them." " This presented the subject," continues Dr. Bangs, " in a new and very clear light." * That it was new, there could be little question: its clearness depends somewhat on the angle of vision.

However, the report of the first committee having come to naught, William Ryerson, on behalf of the Canadians, submitted, May 17, a preamble and series of resolutions, based on the " voluntary compact" doctrine. His first resolution was adopted by a vote of 104 for to 43 against, as follows:

Resolved, etc., 1. That the compact existing between the Canada Annual Conference and the Methodist Episcopal Church in the United States be, and hereby is dissolved by mutual consent, and that they are at liberty to form themselves into a separate Church establishment.

Mr. Ryerson's remaining resolutions, four in number, were referred to a new committee, consisting of five members, Messrs. Emory, Fisk, Jones, Waugh, and Paine. May 21, the report of this able committee was adopted by a vote of 108 for and 22 against. Later, Mr. Emory moved that the vote by which Mr. Ryerson's resolution, recited above, had been adopted should be reconsidered. His motion prevailed, and the resolution was rescinded.†

By some oversight this report as adopted was not inserted in the Journal of 1828. In 1832 Roszel moved its insertion in the Journal of that year, and it so appears, as follows:

Resolved, by the delegates of the annual conferences in General Conference assembled, that whereas the jurisdiction of the Methodist Episcopal Church in the United States of America has heretofore been extended over the ministers and members in connexion with said Church in the province of Upper Canada, by mutual agreement, and by the consent and desire of our brethren in that province; and whereas this General Conference is sat-

---

* Hist. M. E. Church, III. 391, 392; Dr. Emory's Life of Bp. Emory, pp. 107, 108.

† For all the above proceedings in regard to Canada, see Gen. Conf. Journals, I. 311, 312, 322, 323, 335, 336–338, 340, 346, 354.

isfactorily assured that our brethren in the said province, under peculiar and pressing circumstances, do now desire to organize themselves into a distinct Methodist Episcopal Church, in friendly relations with the Methodist Episcopal Church in the United States, therefore be it resolved, and it is hereby resolved by the delegates of the annual conferences in General Conference assembled,

1. If the annual conference in Upper Canada at its ensuing session or any succeeding session previously to the next General Conference, shall definitely determine on this course, and elect a general superintendent of the Methodist Episcopal Church in that province, this General Conference do hereby authorize any one or more of the general superintendents of the Methodist Episcopal Church in the United States, with the assistance of any two or more elders, to ordain such general superintendent for the said Church in Upper Canada, provided always, that nothing herein contained be contrary to or inconsistent with the laws existing in the said province; and provided that no such general superintendent of the Methodist Episcopal Church in Upper Canada, or any of his successors in office, shall at any time exercise any ecclesiastical jurisdiction whatever in any part of the United States, or of the territories thereof; and provided also, that this article shall be expressly ratified and agreed to by the said Canada Annual Conference, before any such ordination shall take place.

2. That the delegate who has been selected at this General Conference to attend the ensuing annual conference of the British Wesleyan Methodist Connexion be, and hereby is, instructed to express to that body the earnest and affectionate desire of this General Conference that the arrangement made with that connexion in relation to the labors of their missionaries in Upper Canada may still be maintained and observed.

3. That our brethren and friends, ministers or others in Upper Canada shall, at all times, at their request, be furnished with any of our books and periodical publications on the same terms with those by which our agents are regulated in furnishing them in the United States, and until there shall be an adjustment of any claims which the Canada Church may name. On this connexion the Book Agents shall divide to the said Church an equal proportion of any annual dividend which may be made from the Book Concern to the several annual conferences respectively; provided that however the aforesaid dividend shall be apportioned to the Canada Church only as long as they may continue to support and patronize our Book Concern as in the past. Respectfully submitted as agreed.   W. FISK, *Chairman.*

PITTSBURG, *May* 26, 1828.[*]

The parallelisms between this and a later division of the Church we need not now point out. The contrast between this peaceful separation and the stormy departures of the two African Churches and of the Methodist Protestants and the Wesleyans is delightful. We can conceive, also, of a

---

[*] Gen. Conf. Journals, I. 406, 407.

technical definition by which this separation of the Canadians might be styled a " secession," since the action of the General Conference is expressly based on the Canadian initiative; but, as a matter of fact, we are not aware that this hard and ugly word has ever been applied to it. Bishop Hedding presided at the last session of the Canada Conference of the Methodist Episcopal Church. After the usual business of such a body had been transacted, resolutions were adopted declaring the connection of the Conference with the Methodist Episcopal Church in the United States dissolved, and organizing an independent Church in Canada. Bishop Hedding thereupon vacated the chair. The next year he attended as a visitor, and ordained the first elders and deacons of the new Church.*

There is little else in the action of the General Conference of 1828 that demands attention in these pages: the body adjourned Saturday, May 24.

* Clark's Life of Hedding, pp. 364, 365, 380.

CHAPTER XXIII.

THE SIXTH AND SEVENTH DELEGATED GENERAL CONFERENCES, 1832 AND 1836: CONCLUSION.

THE Sixth Delegated General Conference met at Philadelphia, May 1, 1832, and was composed of about two hundred and twenty five delegates, representing nineteen Conferences. No less than six of the future Bishops of the Methodist Episcopal Church, South, were among its members: James O. Andrew, elected at this time; William Capers, Robert Paine, Henry B. Bascom, Hubbard H. Kavanaugh, and John Early.

The membership of the General Conference was becoming too large. This Conference unanimously recommended that the ratio of representation be one in fourteen, and, in addition to the constitutional amendment previously noticed, recommended, also by a unanimous vote, an amendment which recognizes the principles of fractional representation and that no Annual Conference shall be without representation; all of which was concurred in by the Annual Conferences as follows:

Resolved, 2. That the Second Article of the Restrictive Rules be so altered as to read: "They shall not allow of more than one representative for every fourteen members of the Annual Conference, nor allow of a less number than one for every thirty; provided, nevertheless, than when there shall be, in any Annual Conference, a fraction of two-thirds of the number which shall be fixed for the ratio of representation, such Annual Conference shall be entitled to an additional delegate for such fraction; and provided, also, that no Conference shall be deprived of the privilege of two delegates."*

At the Conference of 1836, on motion of John Early, the ratio of representation was changed to one in twenty-one—so rapid was the increase in the ministry and membership of the Church.

The Committee on Episcopacy, in the eighth item of

---

*Gen. Conf. Journals, I. 402.

their report, said that, considering the great extent of the work, "the committee deem it inexpedient to require each of our bishops to travel throughout the whole of their extensive charges during the recess of the General Conference," etc. As this action was somewhat ambiguous, the bishops, May 28, asked for an explanation by vote of the Conference, without debate, in answer to the following question:

> Was it the intention of the General Conference, by the resolution above alluded to, simply to relieve the bishops from the influence of the resolution passed at the last General Conference on the same subject, and to leave them now at liberty on their joint and several responsibility to make such arrangements among themselves for the entire administration, and for the visitation of the Annual Conferences as they shall judge most conducive to the general good; and without designing to give any direction or advice whether it be or be not expedient for each of the bishops, in the course of the four years, to visit each of the Annual Conferences, should they themselves find it convenient and practicable, and judge it for the general good so to do?*

The Conference responded in the affirmative. Tuesday, May 22, the episcopal election had resulted in the choice of James Osgood Andrew and John Emory, the former receiving 140 and the latter 135 votes, out of 223, on the first ballot.†

The Conference adjourned, Monday evening, May 28. The closing session was presided over by Bishop Emory. It was the only time he ever occupied the chair in a General Conference; but, amid the rush and confusion, his presidency was distinguished by perfect coolness and self-possession, promptness and impartiality. "It was the most harmonious and conservative session," says Bishop Paine, "held since the organization of the delegated body in 1808." It was the last General Conference at which Bishop Mc-Kendree was present,—a peaceful close after the storms of his later episcopate. "Leaning on his staff, his once tall and manly form now bent with age and infirmity, his eyes suffused with tears, his voice faltering with emotion, he exclaimed, 'Let all things be done without strife or vainglory, and try to keep the unity of the Spirit in the bond

---

* Gen. Conf. Journals, I. 419, 420,   † *Ibid.*, I. 401.

CPSIA information can be obtained at www.ICGtesting.com
Printed in the USA
LVOW03s0947301113

363239LV00004B/29/P